GEORGE MEREDITH

George Meredith

GEORGE MEREDITH

*From the original pencil portrait by the
Duchess of Rutland*

LIST OF ILLUSTRATIONS

7

PREFACE

MANY friends have expressed the wish that I would reprint, in book form, certain articles on George Meredith which I contributed to *The Fortnightly Review* and *The Saturday Review*; and so, when Mr Grant Richards proposed that I should write a book on the subject of Meredith and his work, I decided it should follow the lines of these articles. The primary object of the latter was to relate and preserve such information as I possessed concerning the early life of George Meredith, who was my father's first cousin, and to reconsider as a corollary the inner or personal history of some of the novels—in particular, *Evan Harrington*, *Beauchamp's Career*, *Vittoria*, and *Diana of the Crossways*.

Consequently the present work is primarily a record of Meredith's early life and meridian, and of his books and the originals of his characters. It essays to show the intimate association between his private life and his literary work, for most of his creations were drawn from or inspired by living models, and his descriptions of scenery and the forces of nature were transcripts from the surroundings of his various homes and places he visited at home or abroad, and reflections of actual experiences. What I term the personal history of all the novels, and of many of the poems, will be found in the following pages, connected by the necessary biographical links, and a brief account of Meredith's last years, when his work was done, is added in order to make this book a more or less complete survey of the author's life and literary achievement.

There are no profundities of criticism in this work, and such light criticisms as I venture to offer need cause no fluttering in the dovecotes of Meredithian culturists, for they are simply the individual views of one unimportant person; and that, after all, is the truth about most so-called "literary" criticism. Meredith considered himself a lifelong victim of adverse and incompetent criticism. If that be so, the pendulum has now swung to the other extreme. He is now over-criticised—in the sense that subtleties of thought and meaning are discovered in his work which he, probably, never intended or conceived. His "Message" is obscured and made absurd by these inspired

9

commentators: his real study and "Message" were ever Human Nature and Beauty. Human Nature he liked to dissect, and examine its variable behaviour in certain situations. Beauty in scenery and atmospheric effect and in physical form inspired him to transcribe it in poetry, idealised by his own personality, just as a painter would transmute the same into colour and design on canvas. Surely this is finer than any intense and intentionally " difficult " interpretation of his aim and work.

In this book will be found a requoting of some of Meredith's most exquisite verbal pictures of beauty in Nature ; and throughout, in every personal description of an event in his life, or in the expression of his opinions, I have let him speak for himself in his own words. Only thus can we see correctly the lights and shades in a man's character.

I am indebted to my cousin, W. M. Meredith, for permission to quote from his father's letters ; and to Mrs Arthur Croome and Mr A. N. Bonaparte Wyse for granting me the use of interesting new letters from Meredith to, respectively, Sir William Hardman and W. C. Bonaparte Wyse.

I wish also to thank the Duchess of Rutland, the artist, and Colonel J. G. Adami, A.D.M.S., the owner, of the fine pencil portrait of Meredith, which by their permission is reproduced in this work : the original drawing, I understand, is to find a place in the Art Gallery at Montreal. To Mr F. J. Williamson, the sculptor, I am greatly indebted for the contemporary photographs of Esher and Copsham as in Meredith's time.

For the loan of other illustrations, or help in many ways, I thank Mr A. St John Adcock, Mrs Banks, Mr F. B. Barwell, Mr Reginald Blunt, Mr G. Buckston Browne, Miss Hilda Chester, Mrs Clarke, Mr Herbert Cook (of Copseham), Mr A. T. Everitt, Mr J. J. Freeman, Mr H. M. Hyndman, the Rev. Dr. F. J. Foakes Jackson, Mrs Frederick Jones (of Kingston Lodge), Mr J. Brooke Little, Mr L. J. Maxse, the Rt. Hon. Sir William Pickford, Mr A. Gordon Pollock, Miss Ella Pycroft, Mr Lionel Robinson, Mrs Ross, Miss de St Croix, Mr C. K. Shorter, Miss Tupper, the Rev. W. B. Vaillant, Mrs Woolf, and Mr and Mrs Ralph Wood (who so admirably preserve the amenities of Flint Cottage, Box Hill). S. M. ELLIS.

16 DEFOE AVENUE, KEW GARDENS.
April, 1918.

CHAPTER I

DURING his lifetime an impenetrable veil of reticence, and, in consequence, of mystery also, hid the facts of George Meredith's origin and family history and his own early days from public knowledge. The world has a pardonable weakness for desiring to learn the personal details of a great man's life, and gratification is generally supplied freely, in full measure and unasked, by the subject himself : but in this case there was no information forthcoming either from Meredith or his friends. He had arrived in London a friendless youth, and the friends he began to make then, and all those through the subsequent years, were told nothing definite about his parentage or whence he came. In later days the contemporary books of reference, such as *Men of the Time* and *Who's Who*, merely stated he was born in Hampshire, and made no allusion to his family. Various authors who produced appreciations of Meredith during his lifetime shied as they neared the danger zone of his origin, and slid warily over their thin ice with a few words of polite nebulosity. Mr Edward Clodd has related [1] that when he was filling in a census paper for Meredith, and the place of birth had to be mentioned, he was told to put " near Petersfield " : as a matter of fact, Meredith was born some twenty miles distant from that town. In the obituary notice of Meredith in *The Daily Telegraph* the novelist was stated to have been born at Winchester. It is needless to labour the point that it was not until some time after his death that it became publicly known that Portsmouth was his birthplace.

The reasons for all this mysterious reticence are very difficult to fathom. That it was entirely owing to a desire to hide the fact that his father and grandfather were naval outfitters

[1] *The Fortnightly Review,* July, 1909.

or tailors I decline to believe. No man of a sane mind—to say nothing of one of vast intellect—could attach shame to the knowledge that his immediate ancestors had followed an honest trade. Both his father and grandfather were uncommon men, quite unlike the provincial tradesmen of their time ; and the fact that Meredith recounted many incidents of their lives, and used actual names, in his family history of *Evan Harrington*, refutes the theory that he was literally ashamed of the tailor's shop, which he proclaimed, and eventually immortalised, to all the world. No ; although disliking his origin, the cause of his reticence must be attributed to some deeper source—an abnormally acute sensitiveness of mind which strove to put aside and forget the memories of old, unhappy things. For his own personal experiences in early days were unhappy. " In youth I looked out under a hail of blows," he said metaphorically. His unhappiness, as I shall hope to demonstrate presently, was mainly caused by his own temperament and uncongenial surroundings : the boyhood of a genius is not often appreciated by his family. The point I am trying to establish now is that Meredith, having carved his own career and made his fame, unaided and alone, regarded his early life only with bitterness and pain ; and, perhaps by some twist of unkindly thought, he was unwilling that any portion of his abilities should be attributed to the influence, or training, of those who, as he imagined, treated him unsympathetically in youth. He used to say : " When I was young, had there been given me a little sunshine of encouragement, what an impetus to better work would have been mine." The fact may be granted at once that he owed very little to immediate heredity and so-called education for the upspringing of his literary gift. His genius was innate, and able to hew its own way to consummation. He was certainly the most amazing product that ever came out of a provincial shop, but this was merely a freak of Fate. His birthplace, though of great interest for biographical reasons, is immaterial in tracing the intellectual development and expression of his mind and rare personality.

Whatever the causes that prompted Meredith's reticence on the subject of his origin, he was singularly ill-advised in preserving that silence to the end ; for the sake of his mother's reputation he would, presumably, have refuted the absurd rumours—if they ever reached his ears—that were current about his paternity. For, baulked of any authentic information, public curiosity was titillated, and speculation rife as to the causes or necessities for this strange and mysterious reserve. Consequently, legends arose—a varied assortment, whose only point of agreement consisted in assigning to Meredith high-born but illicit paternity. He was a son of George IV., or, more probably, of the sailor prince, the Duke of Clarence (William IV.), or at any rate of some aristocratic and amorous admiral ashore. He was a son of Bulwer Lytton, and here the evidence was conclusive : Bulwer Lytton's son, Robert, subsequently the first Earl of Lytton, had adopted the literary pseudonym of " Owen Meredith," and so it followed, as the night the day, that George Meredith must be his brother. Most general of all was the suggestion that he was of " noble Welsh descent " ; perhaps he was, very remotely, but there is no evidence.[1] For three generations at least, his immediate ancestors were Hampshire people ; and it was mainly to dispel the ridiculous rumours mentioned above that I was constrained, originally, to make known the real facts of Meredith's parentage ; to point out, for the first time, how much of his family history had been adapted to the story of *Evan Harrington* ; and to relate the history of his own early days in Portsmouth.

In addition to Meredith, Portsmouth was the birthplace of Charles Dickens (in 1812) and of Walter Besant (in 1836), and it is curious that their interesting and historic native town does not appear more frequently as the locale or background of their novels, though it is the case that each of these three writers has dealt with the place in at least one of his books. Besant, in *By Celia's Arbour*, approaches most nearly to what would be expected from a literary son of Portsmouth. In the case of Dickens, his impressions of Portsmouth were faint, of course, for he was removed from the town in early childhood ; but nevertheless he retained some recollections of its topography — or refreshed his memory on the subject—because, in *Nicholas Nickleby*, Mr Crummles and his theatrical company are con-

---

[1] Possibly this rumour had its origin in a remark Meredith places in a letter of the Countess de Saldar's in *Evan Harrington*, where, alluding to the Great Mel., she says : " Had poor papa been *legitimitized*, he would have been a nobleman."

veniently lodged in St Thomas's Street and Lombard Street, close
by the old theatre.　Meredith, who remained in his birthplace
until he was about thirteen or fourteen, in *Evan Harrington*
depicted various scenes at the paternal and grand-paternal shop
in Portsmouth, here thinly disguised as " Lymport " ;　but,
apart from its biographical interest, the novel is subjective rather
than objective, and the situation of the tailor's shop, and the
incidents that happen there, could equally well be placed in
any other town without much loss of pictorial transcription :
the book is no picture of Portsmouth as Portsmouth, with all
its stirring naval interests.

Although Portsmouth failed to inspire her two most famous
sons, the old seaport has no lack of history and romance (of all
periods), for its record runs concurrently with that of civilisation
in England.　The Romans perceived the advantages of this
great inlet of the sea, and established a settlement on the
northern side, at Portchester.　When the sea receded from here
the inhabitants migrated a little way south and founded Portsmouth, which is mentioned as a landing-place in *The Saxon
Chronicle*, A.D. 501.　By the time of Henry I. the place was of
importance.　Both Robert of Normandy and the Empress
Matilda landed here on their aggressive expeditions to claim the
Crown.　Portsmouth became a naval station in the reign of John;
strong fortifications were added in succeeding reigns, and completed in that of Henry VII. ; and during the time of Henry VIII.
the port became the principal station of the English Navy, a
position it has ever since retained.　Tragedy and romance were
mingled here in Stuart days, when the Duke of Buckingham
was assassinated at a house in the High Street, and Charles II.
was married to Catherine of Braganza in the chapel of the
hospital of Domus Dei (now the Garrison Church).　In the
eighteenth century, and for the first part of the nineteenth,
Portsmouth attained its highest renown, during the long American and Napoleonic Wars, when there was ceaseless naval
activity, and the presence of great sailors (now historic names)
an everyday occurrence.　Portsea (which includes the Dockyard), Gosport, and Landport, were of later origin than Portsmouth proper, but all these neighbouring townships assumed
the distinctive " port " in their nomenclature, and to-day form
one great town, popularly known as Portsmouth—though the

actual ancient place covers no more than one hundred and ten acres, and up to the middle of the last century kept severely aloof from its suburban offspring behind armed fortifications, moats, and defensive gates.

How it came about that the ancestors of George Meredith migrated from Wales to Portsmouth will now never be known. Judging by the name, the family certainly was of Celtic origin, and, characteristic of that race both in Ireland and Wales, the Merediths preserved a vague tradition of princely progenitors quite in the style of The Mulligan. George Meredith alludes to this amiable weakness of his relatives in *Evan Harrington*, where he says: " Mr Melchisedec was mysterious concerning his origin; and, in his cups, talked largely and wisely of a great Welsh family, issuing from a line of princes." And again, when the Countess de Saldar asks: " Was it out of Glamorganshire —were we Tudors, according to Papa? Or only Powys chieftains? " Alack! These pleasing speculations are as nebulous as an aerial Spanish—or should it be Welsh?—castle, for the Merediths of Hampshire had no princely possessions and appanages beyond great beauty and distinguished carriage, and a glorious prodigality in money matters.

The first of the name, the novelist's great-grandfather, John Meredith, is merely a name. He apparently lived at Portsea in the middle of the eighteenth century, for his son was baptized in the parish church there, St Mary Kingston, in June, 1763. This son, Melchizedek, was as vivid and picturesque a personality as any of his putative progenital princelings in Wales: " A fine figure of a man, and there ain't many Marquises to match him," as Mr Kilne, the publican, remarked of him in *Evan Harrington*. It was an unkind fate that destined Melchizedek Meredith to a shop. Tall, handsome, and gallant—in both senses of the word—he was cut out for what he considered higher things—county society, hunting and so forth—which pleasures, in time, he did partake of. But in early life he had to attend to his business, and it was about 1784, having attained his majority, that he started his career as a tailor, and more particularly as a naval outfitter, at No. 73 High Street, Portsmouth, the house in which his famous grandson, George Meredith, was to be born forty-four years later.

The High Street runs at right angles to the sea, and at its

sea end, by the Signalling Station and Platform, the road curves round, passing the ancient landing-place known as the Sally-port, to join Broad Street, and so on to the Point. No. 73 is on the right-hand side, just before this curve commences. It is a very old house, for the present grafted stucco front merely masks a far more ancient building of red brick. At the back the original colouring is still visible, and three picturesque dormer windows break the line of mellow red tiles on the roof. In the Merediths' time, the ground floor of the house was occupied by the shop, a door dividing the two windows glazed with old-fashioned small panes of glass. The tailoring work-shop was at the back and reached as far as White Hart Road, but no longer exists. These, then, were the premises where matured that famous naval outfitting establishment, which was to become the premier one of its kind in Portsmouth, and as such was mentioned by Captain Marryat in *Peter Simple* : "We called at Meredith's, the tailor, and he promised that, by the next morning, we should be fitted complete." [1] Without doubt the customers and patrons of this establishment in-cluded Nelson, Collingwood, Jervis, the Hoods, the Troubridges, Rodney, and all the other great sailors of that most resplendent epoch—in both a fighting and sartorial sense—of the British Navy.

Melchizedek Meredith married about the same time as he started in business and came of age. His wife was some ten years older than he, and, though her surname has not been definitely traced in the family records, she is believed to have been Anne Mitchell, daughter of a lawyer in Portsmouth. Her strong personality and physical appearance, however, survive in portraits painted by both brush and pen. She was a tall woman of ample figure, with great stateliness of carriage, and, like her husband, very handsome. They were a splendid couple, and reared a fine family. All their seven children—two sons and five daughters—were born at No. 73 High Street ; for thirty years the old house witnessed all the joys and sorrows of their married life—until inevitable Death knocked at the door and severed the partnership. For sixty years Merediths—to the third generation in the person of the novelist—lived here.

The situation of the house was pleasant, for it commanded

---

[1] Vol. II., chap. vi.

a view of the sea and the Isle of Wight across Battery Row and the Platform ; and to the left was the open space of the Grand Parade, where many stirring military and naval events took place in those days. Here, we may conclude, the Merediths witnessed from their parlour bow-window the brilliant assembly of the Allied Sovereigns with Wellington and Blucher in 1814, after the overthrow of Napoleon ; and nine years earlier Nelson had left the George Inn, a little lower down the High Street, after his last night in England, and, passing along Penny Street and by the cheering and weeping and kneeling townspeople, had embarked from the beach beyond Battery Row. For certain, Melchizedek Meredith knew Nelson, for did he not " shake hands with his customers " ? Nelson's Hardy came to lodge with the tailor's widow and son, Augustus, some years later, for on September 7th, 1827, Admiral Sir Thomas Hardy wrote to his brother Joseph : " PORTSMOUTH. . . . I can give you a bed. I am at Meradith's (*sic*), the tailor, 73 High Street, opposite the Parade Coffee House." [1]

Not far down the High Street stands St Thomas's Church, which has many associations with the Merediths, for here they were christened, married, and buried, for three generations. Here, too, Melchizedek Meredith officiated as churchwarden in 1801 and in 1803-1804, and, on retiring from office, he and his fellow-warden, Lawrence Smith, presented to their parish church two silver offertory plates, which are still in use and have the donors' names engraved upon them.

How Melchizedek Meredith came by his extraordinary Biblical appellation is unknown (John, his father, must have been a sacerdotal enthusiast), but that he himself approved it and desired its perpetuation is evidenced by the fact that he bestowed the name on two of his unfortunate children, to the utter rout of the spelling powers of the clerks at St Thomas's Church, whose entries in the registers varied from Mellchisidick to other original and clerkly phonetic versions. The youthful Melchizedeks, however, seem to have found the ponderous burden of their second name more than they could bear, for, by a curious coincidence, both died young : Charles Melchizedek,

---

[1] I am indebted to Mr Thomas Hardy, O.M., for drawing my attention to this interesting reference in a letter quoted in the late Mr A. M. Broadley's book on Nelson's Hardy.

the elder son, died as a small boy in 1794, and Caroline Melchizedek only survived to the age of twenty-four, dying three years after her marriage, in 1809, with William Price Read (who, it is believed, held a post in the Dockyard). In the same year, 1809, her eldest sister, Anne Elizabeth Meredith, was married to Thomas Burbey, a prosperous banker and wholesale grocer, who lived at No. 46 High Street, a large house on the opposite side of the way : Mr Burbey was Mayor of Portsmouth in 1833.

As Kilne, the publican, observes, in *Evan Harrington*, of the Great Mel.'s beautiful daughters, they were " a fine family, every one of 'em ! and married well ! " And this remark may be particularly applied to the three remaining daughters, Louisa, Harriet and Catherine. Possibly, as their nephew suggested in *Evan Harrington*, " the marriages had happened in this way. Balls are given in country towns, where the graces of tradesmen's daughters may be witnessed and admired at leisure by other than tradesmen . . . the classes of our social fabric have, here and there, slight connecting links, and provincial balls are one of these."

But it must also be borne in mind that the father of the girls had an extensive social acquaintance. Melchizedek Meredith's aspirations were not centred in his shop. He was on friendly terms with many of his distinguished naval patrons, and was a welcome guest in some of the best houses of the locality and further afield in Hampshire. In those days the upper classes were very reluctant to admit that a tradesman could also be a gentleman, so it is very evident that Melchizedek had special qualities which procured him admittance gladly to the high and disdainful regions of county society. His grandson proffered the genial suggestion that Melchizedek's good looks and fine figure found favour with certain great ladies of the neighbourhood. Possibly it was so, for the portrait of his grandfather in *Evan Harrington* is in other respects very accurate. It is true there is no evidence that Melchizedek Meredith ever essayed to stand as parliamentary candidate for " Fallowfield "—Petersfield—or that he was often taken to be a member of the Upper House. Still, it is very likely that the story related in the novel, of how he passed as a marquis during a visit to Bath, is true. It may be a confirmatory, or

St. Thomas's Church, Portsmouth

trivial, point that I possess a little enamel snuffbox, bearing a view of Bath on the lid, which was the property of this great-grandfather of mine. As for the real Melchizedek Meredith, he kept horses and hunted ; in 1796, when he was initiated as a Freemason in the Phœnix Lodge, he was described as " a gentleman " ; and in 1801 he was an officer in the Portsmouth Yeomanry Cavalry, at a time when patriotism was paramount owing to the threatened invasion of England by Napoleon. Consequently, he had many opportunities of meeting and entertaining men of the superior social class who married his three younger daughters.

The most remarkable of these girls, Louisa Mitchell Meredith, was the original of her nephew's famous creation, the Countess de Saldar, in *Evan Harrington*. Needless to relate, she was brilliant and the wit of the family. Ambitious too, her actual career was perhaps even more romantic than adumbrated by George Meredith. At the age of eighteen, in March, 1811, she was married, in St Thomas's Church, to William Harding Read (born in 1775), who, after serving twenty years in the Royal Navy, as purser, and doing consular work abroad, became Consul-General in the Azores, about 1832. Read was a personal friend of Pedro, Emperor of Brazil and sometime King of Portugal, who created him a Knight of the Order of the Tower and Sword as a mark of royal esteem ; and, when in Portugal, Read and his wife maintained a high position in Court circles. In addition to three sons—one being named Guglielmo Meredith —the Reads had a daughter, called Luiza Mitchell after her mother. This girl, born at Ponta Delgada in 1816, was married in 1834, in the island of St Miguel, to Antonio da Costa Cabral, subsequently Marquis de Thomar, the well-known Minister of State during the reign of Donna Maria, second Queen of Portugal. At the time he met his wife he was acting as Judge in the Azores. Later on he held the office of Minister of Justice at Lisbon ; and in 1870 the Count de Thomar (he was created Marquis in 1878), was appointed Ambassador to the Vatican. Thus it came about that the granddaughter of Melchizedek Meredith the tailor died in Rome an Ambassadress—the only lady of that high rank at the Papal Court, where Portugal alone has an Embassy, the other countries being represented by Legations. The Ambassadress's son, Antonio Cabral, second

Count de Thomar, was an attaché at the Portuguese Legation in London in 1858, and his son, in turn, was, until recently, in the Portuguese Legation at Berlin. Other members of the family were officers in the army and navy of Portugal. Such were the appropriate descendants of the diplomatic and strategic " Countess de Saldar "—she whose airs and graces and flapping laces, and talk of courts and nobilities, must indeed have created an excitement when she revisited, at rare intervals, her old home in Portsmouth. That is an aptly characteristic scene in *Evan Harrington*—where the Countess arrives after the demise of her father, and, " in low society," turns, tactfully, the conversation to the most welcome topic of that strata of humanity. " She broached death and corpses ; and became extremely interesting, and very sympathetic ; the only difference between the ghostly anecdotes she related, and those of the other ladies, being that her ghosts were all of them titled, and walked mostly under the burden of a coronet." Somehow, the incongruous figure of the aforetime Louisa Meredith always seems one of the most familiar of the many personalities that haunt the bow-windowed parlour of the old family house in the High Street. The memory of Mrs Read survived in later years among her nephews and nieces as a sort of fairy godmother. She used to send them handsome presents—particularly boxes of rare fruits and sweets from Portugal, where she settled after the death of her husband in 1839—and ever there attached to her an atmosphere of romance, the conception of one who had early used her wings and flown away from the bourgeois to loftier realms. " She seemed so entirely to have eclipsed tailordom or ' Demogorgon ' as the Countess was pleased to call it." Mr Lionel Robinson, an early and intimate friend of George Meredith, told me that the novelist said to him " on more than one occasion that he owed much to one of his aunts who had lived for some time abroad, in Portugal, and that to her he was indebted for his ' manners ' and courteous bearing towards women. He always spoke of her with respect and admiration."

The Marquis de Thomar (Louisa Read's son-in-law) had a brother called Silva Cabral, and here is found the source of the name of " Count Silva," used by George Meredith in *Evan Harrington* to designate his uncle-in-law Read. Only once, in later years, did Meredith come near meeting his Portuguese cousins. In 1881 he wrote to his son Arthur : " Did I tell you of my receiving a letter from one signing himself Guglielmo Read Cabral,[1] claiming me for his cousin. He writes from Lisbon. His sister married Costa Cabral, formerly Prime Minister, now Marchese and Ambassador of Portugal at Rome. I knew of them. It seems that Madame Cabral got sight of one or other of my works and hit on the idea that I was a cousin worth noticing. Of course I wrote courteously, and groan now under the debt of another letter." But apparently George Meredith never met these children of his " Countess de Saldar."

In September of the same year, 1811, that witnessed the wedding of Louisa Meredith, her sister, Harriet Eustace, was married to John Hellyer of Newington, Surrey, a brewer. Little authentic information is available concerning the Hellyers beyond the fact that they were the originals of the Andrew Cogglesbys in *Evan Harrington.*

Although Melchizedek's youngest and most beautiful daughter, Catherine Matilda Meredith, was not married until some years after her father's death, it is more convenient to record now that it was on 28th October, 1819, that she was wedded, in St Thomas's Church, to Samuel Burdon Ellis, then a lieutenant in the Royal Marines, who subsequently rose to the rank of General and Knight Commander of the Order of the Bath. The Ellises, of course, were the originals of Major and Mrs Strike in *Evan Harrington.* How much the characters of my grandparents were misrepresented I shall point out, in a few words, when dealing with that book later on. My grandfather, S. B. Ellis, was born in 1782 and was twelve years older than my grandmother. He entered the Royal Marines at an early age, and at once took part in many of the naval engagements of the Napoleonic War, including Sir Robert Calder's action, the capture of Guadaloupe, and Trafalgar. In the last-named battle he fought on H.M.S. *Ajax,* and before the action commenced it fell to him to announce to the sailors Nelson's famous signal. He relates in his *Memoirs* :

---

[1] Apparently this son of Louisa Read took the married name of his sister, if George Meredith was not in error in adding Cabral to Read.

" There was scarcely any wind at the time, and we approached the enemy at not more than a knot and a half an hour. As we neared the French fleet, I was sent below with orders, and was much struck with the preparations made by the blue-jackets, the majority of whom were stripped to the waist ; a handkerchief was bound tightly round their heads and over the ears, to deaden the noise of the cannon, many men being deaf for days after an action. The men were variously occupied : some were sharpening their cutlasses, others polishing the guns as though an inspection were about to take place instead of a mortal combat, whilst three or four, as if in mere bravado, were dancing a hornpipe ; but all seemed deeply anxious to come to close quarters with the enemy. Occasionally they would look out of the ports, and speculate as to the various ships of the enemy, many of which had been on former occasions engaged by our vessels. It was at this time that Nelson's famous signal, ' England expects every man to do his duty,' was hoisted at the mast head of the Admiral's ship. These words were requested to be delivered to the men, and I was desired to inform those on the main-deck of the Admiral's signal. Upon acquainting one of the quarter-masters of the order, he assembled the men with ' Avast there, lads, come and hear the Admiral's words.' When the men were mustered, I delivered, with becoming dignity, the sentence,— rather anticipating that the effect on the men would be to awe them by its grandeur. Jack, however, did not appreciate it, for there were murmurs from some, whilst others in an audible whisper muttered, ' Do our duty ! Of course we'll do our duty. I've always done mine, haven't you ? Let us come alongside of 'em, and we'll soon show whether we will do our duty.' Still, the men cheered vociferously—more, I believe, from love and admiration of their Admiral and leaders, than from a full appreciation of this well-known signal." [1]

S. B. Ellis's numerous other services, during nearly sixty years, in all parts of the world, included the war with China, 1840-1842, when he was senior officer in command of the Royal Marines during the frequent actions the corps engaged in, and for which he received many encomiums and rewards.

[1] *Memoirs of Sir S. B. Ellis, K.C.B.* Edited by Lady Ellis. 1866.

GENERAL SIR S. B. ELLIS, K.C.B., R.M.L.I., THE ORIGINAL
OF MAJOR STRIKE IN "EVAN HARRINGTON"

He eventually became Commandant of Woolwich, was granted a special augmentation of armorial bearings for his services, was created K.C.B. and knighted, and died in 1865. He came of a family whose long record of military and naval distinction, through many generations, is unique. His three brothers all entered the navy. Captain John Ellis fought at Cape St Vincent and at Cadiz under Nelson ; George Ellis was wounded in action off Calais, and in 1808 his ship was captured near Toulon by a French frigate, and he remained a prisoner of war at Verdun for six years, eventually dying from the effect of hardships experienced there ; and Lieutenant Francis Wilson Ellis's many services included the Baltic and the Bombardment of Copenhagen in 1807, when the Danish fleet surrendered. The father of the four brothers, Commander John Ellis, served with the Naval Brigade at the battle of the Plains of Abraham, when Wolfe was killed, at the taking of Quebec, 1759, and through the American War of Independence ; and their uncle, Captain Stephen Ellis, Royal Marines, was killed in the attack at the battle of Bunker's Hill, in 1775. Their grandfather, Samuel Ellis, was a lieutenant in Barrel's Regiment, and lost an arm at Culloden, 1745. Their great-grandfather, Samuel Ellis, served in the Low Countries under the Duke of Marlborough, and was captain in the Duke of York's Maritime Regiment at Oudenarde. Earlier direct ancestors included Philip Ellis, a noted cavalier, who defended Rose Castle, in Cumberland, against the Parliamentarians ; Sir John Ellis, who was at Marston Moor, and, later, killed in the service of Charles I. ; Sir William Ellys, who did great execution against the unfortunate rebels of the Pilgrimage of Grace ; Sir Henry Ellys, slain at Bosworth Field, 1485 ; Sir William Ellys, who is mentioned as accompanying Edward III. to France ; Sir William Ellys, who served under Earl Warrenne against the Scots at Dunbar and Stirling ; Sir Thomas Ellys, slain at the assault on Northampton, 1265 ; and Sir Archibald Ellys, a noted crusader in the service of Richard I.

The three sons of Catherine Meredith carried on the fighting traditions of their father's family. The eldest, George Ellis, long years after, had his boyhood's portrait drawn very faithfully by his first cousin and namesake, George Meredith, as Crossjay Patterne in *The Egoist*. George Ellis, like his literary presentment, was a restless, high-spirited lad, with a passion for the navy, which he entered at the age of fifteen. He became purser, but his roving spirit, fretting at inaction—for there was no naval warfare during his time—caused him to leave the Service and emigrate to South Africa. From thence he went to America, where he was eventually killed at the battle of Bull's Run, 1861, in the American Civil War, fighting as a volunteer in the Southern Army, thus closing his adventurous career at the age of thirty-nine. His two brothers entered their father's corps, the Royal Marines; Samuel died, from the effects of service, a lieutenant, in 1847; and Arthur Ellis (my father) rose to the rank of Colonel, after over thirty years' service, including the Crimean War, when he was wounded at the Bombardment of Sebastopol, and died in 1885. George Meredith thus long survived all his English first cousins: he and Arthur Ellis were born in the same year, 1828, and much resembled each other in personal appearance.

To revert to 1811, the year which witnessed two weddings of the Meredith daughters, there soon ensued a period of trouble and death for the family. The Great Mel. (who, I fear, keeps banging up and down this family chapter, "like a pertinacious cracker," much as he did at the dinner-table of Beckley Court), having been long indifferent to money matters and given to much generous hospitality, was now faced by serious financial difficulties for the neglected business. In 1812 his eldest daughter, Mrs Burbey, died, four months after the birth of her only child, Mary Meredith Burbey (subsequently Mrs Pratt Wills). In 1813, five months later, his second daughter, Caroline, Mrs W. P. Read, died; and on 10th July, 1814, Melchizedek Meredith himself expired, in the prime of life, at the age of fifty-one. The demise of him who "had been at once the sad dog of Portsmouth, and the pride of the town" is but unromantically recorded in the local paper, *The Hampshire Courier*, of 18th July, 1814, under Portsmouth: "Died on Sunday, 10th inst., much respected, Mr M. Meredith, aged 51, who for many years carried on a respectable trade in the Men's Mercery line in this town."

It may safely be surmised that some such scenes as are depicted in the first chapter of *Evan Harrington* did in reality follow the death of Melchizedek, for at the very outset George

Meredith gives the actual names of certain neighbouring tradesmen living in the High Street at the time. Robert Kiln was the landlord of the Wellington Tavern, No. 62, exactly opposite the Merediths' shop ; Barnes was a pork butcher near the church ; " Grossby " was intended for William Grossmith, the confectioner, at No. 77, four doors from the Merediths ; Mrs Fiske was the wife of the jeweller of that name at No. 59 ; and Goren was probably meant for Joseph Galt, a rival tailor, at No. 63.

So passed " the gorgeous tailor "—" a robust Brummel and the Regent of low life " ; and after being laid out in his old yeomanry uniform, sword and vast helmet by his side, the house permeated with the cooking odour of funeral baked meats, the body of the Great Mel., attended by his widow and surviving children, was laid to rest in the family vault in St Mary's burial ground. This is close to St Thomas's Church, and an ancient place of sepulture for the parish of Portsmouth. It is now disused and abandoned—like the derelict church of St Mary it surrounds. Barracks and some very poor cottages abut right on to the graves, and the dismal scene reminds one of that ghastly burial ground in *Bleak House* where Lady Dedlock dreed her weird.

The Great Mel. buried, there remained now in the old home his widow ; his youngest daughter, Catherine ; and his only surviving son, Augustus Urmston Meredith,[1] born in 1797, who was but seventeen years of age at the time of his father's premature death. He had been destined and partially trained for the medical profession, for he had no desire for tailoring or any business aptitude. He possessed some measure of the family beauty and *savoir faire*, and was in all ways a presentable

---

[1] The nomenclature of Augustus Meredith has a curious history. He was baptized at St Thomas's Church, 7th February, 1797, and his Christian names were entered in the register as Gustave Urmston ; but a few years later they were corrected to Augustus Armstrong, the alteration being initialled by the Rev. J. G. Bussell, curate in charge of the parish. As the boy grew up he accepted the name of Augustus, but not that of Armstrong, for when he witnessed the marriage of his sister, Catherine Matilda, to S. B. Ellis, in 1819, he signed his name in the register : " A. U. Meredith " ; and when he eventually died, in 1876, the names inscribed on his tombstone were " Augustus Urmston Meredith."

youth, far above his station in life. It is very likely that, as adumbrated in *Evan Harrington*, he was on a visit to his sister, Louisa Read, in Lisbon, when the fatal illness of the father destroyed his ambitions and recalled him to Portsmouth to assist his widowed mother with a—to him—distasteful business and the problem of raising money to pay off the large debts left by the deceased Melchizedek, who " never was known to have sent in a bill." It is to be hoped that his heirs and assigns were able to collect some portion of the long outstanding debts, but whatever accrued did not benefit the daughters of the house, for they, in turn, had nothing to bequeath to their children in the way of money.

For the next few years the tailoring business was in the capable hands of the admirable Mrs Meredith, whilst her son did his best to fit himself and become experienced, more or less as described in the sartorial novel. In 1819, the last of the Meredith girls having married, as we have seen, an officer of Marines, mother and son were left alone in the old home from whence the father and all the five fine daughters had departed —to the grave or distant places, a sad change truly. Mrs Meredith's advancing years made it advisable for her son to look out for a wife and housekeeper. He did not require to look far. Just round the corner had lived a playmate of his in childhood days, Jane Eliza Macnamara, born in 1802, daughter of Michael Macnamara, of " The Vine," Broad Street, one of a row of houses, nearly all inns, just beyond the Sallyport and King James's Gate on the site now covered by the Point Barracks. This was the wife selected by Augustus Meredith, and he chose well, though he probably knew and cared nothing about eugenics. Despite her origin, Jane Macnamara was a refined and talented girl, and no unworthy mother of her famous son, who had a double heritage of personal beauty from both parents. His maternal grandfather, Michael Macnamara (who died, in 1815, " much respected, an old inhabitant of this town," as a Portsmouth paper records), had married Sarah, daughter of Thomas and Catherine Dale, of Portsmouth. Consequently, George Meredith was ignorant of his own pedigree when he stated, as reported : " My mother was pure Irish."[1] His actual link with Ireland was as remote as his paternal one with Wales :

[1] Letter from Mr Coulson Kernahan, *Daily Chronicle*, 4th April, 1912.

KING JAMES'S GATE, BROAD STREET, PORTSMOUTH

From Charpentier's lithograph, 1830

but it is interesting proof of the power of Celtic blood to assert itself that, despite many blendings with English strains, and long association with Hampshire, George Meredith was predominantly a Celt, though, as he said to Mr Clodd, "there must have been some Saxon strain in the ancestry to account for a virility of temperament which corrected the Celtic in me " : the Saxon strains were the more numerous.

So Augustus Meredith brought home his wife to the old family house, No. 73 High Street, Portsmouth, and there, on 12th February, 1828, was born their only child, George Meredith. The boy was baptized on 9th April following, in St Thomas's Church, and presumably he was named George after a cousin, George Meredith, born in 1801. One is tempted to picture in imagination the scene in the dim, musty church : the young parents, and probably some of the beautiful aunts and their husbands, all in the quaint, stiff dresses and uniforms of the period ; and then the return to the spacious, bow-windowed parlour on the first floor, over the shop at No. 73, for the christening refection, presided over by the stately Mrs Mel. ("And a beautiful cook you used to be, dear Mama," as the Countess observed.)

But Anne Meredith's course was nearly run. She died seven months later, on 28th November, 1828, aged seventy-five (six days after the birth of another grandson, Arthur Ellis). As related in *Evan Harrington*: "Ghosts were the one childish enjoyment Mrs Mel. allowed herself," and she "did not care to converse about the dead, save in their practical aspect as ghosts." So, to follow her example, in the absence of record of any ghostly manifestations, we will refrain from further reference to her demise to be found in family letters, only pausing to note, as confirmation of her superstitious nature, that in her old-fashioned net purse there is still preserved a silver coin of the date 1703. This coin was placed in Mrs Meredith's mouth as the moment of mortal dissolution approached. What relic this custom was of some far-away folk-lore superstition, or how it could be expected to speed the parting soul (perhaps it was a sort of entrance fee to Ghostland, or Charon's fare for Styx ferry), it is impossible now to say. Whatever the explanation, the rite was evidently a family tradition, for the coin was carefully preserved by Mrs Meredith's youngest daughter and handed down, together with the story, to her children.

His mother dead, henceforth Augustus Meredith was sole master of 73 High Street, which is now in our family panopticon to be the background of the early scenes in the life of his famous son.

73 High Street, Portsmouth.
The birthplace of George Meredith.
[*From a Contemporary Lithograph.*]

73, HIGH STREET, PORTSMOUTH, SHOWING THE ALTERATION ON
THE GROUND FLOOR SINCE THE MEREDITHS' TIME

Photograph by H. Symonds & Co., Portsmouth

CHAPTER II

CHILDHOOD AND YOUTH

ACCORDING to George Meredith's own statements, his childhood was not a happy time. But that was the fault of his own temperament and constitutional antagonism to his environment, for, despite the immediate circumstances of his heredity, he was an aristocrat by nature and in person—one of the most remarkable examples of atavism. Personally—during his early years at any rate—he was loved and cared for by both his parents, and was, in fact, petted and allowed to have his own way to a degree very unusual at that time, when children were treated in a somewhat Spartan manner, and had little opportunity of doing as they liked or of expressing their own opinions.

As is generally the case with an only child, brought up entirely in the society of his elders, and an auditor of their conversation, Meredith developed early and always had something of contempt or dislike for juveniles of his own age. He was a very reserved and acutely sensitive boy, afraid of ghosts and of being left alone in the dark, and, as I have indicated, a trifle spoilt by his relatives in his position of a solitary little child in a house which had held six or seven lively children in the preceding generation of the family. I discovered a gentleman who well remembered George Meredith at the age of two years, one who had been his neighbour and playmate in those far-away days. In 1830, No. 74 [1] High Street, the house next door to the Merediths', was occupied by David Brent Price, printer and bookseller, and his young family. The youngest son, James Brent Price, born in 1826, when about four years old, was one day invited in to No. 73 to "play with young George"; and here are his recollections of the future novelist as a child of two or three :

[1] Admiral Lord Anson had lived here for a time in the preceding century.

29

" I went up to the large front drawing-room, where I found the boy and a lady who must have been his mother. The boy did not seem to care much about playing with me, and I was rather shy. He brought me his toys and picture books to see, and I was mightily pleased, I remember, with a horse and cart (not like the many cheap ones that I had seen)—a beautiful lifelike white horse, and the cart of superior make, and as George drew it along it made music as the wheels went round. What I remember of the child's appearance is somewhat hazy —a boy in white frock and blue ribbons tied up his sleeves,[1] but he was certainly a pretty child. I spent the afternoon with him, but we did not get on much together as he assumed a sort of superiority.[2]

" In February, 1832 or 1833, there came to us from No. 73 an invitation to a party—' Tea and Ball to keep the birthday of Master George Meredith.' It invited ' The Misses and Masters Price,' so my two sisters, my elder brother and myself went in on the auspicious evening. We have often laughed in after years at the way my brother fulfilled his duties to us. He gave a single knock to the side door, and when a servant came he said, '*Please, we are come!*' We were the first of the visitors, and were shown into the drawing-room, and all four of us sat down on a sofa. Shortly after, knocks came continually, a lady received the company, and introduced the later comers to those who were there. We were removed to a rout seat, many of these being round the room. Tea and coffee and cakes were handed round by servants. I did not know many of the people, but I *did* some of them, viz., the Harrisons of *The Hampshire Telegraph*, the Dudleys, the Pineos, and the Hintons, as they all lived quite near us. There must have been over fifty altogether, but mostly ' grown-ups.' After tea the lady announced that the company were to go to the next room, and that Mr Macnamara [3] would be M.C. The musicians soon struck up, and a first set was announced. I was given a ' grown-up,' as a partner, and pushed through the figures, but

---

[1] See the portrait of Meredith at this age, frontispiece of vol. i. of *The Letters of George Meredith*.

[2] Though he was two years younger than Price !

[3] Presumably Mrs Augustus Meredith's brother, who became a clergyman and lived for some time in Southsea at a later period.

I was such a failure that I had to sit the rest of the evening—a mere spectator. At intervals I was regaled with quarters of oranges, almonds and raisins, and weak negus. I got very sleepy. Supper was announced, and there was a rush to the front drawing-room. I got near my sisters and brother, and was pressed to partake of tarts and cake. At last the lady said, ' It is time those children went home,' so my brother took us home, and as regards myself I was very glad to be there. At this birthday party George was, of course, made much of by everyone. He was then out of the frock-petticoat period. He and I often met after this, but we did not fraternise much. He used just to say, ' How de do,' and nod. I did the same."

It could not have been long after the date of this party that Mrs Meredith died, at the early age of thirty-one. The event is noted briefly in *The Hampshire Telegraph* of 15th July, 1833 : " Portsmouth. Died on Thursday morning, after a short illness, Mrs Meredith, wife of Mr Meredith of this town." She was buried at St Thomas's in the vault of her Macnamara and Dale relatives. To George Meredith in after years his mother was only a shadowy memory. As he wrote to a friend mourning a mother : " I had this shock when I was a little boy, and merely wondered." But Mrs Meredith's early death probably had a share in the mental development of her son, for had she lived during the period of his adolescence he would have been happier and his home conditions very different ; and consequently he would not have been so introspective and lonely in spirit, or so soon have propounded the truth of the words, dear to poets : " They learn in suffering what they teach in song."

The family at No. 73, Augustus Meredith and his small son of five, being now destitute of feminine influences, George was looked after, as far as possible, by his adult cousin, Mary Meredith Burbey, from across the road, and his aunt, Mrs Ellis, at such times as her own family duties enabled her to be in or near Portsmouth. He was now of an age to take notice of things, and his surroundings offered interesting and lively material for his first impressions of life.

The Portsmouth of Meredith's childhood was a vastly different place from the town of to-day. Owing to the removal of the Admiralty offices to Portsea, all trade and traffic are now centred there, and naval life congregates round the Dockyard and Whale Island, leaving the High Street stranded and quiet. Eighty years ago the sea end of High Street was almost entirely composed of shops : now they are converted into private residences, including No. 73. But George Meredith's early years were passed in the very heart and whirl of English maritime life. His home was just at the edge of the world, so to speak, for here at the Sallyport and Point all sailors then landed and took their pleasures without delay, both officers and men. He must have seen many famous seamen, for close by were all the popular resorts of the officers; the George Hotel and the Fountain (where Mr Midshipman Easy routed the first lieutenant) were both in the High Street ; and the Blue Posts (rendezvous of Peter Simple and every other midshipman) was in Broad Street—all in close proximity to the Meredith shop, where an officer could be " fitted complete." As before stated, almost every house in Broad Street was a tavern, and the adjoining purlieus of East Street, Bathing Lane, Bath Square, and Tower Street were devoted mainly to houses of ill-fame. On the site of what is now Tower House (the home of Mr W. L. Wyllie, R.A.) stood a particularly lively tavern where music—of a sort—was provided. Off the High Street, too, were similar places, and in St Mary's Street (now Highbury Street) a most notorious music hall, eventually abolished. All kinds of excitement, from murder downwards, were at hand for the delectation of the boys of the neighbourhood. And there were numerous barracks and much military pomp and circumstance. Portsmouth was then strongly fortified, and defended by walls, bastions, moats, guard-houses, and gates. These last were closed at a certain hour at night, and, after that, belated inhabitants could only obtain admission by giving the countersign to the sentries on guard. A mounted officer went the " Grand Round " of the town, and the conditions were entirely those of a strictly guarded garrison. To stray beyond St James's Gate into Broad Street after dark was to court many dangers, including the activities of the Press-gang.

Opposite the Merediths' house was held, on the Grand Parade, in July, for the most exciting fortnight in the exciting year, the

HIGH STREET, PORTSMOUTH
From Charpentier's lithograph, 1830

annual Fair, a veritable pandemonium which it became necessary to abolish in the " forties." Richardson's Show always had the best pitch, by the Bank at the corner of the High Street, and adjoining it was Wombwell's menagerie of wild beasts. Probably young George Meredith disdained these vulgar entertainments, and he does not seem to have been much interested in the naval and military life that surrounded him, although he came into personal contact with officers who could have given him accounts of their experiences at Trafalgar, Cape St Vincent, the Baltic and in the sinking of the *Royal George*. For his uncle by marriage, S. B. Ellis, and this uncle's brothers, came to Portsmouth and 73 High Street, and a friend of the Ellises was the Commander-in-Chief at Portsmouth in 1837, Admiral Sir Philip Durham, who had been a lieutenant on the *Royal George* when she went down. To illustrate the social conditions George Meredith was familiar with as a young boy, I give a few extracts from the journal of my grandfather, S. B. Ellis, who, *en route* to service in India, had anchored at Spithead, when he took the opportunity to see much of his brother-in-law and other relatives in Portsmouth.

" *6th September*, 1837. Landed after breakfast. Walked with Mrs Burbey [1] and daughters to their garden at Southsea.

" *7th September*. Landed in the afternoon, and dined with the Commandant of Royal Marines, Colonel Hornby, at his house in St Thomas's Street.

" *8th September*. Remained on shore, and dined with Mr Thomas Burbey; in the evening there was music and dancing. Returned at a late hour, and slept at Mr Meredith's in the High Street.

" *9th September*. Had the unexpected pleasure once more to shake by the hand my kind brother Frank, who had come to Portsmouth to see me before my final departure for India.

" *12th September*. Accompanied my brother to Gosport and visited with him the *Britannia*, the flagship of Sir P. Durham, the Commander-in-Chief at Portsmouth. Returned and dined with Mr Meredith in Portsmouth."

[1] This was Thomas Burbey's second wife, Mary Bradley. Her son, George Burbey, born 1829, was one of the few boys George Meredith cared for at this date.

C

As befitted the original of Evan Harrington, Augustus
Meredith was more addicted to the society of those in higher
circles than that of his neighbours, the tradespeople of the High
Street, a characteristic which his young son inherited or very
soon copied. But the real Augustus Meredith was a very
superior man, and scant justice has been done to him by those
who merely echo the crushing dictum of his son that he was
" a muddler and a fool."   If George Meredith really used these
words, it must be remembered that he delighted in imparting
a freakish touch of exaggeration to his statements, and, like
all great men, he suffers the penalty of too meticulous records
of his conversation, whether in grave or light mood. Augustus
Meredith and his son were alike physically, and they both had
the love of walking many miles in the country over hill and
dale. Augustus was a great chess-player and very fond of
reading. He was a member of the Portsmouth Literary and
Philosophical Society. There is other evidence that he was a
cultured, generous man : " a perfect gentleman and not in the
least like a tailor " is the report of one who knew him well,
though, in view of the fact that he never wanted to be a tailor,
the latter part of the statement is not surprising. But why
the highly honourable and necessary calling of a tailor should
bring any discredit or opprobrium upon its professor, and a
hatter, a hosier, and a bootmaker be exempt from disgrace
and disdain and division into a fractional ninth of a man, with
concomitant goose and cabbage, is a profound sartorial mystery
which neither Sir Piercie Shafton nor the Harringtons satisfactorily explain.[1]

It must be admitted that, like his father before him, Augustus
Meredith was very careless in money matters, and very hospitable. He entertained his friends often, and he had a curious
habit of retiring from the head of his table early, leaving his
guests with wine without stint—certainly not an economical
plan in those days of two-or-three-bottle-men. Money was
accordingly short at No. 73, for the incubus of the Great Mel.'s
debts still remained, and the income from the neglected business
was much reduced. So it was found necessary to let off part
of the house, and the drawing-room and a large back room

---

[1] John Accutus, the warrior, was originally a tailor, and so were
John Stow and John Speed, the topographists.

(over the workshop) were duly rented by Sir Edward Synge, an eccentric Irish baronet.[1] Perhaps this arrangement enabled Augustus Meredith to provide better schooling, clothes, and amusements for his son than fell to the lot of the other boys round about their home. It is strange that the father never succeeded in winning the affection and sympathy of his uncommon son, for undoubtedly, to the best of his ability, Augustus did all he could to give his child a good education and such pleasures as he liked. He sincerely loved the boy.

About 1837 George Meredith was sent as a day scholar to St Paul's School, Southsea, a seminary—to use the word beloved of pedagogues of that period—which existed from 1825 to 1850. (Long's Memorial Hall, at the corner of St Paul's Square and King Street, is said to be the original school building, though adapted to the purposes for which it is now used.) After becoming a pupil at this superior Fount of Learning, young George was more aloof than ever from his boy neighbours in the High Street—Jem Price from next door, Ned Galt from No. 63, Joe Neale from the Coffee House at the corner of Grand Parade, and many others, for all these lads imbibed knowledge at the far humbler stream of Frost's Academy in St Thomas's Street. Mr Price, before mentioned, related some amusing reminiscences of these schooldays :

" The boys of St Paul's looked down upon us, Frost's boys, but George Meredith and I when we met always exchanged salutations : ' How de do, Price,' in his usual drawling, patronising way. He was certainly a good-looking youth, with bright blue or grey eyes, and a nice, light, curly head of hair, and always well dressed, much better than any of us boys, all sons of tradespeople. We were, however, a jolly lot of boys—trundled hoops, played at marbles, whip and peg-tops, rounders, prisoner's base, pitch-hat, and on winter nights at ' nickey-night ' with flint and steel to strike when told to ' show your light.' To these

---

[1] Sir Edward Synge was a first cousin of the grandfather of J. M. Synge, dramatist and poet. Sir Edward later took a house farther up the High Street. His youngest son, General Millington Synge, remained faithful to Portsmouth, and died at 61 High Street, where also his widow lived until her death in 1915.

sort of things George Meredith never stooped, and, in consequence, he got the name of ' Gentleman Georgy ' amongst us boys. We often waited for the Convict Guard to come to the Guard House on the Parade, where the soldiers had to draw their cartridges, and we boys collected the powder and made what we called ' Devils ' by mixing our saliva with the powder and working it into a pyramid, and then set light to it at the top—it was really a pretty bit of fireworks. Need I say George Meredith did not join in this ?

" It was in 1839 that I saw the last of George Meredith. We Frost boys had been running races on the Governor's Green, and several of us were together talking when George Meredith joined us just opposite the Parade Coffee House, kept by a man named Neale, who owned a racehorse. G. M. was on this occasion very affable to us, as a boy, Joe Neale, son of the Coffee House keeper, was with us. George Meredith said to Neale : ' I was at Stokes Bay races last week and I saw your father's horse come in *second*, but I think he is a grand horse. By George ! he's got some blood in him ! ' *N.B.*—This young gentleman was at the most eleven years old ! "

Despite this dashing comment on horseflesh, evidently a Mendelian echo of Melchizedek, it is to be feared that George Meredith's young contemporaries regarded him in the main as " a cocky prig "—for how could these normal, healthy, common little boys be expected to understand, or sympathise with, the manifestations of a dawning genius as exemplified in the character of this uncommon boy all too conscious of his own rare personality and superior gifts. He looked down upon his young companions and analysed them disdainfully. As he stated in after years, he had the faculty in boyhood of reading the characters of his friends " consummately." [1] He lived in a romantic world of his own imagining, and all normal, conventional things bored him. He has left a vivid picture of the Sunday devotions of his childhood :

" I remember, at that age, how all love of the Apostles was belaboured out of me by three Sunday services of prodigious length and drowsiness. *Corinthians* will for ever be associated

[1] See Letter to Dr Jessopp, 23rd December, 1862.

in my mind with rows of wax candles and a holy drone over-head, combined with the sensation that those who did not choose the road to Heaven, enjoyed by far the pleasantest way. I cannot hear of *Genesis*, or of the sins of amorous David, or of Hezekiah, without fidgeting in my chair, as if it had turned to the utterly unsympathetic Churchwood of yore. In despair I used to begin a fresh chapter of the adventures of St George (a serial story, continued from Sunday to Sunday), and carry it on till the preacher's voice fell. Sometimes he deceived me (I hope, not voluntarily) and his voice bade St George go back into his box, and then ascended in renewed vigour once more ; leaving me vacant of my comforting hero ; who was not to be revived after such treatment. I have known subsequent hours of ennui : but nothing to be compared with those early ones."

As for books, he found his chief pleasure in *The Arabian Nights*, which, as he said, " doubtless fed an imagination which took shape in *The Shaving of Shagpat.*"

But in boyhood, as in all the future, Meredith found his greatest delight in Nature, though in his Portsmouth days the country was somewhat distant from his home. In several of his early poems, written a few years subsequent to the period we are considering, there are allusions to the joys he experienced as a boy amid the beauties of Nature and wild life. Thus :

> Under boughs of breathing May,
> In the mild spring-time I lay,
> Lonely, for I had no love ;
>   And the sweet birds all sang for pity,
>   Cuckoo, lark, and dove.

> O SKYLARK ! I see thee and call thee joy !
> Thy wings bear me up to the breast of the dawn ;
> I see thee no more, but thy song is still
> The tongue of the heavens to me.

> Thus are the days when I was a boy ;
> Sweet while I lived in them, dear now they're gone ;
> I feel them no longer, but still, O still
> They tell of the heavens to me.

And in his lovely *Spring Song* :

My soul is singing with the happy birds,
    And all my human powers
    Are blooming with the flowers,
My foot is on the fields and downs, among the flocks and herds.

Deep in the forest where the foliage droops,
    I wander, fill'd with joy.
    Again as when a boy,
The sunny vistas tempt me on with dim delicious hopes.

The sunny vistas, dim with hanging shade,
    And old romantic haze ;
    Again as in past days,
The spirit of immortal Spring doth every sense pervade.

There speaks the real youthful Meredith. A wonderful
thing, for this was not a country-bred boy imbued in earliest
days with the wonders of Nature. He had to discover and
recover them himself, unaided and alone. For, as we have
seen, this was a town-bred boy, the son of tradespeople, born,
reared, and schooled in a great seaport, distant from woods and
country-side. True, he had the sea, but, unlike the case of
Swinburne, the " fair green-girdled mother " did not influence
him in any degree. The sea and naval history, so paramount in
Portsmouth, never inspired the youthful muse of Meredith.
His love of Nature, birds and flowers, mountain and woodland,
was innate, and he had his own secret dreams and delights amid
the maritime and commercial surroundings of his boyhood, to
him so uncongenial and sordid.

In 1841 came many changes in the life of George Meredith,
now thirteen years old. His father married a second wife,
Matilda Buckett, who, it seems, had previously been housekeeper at No. 73. His financial position not improving,
Augustus Meredith decided to leave Portsmouth and make a
fresh start at tailoring in London. He accordingly disposed
of his business to his neighbour, Joseph Galt, who figures as the
occupant of the old Meredith house in the Directory of 1842.
What became of Augustus during the next three years is not
clear, but from 1846 to 1849 he carried on a tailor's business at
26 St James's Street, London, which ought to have been a profitable speculation, for it may be presumed that many naval
officers who had patronised the Portsmouth establishment in

past years would return to their old tailor now that he was located in the midst of Clubland.[1] But Augustus Meredith's lack of business aptitude always nullified his schemes, and the London venture was not a success. Upon the break-up of the home in Portsmouth, George Meredith was sent to a boarding-school in the country for a year. Personally, I think this school is depicted as Rippenger's in *The Adventures of Harry Richmond*, and that some of the youthful adventures of Harry were in fact an echo of those of George Meredith, for he endows his hero with the same airs of superiority and " penetrative capacity " [2] for reading the characters and motives of his companions that he himself possessed even from boyhood, as we have seen. And just as young Harry Richmond went later to Germany, so did Meredith.

Meredith parted from his birthplace and the only home he had hitherto known without any regrets.[3] Portsmouth, apparently, had no happy memories for him : only those of sad or painful things magnified from trifles by his super-sensitive imagination and temperament. He never spoke in after years, with regretful reminiscence, of his childhood, as do most men of the only golden time (if it is happy) of life. Inscrutably he put those " days and dreams out of mind," and Portsmouth never furnished scene or incident for his literary work beyond that bitter transcript of family history in *Evan Harrington*.[4] His father he never cared for, and he did not keep in touch, after

[1] The original house and shop at 26 St James's Street are now gone ; the site is covered by the building known as Ormonde House, adjoining Ryder Street.

[2] Chapter ix.

[3] The tablet placed on No. 73 High Street, at my suggestion, by the Corporation of Portsmouth, in 1913, bears the words : " In this house was born on the 12th of February, 1828, George Meredith, Novelist and Poet, who lived here until his thirteenth year."

[4] The only passage, that I recall, in Meredith's other work that might be construed as an echo from early influences in Portsmouth is in *The Amazing Marriage*, relative to the swearing habits of sailors of the old days : " When I was young the boys relished these dreadful words because they seemed to smell of tar and battle-smoke, when every English boy was for being a sailor . . . those old quiet yet exciting days in England . . . the whole period is alive to you, as it was to me in the delicious dulness I loved, that made us thirsty to hear of adventures and able to enjoy to the utmost every thing occurring."

boyhood, with many relatives. They—commercial and naval people—were not in a position to help him to a congenial livelihood, or likely to sympathise with romantic, literary aspirations, and he, proud, reserved, and intellectually their superior, mutual misunderstandings, and possibly dislike, were not unlikely to ensue. Consequently Meredith faced life in the outer world friendless, poor, and desolate in spirit.

He had inherited a little money from his mother, and the trustee of the small estate was now charged with the educational arrangements of the boy, who accordingly entered the Moravian School at Neuwied, on the Rhine, 18th August, 1842. Here his education really commenced, for at his previous schools, as he said, " I learned very little." The influences of his experiences in Germany were very strongly stamped on his subsequent mental career. His poetry, *Farina* (particularly), *The Adventures of Harry Richmond, The Tragic Comedians,* and *One of our Conquerors,* all bear the impress of his admiration for Germany and some qualities of the people, though he was equally observant of their absurdities and faults. Although in these late sad days the German character has been overwhelmed by a flood of false culture and savage megalomania, it is childish and futile to deny the many charms that the country possesses or has created in the past. German music, some portion of German literature, German wine, German scenery—the stately curves of the Rhine bordered by ruined castles, or the wild, wooded mountains of the north and south, all permeated with legend and romance—such things are essential and will survive the madness of the present German ruling caste. And these were, primarily, the things that appealed so vividly to the plastic imagination of the youthful George Meredith, and to which he gave such beautiful expression in his early poem, *Pictures of the Rhine* :

> The spirit of Romance dies not to those
> Who hold a kindred spirit in their souls.
>
> . . . .
>
> Beauty renews itself in many ways ;
> The flower is fading while the new bud blows ;
> And this dear land as true a symbol shows,
> While o'er it like a mellow sunset strays
> The legendary splendour of old days.
>
> . . . .

About a mile behind the viny banks,
How sweet it was, upon a sloping green,
Sunspread, and shaded with a branching screen,
To lie in peace half-murmuring words of thanks.
To see the mountains on each other climb,
With spaces for rich meadows flowery bright ;
The winding river freshening the sight
At intervals, the trees in leafy prime ;
The distant village-roofs of blue and white,
With intersections of quaint fashioned beams
All slanting crosswise, and the feudal gleams
Of ruined turrets, barren in the light ;
To watch the changing clouds, like clime in clime ;
Oh ! sweet to lie and bless the luxury of time.

   .   .   .   .

To dream of fairy foot and sudden flower ;
Or haply with a twilight on the brow,
To muse upon the legendary hour.

   .   .   .   .

Rare is the loveliness of slow decay,
With youth and beauty all must be desired,
But 'tis the charm of things long past away,
They leave, alone, the light they have inspired :
The calmness of a picture ; Memory now
Is the sole life among the ruins grey
And like a phantom in fantastic play. . . .

George Meredith was fourteen years of age when he became
a pupil at the Moravian School at Neuwied, on the romantic
Coblenz-Cologne section of the Rhineland scenery. The school
had been founded in 1756, and it was ever famous for its excellent
liberal education, and for the instillation of true Christian and
social ideals in the minds of its pupils. During the first fifty
years of its existence the scholars were mainly Swiss. Many
German boys came later, but from 1832 to 1842 British youths
formed the majority, and this decade was known as "The
English Period." The late Professor Henry Morley preceded
Meredith as a pupil by a few years, and throughout his life
retained the greatest interest in his old school. Fifty-five years
after his time there he was editing a magazine which aimed at
keeping in touch with the pupils, past and present, of the
various Moravian Schools abroad ; and at a meeting of
"Old Neuwieders" in London, 1889, he paid this tribute to the
particular establishment which had included Meredith among its

scholars : " No formal process of education had acted upon their lives so thoroughly or so much for their good as the little time they had spent at Neuwied. It had taken all the bitterness out of their lives, all envy and hatred and uncharitableness having been so thoroughly removed from them by contact with the gentle spirit of the old Moravians." Mr J. A. Hammerton, in his useful work, *George Meredith in Anecdote and Criticism*, gives an excellent verbal picture of Neuwied and the school which claims quotation here :

" We may reasonably assume that Meredith's schooldays at Neuwied represent a period of the utmost importance to his after life, and the scene of this early influence on one of the greatest figures in modern literature is worthy of some little notice, for one so observant and vigilant as Meredith must have been, even as a boy, could not have lived there long before he had absorbed the spirit of the place, and doubtless that passion for long walks and hill-climbing, which later characterised his days of lusty manhood, first awoke among the historic heights along the right bank of the Rhine from Neuwied to the Drachenfels. The Moravian Schools at Neuwied have long been famous throughout Europe, and many notable Englishmen have passed through them. Their origin dates from the time of Prince Alexander of Neuwied—the town was formerly the capital of a little principality—who was a shining example of liberalism in an age of bigotry, and who, in 1762, during the religious unrest and intolerance of his time, made free of his little town to all the sects that cared for religion sufficiently to stand by their convictions. Lutherans, Calvinists, Catholics, Moravians, Jews, were all allowed in Neuwied the fullest liberty of thought and worship ; being, as an old writer quaintly puts it, ' children of the same Parent, subjects of the same moral government, candidates alike for a future state, they are taught to reflect that the articles in which they agree are of infinitely greater importance than those on which they differ, and that the minutiæ and speculative opinions cannot annihilate the primary duty of brotherly love.' The partisans of each sect were allowed to maintain their own ministers and conform each according to their established convictions, without any form of interference from the state. A little religious Utopia ! Out of this grew up the remarkable educational establishment of the Moravians, whence so many of the famous missionaries of that small but energetic body have gone out to the far places of the earth. Neuwied was happy in its princes, the little town was beautifully laid out, industries encouraged, and life must have flowed along there with melodious and purposeful rhythm for generations. When Meredith became a Neuwieder, the town had a population of about 5000 ; but to-day it has considerably extended and contains some 10,000 inhabitants. It was the scene of Cæsar's crossing of the Rhine, and the district was rich in Roman antiquities, which the care of Prince Alexander first brought together in the museum of his palace, still one of the features of the place. We may conclude that something of this spirit of liberalism, which must still have been electrical in the air of Neuwied in the earlier years of last century, entered into the young Meredith and conditioned the shaping of his mind."

The religious spirit of the place was also strongly impressed, though only temporarily, upon Meredith's young mind. He was at Neuwied for two years, without any break of holidays at home, and it was during this period that he went through that process of religious unrest and excitement—sometimes introspective and morbid, in other cases enthusiastic or ecstatic— which is a common experience in the development of an imaginative boy or girl at about the age of fifteen. As he told Mr Clodd : "When I was quite a boy I had a spasm of religion which lasted about six weeks, during which I made myself a nuisance in asking everybody whether they were saved." Interesting evidence on this point is furnished by the earliest letter of Meredith's that has been traced, one written at the time of his departure from Neuwied to a boy named R. M. Hill, his schoolfellow there :

" Neuwied,
" 8th July, 1844.

"My dear Hill,—During the time that we've lived together, one feeling, whether in union, or shall I say enmity—no, that is too harsh—has agitated our respective bosoms. It is fellowship. O may God grant that all may have the same feeling towards you to make your life happy. But true fellowship is not to be had without Christianity; not the name but the practice of it. I wish you the greatest of all things—' God's blessing,' which comprehends all I would or could otherwise say.

"Yours,

"GEORGE MEREDITH."

Curious to think that the mortal ashes of him who wrote this letter in youth should, sixty-five years later, be denied interment in Westminster Abbey on account of religious views presumably not up to a decanal standard. But then, of course, this was the dust of him who had said : "Parsondom has always been against progress; they treat Christianity, not as a religion, but as an institution."

CHAPTER III

GEORGE MEREDITH left Neuwied in 1844, and the next two years of his life are a blank. What he did between his sixteenth and eighteenth year and where he lived is unrecorded, though it is permissible to presume he was with his father in London, and possibly attended to the account work of the business. As we have seen, Augustus Meredith was at 26 St James's Street in 1846, the year which provides the next authentic fact of his son's career, for it was on 3rd February that George Meredith commenced his duties as an articled clerk with Richard Stephen Charnock, a solicitor and Fellow of the Society of Antiquaries, whose offices were at 44 Paternoster Row, and later at 10 Godliman Street. Charnock belonged to the Arundel Club, whose members included Dickens, R. H. Horne, and Lord John Manners.

According to Meredith's account, during his absence in Germany his little legacy from his mother had suffered serious diminution by the mismanagement of his trustee. He was made a ward in Chancery, and the residue of his money was mainly devoted to fitting him for the profession of the Law. Although he said his legal employer " had neither business nor morals," Charnock was an interesting and cultured man of literary gifts who did not discourage similar tastes in his pupil ; and though George was articled and bound to him for five years, Charnock seems to have released the boy from legal obligations when Meredith decided to act like Scott, Disraeli, Harrison Ainsworth, Charles Reade, Sheridan Le Fanu, F. C. Burnand, and many other writers, who all abandoned the Law for the lure of Literature.

Charnock, indeed, had some considerable share in starting Meredith on his literary road, for he introduced the lad to his own set of intimates, mainly writers and artists, including

45

Edward Peacock and Mrs Nicolls, son and daughter of Thomas Love Peacock, the polished novelist and former friend of Shelley. This was an intensely appreciated sequence of associations for the eager boy, compact of dreams and aspirations. Further, Charnock was mainly instrumental in giving expression to the work of his little literary coterie by starting, about 1848, a manuscript magazine, entitled *The Monthly Observer*. The various contributions, written on quarto sheets, were bound together, and then circulated among the contributors, each of whom, in turn, acted as editor and critic. Here, in the number for April, 1849, appeared George Meredith's earliest published poem, *Chillianwallah*. It was criticised by the editor for the month, Austin Daniel, and several of his suggestions were adopted, and the third stanza omitted, when the poem attained the glory of actual print in *Chambers's Journal* for 7th July, 1849, three months after the original manuscript circulation in the amateur magazine. Five numbers of *The Monthly Observer*, including two edited by Meredith, were sold for £80 at Sotheby's a few years ago, and crossed the Atlantic to join the famous bibliographical collections of Mr H. E. Widener.[1] Meredith's share as critic of his fellow-contributors' work included this pungent observation, which adumbrates the style of the years to come : " Inspiration, like Balaam's Ass, suddenly stopped short of itself, despite all the whipping and spurring of the infatuated jockey, who comprehended not the divine instinct of his Pegasus."

It was in this same year, 1849, that Augustus Meredith gave up his business in St James's Street and emigrated with his wife to South Africa, a very adventurous undertaking in those early days of travel and colonisation. He established himself as a tailor in St George's Street, Cape Town, where we will take another glimpse of him a little later on, when considering *Evan Harrington*. George Meredith was now homeless in London, and was obliged to take lodgings—or probably only one room—at No. 7 Upper Ebury Street, Pimlico.[2] It was

---

[1] See *The Athenæum*, 24th August, 1912.

[2] Upper Ebury Street commenced at Elizabeth Street and ran west to Grosvenor Road. It is now part of Ebury Street, and renumbered. No. 7 Upper Ebury Street would probably now be No. 153 Ebury Street, but this particular house looks as if it had been refronted since 1849.

from here that he wrote, on 4th June, 1849, to Messrs Chambers respecting his poem *Chillianwallah* :

"I have sent you the enclosed poem in the hope that it will be acceptable to your Journal. It was written immediately on receipt of the intelligence which it chaunts, and will, I think, even now find many an echo in hearts akin to the subject and the name which christens it."

The poem, though mediocre, found immediate acceptance, for it was topical and commemorated, of course, the sanguinary battle fought on 13th January, 1849, in the Second Sikh War, when the English lost 2400 killed and wounded in defeating the natives, preliminary to the annexation of the Punjab. A week after sending in his manuscript, Meredith wrote, on 12th June, to Leitch Ritchie, the editor of *Chambers's Journal* :

"I am obliged by your acceptance of the Poem. Would a translation of the life, etc., of *Kossuth the Magyar* suit the columns of your Journal ? . . . The accounts of the man now afloat are flimsy and unconnected. . . . May I beg you to substitute for '*hearts*' in the 7th line of the last verse of *Chillianwallah* '*hopes*.' Thus—

"'And the *hopes* of all will languish.'"

Nearly half a year went by, and then, on 30th November, 1849, having made a start with his study of Kossuth, Meredith wrote again to Leitch Ritchie :

"I send you four sheet pages of *Kossuth*. . . . I trust it is not too late—but the fact is I was determined to ascertain if the character of Kossuth was as fine as . . . I had imagined. . . . You are at liberty to erase *all* passages which suit not the purpose or politics of the Journal.

"I accompany this with some Sonnets on Two Kings of England, which may if you like form a series.

"I have been contemplating a sketch of the life of Hermann [1] who has lately died. There is as yet no English account."

[1] Johann Hermann, 1772–1848. German humanist and Greek scholar.

And the next day he added :

" I find I have forgotten to enclose the Sonnets mentioned in my letter of yesterday's date. . . . I think they would do very well if taken in a series, and I have a great many already finished, etc. Let me know about the article on Hermann as early as you can."

For some unexplained reason, the study of Kossuth and the other proposed work never appeared in *Chambers's Journal* ; and the " great many " Sonnets must have been eventually destroyed in manuscript, though possibly the early poem, *John Lackland*, may be a solitary survivor from the royal galaxy. Meredith, however, preserved no sentimental interest in his early poetry or his first published work, for when, towards the end of his life, Mr C. E. S. Chambers wrote to him, reminding him of his early association with the famous *Journal*, and expressing a hope that they might, perhaps, meet in London, no reply was forthcoming.

At the time he came of age, 1849, Meredith was, of course, exceedingly poor. He had merely the remnant of his mother's small property by way of income, for his literary earnings in this first year of publication could only have amounted to a few pounds. Journalistic " biographers " are very fond of the legend that Meredith started his literary career in London with one guinea and lived entirely on cold porridge. This popular delusion has been succinctly preserved for future use by the brethren of " scissors and paste " thus :

" There is a legend current in literary circles that Mr Meredith first started his career as a writer in the possession of one guinea. This he invested in a sack of oatmeal. Since he was too poor to buy fuel to cook it, during the whole of the time he wrote his first work, *Evan Harrington*, he subsisted on oatmeal and water, in the form of a most unpalatable drink."

Without doubt a very unpleasant beverage, but there is no reason to believe that Meredith patronised it. The slight discrepancy in the above statement, which places the commencement of his literary career in 1860, when he published his *fifth* work, *Evan Harrington*, renders the rest of the story valueless. Indeed, by 1860 Meredith was a connoisseur in wines, and had the means to offer good vintages to his friends, and always he was, rightly, an appreciator of good food and good cooking. Even as early as 1849, as a member of Charnock's hospitable coterie of friends, he would often be asked out to dine, so the oatmeal fable must be consigned to the limbo of foolish and unprofitable parables invented for our behoof or chastening. Still, it may be granted that Meredith had very little money to spend on himself at this period, and no doubt often went short of rations in his own room at 7 Upper Ebury Street. He was in the bloom of his splendid young manhood, and the long walks in the country he delighted to take must have engendered a healthy appetite that needed substantial appeasement. His footsteps always turned to Surrey, the beautiful county which called to him ever, and where nearly all his subsequent life was to be spent. So, let us picture him, his tall, strong figure crowned by a mass of curly hair (red chestnut in colour then), striding through Brompton, Chelsea, or Kensington—then distinctive village-like suburbs compact of market gardens and good residential houses—away to the hills and heaths of Surrey :

> The sun bursts broad, and the heathery bed
> Is purple and orange, and gray :
> Away, and away, we'll bound old hound,
> Over the hills and away.

He was sometimes accompanied on his long walks—even as far as to Brighton—by Edward Gryffydh Peacock,[1] whose acquaintance, as we have seen, he had made through Charnock, and the little manuscript magazine run by the lawyer's friends. And it was at Peacock's rooms, near the British Museum, that on one fateful day Meredith was introduced to his friend's sister, Mary Ellen, the eldest daughter of Thomas Love Peacock. She was a brilliant, witty, beautiful woman, thirty years of age,

---

[1] Edward Peacock in early life went to sea. He subsequently became a clerk in the East India House, and a barrister. He was a great athlete, a champion sculler, and fond of boxing. He married, and left one son, named Thomas Love Peacock, who was much at Lower Halliford in the Merediths' time as a playmate for Arthur, his cousin.

D

and a widow. She had married, in 1844, Edward Nicolls, a lieutenant of the Royal Navy, who commanded H.M.S. *Dwarf*; he was drowned at sea four months later, and the posthumous child of the marriage, Edith (subsequently Mrs Clarke), was born in the same year.

Meredith was immediately attracted by Mrs Nicolls and she by him, but the mutual attraction was probably only of a physical nature. Their personal qualities and temperaments and the story of their courtship and disastrous marriage much resemble the similar tragedy of Bulwer Lytton and Rosina Wheeler. Just as the latter declined Bulwer's proposals at first, three or four times according to her own account, so Mrs Nicolls refused Meredith six times. If she had only persisted in her refusal, both would have been saved from an immensity of grievous pain and sorrow. From the material point of view even, there were many objections to the marriage. The disparity in age of nine years' seniority on Mrs Nicolls's side, and the fact that Meredith lacked position, profession, and any income worth considering, might well have made them pause. But he had rare personal gifts and beauty, and Mrs Nicolls, casting discretion aside, yielded to her persistent young admirer.[1] They were married on 9th August, 1849, in St George's Church, Hanover Square, by the Rev. Henry W. Blacket, curate. Meredith was described in the register as of Maddox Street—so he must have moved to lodgings there prior to the ceremony—and son of Augustus Meredith, whose profession was given as "Esquire." The bride was described as of Devonshire Street, and the register was also signed by her father, T. L. Peacock. Probably Peacock's second daughter, Rosa, was also present. She later became Mrs Collinson, and died in 1857, at the age of thirty. His youngest daughter, Margaret, died in 1826, aged three years ; and Peacock wrote for her tombstone in Shepperton Churchyard the poem commencing " Long night succeeds thy little day."

Soon after the marriage, the Merediths went to the Continent on the proceeds of a legacy which had come to George from a relative in Portsmouth ; but they were back in London by November, when they stayed with Thomas Love Peacock at

---

[1] " The combination of cleverness and beauty in men was never to the advantage of women,'' Meredith wrote over half-a-century later.

his house, No. 22 John Street, Adelphi.[1] It was from here
that Meredith addressed his later letters to Leitch Ritchie,
on the subject of his Sonnets and Kossuth study. At first
the Merediths seem to have been tolerably happy together,
just as the Bulwers were in the early years of marriage. They
passed their time between Peacock's homes and various
lodgings and boarding-houses by the seaside (particularly at
Felixstowe and Seaford) and in Surrey. For a considerable
time they boarded with Mrs Macirone, at The Limes, Weybridge, a pleasant house with a large garden. Mrs Macirone
(formerly Miss Elizabeth Williams) was a woman of considerable
culture and charm. She was the widow of Colonel Francis
Macirone, A.D.C. to Murat, King of Naples, and a versatile
man of inventive powers who was an early pioneer in the study
of aviation. Mrs Macirone had two very beautiful daughters,
who were, of course, half Italian. The elder, Emilia, as will
be seen later, in some degree suggested to Meredith his Emilia
Sandra Belloni. Miss Emilia Macirone became the wife of
Sir Edmund Hornby, and was later the author of *In and
Around Stamboul during the Crimean War*; and her sister
Giulia married Major Albert Vaillant. The Limes was an
exceedingly pleasant abode for the Merediths, for Mrs Macirone
and her daughters knew many interesting people, their guests
including Bulwer Lytton; Tom Taylor; Eyre Crowe, A.R.A.
(Thackeray's secretary); Samuel Lucas, the journalist; and
R. H. Horne, the peculiar author of *Orion* and *A New Spirit
of the Age*. With most of these men Meredith became on
friendly terms, with some important results; and through the
introduction of Tom Taylor he formed an eventful friendship
with Sir Alexander Duff Gordon and his wife (a woman of
literary and linguistic gifts), who were then living at Nutfield
Cottage, Weybridge. To their daughter Janet (later Mrs
Ross), then a little girl about eight years old, Meredith was
devoted, and his affectionate regard for her never wavered
throughout life. In the early days she gave him the name of
" My Poet "; and she has related how Meredith used to take
her for long walks, perched on his shoulder, telling her wonderful
fairy tales all the way. Meredith loved children. His own

[1] This is the last house on the north side of John Street, at the corner
of Adam Street and facing the Adelphi Hotel.

little step-daughter, Edith Nicolls, speaking of the time when
she was seven years old, says : " He and I were great friends
in those early days even. We played cricket together ; he
was a splendid playfellow."

In the first years of their married life, Meredith and his
talented wife found a congenial link in their literary pursuits.
They were both writing a good deal of poetry, and sometimes
they collaborated. Through R. H. Horne, who was at that
time a member of the staff of *Household Words*, Meredith
obtained an introduction to Charles Dickens, and it was in this
journal that a number of these early poems appeared during
a period of six years. Mr B. W. Matz, by means of the contributors' book of *Household Words*, was able to attribute
twenty-three poems to Meredith.[1] The two first, *Sorrows
and Joys* and *The Two Blackbirds*, appeared in 1850, and the
last, *Monmouth*, in 1856. It is possible some of the intervening
numbers were the work, wholly or in part, of Mrs Meredith.
About this date she and her husband compiled a treatise on
Cookery, an art they were both practised in, and of which they
were appreciative—as befitted the daughter of Peacock, the
Epicurean novelist, and the son and grandson of those Merediths
who, as we have seen, were given to much hospitality and good
cooking. In addition to recipes, the manuscript, in Meredith's
writing, comprised many entertaining notes on domestic
management, apt quotations from poetry and prose, and some
sapient bits of advice presented to the female sex. Thus :

" A small portion of the time which young Ladies sacrifice
to torturing the strings of their Pianoforte, employed in obtaining Domestic Accomplishments, might not make them worse
wives, or less agreeable Companions to their Husbands. We
hope our fair readers will forgive us for telling them, Economy
in a Wife is the most certain Charm to ensure the affection and
industry of a husband."

" The Editor has considered the Art of Cookery not merely as
a mechanical operation, fit only for working cooks, but as the
Analeptic part of the Art of Physic. Philosophers of the highest
class, such only, can comprehend its Importance, which amounts
to no less, than not only the enjoyment of the present moment,

[1] See *T. P.'s Weekly*, 17th February, 1911.

The Limes, Weybridge. Here Meredith wrote much of his early work and commenced "The Shaving of Shagpat"

but the more precious advantage of improving health and prolonging life, which depends on duly replenishing the daily waste of the human frame with materials pregnant with nutriment and easy of digestion."

" I have written for those who make Nourishment the chief end of Eating, and do not desire to provoke Appetite beyond the powers and necessities of Nature ; proceeding, however, on the finest Epicurean principles of indulging the Palate, as far as it can be done without injury or offence to the stomach, and forbidding nothing but what is absolutely unfriendly to Health."

" These rules and orders for the regulation of the business of the Kitchen have been extremely beneficial to the Editor's own Health and Comfort. He hopes they will be equally so to others, they will help those who enjoy health to preserve it ; teach those who have delicate and irritable stomachs how to keep them in good temper, and, with a little discretion, enable them to indulge occasionally, not only with impunity but with advantage, in all those alimentary pleasures which a national epicure can desire."

And on the Eternal Servant Question the Editor propounded in the same Johnsonian style :

" Avoid all approaches to Familiarity, which according to a proverb is accompanied by contempt, and soon breaks the neck of obedience. Servants are more likely to be praised into good conduct than scolded into bad, always commend them when they do right, to cherish the desire of pleasing in them you must show them that you are pleased :

> " Be to their faults a little blind,
> And to their virtues very kind."

And he sums up the Cuisine with the couplet :

> " The tender morsels on the palate melt,
> And all the force of Cookery is felt." [1]

To *Fraser's Magazine* for December, 1851, Mrs Meredith had contributed an interesting article entitled *Gastronomy and*

---

[1] The original manuscript, in George Meredith's holograph, extending to fifty pages, was recently in the possession of Maggs Brothers, who priced it at £195.

Civilisation, tracing the history of cookery from the earliest times, and which gives evidence of such erudition and wide classical reading as to suggest that some aid was rendered by the writer's husband. The article was pessimistic on the matter of contemporary cooking (both in France and England), and methods of serving, and lamented the declension of hospitality—a curious commentary in face of the descriptions of Dickens and Thackeray, who have pictured the " forties " and " fifties " as a period of much good solid dining and constant hospitality. In the same magazine, 1851 and 1852, appeared two of George Meredith's poems, *Invitation to the Country* and *The Sweet o' the Year*. *Fraser's Magazine* was published by John W. Parker, of West Strand, London, and Meredith had previously arranged with this publisher to produce, at the author's cost, his first book—his collected *Poems*, 1851. Writing to Parker from Weybridge, on 12th December, 1850, Meredith said :

" I send you a Selection of Poems completed, and a List of others from which I intend selecting for the projected volume. Of the latter I prize the *Cassandra* as my best work, but it is not yet finished.[1] *The Shipwreck of Idomeneus* is blank verse and 17 pages. The rest, with the exception of one or two of the ballads, are ready. Of the Poems I forward you, I wish to have your opinion as early as you can give it. If you think the specimens I forward you inferior to the ' requirements of the age,' ' not saleable ' and so forth, I shall very likely be content to abide by your decision for a time. Mr Horne speaks very favourably of those he has seen, but he has only seen the classical Poem and a few others, and consequently insists on Ballads and modern ingredients which I have endeavoured since then to supply.[2] *Sorrows and Joys*, *The Two Blackbirds*, *Infancy and Age* are a selection from those published in *Household Words*. The two ' blank verse metres ' beginning ' How sweet on sunny afternoons ' are selections from half a dozen of

[1] Apparently *Cassandra* was not completed in time for this volume. It was published with *Modern Love, and Poems of the English Roadside*, 1862.

[2] *Daphne* was sent to R. H. Horne with some lines, commencing : " That you will take the meaning of this verse I know, deep-hearted friend and earnest man, Poet ! " See *Letters of George Meredith*, p. 5.

the sort,[1] and will be, I think, the most original features in the volume. Also *London by Lamplight* has two or more numbers to follow (but shorter ones), if you think fit. Besides these I am writing a Ballad for *Household Words*, which I think will be liked. I will tell you the subject when I see you. You will see that in *The Rape of Aurora* I have followed the idea of Ariosto, and inserted a little mythology—the union of the Sun and the Dawn—and in *Daphne* I have avoided mention of ' Don Cupid.' I have other *Pictures of the Rhine*, but I thought six enough.

"Thus far, then, I have explained the Contents of the parcel, which as soon as you can peruse, do, and let me know your opinions thereon and thereafter, when I will have the pleasure of calling on you and consulting as to the birth and baptism of my first-born of the Muse."

Shortly before publication, the author wrote from Weybridge to James Vizetelly :

" If possible put the enclosed *Hexameters* among the *Pastorals* —that is to say if not too late. Also *Love in the Valley*—but separate the two—and put neither first among the Pastorals— and let the Songs, *Spring, Autumn,* be last among them. *July* is to follow *Antigone,* and then *Beauty Rohtraut.*

" I hope to hear from you to-morrow about *Idomeneus* and that the volume will soon be finished.

" Very truly,

" GEORGE MEREDITH."

But the young poet had to suffer the usual annoyances in the way of errors in printing, and on the eve of the public appearance of his first-born he wrote again to Vizetelly :

" *26th May,* 1851.

" I am sorry to say I discover a great many new and original mistakes in my Book, of which both the MS. and proofs were utterly guiltless."

The little volume, now so valuable, of 159 pages, bound in green cloth, was published about 30th June. It was dedicated " To Thomas Love Peacock, Esq., with the profound admira-

---

[1] *The Pastorals.*

tion and affectionate respect of his son-in-law. Weybridge, May, 1851." Reviews appeared on 5th July in *The Leader* and *The Speaker*, and others followed. These were not enthusiastic, of course, and the book was not a financial success : how seldom a volume of verse by a new writer ever fares otherwise. Meredith had expended and lost some sixty pounds on his preliminary flight up Parnassus, and he seems to have judged his resultant position, his poetical gifts at that stage of their development, and his future prospects, very fairly. He had received a letter in commendation of his book from Charles Ollier,[1] and in reply wrote :

"*July*, 1851.

"It is the appreciation you give that makes Fame worth asking for ; nor would I barter such communication for any amount of favourable journal criticism, however much it might forward the popularity and sale of the book. I prepared myself, when I published, to meet with injustice and slight, knowing that the little collection, or rather selection, in my volume was but the vanguard of a better work to come ; and knowing, also, that the strictest criticism could scarcely be more unsparing than myself on the faults that are freely to be

[1] As Charles Ollier was the first writer of note to appreciate George Meredith's work and the first critic to encourage him in his literary path, it may not be supererogatory to recall briefly Ollier's career. This man of many literary friendships was born in 1788. Early in life he, with his brother James, was a publisher in Vere Street. He was the friend of Shelley, Keats, Lamb, Leigh Hunt, Peacock, Harrison Ainsworth, and many other writers. He published for Shelley. In 1829 he was connected with *The New Monthly Magazine*. Later, he was principal reader for Richard Bentley. Charles Ollier was the author of novels entitled *Altham and his Wife* and *Ferrers*, and many contributions to magazines. But, as Ainsworth wrote to Ollier's son : "From circumstances he never achieved the position in literature which he ought to have obtained. He had a fine critical taste, and a genuine relish for the broadest humour, as well as a susceptibility of the tenderest pathos. He had a thoroughly masculine nature, and I never knew a man with a keener sense of existence nor one more alive to the beauties of external nature. He was a lover of art—indeed, a critic in art, and accomplished in music. His conversational powers on all subjects were very great. . . ." Charles Ollier died in 1859, so his encouraging appreciation of Meredith's first work was one of the last episodes in his useful and well-spent life devoted to the best interests of literature.

found ; knowing, lastly, that a fresh volume (of poetry) is with the Press a marked book. . . . The poems are all the work of extreme youth, and, with some exceptions, of labour. They will not live, I think, but they will serve their purpose in making known my name to those who look with encouragement upon such earnest students of nature who are determined to persevere until they obtain the wisdom and inspiration and self-possession of the poet."

However, before the year was out, two notable and signed reviews of the *Poems* appeared. In *The Critic* of 15th November, 1851, there was an interesting notice by William Michael Rossetti, who, although but twenty-two years old himself, and a year younger than Meredith, assumed a mentorial attitude of age towards his future friend's work :

"The main quality of Mr Meredith's poems is warmth—warmth of emotion, and, to a certain extent, of imagination. That he is young will be as unmistakably apparent to the reader as to ourself ; on which score various shortcomings and crudities, not less than some excess of this attribute, claim indulgence. . . . Scarcely a perceptive, but rather a seeing or sensuous poet. He does not love nature in a wide sense as Keats did ; but nature delights and appeals closely to him."

Passing on to note *Love in the Valley*, Mr Rossetti observed :

"Surely, it may be said, there is passion enough here, and of a sufficiently personal kind. . . . It is purely and unaffectedly sensuous, and in its utterance as genuine a thing as can be. We hear a clear voice of nature, with no falsetto notes at all ; as spontaneous and intelligible as the wooing of a bird. . . . We have assigned Mr Meredith to the Keatsian school, believing that he pertains to it in virtue of the more intrinsic qualities of his mind, and of a simple enjoying nature. . . . We do not expect ever quite to enrol Mr Meredith among the demi-gods or heroes ; and we hesitate . . . to say that we count on greater things from him ; but we shall not cease to look for his renewed appearance with hope, and to hail it with extreme pleasure, so long as he may continue to produce poems equal to the best in this first volume."

This was not an unfair criticism, and coincided to some extent with the views expressed by Meredith himself in the letter to Ollier. But a critic endowed with more prevision—acquired, no doubt, by longer experience—was Charles Kingsley, who, in an article contributed to *Fraser's Magazine* for December, 1851, and entitled *This Year's Song Crop*, wrote thus of Meredith's *Poems* :

"This, we understand, is his first appearance in print ; if it be so, there is very high promise in the unambitious little volume which he has sent forth as his first-fruits. It is something to have written already some of the most delicious little love-poems which we have seen born in England in the last few years, reminding us by their riches and quaintness of tone of Herrick ; yet with a depth of thought and feeling which Herrick never reached. Health and sweetness are two qualities which run through all these poems. They are often over-loaded—often somewhat clumsy and ill-expressed—often wanting polish and finish ; but they are all genuine, all melodiously conceived. . . . In Mr Meredith's *Pastorals*, too, there is a great deal of sweet, wholesome writing, more like the real pastorals than those of any young poet whom we have had for many a year . . . honest landscape-painting, and only he who begins honestly ends greatly. . . ."

Kingsley's critique was of considerable length, and he gave Meredith much good advice, which the poet, of course, ignored, to the detriment of many later poems. The fact remains that Meredith, with his sensitive and rather unhappy disposition, was disappointed with the results of his first book. He never would speak well of these early verses. " I still think the poems rubbish," he wrote about 1862. In 1890 he said of the volume : "The sole excuse for it, in my mind, is the crude age of the writer. But that does not make it the more comfortable to think that the book is not extinct." And many years later, in 1908, but eight months before his death, in writing to M. René Galland, he said :

" In any case, forbear to touch on my first volume of poems : they are worthless, immature stuff of a youth in his teens, who had not found his hand. I hoped at one time to think of them as dead to the public. Let them be so to you." [1]

There was an implacable element in Meredith's character. He never forgave what had offended him—not even himself when his work failed to come up to the high standard he had erected. Still, the above criticism of his early poetry is unduly severe when one considers that it included the first version of the exquisite *Love in the Valley*—the poem which, on its original publication in 1851, moved Tennyson to write to Meredith saying how much it charmed him, and that he went about the house repeating its cadences to himself. This from the conspicuous poet who had produced *In Memoriam* the previous year, when also he succeeded Wordsworth as Poet Laureate. Tennyson was then living at Chapel House, Montpelier Row, Twickenham, not far, of course, from the Weybridge district of Surrey, where *Love in the Valley* had its scenic setting. F. T. Palgrave notes in his reminiscences of Tennyson : " In G. Meredith's first little volume he was delighted by the *Love in a Valley* (as printed in 1851 : the text in later issues has been greatly changed)."

Meredith, in return, highly praised the earlier verse of Tennyson. He told Mr Clodd : " In *The Lotos Eaters* and *Œnone* (which I could get neither Peacock nor Jefferson Hogg to enjoy) there are lines perfect in sensuous richness and imagery.[2] *The Idylls*,

[1] There is an interesting reference to Meredith's *Poems* of 1851 in a letter of William Hardman's, written about ten years later to a friend. This also shows how reticent Meredith was on the subject of his first marriage :
" You will recollect in one of my previous letters, I ventured to presume that our friend Meredith married a daughter of old Mr Peacock, the author of *Gryll Grange*. Well, I knew that Meredith had published a volume of poems in 1851, 300 copies of which he had afterwards destroyed, and they are consequently very scarce. Of course the British Museum have a copy, so I got hold of it rather against G. M.'s wish, why, I know not. The dedication of the volume is ' To Thomas Love Peacock, Esq., this volume is dedicated with the profound admiration and affectionate respect of his son-in-law.' So I was right."

[2] The late Rev. H. G. Woods, Master of the Temple, possessed a copy of the second edition of Tennyson's *The Princess*, 1848, which contained on the flyleaf an original manuscript poem of ten lines by George Meredith, and his autograph inscription : " To Cornelia—as the Lady most ambitious and best endowed to take fair Ida for prototype." The book was sold in 1915 for £39.

perhaps I should except the *Morte d'Arthur*, will not add to his fame [1]; they are a part of the ' poetical baggage ' of which every writer of a large body of verse must be unloaded. Tennyson's rich diction and marvellous singing power cannot be over-rated, but the thought is thin ; there is no suggestiveness which transcends the expression ; nothing is left to the imagination. He gave high praise to my *Love in the Valley* ; would like to have been its author."

For some of Tennyson's later work Meredith had severe criticism. Writing to a friend in 1864, he said :

" Have you heard that the Countess Guiccioli has two continuation cantos of *Don Juan* and means to publish them ? Likewise more of Byron ! He's abused, so I take to him ; and I'm a little sick of Tennysonian green tea. I don't think Byron wholesome exactly, but a drop or so—eh ? And he doesn't give limp, lackadaisical fishermen, and pander to the depraved sentimentalism of our drawing-rooms. I tell you that *Enoch Arden* is ill done, and that in twenty years' time it will be denounced as villainous weak, in spite of the fine (but too conscious) verse and the rich insertion of tropical scenery."

Concerning *The Holy Grail and other Poems* of 1869, Meredith wrote :

" Have you read Tennyson's last volume ? Are you delighted with it ? Curious that one pretending to the title of great poet should have given so much of his time to such a composition, which is to poetry what vestments are to religion —and he who writes the grand *Lucretius* ! If you have not read Browning's *Ring and the Book*, I recommend the *Caponsacchi, Pompilia, The Pope* and the two *Guidos*."

And on 19th December, 1869, he wrote to Hardman :

" Alack, the Holy Grail ! Did you ever read such lines ? The poet rolls them out like half yards of satin. They look

---

[1] In an early letter, of April, 1857, written from Seaford to a correspondent who had sent him some verses, Meredith said : " I d onot like your idylls (*e.g. The Boat Race*) because both the poem, the matter, and the blank verse recall Tennyson so strongly."

and taste cud-chewn. The figures are Dresden China. If he has hit the mind of his age, as it seems, the age too has hit him and knocked spontaneity out of him. But both are worthier than they show. Gold, the go-between, the abominable Sir Pandarus, has corrupted them."

In a letter (to be found in the published correspondence of Meredith) to Maxse, written on the same day, similar expressions are used, and he adds : " Why, this stuff is not the Muse, it's Musery. The man has got hold of the Muse's clothes-line and hung it with jewelry. But the *Lucretius* is grand. I can't say how much I admire it."

At another time he said : " I can hardly say I think Tennyson deserves well of us ; he is a real singer. Tennyson has many spiritual indications, but no philosophy, and philosophy is the palace of thought."

In later years he liked Tennyson's *Queen Mary* ; and Mrs Meynell relates that Meredith said the high-water mark of English style in poetry and prose was reached in Tennyson's " On one side lay the ocean and on one lay a great water, and the moon was full."

It is interesting to note that as late as 1886 Meredith wrote a poem, *The Young Princess*, which displayed unmistakably the influence of Tennyson :

> The soft night-wind went laden to death
>   With smell of the orange in flower ;
> The night leaves prattled to neighbour ears ;
> The bird of the passion sang over his tears ;
>   The night named hour by hour.
>
> Sang loud, sang low the rapturous bird
>   Till the yellow hour was nigh,
> Behind the folds of a darker cloud :
> He chuckled, he sobbed, alow, aloud ;
>   The voice between earth and sky.
>
> .   .   .   .
>
> When the South had voice of a nightingale
>   Above a Maying bower,
> On the heights of Love walked radiant peers ;
> The bird of the passion sang over his tears
>   To the breeze and the orange-flower.

This is like the Tennyson of the period of *Maud*, who was begotten of Keats and the Romantics. Despite the harsher notes of most of his later poetry, it is evident that Meredith retained an inner and almost unacknowledged love for the sensuous and mellifluous minstrelsy which sang in *Maud*, *The Princess*, and *The Lotos Eaters*, and in his own *Poems* of 1851.

To return to *Love in the Valley*, R. L. Stevenson also paid a fine tribute to the haunting music of this poem. Writing to W. B. Yeats in 1894, he said :

" Long since when I was a boy I remember the emotions with which I repeated Swinburne's poems and ballads. Some ten years ago a similar spell was cast upon me by Meredith's *Love in the Valley* ; the stanzas beginning, ' When her mother tends her ' haunted me and made me drunk like wine, and I remember waking with them all the echoes of the hills about Hyères."

And York Powell, the Oxford historian, described *Love in the Valley* as " the most gorgeous piece of rhythmical work and passion. . . . Meredith has *invented* his great metres."

Leslie Stephen, too, loved the poem, and knew it by heart. Both Stevenson and York Powell may have been more familiar with the later version of the poem than the original form which moved Tennyson to admiration. As is well known, Meredith rewrote, and added many stanzas to, *Love in the Valley* when it was republished in *Macmillan's Magazine*, October, 1878. It is ever matter for surprise and regret that he omitted those last lines of the original poem which hymn the coming of Spring so beautifully :

Then come merry April with all thy birds and beauties !
  With thy crescent brows and thy flowery, showery glee ;
With thy budding leafage and fresh green pastures ;
  And may thy lustrous crescent grow a honeymoon for me !
Come merry month of the cuckoo and the violet !
  Come weeping Loveliness in all thy blue delight !
Lo ! the nest is ready, let me not languish longer !
  Bring her to my arms on the first May night.

On the other hand, the second version contained many improvements and new stanzas of infinite beauty, particularly this oft-quoted word-picture :

> Lovely are the curves of the white owl sweeping
>   Wavy in the dusk lit by one large star.
> Lone on the fir-branch, his rattle-note unvaried,
>   Brooding o'er the gloom, spins the brown eve-jar.
> Darker grows the valley, more and more forgetting :
>   So were it with me if forgetting could be willed.
> Tell the grassy hollow that holds the bubbling well-spring,
>   Tell it to forget the source that keeps it filled.

Despite his condemnation of the early poems, Meredith, at the back of his mind, doubtless exempted *Love in the Valley*, for we find him writing, in 1907, to Mrs Sturge Henderson, to whose book on Meredith Mr Basil de Sélincourt contributed some chapters dealing with the subject's poetry :

" Mr Basil de Sélincourt strikes home in many passages, and the prostrate subject feels it to the quick ; so that he may say at last he has been criticised, which was not expected by him before he passed out. Here and there I could raise a voice : as for instance (I have taken the volume to read again) against the charge of *preciosity* in *Love in the Valley*. But it is good to have my critic's exact impression of the Poems. . . ."

It is, of course, a partial truism that an artist—particularly a literary artist—is a bad judge of what constitutes his best work. Certainly Dickens and Thackeray were exceptions to the rule, for each was fully aware of the superlative merits of, respectively, *David Copperfield* and *Vanity Fair*. But such personal perspicacity is rare, and Meredith rather lacked it. His literary judgments were generally in dissonance with public opinion—and even critical opinion—and in the case of his own work he favoured his later poetry, which to the majority will always be difficult and therefore unpopular. The early poems, if artless and unpolished, were lyrical : this can scarcely be said of the later poems—such as are contained in *A Reading of Life*— and the odes dealing with French history, which leave a sabulous taste on the literary palate : a more saccharine tooth frankly admits preference for *Love in the Valley* and *Beauty Rohtraut*.

Surely the supreme charms of poetry, regarded as a symbol or
expression of Beauty, are its musical cadences which attune the
mind to the thoughts desired, and its art of painting a mental
picture : profound ideas and didactic philosophy are better
expressed in stately prose. Meredith's early poems supply
unsophisticated tonal pleasures in full measure ; and what
beautiful pictures of twilight and night are these :

> When twilight from the dream-hued West
> Sighs hush ! and all the land is still ;
> When from the lush empurpling East,
> The twilight of the crowing cock
> Peers on the drowsy village roofs,
> Athwart the heavens that glimmering line is seen.
>
> Now from the meadow floods the wild duck clamours,
> Now the wood pigeon wings a rapid flight,
> Now the homeward rookery follows up its vanguard,
> And the valley mists are curling up the hills.
>
> Deeper the stillness hangs on every motion ;
> Calmer the silence follows every call ;
> Now all is quiet save the roosting pheasant,
> The bell-wether's tinkle and the watch-dog's bark.
>
> Softly shine the lights from the silent kindling homestead,
> Stars of the hearth to the shepherd in the fold ;
> Springs of desire to the traveller on the roadway ;
> Ever breathing incense to the ever-blessing sky.

Years later, Meredith showed his friend, William Hardman,
the scene which inspired these lines and the spot where he wrote
them—an eminence surrounded by pines on the St George's
Hill Estate, between Weybridge and Byfleet. Hardman notes
" Meredith and I had an argument as to whether he ought not
to have made the second and fourth line to rhyme, and I think
he convinced me that the plan he had adopted was the better
one."

In the delightful *Robin Redbreast* the last stanza conjures up
a picture of young Meredith in the garden of a Surrey cottage

> Merrily, cheerily, joyously still
> Pours out the crimson-crested tide.
> The set of the season burns bright on the hill,
> Where the foliage dead falls yellow and red,

> Picturing vainly, but foretelling plainly
> The wealth of cottage warmth that comes
> When the frost gleams and the blood numbs,
> And then, bonny Robin, I'll spread thee out crumbs
> In my garden porch for thy redbreast pride,
> The song and the ensign of dear fireside.

In striking contrast to this are *Will o' the Wisp*, with its elfin lilts, and the remarkable *London by Lamplight*, which has an elusive suggestion of the impressionist poets of forty years later, together with romantic word painting in rapid antithesis :

> There stands a singer in the street,
> He has an audience motley and meet ;
> Above him lowers the London night,
> And around the lamps are flaring bright.
>
> His minstrelsy may be unchaste—
> 'Tis much unto that motley taste,
> And loud the laughter he provokes,
> From those sad slaves of obscene jokes.
>
> . . . .
>
> This night of gleaming floods and falls,
> Of forest glooms and sylvan calls,
> Of starlight on the pebbly rills,
> And twilight on the circling hills.
>
> This night from which a morn will spring
> Blooming on its orient wing ;
> A morn to roll with many more
> Its ghostly foam on the twilight shore.

Here, to quote Meredith's words from another poem, is " An influence strange and swift as dreams, a whispering of old romance " ; and so there is, in another sense, in the beautiful and musical ballad of *Beauty Rohtraut*, translated from the German of Möricke. It was first published in *The Leader* for September, 1850, and deservedly found a place in *Illustrated British Ballads*, 1881, with an illustration drawn by Henry Marriott Paget.

How fine, too, is Meredith's first expression of his lifelong love of the South-West Wind in the poem of that name :

> For lo, beneath those ragged clouds
> That skirt the opening west, a stream
> Of yellow light and windy flame
> Spreads lengthening southward, and the sky

E

Begins to gloom, and o'er the ground
A moan of coming blasts creeps low
And rustles in the crisping grass ;
Till suddenly with mighty arms
Outspread, that reach the horizon round,
The great South-West drives o'er the earth,
And loosens all his roaring robes
Behind him, over heath and moor.
He comes upon the neck of night,
Like one that leaps a fiery steed.

And round the oak a solemn roll
Of organ harmony ascends,
And in the upper foliage sounds
A symphony of distant seas.
The voice of nature is abroad
This night ; she fills the air with balm ;
Her mystery is o'er the land ;
And who that hears her now and yields
His being to her yearning tones,
And seats his soul upon her wings,
And broadens o'er the wind-swept world
With her, will gather in the flight
More knowledge of her secret. . . .
For every elemental power
Is kindred to our hearts, and once
Acknowledged, wedded, once embraced,
Once taken to the unfettered sense,
Once claspt into the naked life,
The union is eternal.

This poem was an earlier form of *Ode to the Spirit of Earth in Autumn* (1862), which contains many similar thoughts and Nature pictures, as a comparison of the two pieces will demonstrate. But the finest exposition of Meredith's Nature worship and his kinship with things of air and woodland to be found in the early *Poems* is the third Pastoral :

Now standing on this hedgeside path,
Up which the evening winds are blowing
Wildly from the lingering lines
   Of sunset o'er the hills ;
Unaided by one motive thought,
My spirit with a strange impulsion
Rises, like a fledgling,
Whose wings are not mature, but still

Supported by its strong desire
Beats up its native air and leaves
    The tender mother's nest.

Great music under heaven is made,
And in the track of rushing darkness
Comes the solemn shape of night,
    And broods above the earth.
A thing of Nature am I now,
Abroad, without a sense or feeling
Born not of her bosom. . . .

That was the first verse of the life-song whose last lines were to be written nearly sixty years later, in 1908, when the singer was within a few months of death :

    Once I was part of the music I heard
        On the boughs or sweet between earth and sky,
        For joy of the beating of wings on high
My heart shot into the breast of a bird.

    I hear it now and I see it fly,
        And a life in wrinkles again is stirred,
        My heart shoots into the breast of the bird,
As it will for sheer love till the last long sigh.

Apart from the fact that work which contains so much of beauty and music can never merit oblivion, the early *Poems* of George Meredith have their fitting and important place in the history of his mental development, and are thereby secure of remembrance.

CHAPTER IV

"THE SHAVING OF SHAGPAT." HALLIFORD AND SEAFORD DAYS.
"THE HOUSE ON THE BEACH." "FARINA." DOMESTIC
TRAGEDY AND "MODERN LOVE"

ANOTHER lost year in the record of Meredith's life is
1852. He must, however, have been planning and
commencing *The Shaving of Shagpat*, for he once told
Mr Clodd it was written "at Weybridge with duns at the
door." He was also conceiving *Richard Feverel*, but both
works were completed elsewhere. It is interesting to note,
in confirmation of the fact that Meredith was really contemporary with, and one of the band of, the great Victorian
writers, that in this same year, 1852-1853, which saw the
dawn of these two masterpieces, appeared Dickens's *Bleak
House*, Thackeray's *Esmond* and *The Newcomes*, Kingsley's
Hypatia, Charlotte Brontë's *Villette*, Lytton's *My Novel*, Mrs
Gaskell's *Cranford*, and novels by the lesser lights, Charles
Lever, Harrison Ainsworth, G. P. R. James, Frank Smedley,
and Surtees. Browning and Tennyson, too, were producing
fine poetry, so young Meredith had a noble band of rivals in
the field of literary endeavour.

In 1853 he and his wife removed from Weybridge to the
opposite side of the river, Lower Halliford, to live, for a time,
with Mrs Meredith's father, Thomas Love Peacock, whose wife,
Jane Gryffydh, had died the previous year. Peacock was now
sixty-eight years of age, with the most important events of his
life behind him. His earlier years he had passed in literary
dalliance, and his famous friendship with Shelley commenced
in 1812. He accompanied the poet and Harriet to Edinburgh
in 1813 ; and when Shelley was at Windsor and Marlow, where
also Peacock was then living, in 1816, the two men were constantly together. To Peacock, Shelley's fine letters from Italy
were addressed, and it was this friend who endeavoured to bring
about the production of *The Cenci* at Covent Garden Theatre.

Thomas Love Peacock

The first of the delightful series of Peacock's novels, *Headlong Hall*, appeared in 1816, and the last, *Gryll Grange*, in 1860. Those known to Shelley were much admired by him, including *Nightmare Abbey*, wherein he was amusingly satirised ; possibly the author depicted himself as Mr Glowry, for that " very consolate widower " held " that there was but one good thing in the world, *videlicet*, a good dinner "—which was certainly one of the articles of Peacockian belief. The charm of Peacock's novels is increased by the poems and songs scattered through them, *Melincourt* being particularly rich in this respect. In 1819 he became an official at the East India House, and a confrère there of Charles Lamb. Peacock's long association with Lower Halliford commenced in 1822, and he remained faithful to this part of Shepperton until his death, in 1866. His house, in reality two cottages connected by a passage, was only separated from his beloved Thames by a strip of garden, on to which his long, low-ceiled sitting-room opened.

In this house, now called Elmbank, was born, on 13th June, 1853, George Meredith's son and Peacock's grandson, Arthur Gryffydh Meredith, his second name being that of his maternal grandmother. Possibly he was named Arthur after his father's first cousin, Arthur Ellis, then Adjutant at Woolwich, and available as a sponsor. Several children had been born to the Merediths earlier, and died as infants : this was the only child of the marriage who survived to any age : he was destined to bring his parents much joy and, later, great sorrow.

It was soon found that this joint residence was not altogether a successful arrangement. Peacock was getting old, and liked quiet and a domestic régime that ran on oiled wheels of comfort. His infant grandson was, no doubt, in accordance with the immemorial habits of the genus, exigent in his claims upon the time and attentions of the females of the household, and given to making melody of a timbre not appreciated by bachelors and elderly widowers. Further, it has to be stated that although George Meredith had a profound admiration for the literary work of Peacock, and shared his taste for good cooking and good wine, the two men had not much in common in other respects. Meredith was never easy to live with, and his highly-strung temperament and nervous, restless habits—humming snatches of song the while he strode about the narrow rooms of the house, or fidgeted with ornaments and furniture—worried his comfort-loving father-in-law. Consequently Peacock took another little house for the Merediths just across the way on the opposite side of the pleasant Green at Lower Halliford. It was here, Vine Cottage, in the small front room nearest to the entrance, that Meredith finished *The Shaving of Shagpat*. His recreations in this quiet and rural spot took the form of playing cricket with his little step-daughter and other children on the Green in front of the cottage, and his customary long walks through Surrey, when he stored up many impressions of Nature and scenery which found expression in the novels and poems of the years to come.

The Shaving of Shagpat was published by Chapman and Hall at the close of 1855 (though bearing 1856 on the title page), and the author's prefatory note was worded : " December 8th, 1855. It has seemed to me that the only way to tell an Arabian story was by imitating the style and manners of the Oriental story-tellers. But such an attempt, whether successful or not, may read like a translation : I therefore think it better to pre-lude this Entertainment by an avowal that it springs from no Eastern source, and is in every respect an original work."

And yet this wonderful work of art, original and distinctive, though as picturesque and gorgeous as *The Arabian Nights*, and far transcending Beckford's *Vathek*, achieved no success at the outset. Indeed, the first edition sold badly, and was eventually disposed of as a remainder, according to rumour, although the reviews had been quite favourable. It is of interest to recall that two of these notices were written by George Eliot, who had not then attained her own fame, for it was not until 1857 that her *Scenes of Clerical Life* were published. George Eliot was at this period living at No. 8 Parkshot, Richmond. She had some slight personal acquaintance with Meredith, and read his book directly it appeared, for she noted in her diary for 30th December, 1855 : " Read *The Shaving of Shagpat* (George Meredith's)." Her first review of the work appeared in *The Leader* for 5th January, 1856, in the course of which she said :

" *The Shaving of Shagpat* is a work of genius, and of poetical genius. It has none of the tameness which belongs to mere

The House on Lower Halliford Green where Meredith lived in 1854-1855, and here he finished "The Shaving of Shagpat"

imitations manufactured with servile effort or thrown off with sinuous facility. It is no patchwork of borrowed incidents. Mr Meredith has not simply imitated Arabian fictions, he has been inspired by them ; he has used Oriental forms, but only as an Oriental genius would have used them who had been ' to the manner born ' . . . In one particular, indeed, Mr Meredith differs widely from his models, but that difference is a high merit ; it lies in the exquisite delicacy of his love incidents and love scenes. In every other characteristic—in exuberance of imagery, in picturesque wildness of incident, in significant humour, in aphoristic wisdom, *The Shaving of Shagpat* is a new Arabian Night. To two-thirds of the reading world this is sufficient recommendation."

Writing to Miss Sara Hennell, on 18th January, 1856, George Eliot said : " If you want some idle reading get *The Shaving of Shagpat*, which I think you will say deserves all the praise I gave it." Her second notice of the book appeared, in April, in *The Westminster Review*, a periodical she had previously assisted in editing. In view of George Eliot's appreciation and kindly help in these early days, it is unfortunate that Meredith was not more grateful in his estimate of her. It is true that he once wrote of the author of *Adam Bede* as " the greatest of female writers." But in that case Meredith must have had a poor opinion of " female writers " in general, for, as J. Comyns Carr recorded : " For George Eliot's achievement he never professed more than a strictly limited respect. Her more pretentious literary methods failed to impress him, and there were times when the keenness of his hostile criticism bordered upon scorn. I remember when someone in his presence ventured to remark that George Eliot, ' panoplied in all the philosophies, was apt to swoop upon a commonplace,' he hailed the criticism with the keenest enjoyment, and half-laughingly declared that he would like to have forged the phrase himself." And on another occasion he said to Mr Clodd : " George Eliot had the heart of Sappho ; but the face, with the long proboscis, the protruding teeth as of the Apocalyptic horse, betrayed animality." But Meredith, probably, never contemplated the careful preservation and publication of these post-prandial witticisms and criticisms, or he would scarcely have committed himself to such an absurd literary judgment as this : " Not much of Dickens will live, because it has so little correspondence to life. He was the incarnation of cockneydom, a caricaturist who aped the moralist ; he should have kept to short stories. If his novels are read at all in the future, people will wonder what we saw in them, save some possible element of fun meaningless to them. The world will never let Mr Pickwick, who is to me full of the lumber of imbecility, share honours with Don Quixote." [1] If such a thing were possible, a plebiscite on this point a century hence would be of interest. To-day it would probably be found that where ten people prefer *Don Quixote*, fifty would vote for the greater pleasure they have found in *Pickwick* ; and there would not be absent some who consider Cervantes's masterpiece a greatly overrated work.

To return to *The Shaving of Shagpat*. It will ever be matter for debate and divided opinion as to how much of allegory is contained in that immortal fantasy. At first, Meredith denied that the work contained any allegorical signification, for in a note to the second edition (which also contained the fine drawing by his friend, Frederick Sandys, of " Bhanavar the Beautiful ") he said :

" It has been suggested to me by one who has no fear of Allegories on the banks of the Nile that the hairy Shagpat must stand to mean umbrageous Humbug conquering the Sons of Men ; and that Noorna bin Noorka represents the Seasons, which help us, if there is health in us, to dispel the affliction of his Shadow ; while my heroic Shibli Bagarag is actually to be taken for Circumstance, which works under their cheerful guidance towards our ultimate release from bondage, but with a disappointing apparent waywardness. The excuse for such behaviour as this youth exhibits is so good that I would willingly let him wear the grand mask hereby offered to him. But, though his backslidings cry loudly for some sheltering plea, or garb of dignity, and though a story-teller should be flattered to have it supposed that anything very distinct was intended

---

[1] On the other hand, Meredith wrote, in 1899, to Mrs Meynell, concerning her article on Dickens : " I will confess that I am won by her. She hands me a plum, and I must own her client to be a lord outside cockaigne. It was very handsome pleading."

by him, the Allegory must be rejected altogether. The subtle Arab who conceived Shagpat meant either very much more, or he meant less; and my belief is that designing in his wisdom simply to amuse, he attempted to give a larger embrace to time than is possible to the profound dispenser of Allegories which are mortal; which, to be of any value, must be perfectly clear, and when perfectly clear are as little attractive as Mrs Malaprop's reptile."

But writing in 1906 to the Rev. James McKechnie, who has expounded his own reading of the allegorical significance of *The Shaving of Shagpat* in book form very ably, Meredith certainly modified his original disclaimer with these words :

" You have done as much as could be done with the adventurous barber. An allegory is hateful to the English, and I gave it clothing to conceal its frame. But neither that nor the signification availed. Very few even of my friends have cared to read the book, and of those I can count but two who have said a word in favour of it. I regret to think that although you may be indemnified for the cost of publication your labour will go unrewarded."

Meredith also wrote on this point, to Mrs Bovill, in 1892 :

" Wonderful to hear that there is a woman who can read of Shagpat ! I suppose he does wear a sort of allegory. But it is not as a dress-suit ; rather as a dressing-gown, very loosely. And they say it signifies Humbug, and its attractiveness ; while Noorna is the spiritual truth. Poor Sh. Bagarag being the ball between the two. I think I once knew more about them and the meaning, but have forgotten, and am glad to forget, seeing how abused I have been for having written the book."

All readers of the original work should study Mr McKechnie's most interesting exposition of *The Shaving of Shagpat*, even though they may not see, eye to eye with him, the profundities of allegory and symbolism and philosophy he presents for consideration. Personally, I think Meredith intended his book to be primarily an opulent and gorgeous piece of romantic story-telling ; and having adopted the Eastern method and setting, artistic considerations impelled a certain amount of allegory and symbolism, as in *The Arabian Nights* and all Eastern stories. Allegory of an obvious kind there certainly is in *The Shaving of Shagpat*. Its finest portion, "The Story of Bhanavar the Beautiful," is simply a superlatively picturesque version of the world-old parable of the temptation of Woman by the Serpent, and how she immolates Love on the Altar of Beauty and Ambition, and sends lovers to death for the gain of a jewel. And the quest for the mystic Sword of Aklis, with the preliminary tests and trials of the Well of Paravid, the magic Horse Garraveen, and the Lily of the Enchanted Sea ; the Wiles of Rabesqurat ; the Pit of the Roc ; and the fatal lures of the Palace of Aklis—all these suggest analogy with Bunyan's immortal Allegory, for in both stories the Attainment of the Ideal is only achieved by passing through much temptation and pain.   Endurance for Victory.

Mr McKechnie suggested that Meredith would have reached supreme heights as an allegorist if he had been encouraged to continue his work on these lines : " I am prepared to believe that on none of his works did Meredith, to begin with, build such high hopes as on *The Shaving of Shagpat*, and that to the keenness with which he felt the shattering of those hopes is due the fact that though the heart of his genius lay in that direction he never wrote another allegory."

It is certainly matter for regret that Meredith never pursued his course farther as an Eastern story-teller, for if *The Shaving of Shagpat* be considered merely as a fantasque tale it is in the front rank of that category.   Take the scene where Bhanavar calls the serpents to her aid :

> " Hither ! hither
>   Come to your Queen ;
> Come through the grey wall,
>   Come through the green !

" There was heard a noise like the noise of a wind coming down a narrow gorge above falling waters, a hissing and a rushing of wings, and behold ! Bhanavar was circled by rings and rings of serpent-folds that glowed round her, twisted each in each, with the fierceness of fire, she like a flame rising up white in the midst of them.   The black slaves, when they had lifted the curtain of the harem-chamber, shrieked to see her, and Aswarak crouched at her feet with the aspect of an angry beast carved in stone."[1]

And what vivid word-painting conjures up the Genie Karaz at a touch :

"There was a deep growl of thunder, and the palace rocked, tottering ; and the air became smoky and full of curling vapours. . . . Lo ! in its place a Genie of terrible aspect, black as a solitary tree seared by lightning ; his forehead ridged and cloven with red streaks ; his hair and ears reddened ; his eyes like two hollow pits dug by the shepherd for the wolf, and the wolf in them."

That final scene of the great conflict in the air between Karaz and Shibli Bagarag (mounted on the league-long wings of Koorookh " as the moon sits on the midnight ") is almost too overcharged with wild imaginative descriptions of fantastic happenings—a pagan apocalypse.

The wealth of simile in this story is prodigal : " Her laughter

[1] Mrs Ross records that Meredith had the idea of this story of the Queen of the Serpents suggested to him by the tales of a certain M. de Haxthausen, whom he met at the Duff Gordons' house, Nutfield Cottage, Weybridge : " He had fought with the Queen of the Serpents, whose crown he wore in a little red silk bag that hung round his neck from a gold chain. With flashing eyes and vehement gestures he described how he fought with the Queen. ' She called her subjects to her aid with loud, shrill hisses, and the earth became alive with snakes. I killed, and I killed, and I killed, and then ran for my life out of the burning hot gully, followed by hundreds of gliding, writhing, venomous creatures. The owner of this crown is the ruler and the head of all the serpents,' said he, proudly tossing his head. By dint of much persuasion, M. de Haxthausen was induced to show his treasure, which was inside a small gold box in the red silk bag. It looked like a miniature crown fashioned out of dark amber, and a doctor, who was present, said, after careful examination, that it undoubtedly was a bony excrescence from a reptile, and probably from the head. M. de Haxthausen was uneasy until his crown was once more safely hung round his neck, and said it had not been taken out of the gold box for more than twenty years. Meredith never took his eyes off M. de Haxthausen while he told his weird tale, and when next he brought me home he told me a marvellous story about the Queen of the Serpents, which was afterwards developed into Bhanavar the Beautiful in *The Shaving of Shagpat*.'[2]

was like the falls of water at moonrise ; her loveliness like the very moonrise ; and she was stately as a palm-tree standing before the moon." When Meredith was asked by H. M. Hyndman what suggested this particular comparison of a woman to a palm-tree, he replied : " The hair falling over her shoulders and her slender shape." Throughout this work picture succeeds picture. Here is one of sunset blending with moonrise :

" They, when they had lifted the damsel to her steed and placed her in their front, mounted likewise, and flourished their lances with cries, and jerked their heels to the flanks of their steeds, and stretched forward till their beards were mixed with the tossing manes, and the dust rose after them crimson in the sun. So they coursed away, speeding behind their Chief and Bhanavar ; sweet were the Desert herbs under their crushing hooves. . . . By the beams of the growing moon they entered the first gorge of the mountains. . . . These, as the troop advanced, wound and widened, gradually receding, and their summits, which were silver in the moonlight, took in the distance a robe of purple, and the sides of the mountains were rounded away in purple beyond a space of emerald pasture. . . . Then she looked forth on the stars that were above the purple heights, and the blushes of inner heaven that streamed up the sky."

In amusing contrast are little saws of Eastern philosophy : " ' What creature is that, O Kadza, which tormenteth like the tongue of a woman, is small as her pretensions to virtue, and which showeth how the chapters of her history should be read by the holy ones, even in its manner of movement ? ' Cried Kadza : ' The flea that hoppeth.' "

" A Woman's at the core of every plot man plotteth,
And like an ill-reared fruit, first at the core it rotteth."

" What ! thou hast been thwacked, and refusest the fruit of it—which is resoluteness, strength of mind, sternness in pursuit of the object "—words which Meredith often paraphrased when reviewing his own career. The same philosophy is found in this Shagpatian lyric :

Ye that nourish hopes of fame !
Ye who would be known in song !
Ponder old history and duly frame
Your souls to meet acceptance of the thong.

Lo ! of hundreds who aspire
Eighties perish—nineties tire !
They who bear up, in spite of wrecks and wracks,
Were seasoned by celestial hail of thwacks.

Fortune in this mortal race
Builds on thwackings for its base ;
Thus the All-Wise doth make a flail a staff,
And separates his heavenly corn from chaff.

Following the Eastern fashion, there are many of these little
snatches of song and illustrative verse in *The Shaving of Shagpat*.
One has a distinct echo of Tennyson's *Tears, Idle Tears*, which
had appeared a few years earlier (1847). It is in the pathetic
scene of the death of Zurvan, when, with dimming eyes, he sighs,
and sings to Bhanavar :

Sadder than is the moon's lost light,
Lost ere the kindling of dawn,
To travellers journeying on,
The shutting of thy fair face from my sight.

Enough has been said to demonstrate that *The Shaving of
Shagpat* can be read either for the pleasure it gives as a story
of romance and magic or as a profound and subtle allegory ;
and it is this element of elusiveness and mystery, truly Eastern
in character, which enhances in no small degree the piquant
charm of Meredith's solitary excursion into the enchanted realm
of faery.

During 1856 and 1857 the Merediths were living mostly at
Seaford, then a dull and stagnant little place (as it was even
thirty years later, when fowls promenaded the grass-grown
streets with leisured calm), with the nearest railway station
at Newhaven—another Stygian " seaport." But the glorious
range of Sussex Downs at the back were an immense attraction
to Meredith, the mighty walker of those days. Further, he had
here the society of a friend he much appreciated, Maurice Fitz-
Gerald, who owned property at Seaford. Son of the eccentric

and religiously fanatical John Purcell FitzGerald, of Boulge Hall, Suffolk, and nephew of Edward FitzGerald, the translator of *Omar Khayyám*, Maurice FitzGerald was at this period, though only just of age, the ideal bachelor. Sir Francis Burnand, whose intimate friendship with him commenced at Trinity College, Cambridge, has described him as "a first-rate scholar,[1] a gentle Sybarite, and a skilled *gourmet*." Violent sports and long walks he disliked, so literature and the art of cuisine were the bonds that united him to Meredith, who gave him the name of "The Young Mauritius" and took this friend as the model for The Wise Youth in *Richard Feverel*. In these pleasant days at Seaford the Merediths and FitzGerald used to lodge at Marine Terrace with the village carpenter and wheelwright, Richard Ockenden by name, whose wife was a wonderful cook—and the chief attraction for a prolonged stay in Sussex. "That which fine cookery does for the cementing of couples needs not to be recounted to those who have read a chapter or two of the natural history of the male sex," as Meredith wrote of Mrs Ockenden's culinary fame, which has been recorded by her distinguished lodger's pen in several places. In a dialogue sent to Miss Janet Duff Gordon, FitzGerald voices the nice considerations of one of the Ockenden dinners (for, as Sir Francis Burnand states, "his well-thought-out arrangement of every meal, breakfast, lunch, and dinner, was the result of calm study, guided by such sound common-sense"), whilst Meredith himself enacts "Poet":

"Fitz. goes about with a volume of Francatelli in his hand. Thus we have colloquised :

FITZ. Oyster-soup is out of the question with cod and oysters to follow. It must be brown. But if the veal doesn't come from Brighton ! Good G——! What a set of heathens these people are !

POET. Eh ? Oh, yes, brown, of course !

FITZ. You haven't the slightest idea of the difficulties.

POET (*mooning*). She was dressed very becomingly in white sauce.

FITZ. (*taking it naturally*). À la Bechamel. That's what

---

[1] FitzGerald translated *The Crowned Hippolytus* of Euripides, among other work.

MAURICE FITZGERALD, THE ORIGINAL OF ADRIAN HARLEY IN
" RICHARD FEVEREL."

From the pencil portrait, by Samuel Laurence, in the possession of his Son

I'm most anxious about. Do you think Ockenden understood my directions ? The potatoes to be sliced about half-an-inch : sauce poured over : then fresh layer—— (*Becomes excited.*) If well done, I know nothing better in the world than Potatoes à la Bechamel.

POET (*writes*). And you are all I care for in the world, dearest Rose ! I care for nothing but you on earth ! (*Answers a trebly repeated query.*) Oh, yes ! I like Maintenon cutlets very much.

FITZ. (*rubbing his hands*). I can trust to old Ockenden for them, thank heaven ?

POET (*getting awake*). Your wife should be a good cook, Maurice ?

FITZ. Well, if she's at all educated and civilised, she will be.

POET. I know a marriageable young lady who hates potatoes, doesn't understand a particle of the great science, and finishes her dinner in two minutes.

FITZ. Lord help the man who marries her !

POET. I think he'll be a lucky fellow.

FITZ. No accounting for tastes ! (*Pursues the theme.*) The pheasant opposite you. I'll take the plovers. Ockenden says the Jelly has set. Fancy you not knowing how much a gill is !—a gill and a half of Maraschino. I think the Jelly will be a success.

POET. Upon my honour, you look as radiant as if you had touched off an ode !

FITZ. We won't open the Champagne till the second course.

POET. I'll stick to Claret. What's the matter ?

FITZ. (*impatiently*). I have asked you half-a-dozen times whether you think the Ratafias should garnish the Jelly !

POET (*indifferently*). Just as you like. (*Writes.*) But a misfortune now befell our hero.

FITZ. (*with melancholy*). I've given up all hope of the plovers' eggs ! Heigho ! (*Stretches himself, in a chair, in a state of absolute mental depression.*)

POET (*regarding him, takes out notebook, writes*). Life is a thing of Circles, like Dante's Hell. In the narrowest of them Despair may be as abysmal, Hope as great as in the widest ! The patriot who sees his country enslaved : the lover who wins a smile from his mistress one day, and hears the next that she has bestowed the like on another gentleman : these sorrow not, or joy not more violently than one who is deprived of plovers' eggs, expectant of them, or greets a triumphant dish of potatoes à la Bechamel ! "

But Mrs Ockenden's fame is chiefly preserved in Meredith's excellent little story, *The House on the Beach*, wherein she and her husband figure under the slightly changed name of Crickledon, the village carpenter and his wife, with whom lodged the Van Diemen Smiths and Herbert Fellingham at Crikswich, which place is, of course, intended for Seaford. In Fellingham may be detected some resemblance to Meredith himself with his qualities of satire and laughter, his similar profession and pleasures :

" Herbert begged Mrs Crickledon to cook a dinner for him, and then . . . he started for a winter day's walk over the Downs—as sharpening a business as any young fellow, blunt or keen, may undertake ; excellent for men of the pen, whether they be creative, and produce, or slaughtering, and review ; good, then, for the silly sheep of letters and the butchers. He sat down to Mrs Crickledon's table at half-past six. She was, as she had previously informed him, a forty-pound-a-year cook at the period of her courting by Crickledon . . . on the death of her master, Sir Alfred Pooney, who never would have parted with her in life ; and every day of that man's life he dirtied thirteen plates at dinner, nor more, nor less, but exactly that number as if he believed there was luck in it. . . . But it was always a pleasure to cook for him. Mrs Crickledon could not abide cooking for a mean eater. . . . ' Nothing I knows of proves the difference between gentlefolks and poor persons as tastes in wine,' said Mrs Crickledon, admiring him as she brought in a dish of cutlets, with Sir Alfred Pooney's favourite sauce Soubise, wherein rightly onion should be delicate as the idea of love in maidens' thoughts, albeit constituting the element of flavour."

Although *The House on the Beach* was not published until 1877 (in *The New Quarterly Magazine*), it was commenced some sixteen years earlier, in the days when Meredith frequently stayed at Seaford. Writing to Mrs Ross in May, 1861, he mentioned three literary works he then had in hand : " The

Marine Terrace, Seaford, where Meredith frequently stayed in 1856-1858, and in 1863. Here he wrote "Farina," and part of "Richard Feverel." The place is described in "The House on the Beach"

third is called *Van Diemen Smith*—is interesting as a story. Nous verrons."

It is a most entertaining story, too. The absurd Mr Tinman, with his bad wines, is an early study in egoism, a subject later to be developed so consummately. Truly humorous is this precious person's practice preliminary in the delivery of his Address to the Throne when " his sister Martha sat vice-regally to receive his loyal congratulations " ; and truly mordant is the brush which paints the picture of melancholy little Seaford :

" Marine Parade . . . shaded sickly eyes, under a worn green verandah, from a sun that rarely appeared, as the traducers of spinsters pretend those virgins are ever keenly on their guard against him that cometh not. Belle Vue Terrace stared out of lank glass panes without reserve, unashamed of its yellow complexion. A gaping public-house, calling itself newly Hotel, fell backward a step. Villas with the titles of royalty and bloody battles claimed five feet of garden and swelled in bow-windows. . . . Shavenness, featurelessness, emptiness, clamminess, scurfiness, formed the outward expression of a town to which people were reasonably glad to come from London in summer time, for there was nothing in Crikswich to distract the naked pursuit of health. The sea tossed its renovating brine to the determinedly sniffing animal, who went to his meals with an appetite that rendered him cordially eulogistic of the place, in spite of certain frank whiffs of sewerage coming off an open deposit on the common to mingle with the brine."

Apparently, Meredith, having commenced and then laid aside *Van Diemen Smith* in 1861, was induced to resume and complete the tale on hearing of the Great Flood at Seaford in 1876, an incident which forms the dramatic *dénouement* of *The House on the Beach*. During this encroachment of the sea, Richard Ockenden's wheelwright shop, adjoining Marine Terrace, was much damaged, and his timber floated about as battering rams, one great wheel entering a house in Marine Terrace. The news of Neptune's escapades at the expense of old friends gave Meredith the suggestion for the remarkable ending of his story of Seaford as he knew it sixty years ago.

Seaford and gastronomy were ever allied, and consequently, on the strength of the cook, Meredith entertained many visitors

F

during his sojourns in Sussex, including one of his aunts and her son, which seems to have been the last occasion on which he had any intercourse with his blood relations of the older generation. Here is an invitation to Eyre Crowe, A.R.A., which gives a good idea of Meredith's life at Seaford :

"Will you come down here to us to-morrow ? We shall be glad to have you. Come and stay a week. The weather is lovely. The heat quite sweltering. . . . Mrs Meredith joins in kind regards. She says you must come under pain of her displeasure. Come, O Crowe ! Here is fishing, bathing, rowing, sailing, lounging, running, pic-nicing, and a cook who builds a basis of strength to make us equal to all these superhuman efforts. So come !

"There is a train at ten A.M., First and Second Class, the latter costs to Newhaven 9s. 8d. In the evening there is one at 6 P.M. with a Third Class, the latter being 5s. 11d. It reaches Newhaven at ½ past 8. From Newhaven to Seaford is a walk of two miles. If you walk, go on to the Hotel at Newhaven, anyone will direct you the way. You can go on the train. I may perhaps meet you ; but on second thoughts this is unlikely as I may be over the hills at a pic-nic. But I shall be at home by the time you arrive. Let no excuse delay, and trust me.

"Anticipatingly yours,

"GEORGE MEREDITH."

Meredith spent Christmas of 1856 alone at Seaford. He remained on as he was busy with literary work. Here, no doubt, he wrote *Farina* and some further portion of *Richard Feverel*, for, writing to Edward Chapman, of the firm of Chapman and Hall, who were the publishers of the last-named work, he said :

"SEAFORD, SUSSEX,
"*December* 15, 1856.

"MY DEAR MR CHAPMAN,—Will you send me, this week, the £25 for which I made application, to sum the £70 requested in advance, and so doing oblige your faithful poet. . . .

"I remain here, as I can work better than elsewhere, though, engaged as I am, the DULNESS is something frightful, and hangs

on my shoulders like Sinbad's Old Man of the Sea. I dream of
Boltons. I promise myself a visit there at Christmas just for
a beguilement ; but it is doubtful if I shall quit hard work for
a day, till the book is finished. I will come Manuscript in
hand. . . . The name of this novel is to be *The Fair Frankincense.* Tell me what you think of it ? There are to be two
Prophets in the book, and altogether a new kind of villain ;
being Humbug active—a great gun likely to make a noise, if I
prime him properly.

" Have you, or do any of your people know of, a book of
Hampshire Dialect ? I have a Sussex. Ballads, or Songs,
with the provincialisms will serve. Perhaps Mr Frederic
Chapman may know of such a thing. Also a Slang Dictionary,
or book of the same with Gloss. And if you have, or can get
these, will you forward them by post ? [1]

" Mrs Meredith is staying at Blackheath. Don't wait to
send by her, as I am anxious she should spend Xmas in town.
Dulness will put out the wax lights, increase the weight of the
pudding, toughen the turkey, make lead of the beef, turn the
entire feast into a nightmare down here, to one not head and
heels at work. . . .

" I am glad *Aurora Leigh* [2] is so well received. I have not
read it, but the extracts promise. Confirm to me the news of
Bailey's pension.[3] Will that £100 per ann. chain him to earth,
or only give him firmer spring into the empyrean ? I should
like to spin on the talk ; but the paper contracts, and the
Grave Man of Business frowns already at four pages of it. So
farewell."

The spring of 1857 found Meredith still at Seaford ; and in
the autumn of this year *Farina : a Legend of Cologne* was

[1] These dialect books were no doubt required for the conversation
of Farmer Blaize, Tom Bakewell, the Bantam, etc., then evolving in the
pages of *Richard Feverel.*
  The Fair Frankincense, as the title first adopted, adumbrated the
sacrifice of Lucy.
[2] Mrs Browning's poem was published this year, 1856, after the loss,
and subsequent recovery, of a box containing the manuscript at
Marseilles.
[3] Philip James Bailey, 1816–1902. His *Festus* was published in 1839.
The pension mentioned was from the Civil List.

published by Smith, Elder and Co.[1] This short romance met with no success financially, and it has never been widely popular among admirers of Meredith's later work. Even George Eliot, who reviewed the story in *The Westminster Review*, October, 1857, despite her desire to help Meredith, admitted some disappointment in the matter of *Farina* as a story. And as for the style and grammar, she said : " The author has sacrificed euphony, and almost sense, to novelty and force of expression " —an early example of tilting at Meredithese, which became quite a cult with later generations of critics. Still, George Eliot concluded : "*Farina* is both an original and an entertaining book, and will be read with pleasure by all who prefer a lively, spirited story to those dull analyses of dull experiences in which the present school of fiction abounds."

A liking, or the reverse, for *Farina* is entirely a matter of individual taste. Those who desire an analytic and philosophic novel can leave it unopened : but those who like a Gothic romance, with a dash of demonology and ghosts, can read it with pleasure and find a welcome niche for the volume beside Walpole's *Castle of Otranto*, Lewis's *Monk*, Mrs Radcliffe's *Italian*, and that fascinating volume of 1826 entitled *Legends of Terror and Tales of the Wonderful and the Wild*, to say nothing of the essays in the same school of romance by Walter Scott, G. P. R. James, and Harrison Ainsworth. The supernatural scenes in *Farina* are not very successful and convincing, because they are not treated impressively or with due seriousness : ghosts and humour never blend well. The best parts of the book are those describing the doings of Werner and his men, either in Cologne or in the Robber Baron's castle. There are picturesque descriptions of old Cologne and the Rhine, and the vivid presentment of the storm on the Drachenfels is worthy to rank with the magnificent storm in Dickens's *Martin Chuzzlewit* ; with that in Hardy's *Far from the Madding Crowd* ; with that in De Morgan's *An Affair of Dishonour* ; and with those to be found in the romances of Ainsworth—pre-eminently the word-painter of storms. Here is Meredith's picture :

" By an expiring blue-shot beam of moonlight, Farina beheld

---

[1] A presentation copy, from the author, of this first edition has realised £24 in the sale-room.

a vast realm of gloom filling the hollow of the West, and the moon was soon extinguished behind sluggish scraps of iron scud detached from the swinging bulk of ruin, as heavily it ground on the atmosphere in the first thunder-launch of motion. . . . Now there was nothing to illumine their path but such forked flashes as lightning threw them at intervals, touching here a hill with clustered cottages, striking into day there a May-blossom, a patch of weed, a single tree by the wayside. Suddenly a more vivid and continuous quiver of violet fire met its reflection on the landscape, and Farina saw the Rhine-stream beneath him. . . . Crimsoned above the water glimmered the monster-haunted rock. . . . Scarce had they got footing on the winding path of the crags when the whole vengeance of the storm was hurled against the mountain. Huge boulders were loosened and came bowling from above ; trees torn from their roots from the fissures whizzed on the eddies of the wind : torrents of rain foamed down the iron flanks of rock, and flew off in hoar feathers against the short pauses of darkness : the mountain heaved, and quaked, and yawned a succession of hideous chasms. . . ."

The year 1858 brought tragedy to Meredith at Seaford. For some time past the brief happiness of his marriage had been overclouded. The bitter analogy with the Bulwer Lyttons' disastrous marriage was complete. In each case husband and wife were too much alike in temperament and character and gifts to find permanent happiness together : if one partner in either of the inauspicious unions could have submitted to the stronger will of the other, final catastrophe might have been avoided. But Meredith and his wife were equally strong-willed, equally talented. Both were highly-strung, nervous, emotional, restless in mind and body. Both were hot in temper, satirical and violent in argument and dispute, quick to imagine offence. Consequently, peace was never of long continuance in that unhappy " home " in lodgings. Terrible quarrels and scenes took place, and yet in their own strange way these two sad people had loved each other.

In 1858 came the irreparable breach, when Mrs Meredith went to Capri with Henry Wallis, the painter. He found her alone at Seaford, in difficulties and debt and distress of heart.

He helped her—and she yielded. But the poor woman never found happiness, and her short, tragic life was nearing the end. She seems to have had a prevision that Death was approaching, for she constantly repeated aloud certain verses which she said she desired to have inscribed on her tombstone. Ever restless, she wandered from place to place, seeking to drown bitter memories and regrets. Her supreme sorrow was the loss of her little son, Arthur Meredith, now five years old, who had, of course, been claimed by his father : the passionate devotion of both parents to the child was intense, and deepened the tragedy. The unhappy mother, in the hope of seeing her son, returned to England in 1859, and lived at 4 Crown Crescent (just opposite Orleans House), Twickenham. Sometimes, during the father's absence, she used to meet the boy for a short time in London or at Petersham, in the avenue leading to Ham House : but he was not allowed to go to her cottage in Twickenham.

All those who remember Mrs Meredith in the last years of her life state that she was always sad and constantly in tears. Her warm, vehement nature could not meet sorrow with resignation, or be softened by it. She would pace up and down the room in uncontrollable emotion. She treasured up every little relic that had belonged to her son, and always wore a lock of his hair against her heart.

Mrs Meredith went to Seaford again, and to Hastings, but in 1860 she was living at 2 Sussex Villas, Cambrian Road, Richmond Hill. Like her husband, she seems to have been devoted to Surrey, and her last home was at Grotto Cottage, Oatlands Park, Weybridge—not far from where she had spent the first years of her married life with Meredith. Here she died in October, 1861, at the age of forty-one. Not long before the end she sent a message to her husband begging him to come and see her. He did not go : he had that horror of illness and the circumstances of death which is generally found in a man of imaginative temperament : that is the only excuse that can be offered in mitigation of censure.

Through the mediation of Lady Hornby (formerly Miss Emilia Macirone) Arthur Meredith was with his mother during her last days. Lady Hornby drove over to Copsham Cottage late one night to fetch him when Mrs Meredith was dying : but the

ARTHUR MEREDITH AND HIS STEP-SISTER, EDITH NICOLLS
(MRS. CLARKE)

father would not let the boy go then. He relented, however, the next day, or soon after, for in a letter to Mrs Ross, written at the end of September, 1861, he says: "Arthur is now at Weybridge seeing his mother daily." So the poor mother had the belated joy of seeing her child as mortal shadows closed in upon her. Meredith was in Suffolk at the time of her death. The only comments on the event to be found in his correspondence are contained in a letter to William Hardman:

"I received the Cartes-de-visite on the day I was quitting Copsham for Suffolk, the 'Giles' of Counties, I always think, where I lived in a dumpling state for a week. When I entered the world again I found that one had quitted it who bore my name: and this filled my mind with melancholy recollections which I rarely give way to. My dear boy, fortunately, will not feel the blow, as he might have under different circumstances."

And in another letter to W. C. Bonaparte Wyse: "My wife is dead. All is much the same here. Arthur flourishes."

The curious analogy between the tragic fate of Lady Lytton and that of Mrs Meredith was preserved to the end. Lady Lytton died alone, with no relatives near, and devoted friends were her only mourners. She desired that the text, "The Lord shall give thee rest from thy sorrow, and from thy fear, and from the hard bondage wherein thou wast made to serve," should be placed over her grave. But no tombstone has ever been erected over the spot where she lies in the churchyard of Shirley, Surrey (though her name is recorded on the neighbouring vault of her friend, Miss Devey). Mrs Meredith died alone, and her only mourners were a Mr Howse, and a Miss Bennett, and her former maid, Jane Wells. No tombstone has ever been placed over her grave, and the spot, to the left, near the top of the main path in the churchyard of Weybridge, Surrey, is not marked even by a grass mound. The lines which she hoped might have been inscribed over her grave were these:

> Come not, when I am dead,
>   To drop thy foolish tears upon my grave,
> To trample round my fallen head,
>   And vex the unhappy dust thou wouldst not save.

There let the wind sweep and the plover cry ;
    But thou, go by.

     .   .   .   .   .

          I am sick of Time,
       And I desire to rest.
Pass on, weak heart, and leave me where I lie :
    Go by, go by.

Thus ended the sad life of Mary Ellen Meredith. There is no condemnation for her, for, whatever her errors, they were blotted out by her tears. Meredith himself never blamed her, for he realised his own share in the mistakes and misunderstandings that finally led to ruin. All he permitted himself to say was : " No sun warmed my roof-tree ; the marriage was a blunder ; she was nine years my senior." And " Peacock's wife became mad, and so there was a family taint." But these words do not explain all. Meredith, after his bitter experience, subjected himself to a rigorous mental examination, and the expression of his regret and remorse is to be found in *Modern Love,* written soon after his wife's death. In that fine poem can be traced the whole and gradual course of his marriage tragedy :

    In our old shipwrecked days there was an hour,
    When in the firelight steadily aglow
    Joined slackly, we beheld the red chasm grow
    Among the clicking coals. Our library-bower
    That eve was left to us : and hushed we sat
    As lovers to whom Time is whispering.
    From sudden-opened doors we heard them sing :
    The nodding elders mixed good wine with chat.
    Well knew we that Life's greatest treasure lay
    With us, and of it was our talk. "Ah yes !
    Love dies !" I said : I never thought it less.
    She yearned to me that sentence to unsay.
    Then when the fire domed blackening, I found
    Her cheek was salt against my kiss, and swift
    Up the sharp scale of sobs her breast did lift :—
    Now am I haunted by that taste ! that sound !

    At dinner, she is hostess, I am host.
    Went the feast ever cheerfuller ? She keeps
    The Topic over intellectual deeps
    In buoyancy afloat. They see no ghost.

With sparkling surface-eyes we ply the ball.
It is in truth a most contagious game :
HIDING THE SKELETON shall be its name.
Such play as this the devils might appal !
But here's the greater wonder ; in that we,
Enamoured of an acting nought can tire,
Each other, like true hypocrites, admire ;
Warm-lighted looks, Love's ephemerioe,
Shoot gaily o'er the dishes and the wine.
We waken envy of our happy lot.
Fast, sweet, and golden, shows the marriage-knot.
Dear guests, you now have seen Love's corpse-light shine.

Dead ! is it dead ? She has a pulse, and flow
Of tears, the price of blood-drops, as I know
For whom the midnight sobs around Love's ghost.

But she is mine ! Ah, no ! I know too well
I claim a star whose light is overcast :
I claim a phantom-woman in the Past.
The hour has struck, though I heard not the bell !
All other joys of life he strove to warm,
And magnify, and catch them to his lip :
But they had suffered shipwreck with the ship
And gazed upon him sallow from the storm.
Or if Delusion came, 'twas but to show
The coming minute mock the one that went.
Cold as a mountain in its star-pitched tent,
Stood high Philosophy, less friend than foe :
Whom self-caged Passion, from its prison-bars
Is always watching with a wondering hate.
Not till the fire is dying in the grate,
Look we for any kinship with the stars.
Oh ! wisdom never comes when it is gold,
And the great price we pay for it full worth :
We have it only when we are half earth.
Little avails that coinage to the old !

But where began the change ; and what's my crime ?
The wretch condemned, who has not been arraigned,
Chafes at his sentence. Shall I, unsustained,
Drag on Love's nerveless body thro' all time ?
I must have slept, since now I wake. Prepare,
You lovers, to know Love a thing of moods :
Not, like hard life, of laws. In Love's deep woods,
I dreamt of loyal Life :—the offence is there !
Love's jealous moods about the sun are curled ;

At least, the sun far brighter there did beam.
My crime is, that the puppet of a dream,
I plotted to be worthy of the world.
Oh ! had I with my darling helped to mince
The fact of life . . .
Where came the cleft between us ?   Whose the fault ?
My tears are on thee, that have rarely dropped
As balm for any bitter wound of mine :
My breast will open for thee at a sign !
But no ! we are two reed-pipes, coarsely stopped :
The God once filled them with his mellow breath ;
And they were music till he flung them down,
Used ! used !   Hear now the discord-loving clown
Puff his gross spirit in them, worse than death !

Looking through their dead black years,
By vain regret scrawled over the blank wall.
Like sculptured effigies they might be seen
Upon their marriage-tomb, the sword between ;
Each wishing for the sword that severs all.

Her tears fall fast as oak-leaves after frost,
She will not speak.   I will not ask.   We are
League-sundered by the silent gulf between.

Our eyes dart scrutinising snakes.   She's glad
I'm happy, says her quivering under-lip.
" And are not you ? "   " How can I be ? "   " Take ship !
For happiness is somewhere to be had."
" Nowhere for me ! "   Her voice is barely heard.
I am not melted, and make no pretence.
With commonplace I freeze her, tongue and sense.

It is no vulgar nature I have wived.
Secretive, sensitive, she takes a wound
Deep to her soul, as if the sense had swooned,
And not a thought of vengeance had survived.

Thus piteously Love closed what he begat :
The union of this ever-diverse pair !
These two were rapid falcons in a snare,
Condemned to do the flitting of the bat.
Lovers beneath the singing sky of May,
They wandered once ; clear as the dew on flowers :
But they fed not on the advancing hours :
Their hearts held cravings for the buried day.
Then each applied to each that fatal knife,
Deep questioning, which probes to endless dole.

The whole tragedy of Meredith's first marriage was a grievous experience for such an acutely sensitive and proud spirit. The iron entered into his soul, and, for some years after, he eschewed the love of women. His attitude to the sex at this time is expressed in a letter to a friend, Bonaparte Wyse.

" As to the question of misogyny, why can't you see that I'm on no side but the laughing side ? Your view is the heroic, if not the right one, for it's against the world's experience, and smacks entirely of chivalrous youth. . . . Women, my dear fellow, can occasionally be fine creatures, if they fall into good hands. Physically they neighbour the vegetable, and morally the animal creation[1] ; and they are, therefore, chemically good for man, and to be away from them is bad for that strange being, who, because they serve his uses, calls them angels.

" I respect many. I dislike none. I trust not to love one. For what if you do ? Was there ever such a gambler's stake as that we fling for a woman in giving ourselves for her whom we know not, and haply shall not know when twenty years have run ? I do blame Nature for masking the bargain to us. The darlings ought all to be ticketed. Nevertheless, I envy your state of mind with regard to them immensely. I have seen infants fed with pap-spoons. They took all in faith, and they were nourished. If I thought myself superior, I who looked at them loftily, and drank more than was good for me that night, was I not an ass ? "

And in another letter (1861) : " I am so miserably constituted now that I can't love a woman if I do not feel her soul, and that there is force therein to wrestle with the facts of life (called the Angel of the Lord). But I envy those who are attracted by what is given to the eye ; yes, even those who have a special taste for woman-flesh, and this or that particular

---

[1] " Has it never struck you that Woman is nearer the *vegetable* than Man ? " *The Ordeal of Richard Feverel*, chap. xxii. In one of the early passages of this book, subsequently suppressed in later editions, Woman is compared to a wild cat. See also *Rhoda Fleming*, chap. xxviii., where Edward Blancove inveighs against the " animal vagaries " of the sex.

little tit-bit—I envy them ! It lasts not beyond an hour with me."

But this caustic mood was only a passing phase, and, a few years later, with a new and happier female influence came a complete revolution of views.

CHAPTER V

AFTER his marriage debacle, Meredith returned to
London with his son Arthur, who was now, and for
the next six years, the idol of his life, the object on
whom he showered all the wealth of his love ; for his sensitive
and stricken heart, in the first bitterness of domestic tragedy,
recoiled, as we have just seen, from any intimate association
with the other sex. They lodged at 7 Hobury Street,[1] Chelsea ;
and it was in this rather drab house, a typical London building
in the second-rate style of its period, that *The Ordeal of Richard
Feverel* was resumed and completed in the course of a year.[2]
The story was published in 1859 by Chapman and Hall, and
attracted more attention at the outset than the author's previous
works had secured. *The Times* gave a three-column review.
In this book, of course, Meredith first found himself. His
previous essays in fantasy and the supernatural not having

[1] Mr Clodd has stated it was at No. 7 ; but Mr Thomas Seccombe,
on the authority of two old friends of Meredith, changed the number to 8 in his memoir of Meredith in *The Dictionary of National
Biography*.

[2] It was probably during this period that Meredith and Arthur also
visited Lynmouth, for Mr F. B. Barwell recollects meeting the two there
about the year 1859. He had previously met Meredith, about 1855, at
the table of Mrs Edward Chapman. Mr Barwell states : " I was staying
in lodgings at Lynmouth. Meredith and his boy came to stay there, and
he and one or two other men often spent an evening together at my
rooms, and his conversation was very amusing and often witty.
Meredith had his boy with him at Lynmouth but no nurse, for he considered that a good lad who could wash and dress the child was better
than a woman. He was himself devoted to the little fellow, whom I
often saw with his boy-nurse. Many years later I went to see Meredith
near Dorking. I asked him which of his books I should recommend to
a young Russian who knew a good deal of our literature, and he said
The Egoist as the best specimen."

93

proved popular and financial successes—for in those days he was compelled to remember he was writing for a living—he turned to a deeper seam in his mental equipment, and produced the first of his philosophic novels, wherein the study of character and actions predominated over incident and adventure, which had been the bases, combined with some allegoric intention, of *The Shaving of Shagpat* and *Farina*. *Richard Feverel* had some notable contemporaries, for this year, 1859, also witnessed the first appearance of *A Tale of Two Cities*, *Adam Bede*, *Idylls of the King*, and *The Virginians*—a memorable year in the history of English literature.

As in many of Meredith's stories, one can trace some autobiographic reflections in *Richard Feverel*. The hero in boyhood is not unlike what his creator was during the same period. Proud and handsome and elusive, Richard also had his " religious-propagandist " phase (when, in addition to the heathen round and in Raynham Abbey, he tried to convert Adrian Harley !). Next came his imaginative sojourn in the land of romance and beauty ; and perhaps that scene where Sir Austin Feverel makes the boy burn his manuscript literary lucubrations may have had its origin in Portsmouth days and account for that lack of affection and sympathy which Meredith felt for *his* father : " And so Farewell my young Ambition ! and with it farewell all true confidence between Father and Son." And again : " The boy did not understand his father : his father frequently thwarted him : at times he thought his father foolish : but that paternal pressure of his hand was eloquent to him of how warmly he was beloved." [1]

Lady Feverel's case resembles that of Meredith's wife and her sorrows : " What heart-broken abnegation. . . . What anguish of soul ! " The tinker's philosophy, in the chapter entitled *The Magian Conflict*, concerning the wisdom of preferring tobacco to a wife, finds an echo in the poem of *The Beggar's Soliloquy*, written not long after :

> Now this, to my notion, is pleasant cheer,
>   To lie all alone on a ragged heath,
> Where your nose isn't sniffing for bones or beer,
>   But a peat-fire smells like a garden beneath.

---

[1] The sub-title of the book is *A History of Father and Son.*

The cottagers bustle about the door,
   And the girl at the window ties her strings.
She's a dish for a man who's a mind to be poor ;
   Lord ! women are such expensive things.

  •   •   •   •   •

She pulls out your hair, but she brushes your hat,
   Appearances make the best half of life.

We don't marry beggars, says she : why, no :
   It seems that to make 'em is what you do ;
And as I can cook, and scour, and sew,
   I needn't pay half my victuals for you.
A man for himself should be able to scratch,
   But tickling's a luxury :—love, indeed !
Love burns as long as the lucifer match,
   Wedlock's the candle !   Now that's my creed.

                  •

And the poet's too at that time. The candle of Richard
and Lucy Feverel's wedlock was certainly a " short six." Dis-
satisfaction will probably always be expressed by each generation that reads the book at the tragic *dénouement*. Poor Lucy
deserved a better reward after her long martyrdom. It may be
fatalistic in the classical style, and a tribute to the author's art
that he can so acutely arouse in the reader's mind distaste and
irritation at the fate of his creations, but the fact remains that
the double tragedy of the story serves no purpose. If in the
weaving of Richard's destiny by Fate it was necessary for him
to cause the deaths of the two women who loved him best, the
result should have been portrayed. But we are not told what
was the ultimate effect upon his character. He felt remorse, at
the time, for the untimely end of Clare, and grief for that of
Lucy ; but what of the after years of this ridiculous " hero "—
victim of a ridiculous System ? Which had him in the end—
the sorrowful experiences of his Ordeal or the System ? If ever
a novel with a purpose called for a sequel it was *Richard Feverel*.
   I think all the critics of this book have overlooked the proposition that, in addition to tilting at absurd Systems of Education, Meredith was attacking the conventional hero of fiction
at that time. Richard Feverel had many brethren born a few
years earlier. Those unpleasant young men, masterful and
muscular, with their curling hair and curling lips ; their proud,
quivering nostrils ; their high-flown schemes to redeem the
world ; their drastic thrashings and slayings (in duels) of

hapless males " who cross their path " ; their quixotic chivalry, but despotic, heartless treatment of the unfortunate women they " love "—they figure in almost every novel of the early Victorian period. They abound in Dickens—James Steerforth, John Westlock, Nicholas Nickleby, Eugene Wrayburn, Edwin Drood. They were idealised by Lytton, heroised by the author of *Guy Livingstone*, and brought to a fine art by Frank Smedley, whose vivid creations of Lewis Arundel, Harry Oaklands, and Harry Coverdale enable us to examine the popular hero of the " forties " and " fifties " at his best or worst. And even the satiric Thackeray used the mould for Clive Newcome. The elderly monsters of the Brontës were preferable to these impossible young men.

Sir Austin Feverel, another and earlier Egoist, bears some resemblance to Mr Dombey, for both men, cold and remote to the world, centred their deep affections ardently upon an only son, in each case destined to disappoint parental hopes, each the victim of an absurd system. Dombey's faulty armour was pierced by Edith, Sir Austin's by Lady Blandish. Another Dickensian influence may be traced in Mrs Berry, who is certainly a younger, and much more refined, sister of Mrs Gamp, and a cousin of Mrs Lupin, Peggotty, Polly Richards, and others. All these good women, of course, were lineal descendants of the nurse in *Romeo and Juliet*. Mrs Berry is particularly Gampian at the wedding, and when she visits Lucy in the Isle of Wight and descants on the advent of the heir of the Feverels : " Now I say this angel-infant come from on high. It's God's messenger, my love ! And it's not wrong to say so. He thinks you worthy, or you wouldn't 'a' had one—not for all the tryin' in the world, you wouldn't, and some tries hard enough, poor creatures ! Now let us rejice and make merry ! I'm for cryin' and laughin', one and the same. This is the blessed seal of matrimony, which Berry never stamp on me. It's to be hoped it's a boy. . . . Oh ! this is what I call happiness, and I'll have my tea a little stronger in consequence. I declare I could get tipsy to know this joyful news."

She is even finer on the subject of predestinating the characters of coming infants : " ' Why, to be sure, didn't I know a lady, a widow of a clergyman : he was a postermost child, and afore his birth that woman read nothin' but Blair's *Grave* over and over again, from the end to the beginnin' ; that's a serious book !—very hard readin' !—and at four years of age that child that come of it reely was the piousest infant !—he was like a little curate. His eyes was up ; he talked so solemn.' Mrs Berry imitated the little curate's appearance and manner of speaking."

If Mrs Berry was one half Dickens, undoubtedly the other half was Mrs Ockenden, of Seaford. This was, of course, Meredith's first presentment of that famous cook who, as we have seen, enchained him so long in the dismal little town where her lodgings were situated, and who reappeared a few years later as Mrs Crickledon in *The House on the Beach.* Mrs Berry's wedding present to Lucy was a cookery book ; the very bedrock of her sapient philosophy was the art of cookery. I am not sure if she predated Mr Punch's famous advice for How to be Happy though Married—" Feed the Brute "—but she voiced that Eternal Verity in terms equally exquisite.

" ' When the parlour fire gets low, put coals on the kitchen fire ! and a good saying it is to treasure. Such is man ! no use in havin' their hearts if ye don't have their stomachs.' Perceiving that she grew abstruse, Mrs Berry added briskly : ' You know nothing about that yet, my dear. Only mind me and mark me : Don't neglect your cookery. Kissing don't last : cookery do ! ' "

Apropos of this great aphorism, Sir William Hardman in after years related an entertaining anecdote concerning Meredith's second wife, which deserves a place in any future compilation of the Curiosities of Coincidence. The Hardmans and Merediths were dining out together, and among the guests was Mrs Andrew Crosse, the widow of the celebrated electrician. She was a lively and talkative woman, and during the meal chaffed Meredith about a passage in *Richard Feverel* which had prejudiced her against the author. It was " Kissing don't last : cookery do," as a piece of advice to " persons about to marry." On the drive home the Hardmans and Mrs Meredith (George Meredith was sitting outside in order to smoke) discussed the matter ; and Mrs Meredith related that when she was preparing to get married, an old aunt wrote to her a letter

G

of mingled emotions and advice, discouraging and encouraging, adding that she, the aunt, had read somewhere, in a book whose title she had forgotten, that " Kissing don't last : cookery do." As Sir William Hardman observes : " Was not this singular, when she (the niece) was going to be married to the very man who had written it ? "

There is another apt aphorism from *Richard Feverel* : " The task of reclaiming a bad man is extremely seductive to good women. Dear to their tender bosoms as old china is a bad man they are mending." The Asquithian phrase, " Wait and See," can be found in this book,[1] in the mouth of Farmer Blaize, though I fancy it made an earlier appearance somewhere in *Pickwick*.

As already intimated, Adrian Harley, the most humorous creation in the book, was drawn to a large extent from Meredith's intimate friend, Maurice FitzGerald. As he was the gourmetic instrument that brought Mrs Ockenden's art to perfect expression, he appropriately attained immortalisation jointly with her at the hands of the friend who had shared with him the joys of that good woman's superlative cookery in Seaford days. One might compile a handbook of wise aphorisms culled from The Wise Youth's entertaining philosophy. His sardonic humour is perhaps at its best in that inimitable scene where he presents portions of Richard's wedding-cake to reluctant relatives, in particular to Uncle Hippias, who terms the stuff poison.

" Adrian rang the bell for a knife. ' To present you with your due and proper portion. You will have friends and relatives, and can't be saved from them, not even by miracle. It is a habit which exhibits, perhaps, the unconscious inherent cynicism of the human mind, for people who consider that they have reached the acme of mundane felicity, to distribute this token of esteem to their friends, with the object probably ' (he took the knife from a waiter and went to the table to slice the cake) ' of enabling those friends (these edifices require very delicate incision—each particular currant and subtle condiment hangs to its neighbour—a wedding-cake is evidently the most highly civilised of cakes, and partakes of the evils as well as the advantages of civilisation !)—I was saying, they send us

[1] Chapter xxiii.

these love-tokens, no doubt . . . that we may the better estimate their state of bliss by passing some hours in purgatory.' ''

One is tempted to follow the further "Procession of the Cake," and quote how Adrian was not disappointed in woman when the edible " exploded " amid Richard's female relatives. But we must be content with remembering one of Adrian's early *obiter dicta* on the sex : " Mystery is the great danger to youth, my son ! Mystery is woman's redoubtable weapon, O Richard of the Ordeal ! I'm aware that you've had your lessons in anatomy, but nothing will persuade you that an anatomical figure means flesh and blood."

In spite of being the " ideal bachelor," Adrian's original, Maurice FitzGerald, whose creed comprised gastronomy, whist, and literature, eventually succumbed to matrimony. In accordance with the eccentricities of his family he married secretly, in 1860, and an entertaining—though probably elaborated —account of the matter will be found in F. C. Burnand's *Records and Reminiscences*.

Maurice FitzGerald seems to figure also in Meredith's remarkable poem, *Phantasy*, 1861, and takes part in the Bruges nightmare of that terpsichorean divertisement in waltz metre :

> With cynical Adrian then I took flight
> To that old dead city whose carol
> Bursts out like a reveller's loud in the night,
> As he sits astride his barrel.
>
> . . . .
>
> The mock-priest grinned
> And quickly his mask unriddled ;
> 'Twas Adrian ! loud his old laughter dinned ;
> Then he seized a fiddle and fiddled.

Maurice FitzGerald died at the early age of forty-three, in 1878 ; which suggests that longevity is not always to be attained by philosophy and good cookery, though as a general rule they may aid in warding off the inevitable hour.

The dyspeptic uncle, Hippias, in *Richard Feverel*, is said to have been suggested by R. S. Charnock, the bon-vivant, to whom Meredith had been articled in his legal days.

Meredith described the country of *Richard Feverel* as in a " Western county folding Thames " ; the scenes he had in mind were really south of that reach of the river between

Shepperton and Chertsey so familiar to him when living in the former village and at Weybridge. Raynham Abbey can be identified with Woburn Park, near Addlestone, and Farmer Blaize's farm, Belthorpe, with Ham Farm, though the latter place seems to have been considerably changed and modernised since Meredith thus described it :

" Night had come on as Richard entered the old elm-shaded grass-bordered lane leading down from Raynham to Belthorpe. The pale eye of twilight was shut. The wind had tossed up the bank of Western cloud, which was now flying broad and un-lighted across the sky, broad and balmy—the charioted South-west at full charge behind his panting coursers. . . . The smell of late clematis brought on the wind enwrapped him, and went to his brain, and threw a light over the old red-brick house, for he remembered where it grew, and the winter rose-tree, and the jessamine, and the passion-flower : the garden in front with the standard roses tended by her hands ; the long wall to the left striped by the branches of the cherry, the peep of a further garden through the wall, and then the orchard, and the fields beyond—the happy circle of her dwelling ! it flashed before his eyes while he looked on the darkness."

The old lock at Shepperton was the scene of the meeting of Lucy and Richard at the weir, and the neighbouring country, irradiated by sunset, inspired that famous passage :

" Golden lie the meadows : golden run the streams ; red gold is on the pine-stems. The sun is coming down to earth, and walks the fields and the waters.

" The sun is coming down to earth, and the fields and the waters shout to him golden shouts. He comes, and his heralds run before him, and touch the leaves of oaks and planes and beeches lucid green, and the pine stems redder gold. . . . The plumes of the woodland are alight ; and beyond them, over the open, 'tis a race with the long-thrown shadows ; a race across the heaths and up the hills ; till, at the farthest bourne of mounted eastern cloud, the heralds of the sun lay rosy fingers and rest."

Meredith's powers of scenic description found full develop-ment in *Richard Feverel*. The storm on the Rhine is as fine as that in *Farina* :

"Up started the whole forest in violet fire. He saw the country at the foot of the hills to the bounding Rhine gleam, quiver, extinguished. Then there were pauses ; and the lightning seemed as the eye of heaven, and the thunder as the tongue of heaven, each alternately addressing him ; filling him with awful rapture. . . . Lower down the lightened abysses of air rolled the wrathful crash : then white thrusts of light were darted from the sky, and great curving ferns, seen steadfast in pallor a second, were supernaturally agitated, and vanished. Then a shrill song roused in the leaves and the herbage. Prolonged and louder it sounded, as deeper and heavier the deluge pressed. A mighty force of water satisfied the desire of the earth."

The late Justin McCarthy, in his article entitled *Novels with a Purpose*, which contained one of the ablest reviews of *Richard Feverel*, compared the author's style with that of Carlyle. He said :

"*The Ordeal of Richard Feverel* is a novel of the thoughtful, deep, half-cynical, wholly earnest kind which has so often striven, perhaps not with signal success, to arrest the attention of a public only craving for easy entertainment. It is somewhat in the style of Sterne ; a good deal in the style of one who, acknowledging himself a follower of Sterne, had a warmer heart, a purer soul, and a richer, quainter fancy than the British sentimentalist, I mean Jean Paul Richter. Mr Meredith is often strikingly like Richter in style, with, almost as a matter of necessity, a considerable dash of Carlylese phraseology. Here and there, indeed, something of unmistakable and pure Carlyle flashes in."

This being so, it is of interest to recall that Meredith's *Richard Feverel* was read and liked by Carlyle, and made the two men acquainted. They were both living in Chelsea, and in his walks Meredith often met Carlyle and longed to speak to him, but had no excuse for doing so. Then, one day, Meredith's publishers received a letter from Carlyle asking about the new author. Meredith seized his opportunity and called at Cheyne Row. Carlyle told him that Mrs Carlyle, on first reading *Richard*

Feverel, had disliked the story and flung it upon the floor. But she took it up again, and soon began reading passages aloud to her husband, who said : " The man is no fool." They read the book to the end. Carlyle told Meredith that he possessed the attributes of an historian, and advised him to essay work of that description. But the novelist replied that as so much fiction must always enter into history, he would stick to novel-writing as his method of writing history, which aphorism caused Carlyle to ponder, and not argue in reply, for he realised that there was some truth in the statement. It was a pity this verity could not be offered to the unmeticulous Macaulay.

In later years, apparently, Meredith did not admire his excursion into Carlylean style, for writing to Dr Jessopp, in 1873, he said : " I opened a vol. of *Richard Fev.* the other day, and had a sharp distaste. The lumpy style is offensive." [1] Probably for this reason he rewrote the novel to a considerable extent, eliminating and condensing, before the edition of 1878 appeared.[2]

---

[1] Yet at the same time he paid a tribute to Carlyle's style in *Beauchamp's Career*, in words which very well describe Meredith's style too :

" His favourite author was one writing on Heroes, in a style resembling either early architecture or utter dilapidation, so loose and rough it seemed ; a wind-in-the-orchard style that tumbled down here and there an appreciable fruit with uncouth bluster ; sentences without commencements running to abrupt endings and smoke, like waves against a sea-wall, learned dictionary words giving a hand to street-slang, and accents falling on them haphazard, like slant rays from driving clouds ; all the pages in a breeze, the whole book producing a kind of electrical agitation in the mind and joints."

See also page 332 of *Letters of George Meredith*, where a fine tribute is paid to Carlyle, concluding : " He was the greatest of the Britons of his time. . . . Titanic, not Olympian : a heaver of rocks, not a shaper. But if he did no perfect work, he had lightning's power to strike out marvellous pictures and reach to the inmost of men with a phrase."

[2] Meredith made a curious arrangement about this edition. He signed an agreement, dated 3rd November, 1877, with C. Kegan Paul and Co., selling to those publishers the copyright of *The Ordeal of Richard Feverel* for seven years, by which they agreed to issue the novel in one volume at six shillings, and after the sale of 750 copies net to pay to Meredith a royalty of one shilling and sixpence per copy. These certainly were not wonderful terms for an author then at the height of his powers, who had reached the period of *Beauchamp's Career* and was evolving *The Egoist.*

In other letters Meredith refers to the early experiences of the book when, owing to a review in *The Spectator* accusing it of "low ethical tone," *Richard Feverel* was banned for its "immoral tendency" (!) and subversive doctrines, and Mudie's Library, despite having purchased three hundred copies, refused to circulate the book to subscribers in deference to the fiery cross raised on high by Mrs Grundy. Thus in 1861, in relation to a visit from a lady :

"Is she adapting her wisdom to the mind of the British Matron, and of the snuffling moralist so powerful among us ? Does she know that my literary reputation is tabooed as worse than libertine in certain virtuous societies ? . . . that there have been meetings to banish me from book-clubs ? And that Paterfamilias has given Mr Mudie a very large bit of his petticoated mind concerning me ? These are matters to be thought over. In the way of Art I never stop to consider what is admissible to the narrow minds of the drawing-room. . . ."

And to Mr Edmund Gosse in 1889 : "My first novel dealt with your question. It was, I heard, denounced over the country by clergymen, at book-clubs, and it fell dead. They have since had their drenching of the abominable—as all do, who stand against the plea for the painting of what is natural to us. It may be shown recurring through literary history."

In 1858 Meredith commenced his memorable and lasting friendship with Captain (subsequently Rear-Admiral) Frederick Augustus Maxse (1833-1900), second son of James Maxse by his marriage with Lady Caroline Fitzhardinge, daughter of the 5th Earl of Berkeley (whose matrimonial affairs formed a *cause célèbre* at the beginning of the nineteenth century). Maxse, when Meredith first met him, was a young naval officer who had recently served with distinction and gallantry in the Crimean War. He also had marked literary tastes, and was a deep thinker, much concerned with social questions. It was, no doubt, to be near this new and congenial friend—subsequently to be the hero of *Beauchamp's Career*—that Meredith, with his son Arthur, went in 1859 to live in lodgings at Esher. For Maxse's home with his mother, Lady Caroline, was in Surrey ; and a little later he took for his own use a cottage at Molesey, when he and Meredith were constantly together and enjoyed long walks over the heaths and hills of their beloved Surrey. Meredith accompanied his new friend on a trip to Cherbourg in Maxse's cutter-yacht, the *Grebe*, in 1858.

The house (now called Faireholme) where Meredith lodged in Esher is situated on the left-hand side of the main street between " The Bear " Inn and the Post Office. It is a very ancient building, and was formerly a coaching inn known as " The Grapes." The low-ceiled, narrow rooms still preserve the aspect of an old-fashioned tavern. Meredith's sitting-room (where he wrote the commencement of *Evan Harrington*) was that to the right on the first floor, and his bedroom behind it looked on to the pleasant informal garden and Claremont lands beyond. At this period the house was occupied by Mrs Smith, and it is interesting to note that her son-in-law, Mr F. J. Williamson, the distinguished sculptor, is still (1918) living there, and well remembers the time, fifty-nine years ago, when he and Meredith were under the same roof and constantly meeting. Esher, of course, has other literary associations in addition to Meredith. A few doors from his lodgings is the house where the beautiful sisters, Jane and Anna Maria Porter, had lived with their mother. Their family vault is in the old churchyard. Samuel Warren, the novelist, is buried near the new church ; his son was Rector of Esher. William and Mary Howitt lived at The Cedars, Esher, at one time.

At this date, 1859, Meredith had commenced his activities as a journalist, and his connection with *The Ipswich Journal* ensued the following year ; 1860 also marks the date of his securing the post of publisher's reader to Chapman and Hall, which he held for many years : it will be more convenient to deal with these phases of his life in a separate chapter, merely stating now that at this time he was also glad to add to his income by reading aloud to an old lady who, it is to be hoped, appreciated her singular advantage in securing the services of the author of *Richard Feverel*. No doubt she did, for she was a woman of intelligence, Mrs Benjamin Wood, of Eltham Lodge. She was the sister of Sir Evelyn Wood's mother.

At Esher, Meredith unexpectedly met again his friends the Duff Gordons, who had lost sight of him after he left Weybridge for Lower Halliford and Seaford. The resumption of friendship was brought about in a remarkable way. Miss Janet Duff

FAIREHOLME, ESHER. HERE MEREDITH LIVED 1858-59, AND
COMMENCED "EVAN HARRINGTON"

Contemporary photograph by Mr. F. J. Williamson

Gordon, now grown to a girl of sixteen, was riding down to Esher Station one day when a little boy, some five years old, in trying to run across the road in front of her horse, stumbled and fell. He was much frightened, and the young lady, dismounting, picked him up and strove to reassure him. The boy, who was Arthur Meredith, bravely forced back his tears, gasping out : " Papa says little men ought not to cry." He pointed out the house where he lived, and Miss Duff Gordon, taking the child to the door, was met by a tall, handsome man, who, to her utter amazement, after gazing at her for a moment, and asking : " Are you not Lady Duff Gordon's daughter ? " clasped her in his arms, exclaiming : " Oh ! my Janet ! Don't you know me ? I'm your Poet ! " And then she remembered her friend of the fairy tales in old days at Weybridge, when she was a little girl. Meredith went that night to dine with the Duff Gordons at Bellvidere House, Esher, near Claremont Park. He was now again constantly with his rediscovered friends, whose house was known as " The Gordon Arms " on account of their ever warm hospitality to troops of friends who visited them there.

Maurice FitzGerald was much with Meredith at Esher, where they lived together in the same house, as in Seaford days ; and it was through his introduction of F. C. Burnand, then a young man of twenty-two, that we obtain a delightful picture of Meredith at this period (1859-1860). Sir Francis Burnand thus vividly related, in his *Records and Reminiscences* :

" ' 'Twas in the prime of summer-time,' as the Eugene Aram poem commences, when I paid my first visit to Esher. As we walked across the common, Maurice expatiated on the beauty of the country, of the advantages of rural life over existence in town. . . . ' I thought,' he observed, breaking off in the midst of a vivid description of the beauties of the Box Hill and Dorking country—' I thought we should have met George.'

" ' Who is George ? ' I asked.

" ' George Meredith,' he answered. ' I forgot to tell you that he is stopping with me, or I am with him. It doesn't much matter. We've been together for some time. You know him ? ' No, I didn't. ' You know,' Maurice put it to me inquiringly, ' his *Shaving of Shagpat* and his poems ? '

" I regretted to say that, owing to my studies having been for the last year or more on subjects removed far away from modern literature, I had scarcely looked at any new books for the past eighteen months.

" ' Ah ! ' said Maurice, reflectively. ' You must read his *Richard Feverel*. I've got it and the others at home.'

" Then we saw a figure standing in front of a white gate on our left, about a quarter of a mile distant, waving to us. ' There he is,' said Maurice quietly (he was always quiet) ; ' we shall meet him where the roads join at the corner.'

" As we neared the ' crossways ' (no ' Diana ' there as yet), George Meredith was shaking hands with a stoutish, jovial-looking, rubicund-visaged, white-haired gentleman, who, if he had only been attired in gaiters might there and then have been easily taken for the original of Phiz's delineation of the immortal Mr Pickwick.[1]

" George Meredith and this genial elderly gentleman waved their hands encouragingly to one another as the latter disappeared within the gate, and George strode towards us. George Meredith never merely walked, never lounged ; he strode, he took giant strides. He had on a soft, shapeless wide-awake, a sad-coloured flannel shirt, with low open collar turned over a brilliant scarlet neckerchief tied in loose sailor's knot ; no waistcoat ; knickerbockers, grey stockings, and the most serviceable laced boots, which evidently meant business in pedestrianism ; crisp, curly, brownish hair, ignorant of parting ; a fine brow, quick observant eyes, greyish—if I remember rightly ;—beard and moustache, a trifle lighter than the hair. A splendid head ; a memorable personality. Then his sense of humour, his cynicism, and his absolutely boyish enjoyment of mere fun, of any pure and simple absurdity. His laugh was

[1] Mr Pickwick was the pictorial creation of Robert Seymour, who, discarding his first design of a long, thin man, drew the portrait of a short, stout one from the description by Edward Chapman of an actual person, named John Foster, he, the publisher, knew at Richmond. It was the suicide of Seymour in 1836 that gave Phiz his great opportunity, for at the age of twenty-one he was selected to fill the vacant post of illustrator to *Pickwick* (then appearing in monthly parts). He very skilfully continued Seymour's conceptions of Pickwick and his three friends, and of Jingle ; all the other presentments of the prominent characters of the book were the pictorial creations of Phiz.

something to hear ; it was of short duration, but it was a roar ; it set you off—nay, he himself, when much tickled, would laugh till he cried (it didn't take long to get to the crying), and then he would struggle with himself, hand to open mouth, to prevent another outburst.

" Two more delightful companions for a young man, trembling on the brink of literature and the drama, it would be difficult to imagine. They were both my hosts. I was at home at once.

" 'Who were you talking to as we came up ? ' asked Maurice. 'That,' said George—'Why you've met him '— ' No,' Maurice didn't remember—' that's Evans, dear old Pater Evans.'

" And it was in this company, in these circumstances, that I first set eyes on Mullet Evans, second partner in the old publishing firm of Bradbury and Evans, then known all over the world as the proprietors of *Punch*. At this time they had among other ventures started *Once a Week* as a rival to Dickens's *All the Year Round*, and George Meredith was writing for this opposition his *Evan Harrington*. George scouted the suggestion that his novel should be called *Bradbury-and-Evans Harrington*.[1]

" Our near neighbours were the Duff Gordons, at whose house George was a *persona grata*, As Maurice did not affect society, and as I was ' a person of no importance,' neither of us, though formally introduced, was included in the invitations sent to George Meredith, then a rising star, by Sir Alexander and Lady Duff Gordon."

Meredith, soon after this first meeting at Esher, introduced Burnand to Bradbury and Evans, the proprietors and publishers of *Punch*, of which he, Burnand, was to become editor some twenty years later. It happened thus. Burnand, ever the best of raconteurs, had told Meredith some amusing stories, merely by way of post-prandial entertainment after the excellent dinners provided by his friends at Esher. Some time after, Burnand discovered these anecdotes retold, under the title of *A Story Telling Party*, in *Once a Week* for December, 1859, with

[1] Bradbury and Evans had published much of Dickens's work originally ; and Mr Evans's daughter married the novelist's eldest son, Charles Culliford Boz Dickens, in 1861.

some clever illustrations by Phiz. The contribution was not signed by Meredith. But, to quote Burnand's words, " seeing a point to be scored for myself I wrote to George, asking him as a set-off against the ' honorarium ' he had received for *my* stories (' only infinitely better told ') to recommend a story of mine to the editor. George replied, expressing his regret, excusing himself by saying that he never thought I was going to make capital out of them (here he was right), and that he would have great pleasure in submitting my story to the *Once a Week* editor." This he accordingly did, and *Mr Lorquison's Story*, signed F. C. Burnand, and illustrated by Charles Keene, appeared in the issue for 12th May, 1860.

It was curious that *Once a Week*, ably edited as it was by Samuel Lucas and Walford, did not have a more prolonged existence. It was particularly rich on the pictorial side, for the most distinguished artists of the time were contributors ; and it thus came about that Meredith's work in the magazine obtained some notable illustrations. His first poem therein, *The Song of Courtesy*, 9th July, 1859, was accompanied by a drawing by John Tenniel, who, consequently, was the first artist to illustrate Meredith. *The Three Maidens, Over the Hills*, and *Juggling Jerry*, all dated 1859, were illustrated by Phiz. For the next three poems, 1859-1860, *The Crown of Love, The Head of Bran*, and *The Meeting*, the drawings were furnished by J. E. Millais, then just of age. *The Patriot Engineer*, 1861, was illustrated by Charles Keene, and *The Old Chartist*, 1862, by Frederick Sandys, whose remarkable drawing is a fine example of the work of the Pre-Raphaelite school.

It was owing to his connection with *Once a Week*, and the artists he thereby came in contact with, that Meredith formed his friendship with Dante Gabriel Rossetti. The latter evidently appreciated his society, for in a letter to Alexander Gilchrist, the art critic, in November, 1861, Rossetti said : " Two or three are coming here on Friday evening at eight or so—George Meredith I hope for one. Can you look in ? I hope so—nothing but oysters and the seediest of clothes." A memorable picture celebrates this new companionship, for Rossetti when painting *Mary Magdalene at the Gate of Simon the Pharisee* studied the head of Christ from Meredith's face ; and this Rossetti portrait is one of the earliest presentments of

GEORGE MEREDITH, ABOUT 1860
By D. G. Rossetti

the poet-novelist in manhood. It was doubtless through Rossetti that Meredith became acquainted with Swinburne, then twenty-three years old, just free from his unfortunate period at Oxford, and already producing one of his first dramas, *The Queen Mother and Rosamond*. As early as October, 1860, Swinburne mentioned in a letter : " I have done some more work to *Chastelard*, and rubbed up one or two other things : my friend, George Meredith, has asked me to send some to *Once a Week*, which valuable publication he props up occasion-ally with fragments of his own." By means of Meredith's interest Swinburne secured acceptance in *Once a Week*, 1862, for his prose story, *Dead Love*, the only one of a series in the Italian style, which he intended to call *The Triameron*, that has been published.

At Esher, Janet Duff Gordon was constantly with Meredith and Arthur (whom she looked after when his father was in London), and on one of their rambles discovered the ideal place for her poet to have his habitation—Copsham Cottage, in the midst of heaths and commons on the way to Oxshott. Hither, in the autumn of 1859, came the Merediths to live in this simple and picturesque little dwelling, old and with low-pitched rooms.[1] Except for the adjacent Copsen Farm, it stood quite alone and low by the roadside, immediately adjoining, without any re-stricting railings or hedges, the wild and extensive Common. Gorse and heather and mossy mounds ; and all around glorious pine and larch woods, and in the heart of them, where their blue misty aisles converged, a romantic little lake, " The Black Pool," fringed by dark trees—here, indeed, was a fitting abode for the poet-novelist.[2] No wonder that amid such lovely surroundings —with Nature and Wild Life at his very door—Meredith was

---

[1] Copsham Cottage, now called " Copseham," has been greatly en-larged by subsequent owners, and new wings added. But the original rooms occupied by Meredith and his son can still be identified in the present library and two small bedrooms over it. The house is now the home of Mr Herbert Cook, who has much improved the place and its charming garden.

[2] Unfortunately, in 1918, the trees in the Esher woods are being ruth-lessly cut down for Government and War purposes, and the banks of Black Pool are disfigured by timber works. It is unreasonable that a beauty spot so near London should have been selected for procuring timber, when supplies are available nearer lading ports.

inspired to produce good work. It was at Copsham Cottage that he wrote *Evan Harrington, Modern Love, Sandra Belloni,* and those *Poems of the English Roadside* so racy of the soil and nomadic life. A few steps from the cottage is a large mound—possibly a place of sepulture in ancient times—whence is commanded a glorious view of hill and dale, and nearer the stately woods of Claremont. This was Meredith's favourite resort. " The Mound "—or " Round Hill " as it is called in the maps —is often mentioned in both his correspondence and literary work. In connection with *Sandra Belloni,* writing to Mrs Ross (Janet Duff Gordon) he reminded her : " I gave you once, sitting on the mound over Copsham, an outline of the real story it is taken from." And it was on this mound, of course, that the party from Brookfield, in the story, discovered Emilia, the mysterious singer of the woods :

" In the middle of the wood there was a sandy mound, rising half the height of the lesser firs, bounded by a green-grown vallum, where once an old woman, hopelessly a witch, had squatted, and defied the authorities to make her budge ; nor could they accomplish the task before her witch-soul had taken wing in the form of a black night-bird, often to be heard jarring above the spot. Lank dry weeds and nettles, and great humps of green and grey moss, now stood on the poor old creature's place of habitation, and the moon, slanting through the fir-clumps, was scattered on the blossoms of twisted orchard trees, gone wild again. Amid this desolation, a dwarfed pine, whose roots were partially bared as they grasped the broken bank that was its perch, threw far out a cedar-like hand. In the shadow of it sat the fair singer."

The final scene of the story takes place at the same spot. The Mound also figures in the death scene of *Juggling Jerry* :

> Yonder came smells of the gorse, so nutty,
>   Gold-like and warm : it's the prime of May.
> Better than mortar, brick and putty
>   Is God's house on a blowing day.
> Lean me more up the mound ; now I feel it
>   All the old heath smells. .... [1]

---

[1] The illustration, drawn by Phiz, for this poem in *Once a Week,* 1859, gives a fair idea of the spot.

COPSHAM COTTAGE, NEAR ESHER. HERE MEREDITH LIVED 1859-1864, AND WROTE "EVAN HARRINGTON," "SANDRA BELLONI," "MODERN LOVE," AND "POEMS OF THE ENGLISH ROADSIDE"

Contemporary photograph by Mr. F. J. Williamson

And the adjoining common is mentioned in *The Meeting* :

> The old coach-road through a common of furze
>   With knolls of pine, ran white ;
> Berries of autumn, with thistles and burrs,
>   And spider-threads, droop'd in the light.

The influences of surrounding Nature were finely expressed at this period by Meredith in the *Ode to the Spirit of Earth in Autumn* ; but more succinctly picturesque is his *Autumn Even-Song*, written during his first autumn at Copsham Cottage in 1859, and which at the close again suggests a personal picture :

> The long cloud edged with streaming grey
>   Soars from the West ;
> The red leaf mounts with it away,
>   Showing the nest
> A blot among the branches bare :
> There is a cry of outcasts in the air.
>
> Swift little breezes, darting chill,
>   Pant down the lake ;
> A crow flies from the yellow hill,
>   And in its wake
> A baffled line of labouring rooks :
> Steel-surfaced to the light the river looks.
>
> Pale on the panes of the old hall
>   Gleams the lone space
> Between the sunset and the squall ;
>   And on its face
> Mournfully glimmers to the last :
> Great oaks grow mighty minstrels in the blast.
>
> Pale the rain-rutted roadways shine
>   In the green light
> Behind the cedar and the pine :
>   Come thundering night !
> Blacken broad earth with hoards of storm :
> For me yon valley-cottage beckons warm.

Merely a matter of individual opinion, I regard this as Meredith's most exquisite poem. What a wealth of observation is here enshrined, and how fine the antithesis of the last line of each verse. This poem is a succession of vividly contrasted pictures. It suggests those wonderful dark-shadowed twilight scenes drawn by Hablot K. Browne at the height of his art, particularly " The Ghost's Walk," in *Bleak House*, where also " pale on the panes of the old hall gleams the lone space between the sunset and the squall."

Copsham Common was a great resort for gipsies, beggars, tinkers, and so forth, and Meredith delighted to converse with them. As he said : " I am an associate with owls and night-jars, tramps and tinkers, who teach me nature and talk human nature to me." Much of his work at this period embodies their elemental philosophy ; and, needless to say, his first-hand knowledge of nomads was to find its most vivid expression a few years later in *The Adventures of Harry Richmond*. He gave some interesting details of his attitude to poetry at this time, and incidentally of his life at Copsham, to the Rev. Augustus Jessopp, a stranger and an admirer of Meredith's work who had written to express appreciation, and who, in result, was to become one of the author's intimate and trusted friends.[1]

" COPSHAM COTTAGE, ESHER,
" *November* 13*th*, 1861.

" MY DEAR SIR,—I have received your letter. Let me tell you at once that I feel it to be most generous, and I should be glad to think I deserved such hearty praise as fully as I do the censure.[2] . . . It is true that I have fallen from what I once

---

[1] Dr Jessopp (1824-1914) was at this period headmaster of King Edward VI.'s School, Norwich. He became Rector of Scarning, Norfolk, 1879, and his book, *Trials of a Country Parson*, contains some illuminating studies on the conditions of rural life.

[2] Writing to Mrs Ross a few days later, Meredith told her about Jessopp : " I am busy on Poems. I think it possible I shall publish a small volume in the winter after Christmas. I have had letters from strangers, begging me to do so. One man, headmaster of a Grammar School, writes a six-page letter of remonstrance and eulogy, concluding, ' I have often said I wished to see 3 men before I died : Humboldt, who is gone : Bunsen, whom I had the fortune to meet : and—— ! ' Guess, my dear ! He says that the ' Enchantress ' scene in *Rd. Feverel* made him ill for 24 hours : and that he and his friends (Cambridge men) rank me next to Tennyson in poetic power : and so forth. . . . I listen to it merely as a sign that I am beginning to be a little known. The man praises my first book of verse, which I would have forgotten. . . . I shall set myself seriously to work on a long poem. For if I have the power to do it, why should I not ? I am engaged in extra pot-boiling work, which enables me to do this ; and besides, I can sell my poems."

hoped to do. The fault is hardly mine. Do you know Vexation, the slayer? There is very little poetry to be done when one is severely and incessantly harassed. My nerves have given way under it, and it is only by great care and attention to the directions of my doctor that I can work at all. I have now more leisure and somewhat better health, and the result is that I have gone back partially to my old mistress.

"As to my love for the Muse, I really think that is earnest enough. I have all my life done battle in her behalf, and should, at one time, have felt no blessing to be equal to the liberty to serve her. Praise sings strangely in my ears. I have been virtually propelled into a practical turn, by the lack of encouragement for any other save practical work. I have no doubt that it has done me good, though the pleasure your letter gives me, and let me say also the impetus, is a proof that I should have flourished better under a less rigorous system. . . .

"One result of my hard education since the publication of my boy's book in '51 (those poems were written before I was twenty) has been that I rarely write save from the suggestion of something actually observed. I mean that I rarely write verse. Thus my Jugglers, Beggars, etc., I have met on the road, and have idealised but slightly. I desire to strike the poetic spark out of absolute human clay. And in doing so I have the fancy that I do solid work—better than a carol in mid air. Note *The Old Chartist* and *The Patriot Engineer*, that will also appear in *Once a Week*. They may not please you, but I think you will admit that they have a truth condensed in them. They are flints, perhaps, and not flowers. Well, I think of publishing a volume of Poems in the beginning of '62, and I will bring as many flowers to it as I can. It may be that, in a year or two, I shall find time for a full sustained song. Of course I do not think of binding down the Muse to the study of facts. That is but a part of her work. The worst is, that having taken to prose delineations of character and life, one's affections are divided. I have now a prose damsel crying out to me to have her history completed [1]; and the creatures of a novel are bubbling up [2]; and in truth, being a servant of the public I

---

[1] *Emilia* (*Sandra Belloni*).   [2] *Rhoda Fleming*.

H

must wait till my master commands before I take seriously to singing.

" This is a long letter for a man to write about himself ; and it is the first time I have been guilty of such a thing. . . .

" I will conclude by saying that, whenever you are in London, if you care to visit me, it will give me great pleasure to welcome you. I must warn you that my cottage has very much the appearance of a natural product of the common on which it stands, ' far from resort of men.' But I can give you a bed and good cookery, of its kind. In the winter it will be difficult to tempt friends to meet you. In the summer they find the place pleasant, and, believe me, I shall hold it an honour if you will take rank among them."

Jessopp promptly accepted the invitation, for a fortnight later, 27th November, 1861, Meredith wrote :

" As I said, my cottage here is of the very humblest kind : so much so that I hesitate to ask ladies to come to it, though there are some who do me that honour. You will find me about as plain a man as you could meet. I do not know many literary men myself : those I do know are among the best : and they are not guilty of overbearing brilliancy at all—unless, haply, one should be conscious of a sucking Boswell at the elbow, which is a rare case, and is possibly seductive. The general feeling is, that it is best to let ' good things ' come as they may, and thus the best point of breeding attained : all have even chance, and one man does not draw a reputation at the expense of the others. Believe me, I have as great a respect for a good scholar as you have for a man who writes books."

These were the pleasant days of many friendships. At the Duff Gordons' house Meredith met Mrs Norton, Millais, Kinglake, and G. F. Watts. He and Maurice FitzGerald and Burnand also much liked the society of Frederic Chapman, the publisher, who had a cottage in the meadows by the river Mole near Wolsey's Tower and Esher Place. But the most memorable friendships Meredith was about to form, in addition to that with Maxse, were with W. C. Bonaparte Wyse, William

WILLIAM CHARLES BONAPARTE WYSE
From a photograph about 1860

Hardman, James Cotter Morison, Lionel Robinson, and John Morley.

William Charles Bonaparte Wyse, born in 1826, was a grand-nephew of Napoleon, being the son of Sir Thomas Wyse, of the Manor of St John, Waterford, by his marriage with Letitia, daughter of Prince Lucien Bonaparte, brother of the Emperor. W. C. Bonaparte Wyse was a poet, particularly versed in Provençal metres. His most famous work, *Parpaioun Blu,* published in 1868, won the enthusiastic approval of Victor Hugo, who wrote : " C'est de la poésie vraie, parfois touchante . . . vous écrivez à merveille, et avec une noble aisance dans ce vivant et lumineux idiome. . . . Nous sommes frères dans la grande fraternité de l'idéal. L'idéal, ciel de l'art, est la patrie des poètes." *Li Piado de la Princesso* was a later collection of Wyse's Provençal poetry. Meredith first met Wyse in the early part of 1861, and he describes him thus in May : " I have made friends with a nice fellow lately, a son of the ambassador at Athens, Sir Thomas Wyse. He married a Bonaparte—a daughter of Lucien, who is what all the Bonaparte women are. Two boys, Napoleon Wyse, and Bonaparte Wyse. The latter I know. He has nice tastes, and is an odd mixture of Irishman and Corsican. He wanted me to go to Athens with him. I may meet him returning and come home through Provence. He is intimate with the new School of Provençal poets there, and wishes me to know them. Mistral I have read. He is really a fine poet."

In addition to the bond of poetry, Meredith found Wyse a man after his own heart in that this new friend shared his love for long walks and pleasant excursions in their county of Surrey, for Wyse was living in Guildford, when not at his rooms in Great Coram Street. Consequently, Meredith's letters to him are full of their mutual poetical interests and pedestrian plans, though they soon voice one of the most intimate notes that was ever sounded in his correspondence.

The first letter merely gives directions for reaching Copsham Cottage, when " we may talk over your Provençale Epics." In the second he becomes characteristic :

" MY DEAR WYSE, Hail to you ! Glad must be the release from Coram : into which smutty Elysium I was nigh penetrating yesterday, but had forgotten your number. Now, listen; for this is a thing to be done.

"Shoulder your knapsack to-morrow (Saturday) at 2 o'clock, or 3. March on the London road, asking for *Ripley*; walk through it and straight on, whither leads the Bonapartian nose. I, meantime, will start from Copsham at 3, dining at 2; and on this road, about Ripley Common I'll meet you, and bring you to me. Maxse and another lunch with me on Sunday. Stay till Monday and I will walk back with you, perhaps all the way, returning by rail. Isn't this a decent proposition? Respond to it, and encourage me. I am hoarding up similes from whomsoever I lease to the work of the paper. I must go somewhere soon; for my work is *beastly*.

"Why are you so sensitive about your verse? Let it have air and be seen; or it will never have a skin to stand our atmosphere.

"We have fine suns; but the East I do abominate. It blows my feathers the wrong way ' intirely.'

"I am getting temporarily tired of my *Emilia*. I have read it to Lady Duff, who is satisfied with it : but I am not. I have done little more to it than what you heard. Two chapters. The dawdling dispirits me. Not to have the same effect upon you, I conclude,

"Your faithful   GEORGE MEREDITH.

"The distance from Guildford to Copsham is 12½ miles: not too much. The walk is charming to my mind. Pray, come."

"MY DEAR WYSE,—I think it possible that I shall to-morrow walk *in the morning* to Ripley and *dine* at the Talbot at 2 P.M., so call there : ask : get an answer. Have I made myself clear? This is the effect of the East wind. ' The parting of the Poets at the pond by the Lone Hut.'[1] Look out for that title. The effect of your departing figure, with the East fretting your rear, will linger with me till finally I go. If you are at the Talbot, we will visit Newark Abbey. If not, I perhaps shall meet you on the road.

"Only don't forget *to call at the Talbot*."

[1] At Wisley, by Boldermere.

With the coming of spring, Meredith's spirits rose :

" COPSHAM, *Saturday.*

" It's many a penny you'll pay to go
  To a town beneath the skies,
Where a gentleman dwells whom you may know
  By the name of Bonaparte Wyse.

I was a pote, and *he* was a pote,
  In this town of merchandize :
And we laughed at jests profane to quote
  I and my Bonaparte Wyse.
We cracked our joke improper to quote
  I and my Bonaparte Wyse.

  Chorus—Tol-loddi, tol-loddi ;
   Tol-le-loddi—tolloddi—tollieo.

" Yesterday, being fair, I marched me to the Vale of Mickleham. An English *Tempe*! Was ever such delicious greenery ? The nightingale saluted me entering and departing. The walk has made of me a new man. I am now bather anew in the Pierian Fount.[1] I cannot prose. I took Keats with me to read the last lines of *Endymion* in the spot of composition.[2]

" Now, listen : come here by the afternoon train on Thursday next, and I will return with you for a day through Mickleham, and over the hills. Can you ? Will you ? Perhaps Maxse will join us. The cuckoo has been heard. And through the gates of his twin notes we enter the heart of spring. We will have rare poetizing, no laughter, no base cynical scorn, but all honest uplifting of the body and soul of us to the calm-flowing central Fire of things. Even so, my friend. Or, again, will you, on Friday, come to Burford Bridge at a certain appointed hour, and let me meet you, and let us explore the vale, and sleep in the nightingale vale that night, and roam about next day, and home at night, per train, each his way. These be propositions. Box Hill is your station for Mickleham. How are you ? Give me a sonnet by return.

 " Your faithful

        " GEORGE MEREDITH."

[1] " Drink deep or taste not. That's the Pierian Spring."—*Celt and Saxon.*
[2] At Burford Bridge Inn.

Apparently, on this occasion, Wyse failed to turn up owing to a temporary change of weather, for he is next admonished in rhyme :

" I look'd for my poet—he came not !
    He came not, though much I expected him.
His breach of agreement I blame not,
    But Faith has forever rejected him !

(*Chorus*—Through Eternity, " Forever," etc.)

Yes, tho' the weather be December O !
    Is this a fair excuse, my Bonaparte,
For Friar's Omelettes kill'd in embryo,
    And breakfasts spoilt, or eaten on'y part ?

Lo, the sweet sunshine to shame thee !
'Tis the weather for poets to forage in.
In the clouds I reproachfully name thee,
And they say—Here his promise has origin !
Of us, and in us, see his origin !
His misty, remarkable origin !

" A friend has called to take me to Oatlands Park. I may stay till Monday, and may then drop down on you. Maurice FitzG. wants us to go down to him at Littlehampton for a couple of days. He leaves in a week. Shall we ? The country is nice. I'll if you'll. I want also to go to the Switzerland beyond Godalming. . . .

" COPSHAM, *May 3rd, 4th, or 5th.*"

" *Tuesday, May 7th,* 1861.

" O CORSICAN !—The naval man [1] and the poet of Copsham have combined to arrange an expedition over Mickleham, and along the hills of laughing Surrey, into the heart of pastoral Hampshire, it may be ; and, to be complete, we want thee to join us. This, if the weather be not quite damnable. Or say, in spite of the Gods of Air, if you please. I care not. I am for jollity and snapping of audacious fingers. What tho' Jove frown ? The muse is our'n, and eke the pint of Bass : the comely pipe, the soothing lass, etc.

" We start on Saturday : we lunch lightly at Copsham at 2 P.M. Then like arrows from the Tartar's bow, out we sally, and away we go : knapsack on back. Singing—Hey nonny

[1] Maxse.

nonny ! What will you do ? Reply at once. *I* say, come here. Meetings are always doubtful."

" May 17th, Friday.

" I was hurt to find you gone yesterday. Why do you treat me so ? It might happen that I should not see you ere you leave England, and then——— ?

" Maxse starts with me, if it's tolerably fine, on Saturday. On Sunday morning will you walk to St Martha's Chapel,[1] and we can spend the day together, and walk in such a direction that you can take the train home at night to Guildford. We will be at St Martha's Chapel towards 12 o'clock. If I don't find you there, I shall think there is bad blood in the world and, my dear old boy, I trust you will come. If it rains cats and dogs, of course, I won't hope it. But the cats without the dogs may give us a chance.

" I went to the House—heard Gladstone, and was astounded at the prodigious nature of his yawns. These, with his eloquence, swallow the whole Conservative body."

Wyse again failed to turn up, but Meredith, on his return, went down to see his friend, before the latter set out for France and Italy. Thus :

" My dear Friend,—Only just received your letter—returned from walk with Maxse into Hampshire and Sussex—perfectly charming, and full of fun, etc. But, oh ! how I cursed on St Martha's sacred ground. In Hell I shall repent it. My dear fellow ! I must see you somehow, so I will try, if possible, to run down on Thursday evening from Town, and I'll dine with you at seven, or if you have had dinner, take a chop. Don't *prepare* for me, as press of business makes me uncertain. God bless and prosper you in your expedition. Anyhow you have stuff in yourself to conquer a destiny. Grand-nephew of Napoleon—adieu ! "

" My dear Wyse,—I come to-morrow Saturday—perhaps early, perhaps late, perhaps by rail, perhaps on foot. Anyhow

---

[1] Near Shere.

I come. Isn't the weather glorious ? Is there anything like pastoral England when the Gods are kind to her ?

> " Yes, we'll picnic in the woods,
> And touch on the diviner moods,
> We will forget that we are clay,
> And live the fulness of our day.
> On ladders of pure Niersteiner,
> On Burgundy or simple Claret,
> Than which on Earth there's nothing finer,
> (When waiters stand not by to mar it),
> We'll mount diviner and diviner,
> Until at last on men we glance
> Olympian-like, electively,
> And 'gin to laugh, and shout, and dance,
> And get lock'd up, effectively.

" Mr Wyse, Sir ! I think I'll be early to-morrer, if ye please, Sir. I'll be obliged t'ye not to go out altogether for so long a time as last—at a stretch, ye understann, my worthy friend. With which, God bless ye !

" GEORGE MEREDITH.

" Motto : Pluck up ! Ha ! Ha ! You can't be *cool* in this weather."

So ended this pleasant spring of 1861, with jaunts and nights out—particularly in the nightingale-haunted Vale of Mickleham, for which Meredith had a lifelong love ; here he was to find his romance, and near by he was to spend the last forty years of his life.

When the spring of 1862 came round, Meredith had found a new fellow-pedestrian in the person of William Hardman. Born in Lancashire, Hardman had studied for the Bar, and, subsequently, he acted as chairman of Surrey Quarter Sessions from 1865 until his death in 1890. He was also editor of *The Morning Post* from 1872, and was knighted in 1885. He was a cheerful, humorous man, with wide literary knowledge, and married to a lady of gifted personality and musical talent. Meredith first met the Hardmans in 1861, when they were staying at Littleworth Cottage, Esher.[1] Writing to Mrs Janet Ross on 19th November, he mentioned :

[1] They were introduced by Robert Cooke, of Balham. Mrs Hardman was the daughter of James Radley, of Liverpool.

SIR WILLIAM HARDMAN, THE ORIGINAL OF BLACKBURN TUCKHAM
IN "BEAUCHAMP'S CAREER"

From a photograph of 1863

" I have new friends whom I like, and don't object to call by name. A Mr and Mrs Hardman I met in Esher this autumn. She is very pleasant, and is one of the rare women who don't find it necessary to fluster their sex under your nose eternally in order to make you like them. I gave her private's rank in Janet's Amazonian regiment, with chances of promotion. Also he is a nice fellow : a barrister who does photographs ; of his friends principally."

Fortunately Sir William Hardman preserved his reminiscences of Meredith on paper, and they aid considerably in presenting a picture of the novelist at this period. Hardman thus notes the commencement of his friendship with Meredith, which ripened rapidly owing to their mutual tastes, particularly the love of long walks in Surrey :

" During our stay in Esher we have made the acquaintance of George Meredith, the author of *The Ordeal of Richard Feverel*, *Evan Harrington*, etc. He is very clever, original, and amusing. We soon became great allies. He is a widower of thirty-two,[1] with a boy of eight years—one of the finest lads I ever saw . . . his ' little man,' as he calls him. He is immensely proud of this boy, and the boy is well worthy of his father's pride and affection. . . . Contrary to the usual habit of authors, he is not a silent man, and when he is present conversation goes glibly enough. Although only a new chum, he is quite like an old one. . . .

" Meredith chaffs me, and says I resemble in many ways the man (Cobbett) whose biography I have undertaken. The reason of his opinion is, that I come down in the midst of his many poetical rhapsodies with frequent morsels of hard commonsense. I interrupt him with a stolid request to define his terms. I point out discrepancies between his most recent sentence and some previous one. The consequence of this is that we get into long arguments, and it was only last Sunday, during one of our country rambles, that, in spite of the raw, inclement January day,[2] we stopped a long time at a stile, seated on the top of which he lectured me, quite ineffectually, on his views of the future destinies of the human race."

[1] Meredith was thirty-three at this date.   [2] 1862.

And now follow some delightful glimpses of life at Copsham Cottage and rambles in Surrey during the autumn of 1861 and spring of 1862 :

"We have just returned from a charming little country run of two days and one night. Yesterday morning we left the Waterloo Station at 9.15 for Esher. All our mutual requirements were condensed into a little black bag, which I carried, and we started from the station at Esher triumphantly, regardless of vehicles, for a walk of two and a half miles to Copsham Cottage. We were going to stay all night with our good friend George Meredith. The heartiest of welcomes awaited us at the really humble cottage—for it makes no pretensions to anything, but performs a vast deal more than many great houses that promise so much. Meredith is a man who abhors ceremony, and the ' conventionalities.' After our first greetings were over, we turned out for an hour and a half before lunch. We had exhausted all our superlatives in extolling the day and the walk between the station and the cottage, but we had to begin again now. The scent of the pine-woods, the autumn tints on the elms and beeches, the brilliant sunlight exalted us to a climax of ecstasy. We were children again. Luncheon on our return consisted chiefly of home-made products—bread, honey, jams, marmalade, etc., most delicious. Then came a general lighting of pipes and cigars, and off we started for another walk through lanes and wood to Cobham, a good six-mile business. We got back at five o'clock and dined at six. What appetites we had ! Gracious goodness ! Meredith's two other guests [1] left at eight, to walk home to Walton-on-Thames, and then we put a log of wood on the fire and sat down for a cosy talk. Meredith read some poems which are to form part of a volume shortly to be published. So passed the time till 10.30, when to bed we went, thoroughly prepared to sleep soundly, as you may easily imagine. Up at seven, and away went Meredith and myself for a brisk walk of three or four miles, after taking a tea-cup of hot soup and a slice of bread. After breakfast Meredith retired to work at his book of poems, while we went to call on some friends in the neighbourhood. On our return he read to me the result of his morning's work—portion of a very

[1] Cotter Morison and James Virtue, his brother-in-law.

pretty idyll called *Grandfather Bridgeman*[1] . . . We left Esher by the four o'clock train, carrying with us a pot of honey for consumption in Gordon Street. Hadn't we enjoyed ourselves!"

"On Friday, May 23rd (1862), after dining together at his cottage at Copsham, Meredith and I started about seven o'clock in the evening, intending, if we failed to obtain beds at Mickleham, to walk on to Burford Bridge.[2] I had no bag or pack of any kind, carrying all my necessaries in the capacious pockets of a shooting jacket. Meredith had what the Germans call, I believe, a ' rucksack,' a sort of bag slung by a strap over the back and hanging under the left arm— a most convenient article. In it he carried, besides toilet necessaries, a *Murray's Handbook to Surrey*, and some capital brandy.

"I may as well mention here that we never addressed each other by our real names. He called me ' Tuck,' and I called him ' Robin.' Having enjoyed a good dinner before starting, we walked at a pace befitting the victuals, steady and sober, enlivening the way with snatches of song, reminiscences of overtures, frequent bursts of laughter, and absurd rhymes, as occasion suggested. The evening looked dubious and stormy, and the sunset was red and lowering, but on we went, nevertheless. We avoided Leatherhead by a cut across the fields, coming into the main road by the church. It was quite dark when we reached Mickleham, about twenty minutes past nine. The landlady of the inn was most obliging, and promised us the accommodation we required. After making arrangements, we strolled out to listen to the nightingales in the meadows on the banks of the Mole. While enjoying the cool air, drinking in their music, mingled with the croaking of frogs, ' the monotonous clattering of the brown eve-jar,' and all the varied sounds of a summer night, Meredith recited Keats's *Ode to a Nightingale*, one of Robin's favourite poems. We returned to our inn singing my music to Robin's madrigal

---

[1] This poem duly appeared in Meredith's second volume of verse, *Modern Love and Poems of the English Roadside, with Poems and Ballads*, published by Chapman and Hall in May, 1862.

[2] Meredith had made the same pilgrimage in honour of spring the previous year, 1861. See *ante*, p. 117.

addressed to myself, *Since Tuck is faithless found*, amid peals
of laughter. After large potations of soda-water, flavoured
with the brandy aforesaid, we retired to rest about eleven
o'clock. Our bedrooms communicated by a passage, being shut
out from the rest of the house, and we lay shouting to each
other, and joking about the joviality of the whole affair, neither
of us getting to sleep for an hour or so.[1] My window was wide
open, and I could hear the nightingales singing in the trees by
the meadows. About three o'clock I was awoke by a pertinacious
sparrow who had his house under the eaves close by my window ;
this was followed by the ringing of the stable-yard bell by some
very late or early traveller, with no apparent result to himself.
I could hear the stamp of his horse's feet in the distance, but
the bell was close under my window. After a troubled doze, a
busy cock took up the wondrous tale, and after a few loud crows,
commenced a very noisy commentary on the egg-laying work
of one or more of his wives ; this sound resembled a much
magnified and more andante sort of night-jar. I have omitted
the mention of an earnest dispute between certain village tipplers
in the bar, on the merits or demerits, sayings and doings of one
' Charlie Andrews,' all of which was audible to me and assisted
in keeping me awake when first I went to bed. At last the
sparrow wandered away to seek for food, the eggs were laid,
and I had a snooze in peace, when, about 5.30 A.M., Meredith
enters my room with a suggestion that we should get up. I
recommended him to go to bed again, and he did so. We
eventually got up about seven, and strolled out to see the
immediate neighbourhood while breakfast was being got ready.
   " The church is nearly opposite the inn, and into the churchyard we went. A pet lamb came to us, expecting, as Robin put
it, a gratuity of some kind, but got nothing, as we had nothing
to give it. Beyond the churchyard, which is very lovely, a
stile-road leads across some meadows up the Mickleham Downs.
Meredith declares that here may be obtained one of the most
perfect bits of rustic scenery in this country, and consequently
in any other. The church spire is seen embedded in rich foliage,
backed by the hills crowned by Norbury Hall, with all the

---

[1] It was at the old " Running Horse " Inn that Meredith and Hardman stayed. The place is quite unchanged. In earlier days the stage
coaches stopped here.

noble trees placed there by dear old Evelyn of the *Diary*. The most critical artist—and Meredith has an artist's appreciation of landscape—need not modify one iota of the view ; every tree in its place, and the spire of the church just where it should be. Higher up the scene broadens, and with all the varied greens of May made another view of great beauty. In the midst of our enthusiasm the church clock chimed eight, and warned us of our waiting breakfast.

" After breakfast I wrote a short note to my wife (' Demi-troïa ' as we call her),[1] for which I was duly chaffed by Meredith, who called me an ' uxorious old Tuck,' and finally wrote a note to her himself to tell her that I never thought of writing till I had eaten I know not how many chops, kidneys, eggs, and the etceteras. I posted the letter at nine, and on we went for our day's walk. Striking into the meadows by the Mole we crossed the bridge near the ' Swallows,' and so back into the road near Burford Bridge, revelling in the glory of the morning and the lovely scenery. We followed the high-road to Dorking for some distance, and then struck into a by-path across the fields into the town. After making vain efforts to obtain a *Saturday Review* or any other ' weekly,' we went on towards Guildford, soon emerging on a heath rich with nutty smells of gorse all ablaze, on the right of which was a tumulus. Presently a sudden descent brought us to ' The Rookery,' the birthplace of Malthus, a quaint old house embedded deep in foliage. Soon after this we lost our way, but Meredith made inquiry of certain tillers of the field, and by dint of scrambling over hedge and ditch we at length found ourselves on the right road. Our mishap occurred in consequence of the interest taken by Robin in Malthus's birthplace. In order to get a better view of the house we had turned into a lane, which passed close to ' The Rookery.' Emerging from dense thicket of underwood, we found ourselves on a carriage road which led past Wotton House. Coming to the little village of Shere, we turned into the inn for a rest, and some ale and bread and cheese.

" Soon after leaving Shere we started up a very steep ascent through a deeply embowered lane, terminating in an avenue of beech trees. From the summit we had glimpses of a magnificent

[1] Meredith gave the name to Mrs Hardman because her husband had taken five years to win her—half the period of the Siege of Troy.

view, St Martha's Chapel being a very prominent object. The ascent of the hill took away all my spare breath to Robin's great amusement. Presently we began an abrupt descent into a place called Combe Bottom, one of the most lovely spots in creation. Combe Bottom is one of those basins hollowed out of the chalk, with almost precipitous sides, covered with short grass at the base, but crowned with the most luxurious foliage in every variety of tint. On a bare projecting knob we lay down and smoked our pipes while enjoying the surroundings. Here Robin overhauled his note-books and read to me a number of aphorisms hereafter to be published in ' *The Pilgrim's Scrip*, by Sir Austin Feverel, edited by Adrian Harley.' We discussed them at our ease, for such terse sayings naturally provoke conversation. As Sir Austin says, ' A proverb is the half-way house to a thought.' Having finished our aphorisms and our pipes we descended to the bottom and crossed to the opposite side, on to the Merrow Downs, along which we walked as far as Newland's Corner. Immediately below us on our left lay Albury, where, as Meredith reminded me, the author of *Proverbial Philosophy* resides.[1] At Newland's Corner, by crossing twenty yards to the right, we obtained a magnificent view over Ripley towards St George's Hill and the great valley of the Thames. Returning to the path, we descended to the valley and mounted St Martha's Hill to the Chapel at its summit.

" Getting once more on to the main road we made for Guildford, where, on arriving, we ordered a cold dinner and proceeded to the railway station to get copies of *The Saturday Review*, *Public Opinion*, and *The Spectator* (May 24th, 1862). The last named journal contained an article on Meredith's *Poems* and *Modern Love*, etc., and a regular stinger it was ! Robin was naturally annoyed, for the review was most unreasonable, and was, in my opinion, written with decidedly personal feeling. Meredith did not agree with me in this, and eventually concluded that the review was written by a woman. The disagreeable topic did not interfere much with our pleasure, we were too much determined to enjoy ourselves, and Robin's annoyance soon passed off.

" After our cold collation we started again for Godalming, intending to pass through that town and sleep at a place two

[1] Martin Farquhar Tupper (1810-1889).

miles beyond. The evening was very fine, and defying the critic of *The Spectator*, we found the walk most exhilarating. In passing through Godalming we could not help noticing the number of patriarchal dogs lying about on the doorsteps. Robin was much tickled by my styling one in particular as an ' ancient dog,' he said it sounded so very old. At a small inn near the village of Milford we found a civil and obliging hostess, who recollected Meredith, he having stayed there the summer before with Maxse. She said she could give us beds, so we ordered tea, and took a stroll to an eminence on the wild common adjoining, from which we obtained a fine but desolate view. It was now nine o'clock, and as we had been on our feet for twelve hours we were not sorry to rest. The house filled with hilarious rustics, who sang old tunes with very dolorous choruses. It was Saturday night. They kept it up till midnight. Our bedrooms were very plain, for the house was a small and poor one, but they were clean, and the beds well aired. The following morning (Sunday) we were both up by seven o'clock, took a stroll in the garden, and awaited our coffee, chops, and unlimited bread and butter. Our hostess was very reasonable in her bill, only 3s. 6d. each. We gave sixpence to the little maid who waited upon us, and she was greatly pleased.

" Our course now lay by Thursley over heath, and through hedges white with hawthorn bloom, most beauteous to behold. The sun streamed hotly down upon us. . . . In due time we reached the Devil's Punch Bowl, and ascended to the summit of Hindhead. We lay down and smoked several pipes, enjoying a prospect of from 15 to 30 miles in every direction. We thought we could distinguish the sea through a distant break in the South Downs. At our feet lay Haslemere, and the Black Down, in the distance was Baker Hill, and the high ground about Ashford, and Selborne. We could see the Hog's Back, St Martha's Chapel, and the ridge of downs stretching to Box Hill and Reigate. It was most glorious.

" About noon we started down towards Haslemere, so as to get there by one o'clock, when folks would be out of church and inns open. We knocked at the hostel of the White Horse about ten minutes to one, and had a cut at the family dinner, a breast of veal, washed down by copious draughts of the best pale ale Meredith and I had ever tasted. After dinner we sat on a wall in the garden and smoked. About three we started—ignominiously, as Robin would have it—in a four-wheel chaise for Godalming to catch the train at 5.15, there being no train from Haslemere before 7.20. I arrived in town about seven o'clock, having dropped Meredith at Esher."

I have quoted Hardman's account at length, because his simple, if detailed, language presents an admirable picture of Meredith in these pleasant days when the two friends, still young and compact of health and strength, rambled over Surrey, enjoying the lovely scenery, the good plain fare of homely inns, and many a jest and hearty laugh. Such things go to make the best of life. And this was one of the happiest periods of Meredith's life, and his friendship with Hardman was one of its jolliest features. He regarded "Tuck" with a sort of Shaksperean humour, and the letters to Hardman, the most delightful he ever wrote, are redolent of the mutual pleasures they both so heartily and healthfully enjoyed. Let us quote a few here relating to these good Copsham days.

" COPSHAM,
" *May 5th*, 1862.

MADRIGAL

SINCE TUCK IS FAITHLESS FOUND [1]

Since Tuck is faithless found, no more
I'll trust to man or maid ;
I'll sit me down, a hermit hoar,
Alone in Copsham shade.

The sight of all I shun
Far-spying from The Mound ;
I'll be at home no more,
    Since Tuck,
    Since Tu-a tu-a tu-a
    Tuia Tuck
Since Tuck is faithless found.

[1] Hardman notes : " This was written in consequence of having been obliged to postpone a promised visit to Copsham Cottage. (Mem. ' The Mound,' line 6, is a conspicuous eminence hard by the cottage.) I told him I would immortalise the words by setting them to music, but he begged me not to as he would rather write me something fit to read. No, I would not be persuaded, and I have yesterday composed the music in madrigal style for three voices." See *ante*, p. 124.

" Oh ! What a glorious day. I have done lots of *Emilia,* and am now off to Ripley, or St Demitroïa's Hill, or Tuck's Height, carolling. I snap my fingers at you. And yet, dear Tuck, what would I give to have you here. The gorse is all ablaze, the meadows are glorious—green, humming all day. Nightingales throng. Heaven, blessed blue amorous Heaven, is hard at work upon our fair wanton, darling old naughty Mother Earth.

" Come, dear Tuck, and quickly, or I must love a woman and be ruined. Answer me, grievous man !

" In thine ear ! Asparagus is ripe at Ripley. In haste, your constantly loving friend, GEORGE M."

> " COPSHAM HERMITAGE,
> " *May 6th,* 1862.

" I dare say ! You know how badly you have behaved, and now you praise the poet and cajole the man ! Is it Tuck that sends me a letter of this kind ?—Not a word of repentance for a promise foully broken. No appointment for—or, let me say, expression of humble desire to receive pardon of, Copsham in the flesh next Saturday. I won't come to you on Tuesday. I will emit fresh Anathemas ! Read next page, or no ; rhyme is more kindly.

"TUNE : *Johnny's too late for the Fair*

" Tuck ! Tuck ! Once you would flatter me,
Saying that I in due season should fatter be.
Here is Asparagus—what can the matter be,
Why don't you join in the Fair ?

Ripley's the place with the jolly old Talbot Inn.
Once we two passed there, you know, and were all but in.
Rhyme now commands me to throw here a small ' but ' in.
Why don't you join in the Fair ?

" . . . I won't come to you unless I can be more with you. Now, please come down for some days in this magnificent weather. The nightingales are at their best. I went to see St Demitroïa's Hill yesterday, and saw the great Irrational— the Crystal, Walford's Domicile, Harrow, Windsor, Berks, Bucks, Hants, Hog's Back. Mon Dieu ! And no Tuck near ! To Demitroïa all kindness. Still (through weakness of resolve) your loving GEORGE M."

I

" Copsham,
" *May* 18*th*, 1862.

" Questions and Answers

" Q. What's a continual feast ?

" A. A Day given up to Tuck.

" Q. Why am I of a most vigorous capacity of digestion ?

" A. Because I never can have too much of Tuck.

" Q. Is it true that an Alderman before he finishes his day must necessarily take a bracing walk ?

" A. Necessarily so ; for he makes the circuit of Tuck.

" Confound the Press for its impudence in calling me the pupil of anybody ! Never mind ! If we do but get the public ear. Oh ! my dear old boy ! I rejoice to think that I may soon have you, but grieve for Demitroïa. Come on Tuesday, if you can ; 'cause Wednesday is the day before Black Thursday [1] when George Pegasus, Esq., goes into harness and understands what donkeys feel when they are driven. Also, arrange, if it seemeth fit to you, for a walk with Hinchcliffe, or alone for Saturday next : or arrange to come to me. As you will.

" Gathering up my soul in its might, I say (and damn all consequences) my love to Demitroïa ! There !

" George M."

" *June* 12*th*, 1862.

" My dear First Person Plural,—I wish I could come to you. The rolling seasons seem to have gone round thrice since I (I forgot whom I was addressing) shook your hands.

" I remember one Tuck, a jovial soul, a man after my own heart, whom I loved. I asked Nature for him ; she draws a South-West veil across my eyes, weeping. Francatelli nods a cold and tasteless response ! Tuck ! No answer ! I explore the woods of Copsham Dale, fruitlessly.

" On Friday is the illustrious small man's birthday, and he must not be left.[2] Edward Peacock and his boy are staying

---

[1] The day he went to London to attend to work connected with *The Ipswich Journal*.

[2] Arthur Meredith was nine years old on 13th June, 1862.

with me till Saturday. Rossetti and Swinburne come on Saturday. Will you come the week following ?

" Aha ! As if I cannot see that I am cut, and that the gulf of a tail-coat is for ever more 'twixt me and Tuck.

" Believe me still and ever, my dear F. P. Plural, your loving   GEORGE M."

                                   " *June* 18*th*, 1862.

" WELL-BELOVED TUCK ! — (Though I know I am cut.) 9th progressive station of Ginger Beer to eventful Pop passed pleasantly.[1] Your kind recognition of it was received by me with loud exclamations of delight. Come on Saturday, I prithee. But excuse my attendance on Friday. I am obliged to be here, and indeed, notwithstanding your taunts, Copsham is worth a visit just now. The roses and the Romford ale are in their finest condition. In haste, your faithful,

               " ROBIN SELKIRK.
      " ISLAND OF JUAN FERNANDEZ, COPSHAM."

                                   " *October* 4*th*, 1862.

" DEAR SIR,—I take the liberty to write to you requesting a line of information concerning one, Tuck, a ruddy man and a lusty, with whom I suppose you to be acquainted, and about whom I have recently been feeling a considerable anxiety. He has relations at Hoddesdon, Tunbridge Wells, and Norwich ; but they have no recent knowledge of his proceedings. I have written to him, and can get no reply. You will acknowledge that I have cause for anxiety when I tell you that in a work I have lately been reading, it is said, with regard to fleshpots, that he who giveth his heart to them is on the high road to perdition. Which was truly and sadly the case with this named Tuck. A dangerous man, Sir ! for he tempteth us to love this life and esteems it a cherishable thing : yet, withal, one whom to know once is to desire ever. For indeed such a one is seldom seen. Pity that such roseate healthful bloom as that he wore upon the cheeks of him should be a banner of Repletion ! Alas ! And that the sunny perfection delighting us in him signified verily that Nature, though proud of this, struggled greatly. Even so, the notable rotundity, the fine protuberance, was excess of Potatoe ! Yea, and also the very

---

[1] Arthur's birthday.

perfectness of him partook too largely of Francatelli. Hence my fear for the man : in that he, who was good himself as an egg fresh-laid, had a love of things good, and did attract them to him profusely : which is against one of the decrees. Dear Sir ! Should you see him, and the faithful and loving spouse, be as good as to make known to him these my inquiries ; and that, should he be ill, I recommend any cure but the Epicure : moreover (which he will understand) that I trust among the chief things in his life, that ' WE ' may never be split in 2. . . .

" Yours respectfully,

" GEORGE MEREDITH."

" COPSHAM,
" *February 1st,* 1863.

" DEAR TUCK !—Come, if you can tear yourself away, on Wednesday. Dinner at 6½. Orridge and wife, Wyndowe. Robin, most anxious. . . . We are likely to have a good fine blowing afternoon for the heath and the woods : I say no more. Only

> Write me no pretty note
> Puling excuses.
> Scorned by the Muses,
> Who's tied to a petticoat !

" A new receipt :—I try it on Orridge [1] to-night. ' Lark Pood'n.' ' A bottom of stout juicy steak, topped by 2 doz. ½ bearded oysters, topped by 1 doz. larks.' General sentiment by anticipation—' Gallopschtious ! ' I have an idea that two kidneys might be introduced. I have hitherto refrained from touching a lark : not wishing that divine bird to send reproaches to me from heaven and fill the foundation of my digestion with remorse. Do I degenerate ? Is it recklessness ? Or the noble prosecution of science, the wish to know all ? Adieu ! It is friendship that says ' Come ! ' What reply ?

> No, he wouldn't leave his wife.
> And he shouldn't leave his wife.
> He didn't go to Copsham,
> 'Cause he couldn't leave his wife.

" ROBIN LAURELPATE."

---

[1] Orridge was a barrister. He married a daughter of " Pater " Evans, the publisher (see *ante,* p. 107), and lived at Littleworth Cottage, Esher.

Meredith introduced Hardman to Dante Gabriel Rossetti. Hardman notes :

" Yesterday I went with George Meredith to see Rossetti, the celebrated Pre-Raphaelite painter. He had, unfortunately, no finished works in his studio, but his collection of sketches was most interesting and beautiful. He is a very jolly fellow, and we had a most amusing visit. I am going on Friday to his place again, to a social reunion of artists and literary men, short pipes and beer being, I am given to understand, the order of the day."

Hardman gave Rossetti a far more ambitious entertainment in return. He writes in April, 1862 :

" I had a very select dinner party at the Club last night. Meredith, Dante Rossetti, and Dr Liveing were my party, and I flatter myself they never sat down to a better selected meal in their lives. They were enthusiastic, and I have added fresh laurels to my fame as a dinner-giver. An enviable notoriety, but expensive. We kept it up till 12.30, and Meredith (whom I with difficulty piloted through the Haymarket, he was so very rampant) came home and stayed all night with me."

The menu of this most excellent dinner, and the wines, was quoted by Hardman in full. He mentioned, too, that Meredith at this date had taken to felling trees and sawing up logs at Copsham, to promote circulation and improve his digestion. " A tremendous South-Wester is wakening great woodland hymns. I'm out. My logs are sawed, my song is sung," wrote Meredith to his friend.

It was Hardman who first introduced Lionel Robinson— familiarly known as " Poco "—to Meredith about 1861.

Lord Morley of Blackburn informed me that he first knew Meredith in the early sixties and that he frequently visited his friend at Copsham. This is doubtless the period alluded to by the late W. T. Stead in his character sketch of the then John Morley [1] :

" No living person would hold a higher place in the list of those who had contributed to fashion his mind than Mr George

[1] *The Review of Reviews*, November, 1890.

Meredith. In the early days, before he became famous, Mr George Meredith, then himself neither so popular nor so widely known as he is to-day, took him with a friendly hand. He used to stay with Mr Meredith in a remote country village, and in the evening Mr Meredith would read over the work he had done in the day—the chapter or the poem. It was Mr Meredith who awoke in him the feeling for nature which has ever since remained as one of the great pleasures of his existence, as well as imparting to him a larger concern for the wisdom of life. For many years the long walks across the Surrey Commons, where the south-west wind blows, and when Mr Meredith's genius was at its best, were the delight of Mr Morley's life. ' Much, and very much,' Mr Morley once told me, did he owe to the wise and stimulating friendship of George Meredith in the impressionable times." [1]

Morley, at this date, was in his early twenties, and had not long left Oxford. James Cotter Morison had been at Lincoln College with him, and the two intimate friends often went to Copsham together. Morison (1832-1888), as the author of *The Life and Times of St Bernard*, was soon dubbed " St Bernard " by Meredith, and it is by that name that he is generally alluded to in subsequent correspondence.

But of all the notable friends who came to visit Meredith amid the woods of Copsham one likes most to picture the youthful Swinburne with his aureole of flaming hair, his inspired ecstasies of poetical expression, and his marvellous flow of language which Meredith described as " a torrent of boiling lava." Perhaps the occasion noted in the letter of 12th June 1862, previously quoted, of a forthcoming visit from Rossetti and Swinburne was destined to be that memorable one when Swinburne read aloud his recent discovery—the *Omar Khayyám* of Edward FitzGerald. This had been first published in 1859, but the work met with neglect, and FitzGerald, in disgust, disposed of the two hundred copies he had to Quaritch, telling him to do what he liked with them. The bookseller threw them into the " Twopenny Box "—though fifty years later a single

[1] Lord Morley has also stated that Meredith " lived at every hour of day and night with all the sounds and shades of Nature open to his sensitive perception." [2]

copy could reach the price of £51. But in the early days the little volume came to the notice of Swinburne, firing his enthusiasm and inspiring him to great creation in the same stately metre as *Omar*. Meredith thus described the scene [1] :

" I relish to the full the rhymes of FitzGerald and his beautifully plaintive harmonies, withal so mysterious. . . . I was with some friends at Copsham Cottage, near Esher ; and on a certain afternoon, in full view of all, came Swinburne brandishing a pamphlet which resembled in the distance a Pietistic or Methodist tract. He looked like an ecstatic visionary. Perhaps we should have feared a religious invocation from him, had we not been well aware of his religious beliefs. When Swinburne came near, he began to recite in a high-pitched voice the beginning of that splendid paraphrase which he had just discovered. His enthusiasm infected us ; and so much so, that the shades of night found us still under the trees, reciting those voluptuous and musical verses.[2] Upon our return, after dinner, Swinburne sought for something upon which to write ; and then, under our eyes, in one attempt, he composed the poem *Laus Veneris*, one of the most perfect in our language."

A month before his death, and in one of the last letters [3] he ever wrote, Meredith gave another description of this scene ; the memories of Copsham days were with him to the last :

" It happened that he was expected one day on a visit to me, and he being rather late I went along the road to meet him. At last he appeared waving the white sheet of what seemed to be a pamphlet. He greeted me with a triumphant shout of a stanza new to my ears. This was FitzGerald's *Omar Khayyám*, and we lay on a heathery knoll beside my cottage reading a stanza alternately, indifferent to the dinner-bell, until a prolonged summons reminded us of appetite. After the meal we took to the paper-covered treasure again. Suddenly Swinburne ran upstairs, and I had my anticipations. He returned

---

[1] *George Meredith*, by Constantin Photiadès, in the chapter entitled *A Visit to Flint Cottage*.

[2] " The third line of his quatrains is as the march of a king with his train behind him," Meredith once observed to Mr Clodd.

[3] To *The Times*, 15th April, 1909.

with feather pen, blue folio-sheet, and a dwarf bottle of red ink. In an hour he had finished 13 stanzas of his *Laus Veneris*."

So The Mound by Copsham Cottage can claim to be the spot where Swinburne composed *Laus Veneris* on that long evening of a far-away June when, after the sun had set beyond the woods of Claremont, "Night falls like fire; the heavy lights run low." Surely if ever mortal scenes are revisited by the shades of those who met there in the happy past, in the days of vigorous life and youth and bright mental power, it is a famous company that passes silently along the misty vistas of Copsham woods and lingers regretfully by The Mound and The Black Pool in the wan light of a waning moon.

THE MOUND BY COPSHAM COTTAGE

Photograph by Mr. F. J. Williamson

CHAPTER VI

"EVAN HARRINGTON." ARTHUR MEREDITH AND HIS FATHER:
THEIR TOUR ABROAD. "MODERN LOVE." MEREDITH AT
CHELSEA: HIS RELATIONS WITH ROSSETTI AND SWINBURNE

EVAN HARRINGTON, or *He would be a Gentleman*, appeared serially in *Once a Week* from February to October, 1860. A pirated version of the story was brought out in America at the end of the same year. Meredith had contemplated an American edition twelve months earlier, when he wrote to his publisher:

"The story will suit Yankee sentiment and Yankee principles. Exalt me tolerably, and, in fine, I shall be quite satisfied that you will arrange it as well as it can be done: but there should be no loss of time. *N.B.*—Perhaps, should it be needful, you may say that we are going to be guilty of no impropriety in this tale, and will never again offend young maids"—this last being an allusion to the "moral" attacks on *Richard Feverel*.

The three-volume edition of *Evan Harrington* was issued in London by Bradbury and Evans in 1861, and it has now some considerable value, for the author's presentation copy to his friend, W. C. Bonaparte Wyse, realised as much as £29 not long ago.

In *Once a Week* the story was illustrated by Charles Keene, whose drawings are of singularly unequal merit. Some are admirable, particularly *The Death of the Great Mel.* and *Tom Cogglesby's Arrival at Beckley Court*: others could hardly be worse than they are. Those portraying the Countess de Saldar and Mrs Strike convey no impression of the beauty and charm of the ladies, on which such stress is laid in the novel, and poor Rose Jocelyn is represented always as positively ugly by the artist: it is, indeed, amazing that Meredith could ever have passed the drawings of Evan and Rose *On Board the "Jocasta"* and *In the Conservatory*, except as caricatures of his creations.

137

The story, like the illustrations, is also of unequal merit : parts are superb, but others are very poor, and *longueurs* are not unknown. Though superlatively entertaining, the story as a story is absurd and impossible, for no children of tailordom could have kept up the farce of denying their origin, even when they were known to be what they were, in the manner of the Harringtons at Beckley Court ; consequently the Countess's plots and brilliant generalship become supererogatory. Evan's quixotic sacrifice in the matter of taking on himself the onus of his sister's anonymous letter, and his frequent wilful misunderstandings and renunciations of Rose are extremely improbable, and provoke as much exasperation as the follies of Richard Feverel.

Again the influence of Dickens is apparent in some exaggeration of character in this book. Jack Raikes is a fantastic, impossible creature obviously inspired by Jingle and Simon Tappertit, and only the Master of Caricature Character could have rendered him tolerable ; Lawyer Perkins suggests Perker the lawyer in *Pickwick* ; and the Cogglesby Brothers are nearly allied to the Cheeryble Brothers, Martin Chuzzlewit, Mr Jarndyce, and many other old gentlemen of conspiratorial benevolence to be found with beetling brows but twinkling eyes in the great Boz Gallery. Evan Harrington himself is stilted, unsympathetic, and remote from real life ; whilst Laxley, Harry Jocelyn, and George Uploft are so remarkable for illbreeding and insolence that one can only suppose Meredith, at that date, still ignorant of the manners of gentlemen or, more likely, desirous of paying off old grudges against some local Hampshire bloods who may have slighted him in his sensitive youth. It is only when we get to the feminine characters of the story that the sun of Meredith's art rises in full splendour to dazzle the imagination with subtlety and wit and portraiture *in excelsis*. The Countess de Saldar, Mrs Strike, Mrs Mel., Lady Jocelyn, Juliana Bonner, and Rose—these are no puppets, they live, each a distinctive personality and vivid creation.

Very realistic and never to be forgotten are the great scenes of this book. Evan's adventure with the postillion on the way home to Portsmouth—how plainly we see the youth, humiliated yet proud, striding along the white road across the Downs in the moonlight, the chariot dragging some paces behind him ;

the funereal events at the shop ; the race on horseback for
Rose's handkerchief and the resulting accident ; the dinner
party at Beckley Court, when the digesting of The Great Mel.
proved too much for Mrs Strike ; the love scene by the little
stream in Beckley Park ; Mrs Mel.'s dramatic arrival at the
picnic ; the scene, of tremendous power, where Evan wrests
from the Countess the fact that she wrote the anonymous letter,
and in humorous contrast that one where the outwitted Andrew
Cogglesby dines on bankrupt fare and domestic ice ; and, finally,
Evan's renunciation of Rose by the Park Gates, amid the
glamour of a May night in sharp contrast to lovers' pain. *Evan
Harrington* would make a fine play, and it is curious that it has
never been dramatised. Meredith is said to have discouraged
the proposal by asking : " To what English actress would
you entrust the part of the Countess de Saldar ? " To which
one might reply in these days : " Miss Irene Vanbrugh, or
Mrs Patrick Campbell."

There are some very apt aphorisms in the book, such as that
relating to the great British hunger for papers and news—
" second only to that for beef, it seems, and equally acceptable
salted, when it cannot be had fresh,"—and much that reflects
acute observation of life and manners. But the work betrays
ignorance of the peculiar and arbitrary laws which govern the
expression of English titles. For instance, reference is made
to a Knight Companion of the Bath ; the daughter of the Earl
of Elburne is called " the Hon. Miss Jocelyn " ; and the Duke of
Belfield is addressed as " My Lord."

As I have already described in my first chapter, *Evan Harrington* is very intimately connected with the family history of the
author, who took his own father for the hero of the story ;
introduced the characteristics, and personal history, to a certain
extent, of three of his aunts ; and painted a very accurate
picture of his grandparents, Mr and Mrs Melchizedek Meredith,
and their tailor's shop at 73 High Street, Portsmouth. With
this subject I have dealt fully, but there remain one or two
points connected with my grandparents, the originals of Major
and Mrs Strike, that need, in justice to their reputations, to be
put right. For here, it has to be admitted, Meredith was actu-
ated by a petty and long-brooded personal animus against his
relatives. It is no easy task to explain briefly how much fact

and how much fiction go to make up the presentment of the Strikes, for their creator had the subtlety of the serpent in blending verities with falsehoods. He paid full tribute to the beauty of my grandmother and her gentle, clinging disposition (Evan " loved this beautiful creature the best of his three sisters ") ; and it is interesting proof of Meredith's meticulous detail that he remembered and mentioned his aunt's one physical defect—rather too prominent cheek-bones—in the scene where the Countess begs her sister to " dress her hair plain " in order that George Uploft should not recognise her. The habitual curls and the high cheek-bones of Mrs Strike will be seen in the portrait of Mrs Ellis reproduced in this work. Meredith also admits the personal bravery of my grandfather, but after the statement that the Officer of Marines married his wife when he was stationed at Portsmouth, we come mainly to the realm of fiction. Most certainly this one of the Daughters of the Shears was not an " escaped Eurydice " who " never reappeared " in " the gloomy realms of Dis, otherwise Trade." The early years of Mrs Ellis's married life were spent near her old home in the High Street, first at 1 Algier Place, Alverstoke, and later in Great Southsea Street, three of her children being born during this period. The behaviour of Major Strike to his wife in the story is entirely fiction. The Ellis marriage was a moderately happy one (as numerous letters, journals, and other evidences attest), though there was but little money ; a large family was brought up on a Major's pay. It may be superfluous to add that Mrs Ellis did not contemplate an elopement with a duke, and did not become a widow. She died at Chatham, in 1847, at the age of fifty-two, four days after her son Samuel, who was only twenty-two. It is strange that her simple, well-spent life, devoted to the care and interests of her children, should have been so distorted by her nephew, to whom she had shown many kindnesses in his boyhood. Both she and her husband, a particularly distinguished soldier, did their duty, and had many troubles and sorrows. Fortunately my grandmother died long before the publication of *Evan Harrington* ; my grandfather was still living in 1861, but I do not know if he read, or heard of, the book.

It may pertinently be asked in what way had Sir S. B. Ellis offended George Meredith that he should be the victim of such

CATHERINE MATILDA MEREDITH (MRS. S. B. ELLIS). THE
ORIGINAL OF MRS. STRIKE IN "EVAN HARRINGTON"

a bitter attack here, and also in *The Egoist*. I have no definite information, but only a suggestion to offer. My grandfather was induced by some speculators to allow his name to appear as a director of a company formed to run " The Direct Exeter and Plymouth Railway." The scheme became a failure in 1852, and involved the loss of all Sir S. B. Ellis's savings, and also of a large portion of his income, which had to be allocated for many years to meet the claims made upon him in connection with the liabilities of the company. My theory is that the General may have advised George Meredith to invest his small maternal inheritance—or some portion of it—in this unfortunate enterprise, and that the loss of the money brought down upon the uncle his nephew's implacable resentment. Meredith stated his trustee " had by fraud or folly squandered the little estate " ; and it will be recalled that in *Evan Harrington* there is frequent reference to a speculating company in which Major Strike was interested, and that the Duke of Belfield resigned from the Board owing to the unsatisfactory condition of affairs. But, as I have said, this is merely a suggestion, and may be quite unrelated to the causes which engendered the undoubted dislike that George Meredith entertained for his relative.

The author's father, Augustus Meredith, was also living when *Evan Harrington* was published, and he read the story of which he was the hero ; though, of course, most of the incidents of the tale were fictitious and the character of Evan mainly evolved by the creative art of George Meredith, who merely utilised the situation of his father at the time of The Great Mel.'s death, whilst fully emphasising Augustus Meredith's dislike for a trade career and his aspirations for higher stratas of society.

As already related, Augustus Meredith emigrated to South Africa in 1849, and for many years he carried on his business as tailor in Cape Town, his shop being situated in St George's Street, at the corner of Hout Street. His sister's son, George Ellis, R.N., the original of Crossjay Patterne in *The Egoist*, was also in Cape Town at this period, and he married there in 1851. Probably it was owing to the advice of this nephew that Augustus came to try his luck in that quarter of the globe, then so remote.

After the death of George Meredith in 1909, some correspondence was published in *The Cape Times* on the subject of local reminiscences of the novelist's father. A great many erroneous statements were made, but some points of interest relative to *Evan Harrington* transpired. Mr B. T. Lawton, of Rondebosch, who had been a customer and friend of Augustus Meredith, wrote that he well remembered how, in 1860, when *Evan Harrington* was appearing serially in *Once a Week*, he one day entered the shop and found the tailor in very low spirits. As a rule Augustus was very uncommunicative, but on this occasion, with an obvious desire for sympathy, he departed from his usual reserve and asked Mr Lawton if he had seen the new story. " I am very sore about it," said Augustus ; " I am pained beyond expression, as I consider it aimed at myself, and I am sorry to say the writer is my own son." Mr Lawton added that Augustus Meredith was then a handsome man of medium stature, well educated, and exceedingly obliging in business. He told Mr Lawton that in England he walked many miles every day, and this led to Augustus, at the ripe age of the mid-sixties, accompanying his Cape Town friend in an ascent of Table Mountain. Several other correspondents contributed their recollections, one stating that Augustus Meredith lent him a copy of *Farina*, and another relating how the Rev. Dr James Cannon once said to the tailor : " I am much interested in the career of your distinguished son," whereupon the father turned hastily away and made no reply.

On the whole it appears that Augustus Meredith did not like allusions to his son. He eventually returned to England about 1863, and settled near his old home in Portsmouth. He lived first at Argyll Villas, Wish Street, Southsea, and later at 50 Elm Grove (then called 2 Oxford Villas), a house which belonged to his second wife and where he spent the remainder of his years. Occasionally George Meredith came down for a few hours to see his father, merely a duty, for affection there was none. There is only one allusion to Augustus in his son's letters. In October, 1870, writing to his own son Arthur, then a boy of seventeen, at school on the Continent, George Meredith said : " I saw your Grandpapa Meredith on my way to Captain Maxse's ; he had been unwell, but was better ; he asked after you and so did Mrs M. They were anxious as to your situation in the territory of war."

Augustus Meredith died on 18th June, 1876, at the age of seventy-nine, and was buried (in the same vault as his second wife, Matilda Buckett, who died in 1885, at the age of sixty-seven) at Highland Road Cemetery, Southsea. George Meredith was present at his father's funeral. He inherited a few personal effects and family portraits : but these pictures were never seen prominently in his house. To the last, with that strange secretive sensitiveness which made his early days a closed book of mystery, he put out of sight and mind all memories and reminders of his youth in Portsmouth. And yet, in strange contradiction, he had recorded his family history in *Evan Harrington*. As I previously advanced, it could not be actual shame of the shop that prompted his reticence in conversation concerning his origin. Probably *Evan Harrington* was a sort of safety valve whereby he gave vent to much long-repressed emotion—old slights, old humiliations, bitter regrets that he, so aristocratic in aspiration and personal appearance, was "basely born," as he hyperbolically expressed it in the person of Evan. Undoubtedly there are many passages in the book voicing the personal bitterness of Meredith at the circumstances of his birth and youth. Thus :

"Tailordom triumphant was bearing its victim at a rattling pace, to settle him, and seal him for ever out of the ranks of gentlemen : Society, meantime, howling exclusion to him in the background : ' Out of our halls degraded youth ' : . . . We are no longer children, but men : men who have bitten hard at experience, and know the value of a tooth : who have had our hearts bruised, and cover them with armour : who live not to feed, but look to food that we may live ! What matters it that yonder high-spiced kingdom should excommunicate such as we are."

And, again, where Rose doubts " whether it really was in Nature's power, unaided by family-portraits, coats-of-arms, ballroom practice, and at least one small phial of Essence of Society, to make a Gentleman."

How sensitive he was on this question of being " a gentleman," or the reverse, is further proved in an early letter to Mrs

Ross, wherein, alluding to an acquaintance at Esher, he says:
" H—— is a good old boy. He has a pleasant way of being
inquisitive and has already informed me, quite agreeably, that
I am a gentleman, though I may not have been born one.
Some men are always shooting about you like May flies in little
quick darts, to see how near you they may come. The best
thing is to smile and enjoy the fun of it. I confess a private
preference for friends who are not thus afflicted, and get the
secret by influence. As my Janet does, for instance." And on
another occasion he told a correspondent, in 1886: " I am, I
trust, to the full as modest a person as I am bound to be. In
origin I am what is called here a nobody, and my pretensions
to that rank have always received due encouragement." A
small point to trouble a man of genius, it may be objected:
but men of genius have their weaknesses more painfully pronounced than mediocre people. There is a passage in *The
House on the Beach* (written, as we have seen, in 1861, soon
after *Evan Harrington*) which, I think, accurately expresses
Meredith's attitude, as a Son of the Shop, to Trade:

" The English have been called a bad-tempered people, but
this is to judge of them by their manifestations; whereas an
examination into causes might prove them to be no worse
tempered than that man is a bad sleeper who lies in a biting
bed. . . . Once they sang madrigals, once they danced on the
green, they revelled in their lusty humours, without having
recourse to the pun for fun, an exhibition of hundreds of bare
legs for jollity, a sentimental wailing all in the throat for music.
Evidence is procurable that they have been an artificially-
reared people, feeding on the genius of inventors, transposers,
adulterators, instead of the products of nature, for the last half
century; and it is unfair to affirm of them that they are positively
this or that. They are experiments. They are the sons and
victims of a desperate Energy, alluring by cheapness, satiating
with quantity, that it may mount in the social scale, at the expense of their tissues. The land is in a state of fermentation to
mount, and the shop, which has shot half their stars to their
social zenith, is what verily they would scald themselves to
wash themselves free of. Nor is it in any degree a reprehensible sign that they should fly as from hue and cry the title

of tradesman. It is on the contrary the spot of sanity, which bids us right cordially hope. Energy, transferred to the moral sense, may clear them yet." [1]

And now, at last, we are able to depart finally from the shop and Portsmouth, and, following in the track of the Harringtons, arrive at Petersfield ("Fallowfield"), where it would seem the daughters of Melchizedek Meredith had gone to school. Possibly "Dubbins's Seminary for Young Ladies" was located in that ancient building, formerly "The Castle" Inn, where stayed Charles II. and Pepys. "The Green Dragon" Inn was probably intended for "The Anchor," and "The Dolphin" was described under its own name—the scene where "Mrs Mel. makes a Bed." Beckley Court was, I think, intended for Fair Oak Lodge, about fifteen miles, as mentioned in the book, from Petersfield. The place tallies with Beckley, and the river Rother runs through the grounds, as in Meredith's beautiful description :

"Over a length of the stream the red round harvest-moon was rising. . . . The water curved, and dimpled, and flowed flat, and the whole body of it rushed into the spaces of sad splendour. The clustered trees stood like temples of darkness ; their shadows lengthened supernaturally ; and a pale gloom crept beneath them on the sward. . . . The waters streamed on endlessly into the golden arms awaiting them. The low moon burnt through the foliage. In the distance, over a reach of the flood, one tall aspen shook against the lighted sky."

Fair Oak Lodge was occupied by G. P. R. James, the novelist, in 1837-1839.

It is well known that the characteristics of Sir Franks and Lady Jocelyn and Rose were drawn from the author's friends, Sir Alexander and Lady Duff Gordon and their daughter Janet, of whom Meredith saw so much at the time he was writing

---

[1] If Meredith had lived to see the publication of Mr A. M. Ludovici's book, *A Defence of Aristocracy*, he would have appreciated the elaboration therein of this thesis, for the author ably traces the present economic, industrial, and social ills of England to Puritanism with the concurrent rise and development of the shop and trade, and resultant exploitation of labour.

K

Evan Harrington. Particularly successful was he in delineating the rich personality of Lady Duff Gordon. She (daughter of John Austin, Professor of Jurisprudence, and through her mother a descendant of the Taylors of Norwich) was a very remarkable woman and of a distinguished type of beauty. In advance of her time, she possessed a singular masculinity of intellect, was a famous traveller, and a writer of ability and charm, and smoked cigars both indoors and out. She died in 1869 at the early age of forty-eight. It attaches worthily to her name that she was one of the first to perceive Meredith's powers in his early days as a writer. He received many kindnesses from her, and she was one of the few who understood with sympathy and tact his shy, sensitive nature. He was not ungrateful. " O what a gallant soul she is, and how very much I love her ! " he wrote in 1861 ; and he paid a fine tribute to her in the after years in the Introduction he wrote for Lady Duff Gordon's *Letters from Egypt.* How well his estimate blends with the picture of Lady Jocelyn and recalls her sane, serene attitude to life :

" She preferred the society of men, on the plain ground that they discuss matters of weight, and are—the pick of them—of open speech, more liberal, more genial, better comrades. Was it wonderful to hear them, knowing her as they did, unite in calling her *cœur d'or* ? . . . The hospitable house at Esher gave its welcome not merely to men and women of distinction ; the humble undistinguished were made joyous guests there, whether commonplace or counting among the hopeful. Their hostess knew how to shelter the sensitively silent at table, if they were unable to take encouragement and join in the flow. . . . In England, in her day, while health was with her, there was one house where men and women conversed. When that house perforce was closed, a light went out in our country."

That is a pleasant memorial of the old days at Esher. The amusing Miss Current, in *Evan Harrington*, was drawn from Miss Louisa Courtenay, an old friend of Lady Duff Gordon, who often came to Esher. And Pat, the Irish retriever pup, had his original in Peter, the property of Miss Janet Duff Gordon, at whose special request the dog was introduced into the story. Peter, after being broken in, was given to Arthur Meredith.

LUCIE, LADY DUFF GORDON, THE ORIGINAL OF LADY JOCELYN
IN "EVAN HARRINGTON," AND OF LADY DUNSTANE IN
"DIANA OF THE CROSSWAYS"

From the portrait by H. W. Phillips

Miss Duff Gordon seems quite to have entered into the spirit of her progressive immortalisation as Rose Jocelyn, for she relates she would often interrupt Meredith's reading of his latest instalment of " her " story with the remark : " No, I should never have said it like that." And as she expressed it to me : " I ' corrected ' myself in *Evan Harrington*." But Meredith thought otherwise, for he held the model to be the finer part. He wrote to her in 1861 : " Maxse . . . is very anxious to be introduced some day to Rose Jocelyn. I tell him that Janet Ross is a finer creature. If Rose satisfies him, how will not Janet ! Talking of Rose, did you see *The Saturday* ? It says you are a heroine who deserves to be a heroine. And yet I think I missed you. Your Mother tells me that Mrs Austin speaks in very handsome terms of the performance generally, and of the portrait in particular."

Certainly the history of this novel is a curious one, for here was the author drawing from the life the characteristics of his friends with their willing consent, though at the same time those friends were quite unaware that other characters in the book were drawn from the author's own relatives, long since dead or lost sight of, and that the story was the unveiling of part of his own inner sensitiveness.

Needless to say that, like " that brave high young soul— Rose," Miss Duff Gordon was a fearless rider, and relations of her adventures on horseback will be found in Mrs Ross's book of reminiscences, *The Fourth Generation*. When she married and left Esher, Meredith wrote : " The hunt is queenless evermore." Owing to Mrs Ross's permanent residence abroad she did not often meet her old friend again. Forty-three years later she saw him, five years before his death, for the last time. He was aged and deaf, " but the old fire and brilliancy were there, and we talked for two or three hours about old times and old friends, most of them, alas, dead. ' You have something of Rose in you still, my dear,' he said, smiling rather sadly as I got up to go ; ' those were pleasant days.' " And Mrs Ross concludes : " What an uphill fight he had, and how splendidly he won it. I never think of him as the old man I saw at Box Hill. He lives in my memory as the lithe, active companion who so often strode along by the side of my cob over Copsham Common, brandishing his stick and talking so brilliantly."

I have already alluded to the love and devotion Meredith showered upon his little son Arthur in the years immediately following the separation from the wife and mother and the death of that most unhappy of women. This supreme affection of the then lonely father for his lonely child is the most pathetic episode in the life of Meredith ; baffled love and sorrow and retributive tragedy are enshrined in the story, which in its most appealing features only covers a few years. It was, in a way, a repetition of family history. Remembering his own lonely—perchance loveless—boyhood (for his father, Augustus Meredith, as I have related, though indulgent and anxious to win his son's affections and sympathies, never succeeded in reaching that remote and sensitive heart), George Meredith made affecting efforts to recover the mistakes of the past and win the love of his own son—the only thing in the world he then loved ; the handsome boy, ill-fated inheritor of a double portion of warring temperament and talent, was of curious psychology ; he was rather cold and unresponsive to his father ; his sympathies, in turn, were never won, and eventually came long estrangement between these two acutely sensitive natures so much alike, each with a power of wounding the other most pitiful. George Meredith had to suffer the same regrets and pangs which had been the portion of his father before him in relation to his own personality. As he sorrowfully wrote from experience in *Richard Feverel*: " He was fighting with a fate in this beloved boy. . . . If immeasurable love were perfect wisdom, one human being might almost impersonate Providence to another. Alas ! love, divine as it is, can do no more than lighten the house it inhabits."

In both the cases of George and Arthur Meredith the boys were spoilt and brought up in an ill-advised and uncertain manner ; both in the position of an only child, they each lacked the society of other children and were too much imbued with that of adults. How injudicious, at times, George Meredith was in the treatment of his son is evidenced by a story related to me by Sir Francis Burnand, who was a spectator of the incident and said he never could forget the unpleasant memory. It was in 1859, when Burnand was staying with Meredith and Maurice FitzGerald at Esher, and on one occasion, at dinner Arthur Meredith—then a child of some six years of age—

JANET DUFF GORDON (MRS. ROSS). THE ORIGINAL OF ROSE JOCELYN IN "EVAN HARRINGTON," AND, PARTLY, OF JANET ILCHESTER, IN "HARRY RICHMOND"

From the portrait by G. F. Watts, R.A.

wishing to emulate his elders, asked for some wine. The request was refused. The boy persisted, till, at last, Meredith, in a fine irritation, cried : " If you will have it you *shall*," and compelled the boy to drink a tumbler full of wine, with the result that Arthur was rendered almost unconscious, and then very ill, in which state he remained for several days. Certainly an efficacious, if drastic, lesson in obedience and temperance. But in the main, Meredith's life with his little son, in the days when they were all in all to each other, makes a pleasant picture, with the Surrey lanes and heaths and " dear old woods " of Copsham for a setting. As he wrote : " Yesterday I walked to Mickleham with Sons, taking him on my back returning." That is a typical glimpse of their life and relations. The best way to present vividly the father's constant love and preoccupation for his son will be to quote from the letters Meredith addressed to his friends at this period. Thus, in addition to the paramount thought of his mind we shall also obtain a view of his life and movements at home and abroad during the years 1860-1864.

In December, 1860, Miss Janet Duff Gordon was married to Henry James Ross, a banker at Alexandria. Writing to her in the following spring, Meredith said :

" The little man has been in great glee to answer you. He had paper and everything ready to do so a week before your letter came, and his reply is all his own, and from his heart. He must love you. Who could fail to love one so staunch and tender to him ? Here have I waited silently thinking much of you, and incurring I know not what condemnation. I have not thought of you less because I withheld my pen. The truth is, my experiences are all mental—I see nothing of the world; and what I have to say goes into books. However, I am now compelled by my state of health to give it up for a time. . . . In the Academy . . . Leighton has a *Paolo and Francesca*, painted just as the book has dropped and they are in no state to read more. You would scorn it ; but our friendship never rested on common sentiments in art. I greatly admire it. I think it the sole English picture exhibiting passion that I have seen. I have the delight to stand alone in my judgment of this, as of most things, and I shall see the world coming round to my opinion, and thinking it its own. Does that smack of the original George M. ? . . . How I should wish Arthur to conquer a fair position in the world . . . at present he is not brilliant, but he is decidedly hopeful. I don't want to force him yet. I wish to keep him sound, and to instil good healthy habits of mind and body. In writing, spelling, and reading, in memory for what he acquires, few children surpass him. And he really thinks—without being at all instigated to think. I remained at Copsham for his sake, and perhaps shall not quit it for some time to come. He will not go to a regular school till next year. I don't like the thought of his going ; but it must be, and so I submit.

" In conclusion, let me beg you to send to me and tell me anything that you want that I may have the pleasure to get it for you. I rejoice with all my soul that you are so happy. By the way, Maxse introduced me to the Comte de Paris the other day, who said of your husband : ' Mr Ross is a very clever man,' in a tone of conviction and esteem. Of you he spoke as it pleased me to hear. The Orleanists seem looking up, owing to the Aumale pamphlet. The Duke was chairman of the Literary Fund Dinner last night, and spoke capitally."

At this period Claremont was occupied by the exiled Queen Marie Amélie, widow of Louis Philippe, and her younger sons and grandsons. The Orleans princes were fond of hunting, and lived in pleasant social acquaintance with their neighbours, including Meredith, who stated in later years, to M. Constantin Photiadès :

" These sons of Louis Philippe, handsome, brave, polished, elegant and well-read, the Duke of Nemours with his grand air, and the Prince de Joinville so like Francis I. with his hanging lower lip, his square-cut beard and his long, almond-shaped eyes, they explain to me better than all memoirs the charm of ancient France. We had very friendly relationships with them when they lodged at Claremont. But I never felt attracted by the vague and slow intellect of the Comte de Paris. On the day when he spoke to me of making certain reforms when he should be re-established in his hereditary place upon the throne, I mentally hoped that he might never be seated there.

France, that impetuous thoroughbred, needs a more gallant cavalier."

In the summer of 1861 Meredith went abroad with Arthur, and arranged to meet W. C. Bonaparte Wyse there. The following interesting letters to his friend refer to this project :—

"MY DEAR WYSE,—How I miss you and regret not being with you. I saw the doctor yesterday, who says that the ' knot of the nerves ' is irritated and has been long so. I must not smoke, I must not work ; I must go to the college of the sunny Lazzaroni and live as the ephemeræ live that I may not die like them. He says also that at the end of six weeks I must pack my knapsack and away to Switzerland or Tyrol, so haste on your way. I meantime offer sacrifices—a kid, etc. I send you the book of M. Aubanel's lyrics. They are intensely Southern, arid, monotonous, impressive. When you see M. Mistral, pray tell him that it is my earnest wish to be introduced to him. *Mirèio*, the more I look at it, strikes me as a consummate work in an age of very small singing. It has in some parts the pastoral richness of Theocritus and the rough vigour of Homer. I read your translation of the portion describing the mares of the Camargue to Maxse, who was delighted.[1] He spoke of the poem to the Duc d'Aumale. The latter supposed the name of M. Mistral a *nom de plume*! He seemed astonished to learn that France held a living poet, unknown to him and admired in England. Lady Gordon still has your copy. She is too ill to be seen, or I would give you her opinion. You know how highly I esteem her as a critic.

"I am composing gently. Yesterday I met, in Fleet Street, Dante Rossetti, the artist. I went with him to his studio, and there he gave me a translation he has been at work on many years, viz. poems from the Italian poets up to Dante—some are perfectly exquisite : as for the translation, it is so good that he will rank as poet as well as artist from the hour of the publication. Soon may we two drink this pure Italian wine together ! [2]

[1] Forty years later, in 1901, Meredith produced his *Mares of the Camargue,* translated from the fourth canto of Mistral's poem.
[2] Dante Gabriel Rossetti's *Early Italian Poets* was published in 1861.

"The Derby is over and England's annual culmination with it. Exhausted the nation takes breath, and the more ardent spirits look forward to the Derby ensuing. And so on. . . .

"Hoping a few days will bring tidings of you,

"Your friend,

"GEORGE MEREDITH."

"*Sunday June 16th*, 1861.
"COPSHAM COTTAGE.

"MY VERY DEAR L.B. PAT!—Tell M. Mistral that Lady Gordon, an excellent critic, and one whose opinion I value more highly than that of most *men*, is astonished and delighted at the vigour and freshness of his poem. She has taught herself to read it in Provençale, and has now a fair appreciation of the beauty of the instrument M. Mistral touches so wonderfully. When known in England, *Mirèio* is certain to be highly appreciated.

"I have spoken to Chapman and Hall about your projected book on Rabelais. I think you may look on it as determined, if only you keep to your resolution to work. . . .

"Now tell me, why can't you go to Como through Tyrol? And meet me in Belgium quickly? . . . State when you will be at Como, and for what time. But you are more certain of me by catching me now. I, too, am slipping, and my nostril is turning seawards. The summer is on us, and the Goddess Amphitrite, whose long arms are round the margin of Earth, opens them invitingly for me. Yet do I lean to your companionship in preference, and if I make appointments I keep them. So count on me. I have been to the Doctor! He prohibits work; finds me perfectly sound, but with a drag on one organ—promises speedy cure; and has already set me up somewhat. My tabak is cut dolefully short. And I am to see fresh sights and drink novel air for a term of two months. God bless you! Don't lose heart. Write immediately.

"Arthur's birthday was on Thursday, when he entered his ninth year. I spent the whole day in the woods with the dear little man. I wish I could only contrive to bring him abroad with me. Leaving him is all that bothers me."

But, of course, he did "contrive" to take Arthur.

" Copsham.

"My dear Poet,—I hope to be with you by the margin
of Zürich's fair waters on Saturday, or Sunday. We start
Thursday night ; and come, I think, by the Great Luxembourg
Railway, which they say is more direct. Passports are here.
All is ready. The delay has been caused by the newspapers,
knickerbockers for Arthur—and knick-knacks. I am told by
my doctor to get much tonic glacier air : to pass many mountain passes : to keep to the high land. Before we start together,
I want to go to Hofwyl, to see a school to which Arthur may
ultimately be sent.

" I shall bring a knapsack. . . . I shall take to myself two
months and perhaps a week more. Do try and give up so much
time to me. . . . I shall proceed to the Hôtel de Belle Vue on
arriving at Zürich."

"My dear Fellow,—I don't think I can start before
Tuesday next, as there are things to be got ready for Arthur.
I thank you for your readiness to meet my wishes. I suppose
we shall be three days on the route—so meet on Friday or
Saturday. I hope it won't annoy you our being so late. Arthur
is at school, but will chirp when he hears the good news. . . .
Zürich will do capitally. ' By the margin,' etc.

" La-la-laity !

" I have just polished *Cassandra* to my satisfaction. Also
a new Poem—*The Patriot Engineer.* *Phantasy* is remoulded
and made presentable. Best of all, my health is very promising. I shall not bring a hat, or a tail coat. I won't. If needs
must in your society, I will buy one. To our quick and joyful
meeting, my friend ! In great haste, your aff.

" George Meredith."

Father and son duly set forth, and travelled via Ostend and
the Rhine. They stayed, as arranged, at Zürich, in July, and
then on to Innsbrück, and to Meran in the Tyrol. From the
latter place Meredith wrote to F. M. Evans, the publisher :

" My walks of about 30 miles a day under a fiery sun have
improved me, and I think I can go to work now for another

nine months. Have you any idea of what Lucas's intentions were concerning *The Dyke Farm*.[1] I have an autobiographical story in view for *O. a W.* That is if *O. a W.* survives. For I know nothing and hear nothing. Nobody sends me a *Times* or a *Punch*! I am forgotten if I don't set to work all the agencies of science. You write me contemptuously short business paragraphs. It's clear to me that travelling is for great men alone. . . . What the deuce has come to you all ? The moment I leave England all's dead silent to rearward. I'm not of much importance, but still I expect my country to make a little sign. . . . Arthur is quite well. He is here, and a mighty traveller as you may suppose. He says he is happy, and is catching butterflies."

They had joined Bonaparte Wyse without mishap, and Meredith often mentions the latter in his letters. Thus, he tells Maxse, on 26th July :

"We walked from Innsbrück to Landek in three days. Wyse does not walk in rain, or when it's to be apprehended ; nor when there's a chance of nightfall ; nor does he like it in the heat ; and he's not the best hand in the world at getting up in the morning, and he is rather excitable. But still thoroughly kind and good. So we did not come at a great rate. From Landek we took three days and a quarter to Meran, whence I write to you. The country is wonderful. Mountains holding up cups of snow to the fiery sun, who glares on them in vain. The peasantry are a noble race : pious, and with a strong smell. Priests abound and soap flies before them. . . .

"The Rosanna, by the way, put me in mind of you—nay, sang of you with a mountain voice, somehow, I don't know how.[2] Perhaps because it is both hearty and gallant, subtle, and sea-green. You never saw so lovely a brawling torrent. Clear, ice-cold, foaming. You shall have the verses it inspired.

---

[1] This was the title originally intended for the story now known as *Rhoda Fleming*, which was being evolved by the author at this date. *Once a Week*, as edited by Lucas, was discontinued in 1865. Meredith apparently wrote and sent to *Once a Week* two stories, entitled *The Highwayman* and *Paul Bentley*. They were set up in proof, but were never published, and no trace of them has been found.

[2] Compare with the poem *By the Rosanna*.

Tell me : Would you like the dedication of my volume of Poems, when it's ready ? Say no, if you feel no. For my part I feel the honour will be mine.[1] . . .

"This land abounds in falling waters, brooks, torrents, all ice cold. We drank at the wells every ten minutes, sat over the brooks naked legged, dipped our heads desperately. . . . Nothing can be grander than the colossal mountains of porphyry and dolomite shining purple and rosy, snow-capped here and there, with some tumultuous river noising below, and that eternal stillness overhead, save when some great peak gathers the thunders and bellows for a time. Then to see the white sulphurous masks curl and cower round it, and drip moisture on the hanging meadows. . . .

"My first sight of the Alps has raised odd feelings. Here at last seems something more than earth, and visible, if not tangible. They have the whiteness, the silence, the beauty and mystery of thoughts seldom unveiled within us, but which conquer Earth when once they are. In fact, they have made my creed tremble.—Only for a time. They have merely dazzled me with a group of symbols. Our great error has been (the error of all religions, as I fancy) to raise a spiritual system in antagonism to Nature. What though yonder Alp does touch the Heavens ? Is it a rebuke to us below ? In you and in me there may be lofty virgin points, pure from what we call fleshliness. And so forth. Wyse is lost in astonishment at me because I don't look out for a ' woman.' ' You're a pote, and I can't think how a pote can get on without one. I'd go mad.' Mrs W. is very kind to Arthur, and really in love with the Irish-Corsican.[2] They spoon terribly. Perhaps I am getting old, for I don't envy them, though I feel a kind of emptiness— an uncared-for feeling. A good friendship would satisfy me. . . . How is it the Austrians get beaten by the French ? A finer set of men than the Austrian soldiers you can't see anywhere."

---

[1] *By the Rosanna* (" To F. M.") and the volume of collected poems, *Modern Love and Poems of the English Roadside*, were duly " affectionately inscribed to Captain Maxse, R.N."

[2] W. C. Bonaparte Wyse came from Co. Waterford, and was High Sheriff in 1855. He married Ellen, daughter of W. G. Prout, of St Mabyn, Cornwall.

On 16th August he continued from Milan :

" Behold a pretty picture, which is to tell you I have been in Venice, which you know so well, which is a dream and seduction to the soul of me. I wish you had been there with me. Now, mark the Campanile above, for you are to have it reproduced one day in illustrious verse. There did I conceive an Ode.[1] I have followed Byron's and Shelley's footsteps there (in Venice) on the Lido. Do you remember in *Julian and Maddalo*, where the two, looking towards the Euganean hills, see the great bell of the Insane Asylum swing in the sunset ?[2] I found the exact spot. I have seldom felt melancholy so strongly as when standing there. You know I despise melancholy, but the feeling came. I love both those poets ; and with my heart given to them I felt as if I stood in a dead and useless time. So are we played with sometimes. . . . Well, I walked the Lido every day, and bathed with my little man in the tepid Adriatic, and floated through the streets in my gondola, and received charming salutes from barred windows : from one notably where a very pretty damsel, lost in languor, hung with her loose-robed bosom against the iron, and pressed amorously to see me pass, till she could no further : I meantime issued orders to Lorenzo, my gondolier, to return, and lo, as I came slowly into view she as slowly arranged her sweet shape to be seen decently, and so stood, but half a pace in the recess, with one dear hand on one shoulder, her head slightly lying on her neck, her drooped eyelids mournfully seeming to say : ' No, no ; never ! tho' I am dying to be wedded to that wish of yours, and would stake my soul I have divined it ! '—wasn't it charming ? This, too, so intensely human from a figure vaporous but half-discernible. . . .

" I am much better in health, but, you see, I have been somewhat disappointed about the management of Arthur. I have

[1] Apparently never produced.
[2] " I looked, and saw between us and the sun
    A building on an island. . . .
    And on the top an open tower, where hung
    A bell which in the radiance swayed and swung,—
    We could just hear its hoarse and iron tongue :
    The broad sun sank behind it, and it tolled . . . "
                                    Julian and Maddalo.

been able to get only one week's walk, and the rest of the time the little fellow has been on my hands. But what a jolly boy and capital companion he is! Full of fun and observation, good temper and endurance. The tour has sown much fine stuff in him, but I am anxious at last to have him home. As for me, I believe I shall now be in condition for labour of the remunerative kind. The novelty has been worth the money in all ways. Could I but afford to rest and look on man for one year! *Non è possibile.* You must see Arthur's Diary. He is at it now, at my elbow."

On proceeding to Venice, Meredith had parted company with Bonaparte Wyse, who went to Como to see his mother. Meredith joined him there in August. He wrote:

"MILAN. *August* 17*th*.

"MY DEAR WYSE,—Heartily glad to hear good news from you!... To-morrow I'll come by the 9.30 from Milan. This reaches Camerlata at 10.53, but don't fear my disturbing you at that hour. Why don't you meet me and save my looking foolish, when you know I can't Italian and can only just stumble in French; and Frenchwomen have in their souls (in spite of their soft smiles) no mercy for a wretch who looks foolish! I shall sleep at Camerlata, and start for Turin next day early.

"Your faithful

"GEORGE MEREDITH."

Home again once more at Copsham Cottage in September, Arthur Meredith wrote to Mrs Ross an account of his travels in the usual style of a correspondent of eight years. Leaving uncorrected all errors of spelling, the father added the note: "This is entirely as you would wish it to be—the small man's own, I bearing the stamp thereof. He will have a lot more of it to tell you when he has you by the ear."

Some further details of the tour are contained in a later letter from Meredith to Mrs Ross, when again it will be apparent how the father was ever ready to sacrifice his own wishes to pleasure his loved boy:

"Copsham, Esher.
"*November* 19*th*, 1861.

"My very dear Janet,—I plead ill-health : I plead vexation, occupation, general insufficiency : I plead absence from home, absence from my proper mind, and a multitude of things : and now I am going to pay my debts. But are not my letters really three single gentlemen rolled into one ? This shall count for ten. . . . You have heard particulars of our travels. . . . The little man asked innumerable questions about the amphitheatre, and the gladiators, the shows, and the Roman customs. Thence to Venice, where he and I were alone—Wyse parting for Como and his mother. Our life in Venice was charming. Only I had to watch the dear boy like tutor, governess, courier, in one ; and couldn't get much to the pictures ; for there was no use in victimising him and dragging him to see them, and I couldn't quit him at all. We hired a gondola and floated through the streets at night, or out to Malamocco to get the fresh breeze. A fresh Levant wind favoured our visit. To the Lido we went every morning : Arthur and I bathing— behold us for a solid hour under enormous straw-hats floating and splashing in the delicious Adriatic. The difficulty of getting him out of it was great. 'Papa, what a dear old place this is. We won't go, will we ? ' . . .

" I went to Como to see Wyse, who was with Il Principessa.[1] She received me affably at the Villa—Villa Ciani, près d'Este. She has a handsome daughter, fair as a high-born English girl, engaged then and since married to General Türr. Madame la Princesse will be Madame la Princesse, and desires that she should hear it too, as I quickly discovered. I grew in favour. She has no difficulty in swallowing a compliment. Quantity is all she asks for. This is entre nous, for she entertained me, and indeed I was vastly entertained. Look for it all in a future chapter. A good gross compliment, fluently delivered, I find to be the best adapted to a Frenchwoman's taste. If you hesitate, the flavour evaporates for them. Be glib, and

---

[1] Lady Wyse : Letitia, daughter of Lucien Bonaparte (brother of Napoleon). She married Sir Thomas Wyse in 1821. Her daughter Adeline married General Stephane Türr, a Lieutenant of Garibaldi's and the original promoter of the Panama Canal in 1878. Another Miss Wyse married Rattazzi, the Piedmontese minister.

you may say what you please. Should you, in addition, be
neat and ready, they will fall in love with you. Mademoiselle
the fiancée perceived that I was taken with her before I had
felt it. Hence she distinguished me, till the General came.
It's a real love match. She wouldn't sing then—couldn't.
Nor did I press it : for oh ! she sings in the rapid French style :
all from the throat : and such a hard metallic Giordigianic
rang over Como's water as sure as our dear old Muddy Mole
never knew of. . . . King Victor gave Türr some Royal Tokay,
which he brought to the Villa, and we were merry over it. . . .
Before dinner we all bathed in Como, ladies and gentlemen
ensemble. Really pleasant and pastoral ! Mademoiselle swims
capitally, rides and drives well ; and will make a good hero's
wife. She scorns the English for their bad manners, she told
me. The Emperor allows her £1000 a year : her mother gets
£2000. Vive l'Empereur ! [1]

" Thence over the Mont Cenis to Paris. The little man was
in raptures at the thought of crossing the Alps. He would
barely close his eyes. I had him in my arms in the coupé of
the diligence, and then he was starting up every instant, shouting and crowing till dawn ; when I had no chance of getting
him to sleep. When we reached Macon at night I put him to
bed, and gave him a little weak coffee in bed. He slept like a
top till morning. Arthur was impatient to be home, and
cared little for Paris. I gave him a dinner at Véfours and at
the Trois Frères. He appreciated it : but longed for England.
Paris is delightful ! Under the circumstances, with a remon-
strating little man, there was nothing for it but to return
hastily. Thank Heaven ! I got him home safe—a little worn :
but he soon got over that and has improved his young mind
considerably. The journey did me good. I am much stronger,
and am beginning to be able to work much better, but have to
be careful. . . .

" My housekeeper, good Miss Grange,[2] has just had an offer

---

[1] Napoleon III. was, of course, a first cousin of Lady Wyse.

[2] The rated occupier of Copsham Cottage for many years was Thomas
Grange, and it was his daughter who acted as Meredith's housekeeper
and looked after the rooms the novelist rented. Miss Grange continued
to live in the cottage long after Meredith left ((in 1864) and her father's
death.

from Claremont to go and attend the Princess François, and I'm afraid she'll go ; which will be a complete upset here : for she's a valuable person : excellent temper, spotless principles, indefatigable worker, no sex : thoughtful, prudent, and sensible. Where shall I get such another ? Of course I can't advise her to stay. It's a terrible bother. They have been hunting a little ; but the Prince de Joinville has not yet returned from America, so not much is done in that way."

He was now occupied with his poems. Writing to Wyse in December, 1861, he said :

"We have the winter on us. I wish I had you here to read you some of the Poems I have lately written. Fellows say they are my best. I think it likely that in a couple of months I shall publish a vol. : I fancy, judging from what I hear, that they would sell. This, if there's no war with the Yankees, which at this moment looks too probable.[1] You will see the cause for it in the Italian papers. Maxse, though expecting to be married in a month, has resolved to ask for a ship, so anxious is he to teach them manners, if the chance offers. This feeling is universal, and one may be proud of seeing it : so calm, so fixed ! No shrieks of passion ! Such steady facing of every difficulty, and serene strength. If I were abroad, it would bring tears of love to my eyes. Write and tell me what you are doing ; what are your immediate prospects. I was terribly hurt at that letter from Athens to Galignani, and only wish it had been a case where it would have been possible to take up arms for so innocent and sweet a person."

He wrote again on 15th May, 1862.

"MY DEAR WYSE,—I this day get your letter, and am glad to see it, and shall be glad to welcome you. This opening year I have thought of you much, from the contrast of last spring. I am better in health and strength. The little man blooms constantly. I have just published a volume of Poems, of which a copy is ready for you, when you arrive. Let me know the day you are likely to be in England : what are your immediate

[1] Over the *Alabama* incident.

intentions, etc. : when I am likely to see you. I write in great haste, that this may not fail to reach you.

" Know me ever your faithful

" GEORGE MEREDITH."

At this date also he commenced his comedy, *The Sentimentalists*.—" I have a comedy germinating in the brain, of the classic order : *The Sentimentalists*. I fancy it will turn out well," he said, in June, 1862.[1]

Modern Love and Poems of the English Roadside, when published in the spring of 1862, attracted very little attention and shared the fate of the earlier volume of verse in 1851, despite the brilliant championship of Swinburne. Meredith was prepared for an adverse verdict by experience. Writing to Dr Jessopp, he said : " I scarcely expected that these new poems of mine could please you much. I look to a severe drubbing from the Reviewers, and fold my hands. It is worse to think that Mudie (my old enemy, who quashed *R. Feverel*) has hoisted the banner of British Matrondom, and ejected me." And a little later, to the same friend : "As to the Poems : I don't think the age prosaic for not buying them. A man who hopes to be popular must think from the mass, and as the heart of the mass. If he follows out vagaries of his own brain, he cannot hope for general esteem ; and he does smaller work. *Modern Love*, as a dissection of the sentimental passion of these days, could only be apprehended by the few who would read it many times. I have not looked for it to succeed. Why did I write it ? Who can account for pressure ? "

His anticipations of unfavourable reviews were soon realised.

[1] The comedy, apparently, did not develop at this time, and the project was put aside until about 1870, when scenes 6-8 were written. In 1883, when Meredith's *Poems and Lyrics of the Joy of Earth* was published, the book contained a notice of " Forthcoming Publications " which mentioned *The Sentimentalists : a Comedy*. Then after another long interval, it seems Meredith rewrote, in 1895-1900, the first five scenes. After the author's death the comedy was collated by Sir J. M. Barrie. It was produced at the Duke of York's Theatre, on 2nd March, 1910, with Miss Fay Davis, Miss Mary Jerrold, and Mr Dennis Eadie in the principal parts. Although the piece was admitted to be all very exquisite and fragile—a dainty comedy in porcelain, let us say—and the Georgian costumes picturesque, it was found to be both artificial and ethereal, and lacking in the dramatic sense.

L

An adverse notice of the poems appeared in *The Spectator* for 24th May, 1862, wherein it was said :

" Mr George Meredith is a clever man, without literary genius, taste, or judgment. The effect of the book on us is that of clever, meretricious, turbid pictures by a man of some vigour, jaunty manners, quick observation, and some putonal skill, who likes writing about naked human passions, but does not bring either original imaginative power or true sentiment to the task. . . . Meddling causelessly, and somewhat pruriently, with a deep and painful subject on which he has no convictions to express, he sometimes treats serious themes with a flippant levity that is exceedingly vulgar and unpleasant."

By the Rosanna was classified with " spasmodic ostentation of ' fast ' writing. Mr Meredith evidently thinks mud picturesque, as indeed it may be, but all picturesqueness is not poetry."

This rather fatuous disquisition aroused the ire of Swinburne, who, devoting his attention primarily to a defence of *Modern Love*, replied with a long letter which appeared in the issue for 7th June. He protested against " this sort of criticism as applied to one of the leaders of English literature. . . . Praise or blame should be thoughtful, serious, careful, when applied to a work of such subtle strength, such depth of delicate power, such passionate and various beauty, as the leading poem of Mr Meredith's volume ; in some points, as it seems to me (and in this opinion I know that I have weightier judgments than my own to back me), a poem above the aim and beyond the reach of any but its author. Mr Meredith is one of the three or four poets now alive whose work, perfect or imperfect, is always as noble in design as it is often faultless in result. The present critic falls foul of him for dealing with ' a deep and painful subject on which he has no convictions to express.' There are pulpits enough for all preachers in prose ; the business of verse-writing is hardly to express convictions ; and if some poetry, not without merit of its kind, has at times dealt in dogmatic morality, it is all the worse and all the weaker for that. As to subject, it is too much to expect that all schools of poetry are to be for ever subordinate to the one just now so much in request with us, whose scope of sight is bounded by the nursery walls ; that all Muses are to bow down before her who babbles, with lips yet warm from their pristine pap, after the dangling delights of a child's coral, and jingles with flaccid fingers one knows not whether a jester's or a baby's bells."

He might have quoted the words which Meredith prefixed to *Modern Love* : "This is not meat for little people or for fools."

In addition to the poem of *Modern Love*, the volume contained twenty-two other pieces. Most of those which may be classified as genre had originally appeared in *Once a Week*. Of the rest, the finest was the *Ode to the Spirit of Earth in Autumn*, and it is strange that the reviewer in *The Spectator* could not unbend to admit its merits.

Take but a few lines of this brilliant imagery :

> The voice that issues from thy breast,
>   O glorious South-west,
> Along the gloom-horizon holloa'd ;
> Warning the valleys with a mellow roar
> Through flapping wings ; then sharp the woodland bore
> A shudder and a noise of hands :
> A thousand horns from some far vale
> In ambush sounding on the gale.
> Forth from the cloven sky came bands
> Of revel-gathering spirits ; trooping down,
> Some rode the tree-tops ; some on torn cloud-strips
>   Burst screaming through the lighted town :
> And scudding seaward, some fell on big ships :
>   Or mounting the sea-horses blew
>   Bright foam-flakes on the black review
>   Of heaving hulls and burying beaks.

> Still on the farthest line, with outpuffed cheeks,
> 'Twixt dark and utter dark, the great wind drew
> From heaven that disenchanted harmony
> To join earth's laughter in the midnight blind :
> Booming a distant chorus to the shrieks
>   Preluding him : then he,
> His mantle streaming thunderingly behind,
> Across the yellow realm of stiffened Day,
> Shot thro' the woodland alleys signals three ;
>   And with the pressure of a sea
> Plunged broad upon the vale that under lay. . . .

> Pour, let the wines of Heaven pour !
> The Golden Harp is struck once more,
> And all its music is for me !
> Pour, let the wines of Heaven pour !
> And, ho, for a night of Pagan glee ! . . .

The crimson-footed nymph is panting up the glade,
With the wine-jar at her armpit, and the drunken ivy-braid
Round her forehead, breasts, and thighs : starts a Satyr, and they
     speed :
Hear the crushing of the leaves : hear the cracking of the bough !
And the whistling of the bramble, the piping of the weed !

The notices of the book elsewhere were not remarkable.
Maxse wrote the review in *The Morning Post* from proofs,
without seeing the published volume. In letters to him,
written in June, 1862, Meredith said :

" Your article has appeared in the *Post*. It is very good :
but do you think it ? You should have whipped me on the
score of the absurdities, obscurities, and what not. I feel that
you have been sparing me, and though I don't love the rod,
I don't cry mercy. I'm exceedingly sorry that you did not
review from the book. *The Ode to the Spirit of Earth* will, if I
mistake not, catch hold of you. . . . It will suffice for me if you
tell me what you think of it, and not the public. The notices
that have appeared fix favourably on the Roadside poems, but
discard *Modern Love*, which, I admit, requires thought, and
discernment, and reading more than once. *The Saturday R.*
has not yet spoken. One paper calls me a genius—one, a
meretricious, clever bold man ! I find, to my annoyance, that
I am susceptible to remarks on my poems, and criticisms from
whipsters or women absolutely make me wince and flush. I
saw Robert Browning the other day, and he expressed himself
' astounded at the originality, delighted with the natural-
ness and beauty.' Pardon my egotism—I write to please
you !

" *June* 13. Your letter from Lucca. You complain of sun.
The S.W. has been blowing since the middle of May, and this
year has not yet known one day of sunshine. Rossetti is beginning to ask about your Lady, to know when he may have
a sitting.[1] He, dear fellow, is better—still somewhat shaken.
Mention it not—he buried his MSS. poems in his wife's coffin,

---

[1] Frederick Maxse had married, in 1861, Cecilia, daughter of Colonel
Steel. Mrs Maxse died in 1918. The children of the marriage were
Lieut.-General Sir Ivor Maxse, Mr L. J. Maxse, of *The National
Review*, and two daughters, one of whom married Lord Edward Cecil
in 1894.

it is whispered.[1] He, his brother, and Swinburne have taken a house (Sir T. More's) at Chelsea : a strange, quaint, grand old place, with an immense garden, magnificent panelled staircases and rooms—a palace. I am to have a bedroom for my once-a-week visits. We shall have nice evenings there, and I hope you'll come."

It was in connection with his work as Reader for Chapman and Hall, involving attendance for a whole day each week at the office in Piccadilly, which caused Meredith to enter into this arrangement to take a room and some share of the housekeeping expenses at Queen's (then called Tudor) House, 16 Cheyne Walk, Chelsea, during the memorable occupation of the house by the Rossetti brothers and Swinburne. It was manifestly inconvenient to get back to Copsham Cottage late in the evening, particularly in the winter, and the Chelsea proposition seemed a very suitable and pleasant solution of the difficulty, for here was talented and apparently congenial society, and certainly the house was one of the most delightful in London. It was, however, an error of Meredith's to describe the place as Sir Thomas More's house : this had stood further west on the site of what is now Beaufort Street, Chelsea. And Mr Edmund Gosse, in his *Life of A. C. Swinburne*, was also incorrect in stating that part of the house had been occupied by Queen Katherine Parr. No. 16 Cheyne Walk was built in 1717, as recorded in the Survey of Chelsea issued by the London County Council, and its design and architectural features are in conformation with the building style of that date. It was erected upon part of the " Great Garden " of the Manor House, which house in earlier days had covered the ground east of Winchester House up to what is now No. 18 Cheyne Walk—two doors from Rossetti's house. In his time the garden was much larger than it is now. It reached back to Oakley Crescent, and extended east to Manor Street. Meredith, in after years, used to say that so hilarious were the

[1] Rossetti's wife, Elizabeth Eleanor Siddal, died from the effects of laudanum in February, 1862, and the poet-painter was overwhelmed with grief. Mr Edmund Gosse, in his *Life of A. C. Swinburne*, relates: "Swinburne is said to have been present when Rossetti thrust the sole manuscript of his poems into his wife's coffin, and it was to his marvellous memory that Morris, Meredith, and Burne-Jones principally trusted for the reconstruction of those lost lyrics."[2]

post-prandial meetings of Rossetti's guests in the garden that Mrs Carlyle had to send round to beg them to make less noise, as Carlyle was disturbed at his lucubrations. In such case the garden festivities at No. 16 must have been very obstreperous, as No. 5 Cheyne Row was some considerable distance away, with Oakley Street intervening.

The name "Queen's House" arose from three erroneous traditions which associated the house with Queen Katherine Parr, Queen Catherine of Braganza, and Queen Elizabeth, who had a mulberry-tree in the garden dedicated to her name. "Queen's House," without a distinguishing Christian name, avoids invidiousness and no doubt placates the three royal shades : but the place needs no adventitious associations with virtuous queens to render it deeply interesting. It suffices that it is a perfect example of an early eighteenth-century house, and that here the Rossettis, Meredith, and Swinburne lived together in a quaint attempt at joint housekeeping and domestic intimacy which made no provision for the eccentricities of genius and the clash of highly strung nervous temperaments. And even in those days, fifty-five years antecedent to "war work," servant difficulties were not unknown, for we find Dante Rossetti (the managing director of the quartette of two widowers and two bachelors) writing in January, 1863 : "I have been a martyr to unsatisfactory servants here, and have been asking all my friends if they know any desirable ones. Our household consists of four men, two of whom only, myself and Mr Swinburne, are at all constant inmates." The younger brother, W. M. Rossetti, has given some interesting details of the household and of the not altogether sympathetic atmosphere which soon settled over it :

"For the Cheyne Walk house . . . Rossetti was to be the tenant, paying a rent (assuredly a very moderate one) of £100 a year, besides—if I remember right—a premium of £225 upon entry. As his sub-tenants for defined portions of the building there were to be three persons—Mr Swinburne, George Meredith, and myself. Of course, each of us three was to pay something to Dante ; though the latter did not wish me, and in fact did not allow me, to continue any such payment after affairs had got into their regular course. We were all to dine together, if

THE BACK AND GARDEN OF 16, CHEYNE WALK, CHELSEA,
AS IN D. G. ROSSETTI'S TIME
From a contemporary photograph in the possession of Mr. Reginald Blunt

present together in the house. Mr Swinburne was generally present, Mr Meredith much less constantly. I came on three fixed days of the week, but not on any others unless some particular occasion arose. Swinburne, and I think Meredith, had their respective sitting-rooms in which they received their personal visitors.[1] I had, and required, a bedroom only.

" Dante Rossetti was by this time familiar with Mr Meredith, whom he had seen increasingly for some three years past, and whose talents and work he seriously, though not uncritically, admired. . . . Mr Meredith and Rossetti entertained a solid mutual regard, and got on together amicably, yet without that thorough cordiality of give-and-take which oils the hinges of daily intercourse. It would have been difficult for two men of the literary order of mind to be more decisively unlike. The reader of their works—not to speak of the students of Rossetti's paintings—will not fail to perceive this. Rossetti was not at all a mere recluse, incapable of taking very good care of himself in the current transactions of life ; he had, on the contrary, a large share of shrewdness and of business aptitude, and a quick

---

[1] Meredith's sitting-room was that to the right of the entrance hall. It is panelled, like the rest of the house, and contains a remarkable ornamented mantelpiece put in by D. G. Rossetti. This room was used also as the common dining-room. The corresponding room to the left of the hall was assigned to Swinburne as his study. Rossetti's studio was the fine room at the back, and his bedroom was over it, opening on to a balcony. The long drawing-room on the first floor in front was not often used ; the bedroom over it was Swinburne's presumably, and Meredith's an adjoining smaller room on this top floor with a fine view of the river and the charm of sunrise.

There have been other notable occupants of 16 Cheyne Walk. Sir Hall Caine lived here, in 1881-1882, with Rossetti during the last year of the painter's life, and he fully describes the house and garden in his *Recollections of D. G. Rossetti* and *My Story*. The Rev. H. R. Haweis and Jacques Blumenthal, the composer, were subsequent tenants, and the house is now (1918) occupied by Sir William Pickford, Lord Justice, Court of Appeal.

It is also of interest to remember that this is the house Thackeray is said to have had in mind in his description of the residence of Isabel Lady Castlewood in *Henry Esmond* : " They rowed up at length to the pretty village of Chelsey, where the nobility have many handsome country houses ; and so came to my Lady Viscountess's house, a cheerful new house in the row facing the river, with a handsome garden behind it, and a pleasant look-out both towards Surrey and Kensington."[1]

eye for ' the main chance ' in all contingencies where he chose
to exercise it.   He understood character, and (though often too
indulgent to its shadier side) he knew how to deal with it, and
had indeed rather a marked distaste for that inexpert class of
persons who waver on the edge of life without ever throwing
themselves boldly into it, and gripping at the facts.   But Mr
Meredith was incomparably more a man of the world and man
of society, scrutinising all sorts of things, and using them as his
material in the commerce of life and in the field of intellect.
Even in the matter of household routine, he found that Rossetti's
arrangements, though ample for comfort of a more or less off-
hand kind, were not conformable to his standard.   Thus it
pretty soon became apparent that Mr Meredith's sub-tenancy
was not likely to stand much wear and tear, or to outlast the
temporary convenience which had prompted it.   I could not
now define precisely how long it continued—perhaps up to the
earlier days of 1864.[1]   It then ceased, without, I think, any
disposition on either side that it should be renewed.   Friendly
intercourse between the two men continued for some years, and
gradually wore out without any cause or feeling of dissension."

One is constrained to admit the accuracy of the above
diagnosis of the characteristics of this curious Chelsea
" bachelor " coterie.   Meredith was the first to realise the impossibility of its continuance, and he was the first to go.   Many
absurd stories have arisen since to account for his departure,
whereas mental irritability and the heat of what the young
lady in one of Sir Arthur Pinero's plays termed " the Artistic
Temperature " are all-sufficient reasons for the break-up of the
Cheyne Walk arrangement.   The most popular of these
apocryphal legends attributes Meredith's flight to disgust at
the habits of Rossetti, more particularly at his late breakfast,
when the painter was alleged to have " devoured like an ogre
five poached eggs that had slowly bled to death on five slabs of
bacon." [2]   Probably this story had its origin in a humorous

[1] Mr W. M. Rossetti has since informed me : " My brother, Dante
Gabriel Rossetti, with his three sub-tenants, entered on the tenancy of
16 Cheyne Walk in October, 1862.   Meredith was there at times up to
some such date as April, 1863."
[2] Sir Hall Caine relates that Rossetti had " an enormous breakfast of
six eggs or half-a-dozen kidneys."

remark of Meredith's, which he never contemplated being re-corded in the formality of print, and certainly he, as a panegyrist of good feeding, would scarcely be expected to take exception to the National Breakfast in substantial ration. Therefore, when this legend was repeated again he felt constrained to indite an explanation and protest, which appeared in *The National Review*, 1909, signed " George Meredith," in these words :

" Gossip is hard to deal with. Some years back a little book on Chelsea came to me wherein I saw it stated that I had left Rossetti's house because of the appearance of ham and eggs on his breakfast plate : ' it was too much for me.' The publica-tion was obscure, the instance given absurd, and I let it pass, as I do usually with newspaper tattle. These reviewers do not reflect on their chance of wounding. What I must have said to some friend was that Rossetti's habits were ruinous to his health, and I mentioned the plate of thick ham and fried eggs, taken at once on the descent from his bedroom. I ventured to speak to him of the walk of at least a mile before this trying meal. But he disliked physical exercise, and he was wilful, though he could join in a laugh at his ways. The main point is that he came down with a head full of his work, and, not to be disturbed during the day, he chose a dish that would sustain him through it. The system could not continue for long, of which I had the sorrowful prognostic. Devotion to his work in contempt of our nature killed him. On no other subject have I spoken of this dear fellow but with the affection I felt—some-times playfully with regard to his peculiar habits, I daresay ; never in the gossip's manner." [1]

What Meredith actually said—or wrote—is preserved in an unpublished letter to Hardman of October, 1868 :

[1] Another legend of Meredith's departure from Cheyne Walk traces it to his pride being hurt by the attempt of his friends there to relieve his pedal necessities arising from lack of pecuniary means. Mr Ford Madox Hueffer, in his *Ancient Lights*, states : " According to Madox Brown, the end came one day when the benevolent poets substituted for the cracked boots which he put outside his door to be cleaned a new pair of exactly the same size and make. He put on the boots, went out, and, having forwarded a cheque for the quarter's rent, never returned." Madox Brown must have been mistaken. Meredith was making quite a good income at this date, 1863. He received £200 a year from *The*

" Poor Dante Rossetti seems to be losing his eyesight, owing entirely to bad habits—a matter I foretold long ago : Eleven A.M. plates of small-shop ham, thick cut, grisly with brine : four smashed eggs on it : work till dusk : dead tired on sofa till 10 P.M. Then to Evans' to dine off raw meat and stout. So on for years. Can Nature endure these things ? The poor fellow never sleeps at night. His nervous system is knocked to pieces. It's melancholy."

It must regretfully be concluded that there was not much affinity between Rossetti and Meredith. Sir Hall Caine, who knew so much of Rossetti in his last days, tells me that the painter said very little about Meredith either in conversation or correspondence, adding : " I am afraid we must reconcile ourselves to the conclusion that there was very little real sympathy between them, although they bore an outer respect and admiration for each other."

Friction there evidently was at 16 Cheyne Walk, and Mr Edmund Gosse, in his *Life of A. C. Swinburne*, suggests that it was incompatibility between the poet and Meredith which caused the first rift in the lute of harmony at Chelsea., He says : " Meredith was not so much delighted with Swinburne as the poet was with him : Why should it be concealed that the two men ultimately got upon the nerves of each other ? " And again : " The Pre-Raphaelites had not been well advised in sharing their domestic bliss : there were too many plums in their pudding. Swinburne and George Meredith developed, in particular, a remarkable incompatibility of temper. They parted, rarely to meet again until 1898," when, on the occasion of Meredith's seventieth birthday, Swinburne was persuaded by Mr Gosse to sign the Address of Congratulation presented to the novelist. Meredith was much touched by this, and a short time afterwards he asked Watts-Dunton to bring Swinburne over to lunch at Box Hill. After that, presumably final, meeting, friendly messages often passed between them. I may

Ipswich Journal, and no doubt quite another £200 as Reader to Chapman and Hall, to say nothing of what he received from his novels and poems. He was also contributing to *The Morning Post* and other papers. Meredith was always scrupulously well dressed when in London at this period, as will be seen later.

add that Watts-Dunton told me that the real cause of the cool-
ness existing between the two former friends up till the reconciliation of 1898 was caused by Swinburne's lack of appreciation
of Meredith's later novels. Not receiving any congratulations
on the publication of *One of our Conquerors* and *Lord Ormont
and his Aminta* and *The Amazing Marriage* from Swinburne,
the author inquired the reason why, and the poet frankly replied
that he could not read them, could not get through them.
This, from such an omnivorous novel reader as Swinburne, was
stinging comment on the torpitude he found in these last novels,
and Meredith deeply resented it.

With regard to the earlier incompatibility that affected
Meredith's relations with Swinburne, it must in fairness be
stated that there was no actual quarrel when the former left
Cheyne Walk. They exchanged friendly letters in 1867-1868;
Swinburne paid a visit to Meredith, at Kingston, in 1867; and
Meredith stood by Swinburne when the storm aroused by *Poems
and Ballads* burst upon the poet in 1866. Just before that
volume was published Meredith wrote sagely to the young
author :

" I am very eager for the poems. The promise of the essay
on Byron makes me extremely curious, for though I don't
mistrust your estimation of the manliness of his verse, he is the
last man of whom I would venture to foretell your opinion.
As to the Poems—if they are not yet in the press, do be careful
of getting your reputation firmly grounded : for I have heard
' low mutterings ' already from the Lion of British Prudery ;
and I, who love your verse, would play savagely with a knife
among the proofs for the sake of your fame ; and because I
want to see you take the first place as you may if you will."

And on 2nd March, 1867, he continued :

" I have waited to read the Ode [1]—the most nobly sustained
lyric in our language, worthy of its theme. Broader, fuller
verse I do not know. I had a glance at the proofs, and my chief
sentiment was envy. Now I can read without that affliction.
For me there will never be time given even to try the rising to
such a song. I am passionately anxious to see the *Italy* [2] and

---

[1] *Ode on Insurrection in Candia.*　　　　[2] *A Song of Italy,* 1867.

have a thousand spirits of fancy about it. . . . I was in Austria when the heat of the storm was raging.[1]   I returned from Italy in the winter after all was over.   It would not have been my advice to you to notice the reviewers ; but it's certainly better never to keep red-hot shot in store, and perhaps one broadside in reply does no harm.   I wish rather that it had been done in verse.   As for the hubbub, it will do you no harm, and you have partly deserved it ; and it has done the critical world good by making men look boldly at the restrictions imposed upon art by our dominating damnable bourgeoisie."

As early as 1861 Meredith had perceived the powers and limitations of Swinburne when he wrote : "He is not subtle ; and I don't see any internal centre from which springs anything that he does.   He will make a great name, but whether he is to distinguish himself solidly as an artist, I would not willingly prognosticate."   And in 1873 he said of Swinburne : "Take him at his best he is by far the best—finest poet ; truest artist —of the young lot—when he refrains from pointing a hand at the Genitals."   As the years passed, his admiration for the poet's work increased yet more, and it is notable that the two last letters written by Meredith, but a month before his own death, were both in tribute to Swinburne.   To Watts-Dunton he wrote : "The blow was heavy on me.   I had such confidence in his powers of recovery.   The end has come !   That brain of the vivid illumination is extinct.   I can hardly realise it when I revolve the many times when at the starting of an idea the whole town was instantly ablaze with electric light.   Song was his natural voice.   He was the greatest of our lyrical poets —of the world, I could say, considering what a language he had to wield."   And to the editor of *The Times* his tribute ended with these words : "The name of Swinburne is one to shine starlike in English literature—a peer among our noblest."

That is a fine epitaph upon the singer of the silvern voice, and it cancels the petty misunderstandings which arose from the too close contact of two highly strung temperaments during a brief period of swiftly passing mortal life.   Truly *ars longa, vita brevis.*

[1] Over Swinburne's *Poems and Ballads,* 1866.

CHAPTER VII

ARTHUR MEREDITH AND HIS FATHER. MEREDITH'S SECOND
MARRIAGE

IN the summer of 1862 Meredith made several pleasant excursions. In August he accompanied the Cotter Morisons on their yacht, the *Irene*, for a run from the Isle of Wight, touching at Weymouth and Torquay, to the Channel Islands. Writing in high spirits, on the 16th, from Ryde Pier Hotel to William Hardman, he said:

" Free Lover Tuck! To-morrow we shall sail! We are off to the West, Love!

> " And now for a Toast!
> (To Tuck the Toast shall be)
> I am off along the Coast,
> And would he were with me.

Here's Morison drunk with salt water, Mrs M. ditto, G. M. ditto ditto. We swear we'll live in it till we come home pickled. I have got a Pea-jacket and such a nautical hat, and such a roll of the legs already. . . . I am moodily leaning over the bin (2 n's, I think) -acle, thinking of Tuck! "

By 7th September he was staying with his friend, Johnson, a bullion broker, at the George Inn, Marlow, and later at Hoddesdon, whence he visited Hatfield and Panshanger. He was compelled to extend his absence from Copsham Cottage for several weeks longer, owing to his housekeeper's niece developing smallpox there. For the same reason he decided to send his son Arthur, now nine years old, to boarding-school. He came to this decision, to part with the only person he loved, very reluctantly. His choice of a school naturally fell upon that of his friend, Augustus Jessopp, to whom he wrote: " I would trust him, who is my only blessing on earth, to you with full confidence."

Accordingly, after spending a few days with Edward Chapman, at Hollyshaw, Camden Park, Tunbridge Wells, at the end of September, Meredith " pronounced the dread word," and he and Arthur, " already breeched for school," set out for Norfolk, where the boy became a pupil at King Edward the VI.'s School, just inside the Erpingham Gate of the Cathedral Close of Norwich. In the schoolroom, formerly the chapel of St John, with its fine fifteenth-century archway and stone staircase, Nelson had been a pupil just a hundred years before.

Meredith stayed a little while with the Jessopps to see his son settled at school, and accompanied the headmaster on a brief visit to St John's College, Cambridge, whence he wrote to William Hardman :

" Yes, I am here. Meeting of British Ass.—So, why not ? And I've wandered up and down Trinity thinking of Tuck, the radiant, and of others mooning by the Cam, into which classic flood dropped numerous dead leaves. I have dined with Fellows and am to dine with them again : have been cordially received, and inhabit chambers of an absent graduate, whose slave is my slave. Jessopp brought me. We return to Norwich to-night. What a good fellow he is ! His wife takes high rank in Demitroïa's Corps. She is quite charming. She unites worth and sweetness of nature and capacity. They have the same face for the school that they show to the world. I never conceived a place better managed. Jessopp has 25 boys in his house. They have studies where 2 study together and are never intruded upon. He breakfasts and dines with them. We have a good deal of Prayer. Oh, Tuck, have we not led thoughtless lives and snuffed our own conceit ! Tuck !

" In the evening, Jessopp, his wife, a pretty niece, and myself do music, read Molière, and are really happy. I feel so much that I would gladly live near them if it were possible. I particularly wish you to know them. Tuck ! It would do thee good, for an I be not deceived, thou art but a lost sheep and one of the ungodly. . . .

" Well, Sons are wonderfully buoyant in a jiffy. Mrs Jessopp writes to say that she took the boys to Lowestoft yesterday. Sons were so independent that they assured her they were exactly like the other boys and didn't want looking after. This is a fair prospect for my dear man. Jessopp won't let me depart till Monday week. I am very comfortable, so why not ? Then I go to Sussex ; then to Richmond, then to Morison, then to Oxford. . . . After that, Bedlam, I suppose, for I don't know of any other place for which I shall have been such an accomplished graduate."

On returning to Norwich much paternal heart-beating was caused by an accident which befell Arthur Meredith in the school gymnasium, and his agitated parent thus relates the incident to Hardman :

> " *Oct.* 11*th,* 1862.

" Embrace me once more, oh, Tuck ! Thou liv'st ! This is to chronicle the sudden and unexpected descent of the small man from a height of 17 feet to the ground. Poor Sons little intended the feat and therefore performed it satisfactorily. In the Crypt here, there is a Gymnasium, fitted up under a regular professor, who is fifth master. One Reimicke. He did this and that, he went in and out of this and the other, and his pupils did the like. Apparently Sons had their emulation violently excited, for whilst we were all engaged with other wonders, Sons must mount a ladder by himself, and from the top of it make a catch at a pole from whence to slip down naturally, instead of which he came plump on to the floor. I felt him tugging gently at my hand, and could not make out what was the matter with him. He had come to tell me that he felt queer, and what he had ' gone and done.' I took him up and his nerves gave way just a moment (not noisily). Then we rubbed him a bit and discovered him to be sound. He was jolly and ready for fresh adventures in $\frac{1}{4}$ of an hour ; wiser Sons as we trust. My parental heart beat fast under its mask. Jessopp and his wife (who is one of the wives of the generation) do all that is possible to make me happy in my own way. They do not want me to go. They do not poetise me but honour me by treating me as simple flesh, so that one does not feel mounted on a pole and ultimately destined to come down as Sons did."

It is pleasant to picture Meredith entering so simply into the life of the school at Norwich in these few days of recreation snatched from his journalistic and " reader " work and the rather laborious toil which attended the evolution of *Sandra Belloni*, which he was now writing.

He was back at Copsham Cottage by 4th November, when he penned this amusing letter in rhyme to Mrs Jessopp concerning some deficiencies in Arthur Meredith's school outfit :

Dear my friend and honour'd Madam ! of hard facts I'm not a hoarder,
And that you will quite forgive me my forgetfulness I beg !
It had pass'd me what was requisite to stock the little boarder,
But dream we of its feathers when the chick has burst the egg ?

Oh ! the happy Close of Norwich with its towering Cathedral !
Its boys that shout at Prisoner's Base, the envy of a man !
Oh ! the happy " harping " hours when of Confederate and Federal
We talked, what time of Partridge fall, and eke of Parmesan !

Methinks to let the days slip by, it was not noble, Madam,
While my infant was deficient in such necessary things ;
Compell'd to rest on Charity, or else to sleep like Adam,
Without a towel to wipe his face, a spoon to oil his springs.

Ha ! you scorn us ? is it not so ? I am led to think it, certes ;
But so terrible a poet's wrath, I pardon ere I blame.
I see the little fellow who so lovely in his shirt is,
And I swear an oath that this day week the sheets shall own his name.

The pillowcases, likewise towels six, and silver fourchette ;
The tea-spoon—dessert spoon (for I have it all by rote) :
I will send them in a jiffy, but pray tell me (with the door shut)
Do you find him such a darling 'tis no wonder that I dote ?

Oh ! had I but a passion now, to tear it all to tatters,
And storm as doth the limp young man who frightened Geraldine !
I have chattered as that weedy woman's tender ruffian chatters,[1]
May it give you satisfaction ! which remaineth to be seen.

Oh ! Lady of The Three Black Cats ! farewell, and let me hope a
Meeting we may compass, ere in effigy you stand,
In Norwich's Cathedral, our illustrious St Jessopa,
A scroll to tell a Boarder's needs in Heaven, in your hands.

Meredith hoped to get down to Norwich again at the end of the term, for as he told Mrs Jessopp : " I should have liked so much to see the boys and my boy among them. He has grown

---

[1] An allusion to kitchen courtship in Jessopp's household.

AUGUSTUS JESSOPP AND HIS WIFE
From a photograph about 1860

strange to me in the long absence. . . . You know I shall be
happy under the roof that holds my dearest ; and more, among
my dearest friends." But apparently he was prevented, and
great preparations were made at home for the return of the
son and heir together with seasonable Christmas festivities. Of
course Meredith's arrangements with other friends had to be
cancelled if they did not coincide with the wishes of his boy.
Thus Hardman was notified :

"*Dec.* 13*th*, 1862.

"DEAR TUCK,—In reply to your Mandate this day received :
Sons come up on Wednesday and sleep in town that night :
but how can I possibly keep him from Copsham on Thursday ?
I fear me I must take him down. It was his special request
six weeks ago.

> " And tho' my Friar's Mandate is severe,
> The wishes of the Sons of Sons are dear.
>   I really fear
> I must bring my little man home on Thursday :
> (As you would rhyme) that he may in the furze play.

"Acknowledge that a Friar cannot always be obliged. . . .
"Thine, ROB."

And on 23rd December :

"MY CHRISTMAS TUCK !—I am preparing for the pudding
with tremendous exercise. I had made up my mind to go with
you to Boxing Night festivity, with Sons likewise. But he will
not like the Strand. He is ardent for a jolly Clown, a Pantaloon of the most aged, the most hopeless, a twirling Columbine,
a Harlequin with a wand on everybody's bottom. This does
the small man seriously incline to. Can I say Nay ? And he
finds he detests Plays and Burlesques. I remember his last
visit to the Strand. He is too young for puns, so, if you have
taken tickets, sad shall I be : but I am for Drury Lane or
Covent Garden : for uproar ; a pit reeking with oranges ;
gods that flourish pewter-pots and tricks that stick and show
their mortality at starting. Would, would, would that Tuck
were then at my side ! I declare that I have swung my

M

beetle[1] and roared at anticipated headlong fun with Tuck. I would go to both ; but, you see, I have again promised the Son. I must go the following night, and there is the following loss of time, if I disappoint him. I understood you distinctly a Pantomime, bully Tuck ! Do we quarrel ? If so, I send Love to Somebody and snap my fingers at you. If not, my regards of the warmest to both.

" Your affectionate,

" GEORGE MEREDITH."

To Arthur Meredith himself the father wrote, in anticipation of his return :

" MY DARLING LITTLE MAN,—I shall be at Shoreditch Station on Wednesday, to meet the train at 6.30. But you must not be disappointed if I tell you that it will be too late for you to go on to Esher that night ; and you will sleep at Mrs Morison's in Porchester Square. Mr Hardman wants me to dine with him on Thursday, but I have told him I am afraid you won't let me. Copsham will be delighted to see you. All the dear old woods are in their best winter dress. Mossy Gordon has come from Eton.[2] Janet leaves England next week ; but hopes to see her dear boy before she goes. Be careful not to have any larks in the train. Only fools do that. As much fun as you like, but no folly. Look out for Ely Cathedral just before you get to Ely Station. At Cambridge you will see the four towers of King's Chapel, built by Cardinal Wolsey. Tell Angrove[3] that I will get a bed for him if he wishes to sleep in Town on Wednesday night. And give Angrove your address, written down ; that he may let me know when he will come to London from Cornwall, and we will go to the theatre together, and then he will take you to school again.

" Your loving Papa,

" GEORGE MEREDITH."

[1] This was an implement used in violent exercise—a heavy iron weight at the end of a wooden shaft. It was thrown into the air and caught, and the strain it involved is believed to have caused, to a great extent, the weakness of the spine from which Meredith suffered in after years. His " beetle " weighed about nineteen pounds.

[2] Maurice Duff Gordon, then a boy of thirteen, succeeded as 4th Baronet, 1872. Died 1896.

[3] A pupil at the Norwich School.

Meredith had no fault to find with the condition of his recovered treasure, and wrote to Jessopp, on 23rd December :

" I found my little man looking marvellously brisk and clear of eye. All his friends exclaim that his school agrees with him. I am altogether pleased and satisfied, and (quoique pauvre diable, comme vous savez) should ungrudgingly pay double the annual sum to have him with you and your wife, which I consider a privilege not to be measured by money. . . . I am amused from morning to night by Arthur's account of the ' boys.' It is as I suspected : he knows their characters consummately. I had the same faculty when I was young. But whether he gets it from deduction, or nervous feelers, or the conjunction of both, I can't guess. He hopes to get a prize next year : speaks of his success in ' dictation ' ; not boastingly ; but to assure him whom he suspects to be a sceptical Papa, that he is not lazy and not stupid. He is not, absolutely, either of the two. He is pre-eminently a growing boy, and has some characteristics to outgrow. He will never, I fancy, do credit to you by any display of acquired knowledge ; but, after a period, I think you will find that his understanding is as sound as that of any fellow you have had to do with. The one point he evidently a little chafes at (though not complainingly, and with submission, poor martyr !) is the Sunday religious exercise, which you have dared to temper for the poor lambs, and which they must still think severe. . . . Your evening service is a noble relief, your evening discourse most sensible, healthy, and calculated to catch the wandering youthful mind. But, it is the third dose of the day. Is it, therefore, appreciated ? . . . I think the drill an admirable idea for an assemblage of anchorites. The future monk will be most grateful for it. I fear the future man will revenge himself.[1] . . . The best thing

---

[1] Meredith wrote more on this subject, some months later, to Mrs Jessopp : " With regard to the Sunday arrangements at the School. Now, let me assure you, O fair advocate, that I think you make wonderful improvements on a state of things rather hurtful to Nature in her untamed years. Hurtful to her, and therefore she has her revenge : a not unholy thing when we see it to be simply the action of violated laws. Young blood will not sit so frequently and so long, on the seventh day, without a desire to stir, which becomes in the brain a remonstrance. . . . The truth is, that our Puritanism is beginning to weary even the

I can wish you at this season is, Strength to conquer the Christmas pudding ! I would that I dined at home ! I would eat by the dictates of common sense and a discreet appetite. As it is, I plunge with knowledge aforethought into a week's dyspepsia. I shall be ridden all night by a plum-pudding-headed hag : shall taste the horrors without the vacuity of death ! "

Meredith and his son spent Christmas Day at 27 Gordon Street, with the Hardmans, and on Boxing Day Arthur's wishes were duly carried out by a visit to the pantomime at Drury Lane. Edmund Falconer commenced his management of the theatre that night, and is reported to have spent £10,000 on the venture. The opening night was very rowdy, and Hardman relates of this outing with the Merediths :

" We went to Drury Lane on Boxing Night, and such a pandemonium I have rarely witnessed. The first piece was acted in dumb show, not a word could we hear. The fights in pit and gallery were frequent. The shower of orange peel from the gods into the pit was quite astounding. The occupants of the latter place made feeble efforts to throw it back again, but, of course, never got it any further than the first tier of boxes. I was glad to see the thing once, but you won't catch me there again."

On 7th January, 1863, Meredith wrote to Wyse :

" Brief are the oracles ! The Talismanic phrase of Eastern fable is of one syllable. In answer to your stentorian summons, I reply, ' I have been busy.' How small it looks ! And yet, O parturient mountain ! Mr Ridiculus Mus is eloquent enough if you will look into him. Busy, my good sir, so as to drive the pen as fast as Stonewall Jackson is driving the Federals : busy to get money for voracious creditors : battling in the hot whirlwind, with scarce a thought of your golden sward, where you

English world, and much as you are disposed to lighten the claims of worship to poor little fellows, you being in East Anglia must of a necessity keep you behind us. Do forgive me for this ! I feel already that the wind is East on me ! . . . May I beg you to give my little man, on my behalf, five shillings ? He writes for half-a-crown, but we double it."

recline, watching an ever sinking sun across a quivering sea,
with fair eyes over you !

" I hope to finish this dreadful work [1] in six weeks. Then
I shall be free to disport. Why won't you write to me, I may
ask ? My darling boy is home, much improved, likes school,
thanks you for your inquiries after him ; is flourishing, I thank
the Disposer of things ! or the stamped fact !

" The day I had your letter I passed through Coram,[2] with
melancholy. Thence home and to your well-known handwrit-
ing. Coram had whispered as much. Maurice FitzG. was here
the other day. Goes to Ireland this month. I go to try a
friend's yacht next week from Portsmouth to we know not
where.[3] He starts from the Mediterranean in February. I
have promised to be due to him at Nice, or Genoa, or Naples, in
March. But I know not ! "

Despite his work, January was devoted by Meredith to
giving his boy a good time. But the last day of the holidays
inevitably came, when " I saw my little man off on Monday,
after expedition over Bank and Tower. Thence to Pym's,
Poultry : oysters consumed by dozings. Thence to Purcell's :
great devastation of pastry. Thence to Shoreditch, where
Sons calmly said : ' Never mind, Papa ; it is no use minding
it. I shall soon be back to you,' and so administered comfort
to his forlorn Dad "—certainly a reversing of the usual pro-
cedure between parent and child at holiday terminations.

When the philosophic youth came back to Copsham Cottage
in April, 1863, for the next holidays, he developed measles,
whereof his father relates : " Sons are as a mulberry in the
shade, they are spotted like a Pard, they are hot as boiled cod
in a napkin ; they care for nothing but barley water, which I
find myself administering at all hours of the night, and think it
tolerable bliss, and just worth living for, to suck an orange.
I am sorry to say they have a rather troublesome cough,
otherwise all goes well."

This illness served as a pretext for keeping Arthur at home

[1] *Emilia.*

[2] Great Coram Street, where Wyse had rooms.

[3] Meredith, Hardman, and James Virtue were guests of the Cotter
Morisons on board the *Irene* for a trip to Cherbourg and the Channel
Islands. The weather was very rough, and most of the party were ill.

for four months ; not until August was Jessopp informed :
" There is a 10.57 train from London to your City—which
snatches small boys from the hearts of their parents. On
Tuesday next, my little recovered rosy man will journey down,
alone, by that train, chewing the cud of anticipating fancy (I
hope). The Guard will be bribed to keep an eye on him. Will
you send some person to meet him ? He will be somewhat at
sea, with his swollen bag, in the press of an arrival. . . . And
indeed my heart is heavy at parting. I let him go from me now
under a high sense of duty. What strange dispensation is it
which gives you my boy for the best portion of his young years.
I am in alarm about his boating on your river before he can swim.
Is there always some responsible, careful fellow in the boats
with the youngsters ? Pray tell me."

Every allusion to Arthur at this period voices pathetically
Meredith's love and solicitude for his son. During these long
summer holidays of 1863 the boy had an alarming accident,
which greatly agitated Meredith, who thus described the affair
to the Hardmans :

" Yesterday, Wyndowe found Arthur out alone, put him on his
horse, after shortening the stirrups, and suddenly let go the reins,
for some purpose unknown ; my little darling was carried off,
fell, dangled to the stirrup, and was dragged headlong over the
furze. Not killed ! Mercifully spared and no bones broken :
but the shaking has been tremendous. He lies upstairs, and
was miserable till this morning. Had he been kicked or dragged
on a road I should have had a shattered heap of all I loved given
to my arms. He was saved by a short length, and by his boot
being pulled off. (He had elastic sides to them.) Izod [1] says
he is doing well. He can't keep anything on his stomach, and
complains of his head : but he sleeps soundly and calmly :
breathes peacefully. My poor lamb ! ' Oh ! is it a dream ? '
he said, as I undressed him after the accident. He can now
recount all that happened till he was dragged. I think I may
hope that he will recover, and be as sound as he was. Of poor
Wyndowe it is useless to speak. He is sorry of course. Don't be
distressed, for you know I should not be quiet at heart if all
did not look very hopeful. I have had a rude blow. . . ."

[1] The local doctor.

GEORGE MEREDITH AND HIS SON ARTHUR
From a photograph about 1862

Four days later, on 5th August, he was able to convey good news from Copsham :

" Sons are on their legs again ! The poor little fellow is very weak and somewhat shaky ; covered with bruises : but vitally sound, bones all right. Head uninjured, as far as human eye can reckon. This day he was allowed to get up. Yesterday he swallowed food without immediately rejecting it. He is not much the worse for his terrible mishap ; quite cheerfully he slightly damns himself for mounting such a big horse, but excuses Wyndowe. Poor Wyndowe has been in a great way. It is no comfort to me to make another miserable, when I am struck ; and it is of no use to examine a catastrophe which I am sure he will not repeat.

" Well, Tuck, my darling is returned to me out of the jaws of death. Wyndowe says he is thankful I was spared the sight which will haunt him till he dies. He feared to look at Arthur, making sure that he was killed. . . . The distance Arthur was dragged was about 50 yards, as far as I can make out. There, Tuck ! we have put up our Thank-song to the Supreme."

After the boy's return to school, Meredith was acutely anxious about him, as the following letter shows :—

" My dear Jessopp,—You say that you are anxious about my little man. You take the wind out of all my sails. Pardon me, but I shall have no peace till I hear whether I have dwelt on the word too strongly. If you are only anxious as to his mental briskness I am not alarmed ; and I know also that he ' potters ' and plays after his own fashion and is not a boisterous fellow. But I am always open to fear for his physical health. His circulation is not rapid, his stomach is weak. He requires to be watched. . . . I don't want to give trouble, but my heart broods over him, and I am unmanned at a breath of doubt concerning him. I told you that his powers of acquisition would not be marked. But you will find by and by that he has sucked in much and made use of it in his own way. He will never be a gladiator : but he may be a thinker : I expect him to be a man of sense. If only—and here my sails flap the mast miserably. I would come down at once but my fresh work detains me. I have my hands full. . . . I had much to discourse on to you. This, doubtless very silly, perturbation of the parental mind chases the gabble from my tongue. God bless you. I have perhaps scarcely recovered from the shock of the accident during Arthur's holidays. The tone of a word relating to him makes me melancholy. For myself, it takes much to make me hang out that yellow flag for an hour even.

" Your loving

" George Meredith."

To retrace in date a little, it was in July, 1863, that Meredith (and Arthur) again visited Seaford, despite the painful memories of his first wife that place must have conjured up. Once more he was with the modern Amphitryon, Maurice FitzGerald, and enjoying the gastronomy of yore in Marine Terrace. He wrote to Hardman from Seaford—" Hades " as he called it : " Here am I—as an animal. Our life is monstrous. My breakfast would supply a Workhouse : my luncheons are equal to the refections of four fat Friars : my dinner would satiate the soul of a ticket-of-leave man. I go to bed when Apollo lays his red nose over the Eastern hill. . . . Here is Frank Burnand that reeks puns from every pore : Maurice and Gerald FitzGerald, Signor Vignati, Hyndman (Cambridge), Laurence, painter, and others coming. I suppose I shall stop through next week."

Henry Mayers Hyndman, the future leader of Socialism, was at this date a young man of twenty-one, an undergraduate of Trinity College, and a member of the Sussex County Eleven. He had joined the party at Seaford as a friend of Maurice Fitz-Gerald, and in his *Record of an Adventurous Life* he gives some interesting impressions of this sojourn in " a sort of village of the dead " :

" The villagers around us knew nothing and cared less about the laughing, chaffing crew who, with the sons of the chief local landowners, were making merry in one of the few decent houses on the front, or at the New Inn, already some centuries old.

" Though Seaford was the spot at which Meredith's first wife had carried on the intrigue with Wallis, the painter, which led to their separation, Meredith shook off the trouble this had occasioned him and was almost as jolly as Burnand. . . . But Meredith in particular was at his best in those days, and being quite at home with the men around him, and with no audience

he felt it incumbent upon him to dazzle, and waiting to appreciate his good things, he delivered himself without effort or artifice
of all the really profound and poetic and humorous thoughts on
men and things that welled continually within him in a manner
that I recall with delight these long years afterwards. It was
on one of these occasions, when we were all sitting together on
the beach, tossing stones lightly into the sea, and Meredith was
discoursing with even more than ordinary vivacity and charm,
that Burnand suddenly came out with, ' Damn you, George;
why won't you write as you talk ? ' Why Meredith, with such
a wonderful gift of clear, forcible language as he possessed and
was master of, should have deliberately cultivated artificiality
I never have been able to comprehend. He had a perfectly
marvellous flow of what I may call literary high spirits throughout his life, and his unaffected, natural talk, such as this at
Seaford, was altogether delightful. But his writings showed
even then to my eye, young and inexperienced as I was, little
trace of this unforced outpouring of wisdom and wit ; while
Meredith's conversation was almost equally artificial, not to say
stilted, except with men and women he had known well for years.
. . . This show talk and show writing of Meredith was quite as
brilliant as the unconsidered outpourings of the natural man, and
he said perhaps even cleverer things ; but his wit was much
more sardonic, and somehow you could hear the clank of the
machinery all the time."

When Meredith went to stay with him at Cambridge during
May Newmarket week of 1864 (" The Cook of Trinity distinguished himself nightly "), Hyndman states that Meredith
met various undergraduates in his rooms in Rose Street. He
talked volubly to them in an artificial, showy way, entering into
discussion about their pursuits and sports of all kinds without
knowing much about these recreations. At the same time, Mr
Hyndman adds that Meredith was then in very good physical
condition, and threw him in a wrestling bout : " In fact he was
all wire and whipcord without a spare ounce of flesh upon him."
There is confirmation of the statement that Meredith was
artificial in conversation, when with strangers he sought to
impress, in Mrs Ross's book. Alluding to the fact that Kinglake and Meredith did not care for each other much, she says :

" Both were shy in different ways, and both were at their best when alone with one or two friends. My Poet, in the early days when I saw so much of him, was a delightful companion when he knew he was liked ; before strangers his shyness took the form of asserting himself rather loudly, and trying to be epigrammatic and witty ; he gave one the impression that he was not quite sure on what footing he stood."

Sir William Hardman also related an amusing anecdote of Meredith's " show " talk in an incident which happened in 1863, when they both met at dinner a remarkable woman, Mrs Atkinson, widow of the celebrated Siberian traveller. She had been a great traveller also, and had spent twenty years in Russia and carried out a fourteen days' ride into Tartary. She was the author of a book relating her many adventurous experiences. To continue in Hardman's words :

" Mrs Atkinson is a bright-eyed, intelligent woman, small in stature. She polished Meredith off in fine style. He was in high spirits, talking fast and loud. The Surrey hills, the Hind-head, and Devil's Punchbowl, were the subjects of conversation, and G. M. asserted (I know not on what authority) that the view from the Hindhead was very like *Africa*. Mrs A. pricked up her ears, and bending forward across the table asked in a clear but low voice : ' And pray, sir, may I ask what part of Africa you have visited ? ' Alas ! poor Robin ! he has never been further south than Venice. No one could be more amused at his own discomfiture than he was himself, and he gave a very vivid description of his sensations when he saw Mrs A. preparing the inevitable enquiry which he foresaw. As he had talked about Africa without having been there, the great Siberian traveller was disposed evidently to hold him lightly, for later in the dinner the talk was of certain cannibals who are to be imported as the last Sensation Exhibition, and the question of feeding them was mooted. ' Oh ! ' says Meredith, ' there will be no difficulty about that, we shall feed them on the disagreeable people and those we don't like.' ' Yes, indeed,' said Mrs Atkinson, ' and that gentleman (meaning Meredith) would be one of the first to go.' Conceive the chaff, the laughter. We all of us liked the little woman immensely, and mean to improve the acquaintance."

At a later period there is an interesting note on Meredith's conversation by Henry Sidgwick, who writes : " *April* 13*th*, 1886. Last night we dined with Leslie Stephen and met George Meredith, whom I liked, but was somewhat disappointed in his conversation. He was not affected or conceited and talked fluently, but not exactly with ease, nor did his phrases seem to me often to have any peculiar aptness ; once or twice there was an amusing stroke of humorous fancy, as when he talked of an unhappy singer's voice being ' like the soul of a lemon in purgatory ' ; but these things did not come often."

And in 1889 Henry Murray relates how Meredith humorously talked against water-drinking, and cited the horrible case of a fellow-student in Germany who practised the fell habit and died suddenly in great agony, leaving behind a solemn request that the autopsy should be performed by his friend, George Meredith. " When I made the first incision, the glitter of the stalactites in the poor fellow's gastric cavity positively blinded me—I had to wear blue glasses for months after."

Comyns Carr suggested that Meredith cultivated conversation on subjects often outside the province of the novelist's art with the ulterior motive of presenting the matter or problem in his novels :

" He loved to submit his creations to the instant pressure of their time, and with this purpose it was his business, no less than his pleasure, to equip himself intellectually with garnered stores of knowledge in fields into which the ordinary writers of fiction rarely enter. It was not, of course, to be supposed that he could claim equal mastery in all, although his intellect was so active and agile that his limitations were not easily discerned. I remember one day having introduced him to an old gentleman, whose long life had been spent in a study of the drawings of the old masters, to whom Meredith, with inimitable fluency, was expounding the peculiar virtues of the art of Canaletto. Meredith was eloquent, but the discourse somehow failed to impress the aged student. When they had parted his sole commentary to me was : ' Your friend—Mr Meredith, I think you said—endeavoured to persuade me that he understood Canaletto, but he did not.' . . . It must be conceded by all who knew him well that Meredith was not often caught tripping in the discussion of any topic in which his intellect had been actively engaged. Sometimes—and then, perhaps, rather in a spirit of audacious adventure and for exercise of his incomparable powers of expression—he would make a bold sortie into realms of knowledge that were only half-conquered. But this was, for the most part, only when he had an audience waiting on his words. When he had only a single companion to listen, there was no man whose talk was more penetrating or more sincere."

Of course as years went by and Meredith became more and more famous, his conversation was directed increasingly to secure an effect, and there was then more excuse for his didactics in the knowledge that his adulatory auditors, in many cases, intended his remarks for subsequent publication. An even less pleasing trait of Meredith in conversation was his habit, particularly at table when guests were present, of exercising his wit at the expense of his household.[1] It is a curious fact that sensitive and shy people, quick to take offence at any personalities or slights directed at them, are the most prone to wound others by ill-timed humour and personal remarks of a disconcerting nature. Thackeray was another case in point. It is unnecessary to recall examples of Meredith's acutest " wit " at the expense of his family, which often distressed those visitors who were auditors of it. In particular, Grant Allen disapproved. As a specimen of Meredith's lighter and less offensive badinage, one may offer the story told by Mr Clodd of the parlour-maid who, on removing the remains of a dish from table, asked : " If you please, sir, does this puddin' want savin'? " To which Meredith solemnly replied : " Now, my good girl, you, I believe,

[1] Meredith made a remark which has some bearing on this point to Lady Ulrica Duncombe, in 1901 : " I will send you my essay on *Comedy and the Uses of the Comic Spirit*, wherein you will see that an accurate perception of foibles in those whom we love does not lessen the love, or perhaps even the reverence. It is only a vindication of our intellect— the seeing in what way our hero or friend or beloved is a little vanitous and pretentious, or not quite honest at the moment. Our good English know next to nothing of this most instructive and corrective of Spirits."
He presumably refers to the passage in *An Essay on Comedy* commencing : " You may estimate your capacity for Comic perception by being able to detect the ridicule of them you love, without loving them less ; and more by being able to see yourself somewhat ridiculous in dear eyes, and accepting the correction their image of you proposes."

a churchgoer, ask me if this puddin' wants savin'. Do you think that the puddin' has a soul, that it stands in need of salvation, as we are told we all do ? Take it away, Elizabeth, and let me never hear you ask such a funny question again."

To return to 1863, the Seaford visitors went over to Goodwood Races, whereof Meredith wrote to Hardman :

" I have been to Goodwood with the FitzGerald Champagne-Loo party : saw much life, which I wanted : backed wrong horses : lost £5. Certain, however, of knowing my lesson. Wise grows the loser, merely happy the winner. A great pastime ! The scene was glorious. We elbowed dukes : jostled lords : were in a flower-garden of countesses. . . . Of Sons, let me say they are wonderfully browned by Seaford sun and breeze and very jolly. . . . Old Copsham is pretty sound, the Beetle soars.

> " The Beetle soars, the Beetle spins,
>   The Beetle is up in the air, Tuck ;
> 'Twill crack Robin's crown
> As a stamp for his sins,
>   Or make him defy old care.

" Tuck, I am going to bed. If I dream, sail thou across the vision, like a jolly monkish owl.

> " My jolly Friar, now lift thy cowl
> And send me a laugh like a revelling owl.
> Were I lying and groaning in pits of fire
> Thy laughter like water would fall, my Friar."

Meredith was in high spirits at this date, and in another letter relates an amusing anecdote about the late King Edward when, as Prince of Wales, he was staying in Ireland :

" Creyke told me that when Prins was at Curragh he came to the Vice-Regal Lodge, and played cricket. Creyke warned all the opposition bowlers that Royal patronage of the manly game depended on Prins getting at least one run. Having missed, whilst fielding, two fine smack-into-the-hand catches, Wales goes in, and faces an unnamed steady determined Briton of a bowler, round, ruddy—an inevitable creature : one clearly selected by the Gods to do this black business with the utmost satisfaction and comfort. Down went the wicket of your Prins at the first delivery of ball ! To make matters worse, some wretches (not knowing that the wicket was a royal one, or not feeling that the knocking of it over was rank treason to the Throne and to cricket) applauded lustily. Your Prins marched out with his bat amid the thunders.

> " At the first ball his wicket fell, and sins
> No more has batted your illustrious Prins."

Arthur having returned to school, Meredith, on 20th August, 1863, crossed to Paris, where by arrangement he met Hardman, who has left a record of their three days together in France :

" PARIS, *August* 21*st*. Letter from George Meredith announcing his approach. He left via Newhaven last night, and ought to have been in Paris about 11.30. He stopped at Rouen to see the *Joan of Arc*, and to call on an author who had submitted certain work to the Chapmans. He arrived about 2.30. Joyful greetings. We dined by Robin's request at Véfour's, a great mistake. Between Véfour's and the Trois Frères there is such a difference as between the University Club and the ' London ' (corner of Chancery Lane). Meredith and I strolled smoking along the Champs Elysées in the evening—very pleasant, and not offensive like our own beastly Haymarket. Robin brought me *Once a Week* containing my article on *America: An Imaginary Tour*, published August 15, and also put Renan's *Life of Jesus* into his bag for me. We think him not looking well—his son Arthur's accident has naturally been a matter of great anxiety.

" PARIS, *August* 22*nd*. Chartered two carriages, and drove about, visiting the Louvre and other places. Dined at Trois Frères, Robin and I going first to order the dinner, and then returning to our hotel. We were the merriest of parties. Charles, the waiter, was an admirable type of the aristocracy of waiters. . . .

" PARIS, *August* 23*rd* (*Sunday*). We went to Versailles by the Avenue de Passy, through Sèvres, and arrived safely at eleven o'clock. Could not get Meredith past the more modern French pictures of battles. . . . We had a delightful drive back through St Cloud and the Bois de Boulogne. Expressions of admiration at the beauty of the drive were exhausted. Truly the Emperor is a wonderful Œdile."

On the evening of this day, Meredith left to join his friend, Lionel Robinson—" Poco "—at Grenoble. Home again by 16th September, he writes of his travels :

" We went to the Grande Chartreuse, filling all the valleys on approach with the joint names of Tuck and Demitroïa.[1] We slept there. We walked away with 9 bottles of Liqueur, and toiled over mountain passes. Through Dauphiné we walked. We walked ourselves into—silence. Our ordinary course was 10 hours *per diem* : sometimes it went to 13. We crossed Mont Genèvre into Italy : to Turin : to Lago Maggiore, then over Piedmontese mountains and lovely valleys into Switzerland to Geneva : thence to Dijon, where Poco reaching me the hand of friendship and shutting up the tongue of seduction, but parting in fact very prettily, set out for Liége : I for Paris, remaining there four days of delight. . . . We went too fast. We trudged like packmen. Still I have much enjoyed the trip ; am better, fresher."

Back at Copsham, he wrote amusingly to Mrs Hardman :

" I wish to come on Thursday, but don't expect me. We are all in confusion here ; for the rat who troubled us in life is vindictive in death, and there is a successive emigration from all the rooms of the house. We march out formally, and back again. I think that never did the classic maid desire to give her brother's corpse rights of burial so much as I that rat ! . . .

" *Can* you suppose I have given up our plan *à nous trois* ? But a house founded on castors must fall. I prefer to make books my basis, and notably prose. When I write a verse I say ' So many lines, so many leagues from your cottage, my lad ! ' . . . To the ruddy man, the future Cook's Oracle, the sapient Rotundity, kind greeting."

The autumn passed, and though busy with *Sandra Belloni* and other work, Meredith became lonely and unhappy at this period. Writing in December, 1863, to Mrs Ross, he said :

" Now of myself a little. Can I ever forget my dearest and best woman-friend ? And I must be cold of heart not to be

[1] Mrs Hardman.

touched by your faithfulness to your friendships. I, who let grief eat into me and never speak of it (partly because I despise the sympathy of fools and will not trouble my friends), am thereby rendered rather weak of expression at times. The battle is tough when one fights it all alone. And it is only at times that I awake from living in a darker world. But I am getting better both in health and spirit. It is my punishment that I have to tell you what I never prove, that I love you and shall do so constantly. For I hold nothing dearer than your esteem, my dear ! Writing letters seems a poor way of showing it, and yet even that I don't do. But you never vary. If you were like me, our lights would soon pass out of sight of one another, leaving me many regrets certainly, but I acknowledge you to be the fixed star of this union, as you will be one of mine forever. So pardon this sentimentalism."

Momentous changes were impending, but, for the moment, Arthur was still the paramount thought of his father's life. Meredith longed for the boy's return at Christmas, and wrote to him : " Island Pond is frozen over, and all the common looks as you saw it that Christmas morning when we walked over to Oatlands. . . . All your playthings, your theatre, books, etc., are put away, but you can get at them easily when you return. You can imagine how glad I shall be to hear your voice again in this neighbourhood ; and if I were not working very hard I should find the place too dull to live in without you."

And when his boy was home,[1] he wrote to Mrs Jessopp :

" The Son blooms in the air of home. How could I have stopped away from my living heart so long ? But I have him and won't moan that it's only for six weeks. . . . Thackeray's death startled and grieved me. And I, who think I should be capable of eyeing the pitch-black King if he knocked for me in the night ! "

Only six months later came the domestic change which caused Arthur's supreme position in his father's life to suffer inevitable

[1] During these holidays D. G. Rossetti painted a full-length portrait of Arthur Meredith, with a " Futurist " dog in the background. It was not in any way a likeness of the boy.

displacement. In the autumn of 1863 Meredith had made the acquaintance of Mr Justin Theodore Vulliamy, a member of an old Huguenot family,[1] who, in 1857, had settled in Mickleham Vale (a few miles from Esher) at The Old House—a delightful red-brick, gabled house, built in 1636, with a background of woods and hill. Mr Vulliamy's wife had recently died, and he was living here with his three unmarried daughters. By the youngest, Marie, Meredith was at once attracted. She was twenty-four years of age, and very musical. When Meredith paid another visit to the Jessopps, in April, 1864, Miss Vulliamy was also staying in Norwich, and it was in the East Anglian city that he decided that he had at last found the ideal woman for his helpmate ; and here he made his courtship whilst " cathedral-ising "—as he termed those pleasant strolls through the picturesque Close and the meadows by the Wensum and the Yare. Meredith and Miss Vulliamy travelled back to London together, whereof the former wrote to Jessopp :

" I say ! what a charming line of Rail from Norwich to London by way of Ipswich. But apparently little known, for those who took the journey from Norwich on a day last month were alone in the carriage the entire length of the route ; and really it is hard, for a young lady demands all your resources to amuse her : and I wonder whether I did ! She wants a photograph of the little man. Could one be got for her ? She is well, practising music early, and I still wonder why both of you won't think her very handsome. The will is clearly manifested in your refusal to do so. I mean, handsome of that style. Some vitality being wanted ; but the lack of it practically compensated by so very much sweetness. Thus may a cold but friendly spectator speak of her !

" Sandys will have been with me next Friday just three weeks.[2] He is painting country for background of a picture of

---

[1] The introduction took place through N. E. S. A. Hamilton, of the Manuscript Department of the British Museum, author of *The Shakespearean Question*, 1860.

[2] At Copsham Cottage. Frederick Sandys, one of the most remarkable of the Pre-Raphaelite painters, was born at Norwich in 1829, and educated at the Grammar School there. He became intimate with D. G. Rossetti in 1857, and hence arose his friendship with Meredith, which increased when they were both working for *Once a Week*.

the maiden Spring. ' Then came fair May, the fairest maid
on earth,' with heaps of flowers at her feet and immense peri-
wigs of apple-blossom about her poll. She with a look of unconsciousness and a rainbow over her head and such larks in
the sky : a nice girl. We walk hard, though Sandys is not
much of a leg at it and develops groaning feet, etc. At 7½
we dine and are uproarious. Tom Taylor speaks well of his
work in the Academy. I suppose he will be here about a month
longer, he has so much to do. He is going to give me a drawing
of Arthur, and also of—what's the name ? I've forgotten the
name of the person, but am not the less grateful for his kind
ness. . . .

" Since we parted I've been to Tunbridge Wells, to Ventnor,
to Cambridge, and half over Surrey. I came here first with
Sandys, so you may imagine that I haven't had much time to
spare. All kind things to Mrs Jessopp. The young lady who
made her acquaintance in Norwich says innumerable kind
things of her. (I don't mention what is the Norwich return for
this ingenuous heartiness.) "

A few weeks later Meredith definitely announced his engagement in terms expressing how highly he idealised his late-found
happiness, and what bright promise he built upon it for the
future.

" *June 6th*, 1864.

" MY DEAR JESSOPP,—It is time that your friend should show
you a clean breast. He loves a woman as he never yet loved,
and she for the first time has let her heart escape her. She is

Meredith said : " He is one of the most remarkable of the ' brushes ' of our
day, with the quaintest stolid Briton way of looking at general things.
. . . Sandys has a romantic turn that lets me feed on him." Rossetti
called him " the greatest living draughtsman," and Millais said he was
" worth two Academicians rolled into one." Sandys's crayon portrait
of Meredith's second wife, 1864, was one of his finest works. His
Gentle Spring, the picture mentioned by Meredith, was exhibited in 1865.
His *Medea* was crowded out of the Royal Academy Exhibition of 1868,
but vehement protests, Swinburne joining heatedly in the fray, resulted
in the picture being hung on the line in 1869. In his later years, Sandys
was a friend of Aubrey Beardsley and the younger generation of rising
artists of the " nineties." He was ever a Bohemian, thriftless and rather
pugnacious. He died in 1904.

MARIE VULLIAMY (MRS. GEORGE MEREDITH)

*From the Portrait by Frederick Sandys, 1864, in the possession of her son,
W. M. Meredith*

not unknown to you, as you both immediately divine. She is the sweetest person I have ever known, and is of the family which above all others I respect and esteem. Her father is a just and good man ; her sisters are pure gentlewomen : she is of a most affectionate and loving nature. May I be worthy of the love she gives me !

"Your surprise over, you will possibly think me rash. My friends, who know of this, think me fortunate, on reflection. They see that I shall now first live ; that I shall work as I have never yet done ; and that, to speak materially, marriage will not increase the expenses of a man hitherto very careless. My hope stands like a fixed lamp in my brain. I know that I can work in an altogether different fashion, and that with a wife, and such a wife by my side, I shall taste some of the holiness of this mortal world and be new-risen in it. Already the spur is acting, and health comes, energy comes. I feel that I can do things well, and not haphazard, as heretofore. . . . I can hardly make less than eight hundred, reckoning modestly. And I shall now hold the purse-strings warily.

"I shall not speak to Arthur till he is with me. She is very fond of him, and will be his friend. He will find a home where I have found one.

"I cannot play at life. I loved her when we were in Norwich. Cathedralising would not otherwise have been my occupation. I believe that I do her good : I know that she feels it. Me she fills with such deep and reverent emotion that I can hardly think it the action of a human creature merely. I seem to trace a fable thus far developed by blessed angels in the skies. She has been reserved for me, my friend. It was seen that I could love a woman, and one has been given to me to love. Her love for me is certain. I hold her strongly in my hand. Write —I thirst to hear words from you. . . . And if Mrs Jessopp can feel that she can congratulate my beloved and thank her for loving me—Ah ! will she let her know this ? . . . Will two be welcome some day ? She has ventured to say that she hopes so.

"Your loving

"GEORGE MEREDITH."

To Frederick Maxse he wrote, on the same day :

" Pray write to her at once, if you have the kindly impulse.
It will please her, for I have talked much of you and my feeling
for you : of your happiness with your beloved, which she would
rival. And she wishes to feel that my friends are to be hers.
The letter will be a charming surprise to her. An assurance also
I am cared for, here and there, and by worthy men. Your wife
is sure to love her. If God gives her to me, I may certainly say
that our wives will be as much heart in heart as we are. We
shall see one another more. Ah ! when you speak of Ploverfield
for us during the first sweet days of our union, you touch me
deeply and breathe fair auspices. . . . My friend, I have written
of love and never felt it till now. I have much to pass through
in raking up my history with the first woman that held me.
But I would pass through fire for my darling, and all that I
have to endure seems little for the immense gain I hope to get.
When her hand rests in mine, the world seems to hold its breath,
and the sun is moveless. I take hold of Eternity. I love her.
She is intensely emotional, but without expression for it, save
in music. I call her my dumb poet. But when she is at the
piano, she is not dumb. She has a divine touch on the notes.
Yes, she is very fond of the boy. Not at all in a gushing way,
but fond of him as a good little fellow, whom she trusts to make
her friend. As to her family : the old man is a good and just
old man, who displays the qualities he has. There are three
sons, four daughters. The sons are all in business in France—
wool manufacturers, or something. They and the girls were
strictly brought up at home at Nonancourt in Normandy.[1]
Marie was seventeen when seven years ago they came to England.
They have been about five years in Mickleham Vale. On
Saturday next, Kitty, the third—the one preceding my beloved
—is to be married at the little church : Marie being first brides-
maid, and I shall see her. The eldest sister is married to a
French officer,[2] who has an estate in Dauphiné, and is a good
working soldier—' a rough diamond,' says Marie. The eldest
unmarried sister, Betty, is a person of remarkable accomplishments and very clear intellect, vivacious and actively religious :

[1] Mrs Vulliamy was English. She was Miss Elizabeth Bull, a member
of a family settled in Cheshire. She died in 1863 and her husband in
1870.
[2] Commandant Poussielque, of Pont de Beau Voisin, Savoy.

therefore tolerant, charitable, and of a most pure heart.   Kitty, the present bride, takes her Christianity with more emotion : she teaches the children of the parish, while Betty every Sunday evening has a congregation of the men and women in a barn. Do you smile ?   Much good has been done by these two women. . . . To Ploverfield ?   I sound the echoes of the future.   Oh ! is it to be ?   There could not be a fairer, sweeter companion, or one who would more perfectly wed with me.   She tries to make me understand her faults.   I spell at them like a small boy with his fingers upon words of one syllable.   Of course some faults exist.   But she has a growing mind and a developing nature. Love is doing wonders with her. . . . I shall now write in a different manner. . . . Let me know what day you think I may select to present you. . . . Try to give her the whole day, so that you may hear her play in the evening, and see her in all her lights and shades, and know the family—the best specimen of the middle-class that I have ever seen—pure gentlewomen, to call one of whom wife and the rest sisters is a great honour and blessing."

To Hardman he wrote on the next day, 7th June :

" MY DEAREST TUCK,—. . . What do you think of her ?   Is she not worth anything or all in the world ?   And she likes you so much—thinks, I believe, better of me for having such a friend, and hopes that Mrs Hardman may take to her.   I never touched so pure and so conscience-clear a heart.   My own is almost abashed to think itself beloved by such a creature.   The day when she is to be mine blinds me.   Will it come ?   It flickers like lightning in my brain.   It will not burn steadily.   I can't grasp it.   What does this mean ?   I am troubled but can work. " Your loving

" GEORGE M."

Perhaps the most interesting letter on his new life is the following, addressed to W. C. Bonaparte Wyse, on 23rd July :

" I have been for months, and I am now, desperately in love. You know that I am not subject to be smitten.   The wound is all the deeper when it comes.   I am beloved in return.   She is a very handsome person, fair, with a noble pose, and full figure, and a naturally high-bred style and manner such as one meets but rarely. . . . We are to be married in September, and I am thrice a man in the prospect of it, admitting at the same time that some nervous excitement will keep me low till the marriage is complete. When I do love, I love hotly and give the heart clean out of me. She does likewise. . . . I trust I may have strength, as I have honest will, to make her happy. She has money enough to make her independent of me, so she will not be leaning on a literary reed."

On 6th September he wrote again to this same friend:

" COPSHAM, ESHER.

" MY DEAR WYSE,—You will, I know, pardon the silence of a man in love. My bride has the wish that you should come to our wedding. Can you ? Will you ? Write and say ' yes ' at once. The day is the 20th September : a fortnight from this. The place is Mickleham, three miles beyond Leatherhead, and seven from old Copsham, where you may find quarters the previous evening, and a friend will call for you and bring you on in the morning. It will give me great pleasure to see your face and shake your hand on that day. My darling also will remember the friends that day surrounding us. So, do come. I want you to see my Marie blooming. She is a full and perfect rose. You know the Gloire de Dijon ?—of that kind, my friend, with the sweet flush and delicious odour—all the richness of the flower ! Write to me ' care of Justin Vulliamy, Esq., Mickleham, near Dorking, Surrey.' I shall hardly be able to welcome you here before the noble day (would 'twere over !). You have thought of coming to London—contrive the visit to suit the 20th. Jessopp marries the pair. Maxse gives me his house near Southampton for a month or so. We live in an Esher house for six months, and then build or buy a place suitable for modest married lovers. I wish I could read you some of my new novel *Vittoria*. You must come to me in the winter and help me anent certain Italian matter. I am surcharged with work, with but little time at present to accomplish it.

" Your fine Epicurean contempt for the passing show of this life charms me. But, to be rightly and lastingly content, you must work, work ! Set yourself to a task. Uncertainty

has been your storm at sea, but now you are in haven, don't
rot.

" My kindest regards to your wife, and believe me ever your
loving

"GEORGE MEREDITH."

As the wedding day approached his ecstatic mood suffered
no diminution. He wrote to Maxse:

" I write with my beloved beside me ; my thrice darling—of
my body, my soul, my song ! I have never loved a woman
and felt love grow in me. This clear and lovely nature doubles
mine. And she has humour, my friend. She is a charming
companion, as well as the staunchest heart and fairest mistress.
You will not fail us on our marriage day. A goodly host of
friends will be here. Janet and Sir Alec come—and oh ! I
would that the day were over ! "

The marriage took place on 20th September, 1864, in the
ancient little church of Mickleham, which stands so picturesquely
at the foot of the wooded downs. The ceremony was performed by Dr Jessopp, and the witnesses who signed the register
were Lionel Robinson, Annie A. Smith, and the bride's father
and brother, Theodore. (Seventy-one years previously Fanny
Burney and D'Arblay were married in the same church.) The
first part of the honeymoon was spent at Southampton, and
after a fortnight the Merediths went on to Captain Maxse's
house, Ploverfield, Bursledon, a place which Meredith found
very pleasant and where he could work well. As he wrote to
Hardman :

" MY DEAR LORD ABBOT,—I am working mightily. Last
night I awoke, and at 3 o'clock struck a light and wrote a poem
on Cleopatra for *The Cornhill*, to suit Sandys's illustration.[1]
Also an ' Ode ' to the Napiers (part of it) and part of *The Ex-
champion's Lament*. I say, young Copperfield ! I never had

---

[1] Apparently Meredith's poem on Cleopatra was rejected and the
manuscript destroyed. Sandys's drawing of this subject did not appear
in *The Cornhill Magazine* until two years later, in September, 1866, and
it was then accompanied by Swinburne's poem. Meredith described his
own poem as " ' Lines ' merely ! Not of much value, but containing
fire as well as wind."

such a fit on me since the age of 21 ; and my good love, waking too, joyfully assisted by lending notepaper and soothing me for having disturbed her slumber.

" You frisk not in your letters to me.   I pay you due respect, but an you continue this tone of formality, by God, I will unfrock you !   Know that Marie is the wife of a Pantagruel ; she is sublime in laughter.   We sit on a humorous Olympus, and rule over the follies of mortals. . . . Life here is jolly.   I rise, bathe, run, and come blooming to breakfast, having tied up Sam, the vagabond dog, who breaks Maxse's heart, who in return does his best to break Sam's back.   I treat the dog differently, and being a Celt myself, the Irishman comprehends, and loves me, and won't leave me.   To-day we went out fishing in the boat, and Sam would follow, swimming a mile. . . .

" I shall rejoice to see the Hall.[1]   But, my father, in your future letters, date them from the Refectory, as of yore.   I give myself seven years, and then, an I be not a pallid ghost, I will fix here my abode.   By the Nine Gods !   Fancy a salt river, crystal clear, winding under full-bosomed woods, to a Clovelly-like village, house upon house, with ships, and trawlers, and yachts moored under the windows, and away the flat stream, shining to the Southern sun till it reaches Southampton Water, with the New Forest over it, shadowy, and beyond to the left, the Solent and the Island.   This is possible from our window. The air makes athletes.   All round are rolling woods, or healthy hills.   The Roads are hard : but one can't have everything. I am a man of Bursledon, mark you.   Adieu ! I must to work."

The Merediths left Bursledon towards the end of October, and went first to Mickleham, where they spent Christmas of 1864 with Mr Vulliamy, at the picturesque Old House.   Writing from there on December 18th to William Hardman, Meredith said :

" BELOVED TUCK,—The Christmas season causes that contemplation should make you specially its object.   Marie went in the afternoon for a second edition of the Reverend Burmester.[2] I aloft, to Mickleham Downs, where the great herded yews stand on a pure snowfield.   I thought to have fallen on the very

---

[1] Hardman had removed to Norbiton Hall, Kingston.
[2] Rector of Mickleham.

throne of Silence. In a few paces I became a Druid. Time
withered from the ends and all his late writings were smudged
out, till I lived but in the earlier days of Britain, when he with
difficulty made his mark. It was a sublime scene, that long roll
of the unfooted snow, with the funeral black plumes of the
yews spreading in a dumb air, as if all had ceased, or nothing
was begun. Embraced by it, my spirit conjured up a passionate desire to snowball Tuck, till he cried himself a sinner. I
moaned that the man was not there, that I might snowball him,
till fainting he dropped to earth.

" Eh ! What a change in the course of our fortunes, Tuck !
I am married, and thou Lord of Norbiton, and all these things
were dreamed not a year back. . . ."

And what a change from two years ago when Meredith and
Arthur spent that jolly Christmas with the Hardmans in London
before returning to " dear old Copsham." But now Copsham
days were over, for there was not sufficient accommodation at
the cottage for a wife, so whilst they were looking out for
a place of their own the Merediths stayed at "The Cedars,"
Esher, a pleasant house near the river Mole.

His marriage and the departure from Copsham Cottage marks
a distinct change in the life of Meredith. The first phase was
now closed. It had been at times a lonely and perhaps a sad
period, but it had been illumined by much good friendship and
social pleasure, much Nature study and fine work. The new
era of domestic happiness now opened auspiciously, together
with a consciousness of unabated literary power ; but the
change in his life inevitably involved one sad circumstance—
the estrangement of his son Arthur, now eleven years old.
Although the boy had never warmly responded to the love
which hitherto his father had whole-heartedly laid at his feet,
he naturally felt the difference when a large portion of that love
was diverted to another person. And from being the pivot on
which his father's existence turned and one whose slightest wish
had been gratified in his home, he now found himself of secondary
importance, and even less after the advent of his step-brother
in 1865. The juvenile tragedy of an eldest child, who has been
for some years alone and supreme in his home and then is super-
seded, is ever a bitter one ; and in the special circumstances

of Arthur Meredith, who had been his father's sole relation and much noticed in the society of his parent's adult friends, it is not surprising that the boy was jealous and keenly resentful of his altered life and lost autocracy. Unfortunately, as he grew older he did not learn to accept the change with wise philosophy. Inheriting his father's acute sensitiveness and pride, he gradually drifted away from his home, and it was found best for him to be abroad. After leaving Dr Jessopp's school he was sent, in 1867, to a school at Hofwyl, near Berne, conducted on the system of Pestalozzi, which had for its basis graduated object teaching. His education was completed at Stuttgart. His father did not encourage the idea of the boy's return home. Thus he wrote, in 1868 : " I think it quite as well that you should not return to England until you do so finally to begin your apprenticeship to some business—I don't mean trade, unless you like it, nor do I suppose that you much desire to come home at present." It must have pained Meredith to recall how, only four years previously, Arthur's holidays had been the happiest weeks of the year, and so eagerly anticipated. But he went on to say in the same letter : " How much I long to meet you ! Keep pure in mind, unselfish of heart, and diligent in study. This is the right way of worshipping God, and is better than hymns and sermons and incense. We find it doubtful whether God blesses the latter, but cultivate the former, and you are sure of Him. Heed me well when I say this. And may God for ever bless you, I pray it nightly."

At intervals Meredith continued to write to his son long letters containing good advice as to health and morals. " Don't think I preach too much," he said, " I am naturally anxious about you. I have passed through the wood, and know which are the paths to take, which to avoid. By following my directions you will spare yourself many troubles, many a heartache. . . . Virtue and truth are one. Look for the truth in everything, and follow it, and you will then be living justly before God. Let nothing flout your sense of a Supreme Being, and be certain that your understanding wavers whenever you chance to doubt that he leads to good. . . . And do not lose the habit of praying to the unseen Divinity. Prayer for worldly goods is worse than fruitless, but prayer for strength of soul is that passion of the soul which catches the gift it seeks."

This was in 1872, but the rift was rapidly widening, and for the next nine years apparently few, if any, letters passed between father and son. The latter complained of a lack of consideration shown towards him and that he was kept short of money by his father. Meredith, however, seems to have been fairly generous, until a legacy from a grand-aunt made the boy more or less independent. A post was obtained for him in the firm of De Koninck at Havre. Later he was employed in a linseed warehouse at Lille. His health failed, and then, in June, 1881, Meredith broke the silence of years and remorsefully wrote :—

" I have been struck to the heart by hearing ill news of your health from Lionel Robinson. He was here yesterday, and told me of your having had to consult a physician in London about spitting of blood. . . . The account of the nature of your work makes me fully commend the wisdom of your decision to quit it and Lille. It would severely tax the strongest. You should have rest for a year. . . . Your pride, I hope, will not be offended if I offer to eke out your income during the term of your necessary relapse. You have laboured valiantly and won our respect, and you may well consent to rest for awhile, when that is the best guarantee for your taking up the fight again. But come to us in September. . . . When I was informed of your wishing to throw up your situation at Lille that you might embrace the profession of Literature, I was alarmed.[1] My own mischance in that walk I thought a sufficient warning. But if you come to me I will work with you in my chalet (you will find it a very quiet and pretty study), and we will occupy your leisure to some good purpose. I am allowed the reputation of a tolerable guide in writing and style, and I can certainly help you to produce clear English. . . . After all, with some ability, and a small independence just to keep away the wolf, and a not devouring ambition, Literature is the craft one may most honourably love. I do not say to you, try it. I should say the reverse to anyone. But assuming you to be under the obligation to rest, you might place yourself in my hands here with advantage ; and leading a quiet life in good air, you would soon, I trust, feel strength return and discern

[1] Arthur contributed some Travel Sketches to *Macmillan's Magazine*.

the bent of your powers. Anything is preferable to that
perilous alternation of cold market and hot café at Lille.
I had no idea of what you were undergoing, or I would have
written to you before. No one better than I from hard priva-
tion knows the value of money. But health should not be
sacrificed to it. I long greatly to see you. I would at once
run over to Lille, if I could spare the time. Write to me, and
specially of your health, on the day you receive this—a dozen
lines in the case of a press of business. You may rely on my
wife's cordial anxiety to see you well and receive you here. I
shall be troubled until I hear from you. . . .

" We have been long estranged, my dear boy, and I awake
from it with a shock that wrings me. The elder should be the
first to break through such divisions, for he knows best the
tenure and the nature of life. But our last parting gave me
the idea that you did not care for me."

Truly was this a sad aftermath for the love and devotion of
earlier years. Perhaps Meredith perceived there was a touch
of retributive fate in this repetition of family history, and at
last was able to realise the feelings of his father before him in
relation to himself; to understand something of that baffled
affection and cold response from a son, which had been the
portion of Augustus Meredith; to regret the pain with which
he had pierced his own father's heart.

Arthur Meredith did not come home; he preferred to seek
recovery in the mountain air of Switzerland or Italy. Eventually he went to live at Bergamo and Salò on Lake Garda. By
the beginning of 1889 he was in a precarious state, and a voyage
to Australia was resolved upon. But he never would accept
any financial help from his father, although Meredith wrote
to Arthur's step-sister, Mrs Clarke (Edith Nicolls), on the
matter thus :

" I want you to use your influence in getting him to accept
this little sum in part payment of his voyage. Tell him it will
be the one pleasure left to me when I think of his going. It
may not help much—and yet there is the chance. As I sat
chattering yesterday afternoon and noticed how frail he looked,
I was pained with apprehension. . . . I apply to you for an

aid that must needs be powerful with him ; I am sure you are rational ; you have been sister and mother to him, you will induce him not to reject from his father what may prove service-able. As for money—how poor a thing it is ! I never put a value on it even in extreme poverty. He has an honourable pride relating to it ; touch his heart, that he may not let his pride oppose my happiness—as far as I may have it from such a source as money."

Arthur had rather a trying experience on the voyage out, when the other occupant of his cabin proved to be an almost mad inebriate. At Sydney he made a partial recovery ; but after his return to England, in the spring of 1890, he failed again rapidly, and died, on 3rd September, at Woking, in a house temporarily taken by his sister. Mrs Clarke was his best friend, and she tended him to the last with the tenderest devotion. To her Meredith wrote : " I am relieved by your report of Arthur's end. To him it was, one has to say in the grief of things, a release. He has been, at least, rich above most in the two most devoted of friends, his sister and her husband. Until my breath goes I shall bless you both."

Many sad memories must have arisen like wan ghosts in the father's mind as he recalled the past and old days at Halliford, Seaford, and Copsham. As he cried :

> Ask, is Love divine,
> Voices all are, ay.
> Question for the sign,
> There's a common sigh.
> Would we, through our years,
> Love forego,
> Quit of scars and tears ?
> Ah, but no, no, no.
>
> Joy is fleet,
> Sorrow slow.
> Love, so sweet,
> Sorrow will sow.
> Love, that has flown
> Ere day's decline,
> Love to have known,
> Sorrow, be mine.

Arthur Meredith was buried at Woking.   Proud and reserved, yet self-conscious to a degree, gifted with personal beauty and some measure of talent, such was the untimely end, at the age of thirty-seven, of him who was Meredith's son and Peacock's grandson.   Fated without choice to cause both his parents, whom he resembled so much, the most acute sorrow, he never found happiness himself, a victim of heredity.

Arthur Meredith

CHAPTER VIII

"SANDRA BELLONI." "RHODA FLEMING." "VITTORIA."
MEREDITH AT KINGSTON LODGE AND IN ITALY

EMILIA IN ENGLAND (later to be renamed *Sandra Belloni*) was published in three volumes by Chapman and Hall in April, 1864. It was the story which of all his creations caused Meredith the greatest pangs in conception. He took over three years to write it, and he was continuously hacking it about and altering it, sometimes to his satisfaction and sometimes not.

As early as May, 1861, he said he was well " advanced " with *Emilia Belloni,* but by November he had left her " untouched for months." Seven months later, in June, 1862, he cast aside what he had done. " I have rewritten it. . . . I have remodelled the whole, making the background more agreeable and richer comedy," he told Maxse. In August " a dreadful hitch in *S. Belloni* has been distressing me of late. This day tides me over the difficulty." But four months later he was again displeased with his work and wrote to Mrs Jessopp : " My fastidiousness has made me cut to pieces four printed chapters of *Emilia* (who begins to dissatisfy me totally, as do all my offspring that have put on type)." In March, 1863 : " I am overwhelmed with disgust at *Emilia.* Am hurrying her on like Ye Deuce. She will do. But, ahem ! she must pay. I have taken some trouble with her and really shall begin to think her character weak in this respect, if she don't hand in what I think due, speedily." He thought he had finished with the troublesome damsel in July, but he had not by any means, and in November was " dejected as regards this novel." His friends Hardman and Maxse were reading it in proof and giving some useful criticism.[1] To the former he wrote : " On the

---

[1] Hardman notes in November, 1863 : "Meredith . . . is to sleep here, in order to have a fight with me about my criticisms and suggestions anent the second volume of *Emilia,* the proofs of which have just

whole, nothing could be neater than your criticism. Maxse is amusing. Objects to her conduct in going with Gambier ' because every girl is conscious that she should never trust herself alone with a man,' etc. So : the sentimental worshipper will always make them animals. . . . I'll come to talk and fight him : but with full acknowledgement of the soundness of some of his criticism and value of his advice. I am glad that Tuck likes it on the whole. It's impossible to tell him what difficulty I get myself into by altering my original conception of the scheme." In the same month he wrote : " Of *Emilia* I cannot speak. She grieves me. I have never so cut about a created thing. There's good work in her : but the work ? " In January, 1864, all he could tell Jessopp was : " I am not all right. *Emilia Belloni* is not all right. She has worried me beyond measure, and couldn't expect to be all right. She will be, when she's in Italy. As to character, I think you will have no doubt of her flesh and blood. How you will like the soul of the damsel, I can't guess. . . . The book is to be published at my risk and for my profit. . . . Nothing but my carelessness puts me behind in my money accounts. I make, apart from novels, enough for Arthur and myself. It comes and goes. If this novel does not pay well, I shall retrench rigidly, book my bills, deny friends, have no purse, and look above the head of the crossing sweeper. The novel has good points, and some of my worst ones. It has no plot, albeit a current series of events : but being based on character and continuous development it is not unlikely to miss a striking success. . . . I am growing fuller of hope and thirst for work. I begin to believe again that I may do ' something.' Judge me not by this present perform-ance ! . . . I trust all will go tolerably well with the book, though what the public will make of 3 vols. without a climax of incident (Finis waving no nuptial torch)—the climax being all in a development of character—I am at a loss to imagine ; and so wait patiently, hoping for here and there a critic to interpret me to the multitude."

The reason for all this groaning and labour is to be accounted for by the fact that this was the author's first distinctively

passed through my hands. These criticisms mainly relate to an absorb-ing tendency which possesses him for indecent double-entendre. I am determined he shall not offend the public taste, if I can help it."

original work, the embryo of what may be termed the Real
Meredith. Here he cast aside the influences of *The Arabian
Nights* and Dickens, and the arts of the story-teller, and evolved
a novel of striking interest in which incident and drama were
subordinate to play and development of character mainly presented in the form of conversations, and a delicate dissection of
" the Fine Shades " of thought and motive leading to action.
Unfortunately this method of narrative (though it has classical
precedent) often involves the description of some great scene by
the mouths of other characters in the book instead of being
directly and vividly recounted as part of the story proper. How
far finer, for instance, might the dramatic scene in Devonshire
between Emilia, Lady Charlotte, Wilfrid, and Georgiana Ford
have been rendered if told in straightforward narrative instead
of by the disjointed report of Georgiana. And *Sandra Belloni*
suffers, like its two immediate predecessors, by ending inartistic-
ally with a letter. Meredith broke himself of this annoying
habit in his subsequent books (excepting *Lord Ormont and his
Aminta*), though he was seldom at his best with a finale, apart
from *Vittoria* and *Beauchamp's Career*.

Although he had not so much cause for complaint against
the reviewers of his latest book as on previous occasions, he
was annoyed by the notices that had appeared by 18th May,
1864, when he wrote : " I get slaps for having written *Emilia*.
I am ' eminently ' this or that, unpleasant, in review style.
Have you ever met a Reviewer ? It's curious to see how small
this thing that stings can be. She moves, which is good. A
favourable touch to her in *The Saturday* or *Times* would launch
her into more than the middle of a 2nd edition." It is strange
that he makes no allusion to the very full and sympathetic
notice, by Richard Garnett, in *The Reader* of 23rd April, in the
course of which it was said :

" *Emilia in England* is fully equal to the author's former
works in humour and power, and only less remarkable in so far
as it is less original. The plot is a variation on the theme of
Evan Harrington. The comedy of that admirable novel turned
on the struggle of three sisters, upheaved into a higher than
their natural sphere, with the demon of Tailordom ; their
frantic efforts to entomb the monstrous corpse of their plebeian

o

origin beneath the highest available heaps of acted and spoken lies; the vigorous resistance of that ghastly being to this method of disposing of him, and his victorious assertion of his right to walk the earth. . . . In *Emilia* we have three sisters again—the Misses Pole. . . . The situation is fundamentally the same, but so far varied that the ladies have no chance of concealing their mercantile origin, of which, indeed, to do them justice, they are not ashamed. They simply wish to get higher, and, by way of justifying their ambition to themselves, have set up a fanciful code of feelings supposed to be proper to the highest circles . . . and the gist of the present work is a sarcastic but quiet exposure of the evil these ladies wrought against their better nature."

That is a very fair exposition of the aspirations which animated the ladies of Brookfield. For, as Meredith wittily put it : " Flying about with a desperate grip on the extreme skirts of aristocracy, the ladies knew to be the elevation of dependency, not true eminence ; and though they admired the kite, they by no means wished to form a part of its tail. They had brains. A circle was what they wanted, and they had not to learn that this is to be found or made only in the liberally-educated class, into the atmosphere of which they pressed like dungeoned plants."

In July there followed, in *The Westminster Review*, Justin McCarthy's article, *Novels with a Purpose*, wherein *Emilia in England* received high praise : " I remember no character in modern literature that so faithfully pictures the nature which is filled with a genius for music "—so that Meredith's life-long complaint of lack of appreciation had but exiguous justification even in these early days.[1]

In the autumn of 1864 a translation of *Emilia in England* by E. D. Forgues appeared in the *Revue des Deux Mondes*.

As we have seen, Meredith told Mrs Ross : " Emilia is a feminine musical genius. I gave you once, sitting on the Mound

---

[1] The book was immediately appreciated by Henry Sidgwick, who wrote, in February, 1865 : " Beg, borrow, or steal *Emilia in England* ; it had such an effect on me that I employed my spare cash in buying up the man's other works." His biographers add that he was able to obtain first editions of *Richard Feverel*, *Evan Harrington*, and the others, second-hand, at something less than a shilling each.

EMILIA MACIRONE (LADY HORNBY). THE ORIGINAL OF
EMILIA SANDRA BELLONI AND VITTORIA

over Copsham, an outline of the real story it is taken from. Of course one does not follow out real stories ; and this one has simply suggested Emilia to me." Therefore, in dealing with the original of this book it will suffice to say that the character and more particularly the physical aspects of Emilia were drawn to a certain extent from Miss Emilia Macirone (Lady Hornby), whom Meredith had known well when he lived at The Limes, Weybridge, and who, some ten years later, acted as intermediary between him and his dying wife. This painful task adumbrates the good nature and faithfulness which animates the Emilia of the story. Like her, Miss Macirone—a name sounding much the same as Belloni—was the daughter of an Italian by an English wife. She had brilliant eyes, and a splendid complexion of deep, rich colouring. " A superb Italian head, with dark-banded soft hair, and dark strong eyes under unabashed soft eyelids." [1] She was an accomplished musician, and sang exquisitely. She was unconventional for her period, and during her voyage to the Crimea, in 1855, used to sing to a large audience of the soldiers and sailors on board almost every evening. In England, when at Penn, in Buckinghamshire, she would go out at night in harvest time and sing to the reapers and labourers assembled in a barn. This incident was utilised by Meredith in the scene where his Emilia goes to sing in the booth on the Common for the delectation of the members of the rural Junction Club of Ipley and Hillford (Ripley and Guildford), when the harmony of the evening was rudely interrupted by the beer-brave members of a rival club. The name of the younger Miss Macirone (Mrs Vaillant), Giulia, was given to the minor character of Madame Marini in *Sandra Belloni*.

Apparently no Meredithian commentator has observed that Swinburne figures in *Sandra Belloni* under the name of Tracy Runningbrook — a sort of play upon the poet's cognomen. There is no mistaking the portrait drawn : " Tracy's hair was red as blown flame, with eyes of a grey-green hue, that may be seen glistening over a wet sunset . . . he was of the blood of dukes, and would be a famous poet." The date, 1861-1863, when Meredith was writing this book coincided with the time when he was most intimate with Swinburne, the days when they were at Copsham and Chelsea together. Therefore his

---

[1] *Vittoria.*

presentment of the youthful poet has great interest, for no doubt the conversation of Tracy is a literal transcription of the vehement avalanche of words which characterised the original. Take the scene where Tracy discusses with Emilia the libretto he will write for her opera on the subject of their jointly beloved Italy :

" Cast the die for Camillus, and let's take horse. Only, we lose the love-business—exactly where I show my strength. Clelia in the camp of the king : dactyllic chorus-accompaniment, while she, in heavy voluptuous anapæsts, confesses her love for the enemy of her country. . . . Then that scene where she and the king dance the dactyls, and the anapæsts go to the chorus. Sublime ! Let's go into the woods and begin . . ."

And when he proposes to create a daughter for Brennus :

" She's a bony woman, with a brawny development ; mammoth haunches, strong of the skeleton ; cheek-bones, flat-forward, as a fish's rotting on a beach ; long scissor lips— nippers to any wretched rose of a kiss ! a pugilist's nose to the nostrils of a phoca ; and eyes—don't you see them ?—luminaries of pestilence ; blotted yellow, like a tallow-candle shining through a horny lantern."

Undoubtedly here we recover an authentic echo of that flow of Swinburnean language which Meredith likened to a torrent of boiling lava, and a taste of that wealth of violent simile which enabled the poet easily to rout a merely sanguinarily garnished cabman who was dissatisfied with his fare.

Meredith also introduces the matter of Swinburne's spirited defence of *Modern Love* in the press, though he transposes the facts, for it is Tracy Runningbrook's poem which is unjustly reviewed, and the protest is penned by Purcell Barrett. This, via Wilfrid, enabled Meredith to voice his contempt for the recent attack he had endured in *The Spectator* :

" I have just come across a review of your last book, and send it. . . . There will be no necessity to call your attention to the critic's English. You can afford to laugh at it, but I confess it puts your friends in a rage. Here are a set of fellows who arm themselves with whips and stand in the public thoroughfare to make any man of real genius run the gauntlet down their ranks till he comes out flayed at the other extremity."

To which Tracy replies :

" Why the deuce do you write me such infernal trash about the opinions of a villainous dog who can't even pen a decent sentence. . . . Let the fellow bark till he froths at the mouth, and scatters the virus of the beast among his filthy friends."

And this Swinburnean definition of the Teutonic cuisine will, no doubt, now be regarded as prophetic : " German cookery is an education for the sentiment of hogs. The play of sour and sweet, and crowning of the whole with fat, shows a people determined to go *down* in civilisation and try the business backwards."

The character drawing in *Sandra Belloni* varies considerably in merit, as in most of the author's books. Emilia herself is, of course, a superlative study. All the Poles are good. Lady Charlotte is very finely drawn, and her broad-minded philosophy and serene *savoir faire*, lights and shades, are etched with consummate art. Mr Pericles—that earlier and more benevolent Svengali—is a delightfully original creation. But Mrs Chump is a failure and fatiguing ; Gambier, Merthyr Powys, and Georgiana Ford are shadows, who never develop. Purcell Barrett, too, is a disappointment. Up to a certain point he is an interesting study with strong features, and then suddenly he fizzles out in a damp cloud of feeble sentimentality. But perhaps his creator intended him as a dire warning against admitting sentiment into an imaginative and brooding mind. One could almost think that Meredith had taken the character and circumstances of his small son, Arthur, and was tracing out their possible development in the future :

" As a child . . . he had grown up with ideas of filial duty perplexed, and with a fitful love for either (parent) that was not attachment : a baffled natural love, that in teaching us to brood on the hardness of our lot, lays the foundation for a perniciously mystical self-love. He had waxed precociously philosophic when still a junior. His mother died away from her husband's roof. The old man then sought to obliterate her utterly."

There is much humorous observation in this book. One would have liked more *obiter dicta* from the unnamed landlady, thankful Cockney, of Barrett's, who in her one brief appearance is profound on the subjects of metropolitan advantages and wife-beating :

" For market-gardening London beats any country I ever knew ; and if you like creature comforts, I always say, stop in London ! And then the policemen ! who really are the greatest comfort of all to us poor women, and seem sent from above especially to protect our weakness. . . . It seems almost wicked to say it, Sir Purcy ; but it's my opinion there ain't a Christian woman who's not made more of a Christian through her tea. And a man who beats his wife—my first question is, ' Do he take his tea regular ? ' For, depend upon it, that man is not a tea-drinker at all. "

How amusing, too, is Emilia's definition of poetry :

" ' Poetry ? ' said Emilia. . . . ' It seems like talking on tiptoe like animals in cages, always going to one end and back again.'

" ' And making the same noise when they get at the end— like the bears ! ' Sir Purcell slightly laughed. ' You don't approve of the rhymes ? '

" ' Yes, I like the rhymes, but when you use words—I mean, if you are in earnest—how can you count and have stops and— no, I do not care anything for poetry.' "

And yet Emilia could be intensely poetical in expression, as when she wore the gorgeous purple Branciani dress and said : " It seems like a deep blush all over me. I feel as if I looked out of a rose." Naturally she was in tune with her creator's favourite aspect of nature—the clouds that attend a south-west wind : " South-westward she gazed, eyeing eagerly the struggle of twisting vapour ; long flying edges of silver went by, and mounds of faint crimson, and here and there a closing space of blue, swift as a thought of home to a soldier in action.[1] The heavens were like a battlefield."

---

[1] The same thoughts seem to have inspired Wilde's lines in *The Ballad of Reading Gaol* :

> I never saw a man who looked
>   With such a wistful eye
> Upon that little tent of blue
>   Which prisoners call the sky,
> And at every drifting cloud that went
>   With sails of silver by.

THE BLACK POOL, COPSHAM WOODS

Photograph by Mr. F. J. Williamson

Exquisite little scenic cameos gleam in this Surrey novel. When Emilia and Wilfrid were by the Weir they saw " the moon that had now topped the cedar, and was pure silver ; silver on the grass, on the leafage, on the waters. And in the West, facing it, was an arch of twilight and tremulous rose ; as if a spirit hung there over the shrouded sun. . . . They saw the cedar grey-edged under the moon : and Night, that clung like a bat beneath its ancient open palms. The bordering sward about the falls shone silvery. In its shadow was a swan."

Meredith's surroundings at Copsham are all intertwined with this book. It was by the pollard-willow near his favourite haunt, the Black Pool in the wood, that he ended the life of poor Purcell Barrett ; and in his penultimate chapter, *Frost on the May Night*, gazing from his cottage window he summoned his characters [1] for adieu and ranged them, lit by moonlight, in that " fair woodland court," with moss and frosted fern for flooring, that bordered The Mound :

" A sharp breath of air had passed along the dews, and all the young green of the fresh season shone in white jewels. The sky, set with very dim distant stars, was in grey light round a small brilliant moon. Every space of earth lifted clear to her ; the woodland listened ; and in the bright silence the nightingales sang loud."

Writers are sometimes aware when they have achieved good work, and Meredith knew his last scene in *Sandra Belloni* was good. He wrote to Maxse, when reminding his friend of the songs of nightingales they had heard in the past : " Note ' Frost on the May Night ' close at the end of *Emilia*." The memory of the scene and of Copsham Woods remained with Meredith, and thirty years later he recalled again that beautiful experience of the long ago in his poem, *Night of Frost in May* :

> With splendour of a silver day,
> A frosted night had opened May :
> And on that plumed and armoured night,
> As one close temple hove our wood,
> Its border leafage virgin white. . . .

---

[1] They were very real to him. Hardman relates of Meredith's creations in *Sandra Belloni* : "To him they are evidently living beings, in fact, I know he has felt them as such for the past twelve months."

It seemed a single harper swept
Our wild wood's inner chords and waked
A spirit that for yearning ached
Ere men desired and joyed or wept.
Or now a legion ravishing
Musician rivals did unite
In love of sweetness high to sing
The subtle song that rivals light . . .
          It holds me linked
Across the years to dead-ebb shores
I stand on, my blood-thrill restores.

So the influences of Copsham were lovely and enduring.

With the publication of *Sandra Belloni* coincided the turn in
the fortunes of Meredith, who now was making quite a comfortable income by his pen. He was writing *Rhoda Fleming*
and *Vittoria*, and planning *Harry Richmond*; he was writing for
The Ipswich Journal still, and for *The Morning Post*; he was
expecting to make new arrangements with Chapman and Hall
that would secure him a salary of £250 or £300 a year; " a
publisher . . . proposes to give me four figures (with no dot
between) for a novel. Am I rising ? The market speaks ! "
and, in fact, as he put it in the summer of 1864 : " I have laid
lines right and left . . . and in short spread traps for money
everywhere." By October he wrote humorously : " I shall be
a MILLIONAIRE next year. My ' plain story ' (*Rhoda Fleming*)
is first to right me, and then the 3 volumer will play trumpets."
His prosperity continued to increase ; he joined the Garrick
Club, he entertained his friends, and still was able to notify
Hardman a few years later :

Sweet Justice of Norbiton, neighbour of Jones,
    Have you paid in the £15 cheque ?
The account at my banker's has recently grown's
    Fat as the Princess of Teck.

After staying at The Cedars, Esher, during the early part of
1865, the Merediths took lodgings in Kingston-on-Thames ; and
in the spring they entered upon a three years' lease of Kingston
Lodge, Norbiton, a quaint and pleasant little house in pseudo-
Gothic style. It had a good garden, and here stood—and still
stands—a tower, covered with ivy, the freak of some previous
owner with a taste for decorative building. The great attraction
of Kingston Lodge to Meredith was that it stood opposite to

KINGSTON LODGE, NORBITON. HERE MEREDITH LIVED 1865-1867
AND WROTE "RHODA FLEMING" AND "VITTORIA." THE
BATTLEMENTED WING IS A MODERN ADDITION TO THE HOUSE

Norbiton Hall, where lived, since 1864, his valued friends the Hardmans. Apart from this he never liked Kingston. He told Maxse, in a nipped winter frame of mind : " I hate the black East, and I don't like the frost ; I like nothing in Kingston. But I envy you the fine S.W. now showing soft white and blue, and taking you in his arms. . . . But I have determined to save up and put by, and endure this place (if possible) for the three years' term. And when I move I will move to a fixed place.[1] Rich men may be houseless rovers ; it upsets poor ones. Besides, wives don't like foreign houses, and won't let their hearts' fibres cling to any place not their own."

Still, Kingston Lodge has interest for Meredithians, for here he finished *Rhoda Fleming* and wrote most of *Vittoria* and a great part of *Harry Richmond*. Here, too, was born his son, William Maxse Meredith, whose first two names perpetuate his father's friendships with Sir William Hardman and Admiral Maxse. Meredith deals with these matters in a letter to W. C. Bonaparte Wyse, dated Norbiton, 27th July, 1865 :

" My dearest Corsican, and Right Good Friend and Brother of Parnassus,—I delayed to reply, having had to visit Maxse and await the result of my wife's confinement. It's over, and here's a new Boy in the world of uncertainty. And now, mother and child going on as well as at present, I shall be free about a fortnight hence, and may, perhaps, drop down and spend a few days with you, if you can receive me. I have lots to talk about. Just now, I haven't time for a word. There are letters to be written and dispersed among all my wife's relations, that they may know of this marvel. Write to me by return, and tell me whether you will be at home and can give me housing in the middle of August. I shall walk on to Lynmouth and Ilfracombe. Perhaps subsequently run over to Brescia and the Subalpine cities, to see to my colouring in the novel, *Vittoria*, which is to appear in *The Fortnightly Review*. I have just completed a novel called *Rhoda Fleming*."

Like her predecessor, *Rhoda Fleming* was a long time in the making. The book was begun as far back as the spring of 1861,

---

[1] He kept his word. He removed to Box Hill, and stayed there till the end.

when Meredith, intending then to call it *A Woman's Battle*, wrote to Mrs Ross : " Query—good title ? I think it will be my best book as yet." Some months later he seems to have named it *The Dyke Farm*. Then the work was laid aside for a long time while *Emilia* was being wrestled with, and it was not until 1864 that Meredith's " Plain Story " was resumed. He worked hard at it during his honeymoon near Southampton, when he announced : " *Rhoda Fleming* is a right excellent story. . . . I have, during the last month of my stay here, written 250 pages." Meanwhile *Vittoria* came to the fore, and in January, 1865, the harassed author wrote from The Cedars, Esher, to Jessopp, and said he had " put aside *Vittoria* (which contains points of grandeur and epical interest) to ' finish off ' *Rhoda Fleming* in one volume, now swollen to two—and Oh ! will it be three ? But this is my D$^{d.}$ D$^{d.}$ D$^{d.}$ uncertain work-manship. You see, I am three days in town, and I am hustled with moving and can't get my shoulders into a place, but the toe of Fate takes me somewhat lower and away I go ; and this is not favourable to composition, though my dear wife does all that she can for me, and would hush the elements, bidding them know me pen in hand. However, I hope in six weeks to be clear of Miss Rhoda, into whose history I have put more work than she deserves. I wrote in saddest spirits, rare with me. Stomach, my friend. I am not in the bracing air which befits me. . . . *Vittoria* is one-third towards completion. Did you see the translation of *Emilia* by Forgues, condensed, in the *Revue des Deux Mondes* ? He has apparently taken to me ; he sent for *Rd. Feverel* to review. A New Edition of *Shagpat*, with an illustration to *Bhanavar* by Sandys, comes out in a month. Marie has, I believe, written fully anent the Son. We mourn and howl over him. When are we four to meet again ? You see, there is a new witch now, and she's a darling."

On 24th April, 1865, writing from Kingston, he was able to inform Jessopp : " *Rhoda Fleming* is just completed (all but the last two chapters). It is 3 vols., six months' work, minus a week or two. Tinsley offers £400 for it. . . . I don't quite like to sell it for that sum. Chapman bids me wait till November. . . . Faguet, in the *Revue des Deux Mondes*, is now translating *Richard Feverel*, and doing it, after a fashion, well."

It is not clear why Chapman and Hall wanted to wait seven months before securing one of Meredith's most readable works in view of the fact that they had already published four of his books, bringing fame to the firm if not large monetary returns at the time. But Meredith could not wait, and so he accepted Tinsley's rather poor offer, and it was from the house in Catherine Street that the novel issued in this year (1865). William Tinsley relates that it had " a very poor sale," and there were apparently no contemporary reviews of any note. It was not until twenty years later that W. E. Henley's able criticism of the book appeared in *The Athenæum*, wherein he advanced the opinion that of " passion deeply felt and poignantly expressed there is such a feast in *Rhoda Fleming* as no other English novelist alive has spread." William Watson, in his *Fiction—Plethoric and Anæmic*, regarded the work as " an ill-constructed and very unequally written story, having some fine scenes and clever, if equally unattractive, character studies." On the other hand again, Arthur Symons judged *Rhoda Fleming* to be Meredith's *chef d'œuvre* in tragedy and said " the plot is woven with singular closeness and deft intricacy." The partial and enthusiastic R. L. Stevenson committed himself to the rather foolish and indemonstrable statement that *Rhoda Fleming* was " the strongest thing in English letters since Shakespeare died, and if the latter had read it he would have jumped and cried : ' Here's a fellow ! ' "

Literary opinion concerning the story is therefore not sharply divided, but the general opinion must be that *Rhoda Fleming*, like so many of the author's books, is of very unequal merit. Meredith himself did not think much of it in later years, and classed it with his personally despised *Poems* of 1851. He wrote to a correspondent in 1883 : " I have neither the 1st vol. of *Poems* nor *Rhoda Fleming*. If you have not seen the books, I would beg you to take my judgment upon them, that they are not worth reading." [1]

That is a judgment no one who cares for Meredith's work will subscribe to, for, despite its many faults, *Rhoda Fleming* is a fine and tragic story of elemental passions, of dwellers of

[1] But Meredith is reported to have said to someone who expressed admiration for the character of Rhoda Fleming : " Don't you love Dahlia more ? I do."

the soil, and may be said to approximate most nearly of all
Meredith's books to the subsequent mental outlook of Thomas
Hardy. But, unfortunately, the events do not always spring
from the actions of the characters, as in Hardy, for the plot is
a most mechanical and obvious affair, with various puppets
invented to oil the springs of this luculent machine. Such is
Sedgett, such is Percy Waring, such is Mrs Lovell, and, most of
all, such is the melodramatic Anthony Hackbut, who was a
temporary reversion to the Dickensian influence and a jumble
of the Jerry and Newman Noggs types. I do not find Algernon
Blancove the lifeless dummy suggested by Henley. Rather is
he a subtle study of a young fool and a fine foil to the acutely
drawn character of Edward Blancove, who was apparently
based, in some respects, upon Meredith's brother-in-law, Edward
Peacock. At any rate, in addition to the same Christian name,
Edward Peacock, like Blancove, studied as a barrister, and was
much addicted to boxing in his chambers.

Concerning the two sisters, it must be admitted that Dahlia
is rather an anæmic creation, and Rhoda an exceedingly unlovable young person, though, no doubt, her contradictory character and devotion to a person loved is a correct presentment
of a certain feminine type. But these girls talk and write the
language of Meredith and not that of the daughters of a farmer
of 1860, when educational advantages for women were negligible,
particularly in rural districts. Therefore it is a sad blow to
probability when Dahlia writes from Italy such an epigrammatic remark as " Even modesty seems too hot a covering for
human creatures here." And Rhoda's language all through is
entirely too fine. The means by which Sedgett meets Dahlia
is left to the imagination, and there are many missing links in
the story. Farmer Fleming is the best drawn character. He
lives, and so does Farmer Eccles. Also Master Gammon, the
champion dumpling eater and immutable rustic Stoic, and his
interlocutress, Mrs Sumfit, who is a " niece " of Mrs Ockenden
of Seaford. She uses the same words as the latter good
woman voices in *The House on the Beach* in the rôle of Mrs
Crickledon : " But if you only knew how—to cook—it spoils
the temper of a woman ! I'd a aunt was cook in a gentleman's
family, and daily he dirtied his thirteen plates—never more nor
never less." Probably Colonel Barclay was drawn from an

officer Meredith saw at Lord's in June, 1863: "Notably a Colonel
M—— amused me, and shall see himself if he looks one day in
a book of mine."

As to the localities of the story, Queen Anne's Farm is said
to have been intended for Byfleet Manor House : Queen Anne's
Hill is in the neighbourhood. "Greatham" is Cobham. When
the action passes to Hampshire, "Fairly Park" is Beaulieu,
and "Warbeach" is probably a picture of Bursledon, where
Meredith stayed, during his honeymoon, when writing this part
of *Rhoda Fleming*. The book is not rich in scenic descriptions,
but there are some memorable sayings within its pages.
"Silence is commonly the slow poison used by those who mean
to murder love." "Old letters are the dreariest ghosts in the
world." "Inferences are like shadows on the wall—they are
thrown from an object, and are monstrous distortions of it."
"She liked the French . . . she liked their splendid boyish-
ness, their unequalled devotion, their merciless intellects; the
oneness of the nation when the sword is bare and pointing to
chivalrous enterprise. . . . She had her imagination of them as
of a streaming banner in the jaws of a storm, with snows among
the cloud-rents and lightning in the chasms."

That is as appropriate for 1918 as 1860. Meredith ever loved
France and Italy best among the nations, and now he voiced
the epic of Italy.

Although the composition of *Vittoria* (or *Emilia in Italy*, as
it was originally entitled) was interrupted by *Rhoda Fleming*—
"I have an English novel of the real story-telling order, that
must roll off soon and precede it," he wrote—the Italian tale
was the immediate sequel, or rather second part, of *Sandra
Belloni* (*Emilia in England*). The earlier work closed with the
departure of the heroine for her passionately loved Italy.
Meredith had long desired to write a romance typifying the spirit
of modern Italy, in the years of revolt 1848 and 1859, and now
was his opportunity, for the subject was topical by the fresh
development of political events in that country. In May, 1864,
he told friends : "I think I shall have to go to Italy, for everybody says *Emilia in Italy* should be forthcoming as speedily as
may be; and I want a little local colour." "I am hard at
work on *Emilia in Italy*; all story . . . no philosopher present :
action, excitement, holding of your breath, chilling horror,

classic sensation. We may hope to see the damsel of the fiery South (no longer tripped and dogged by philosopher or analyst) by late autumn."

In addition to the heroine, Meredith reintroduced in his new work the characters of Wilfrid and Adela Pole, Merthyr Powys, Gambier, and the delightful Pericles, from *Sandra Belloni*. The earlier portion of *Vittoria* was written, amid the happy associations of his engagement and second marriage, in The Old House at Mickleham. He wrote from here to Maxse in the summer of 1864 : " *Vittoria* does not proceed fast, but the matter is of a good sort. I've half a mind to bring you half-a-dozen chapters to read to you. My Marie copies them regularly." And to Hardman : " Sandys has heard the first 150 pages, and says it is extremely interesting, and likely to be by far the best thing I have done."

Then came the interval when *Rhoda Fleming* was completed ; but later in 1865 the author reported to Maxse : " I am very hot upon *Vittoria*. Lewes [1] says it must be a success ; and it has my best writing. Perhaps I have given it too historical a character to please the brooding mind of Fred. But, we shall see. I think one must almost love Italy to care for it and the heroine. There are scenes that will hold you ; much adventure to entertain you ; delicate bits and fiery handling. But there is no tender dissection, and the softer emotions are not kept at half-gasp among slowly moving telescopic objects, with their hearts seen beating in their frames. . . . As regards Hawthorne, little Meredith admits that your strokes have truth. I strive by study of humanity to represent it : not its morbid action. I have a tendency to do that, which I repress ; for, in delineating it, there is no gain. In all my, truly, very faulty works, there is this aim. Much of my strength lies in painting morbid emotion and exceptional positions ; but my conscience will not let me so waste my time. Hitherto, consequently, I have done nothing of mark. But I shall, and *Vittoria* will be the first indication (if not fruit) of it. My love is for epical subjects— not for cobwebs in a putrid corner ; though I know the fascination of unravelling them. . . . Tell me what you think of *Vittoria*. Lewes is enamoured of her. I know the workmanship is good. Further I am unable to judge."

[1] G. H. Lewes, the editor of *The Fortnightly Review*.

THE OLD HOUSE MICKLEHAM, THE HOME OF THE VULLIAMY FAMILY. MEREDITH
COMMENCED "VITTORIA" HERE

Vittoria appeared first as a serial in *The Fortnightly Review* during 1866, and to the editor, Meredith wrote from Kingston Lodge, on 9th December, 1865 :

" MY DEAR LEWES,—I shall be glad to make over to you the use of the copyright of my novel *Vittoria* for issue in *The Fortnightly Review*, in consideration of the sum of £250 : all subsequent rights to the use of it being reserved by myself. . . . If my progress seems to you slow, remember that I am on foreign ground and have to walk warily. I read a good deal of the novel to Madame Venturi the other day, who says the Italian colouring is correct." (She was the great friend of Mazzini.)

Meredith was much away during 1866. In the spring he paid a visit to Monckton Milnes, Lord Houghton, at Fryston Hall, in Yorkshire : this probably came about through the introduction of Swinburne.[1] In June he proceeded to Italy to act as War Correspondent for *The Morning Post* during the campaign between that country and Austria. This expedition enabled him to obtain some additional and valuable local colour for *Vittoria* before it was republished in three-volume form by Chapman and Hall early in 1867 ; this reason and the financial benefit accruing induced Meredith to undertake the work, for he was not by inclination ever a journalist. In fact, he hated the methods of journalism, which were, of course, in absolute antithesis to his own natural style. Consequently his war articles were unnatural and cramped, and rather dull : he cannot be placed in the front rank of war correspondents. His reports of the war were mainly second-hand, as he did not see much of the actual fighting. But he accompanied the Italian army,

[1] Lord Crewe informs me : " Mr George Meredith's signature in the Fryston Visitors' Book is dated 5th April, 1866. Among the guests a few days earlier appear : T. Carlyle (28th March) ; T. H. Huxley (29th March) ; and Henry Reeve (2nd April) ; but it is not likely that any of these stayed on during his visit. The following were no doubt his fellow-guests : A. C. Swinburne (5th April) ; Samuel and Florence Baker (4th April) ; the Bishop of St David's (6th April—Thirlwall) ; Dr and Mrs Vaughan (6th April—then Vicar of Doncaster) ; J. H. Bridges (7th April—the positivist philosopher) ; Henry J. Selwin (7th April—afterwards Sir H. Selwin Ibbetson). I do not think my father ever saw much of Mr Meredith, though he admired his work, in poetry especially."

driving and camping with the troops. Here he was more in his element, and his narratives, written in haste without time for art and elaboration, and therefore quite un-Meredithian, are not without some interest and value.[1] On 22nd June he was with Cialdini's army corps at Ferrara, and on the 30th at Cremona. By 3rd July he was at Bozzolo, the headquarters of the eleventh division of the Italian army, and on the 7th at Torre Malimberti. Finally he accompanied the troops to the new headquarters at Piadena, and thence to Gonzaga, where he saw a good deal of camp life. Proceeding to Treviso and Venice, he left Italy, reaching Marseilles on 24th July. He returned to Austria and Italy in August, and on 10th September wrote to Tom Taylor from the Hotel Cavour, Milan : " Your letter reached me in Vienna. . . . I came over the Semmering to Venice, remained there three days and worked my way through Padua and Vicenza hitherwards, where from the upper windows of the Hotel Cavour I see the white Alps. Italy is where I would live if I had the choice. Here I am so happy that I only want my wife and little ones with me to wish for nothing further." At the Hotel Cavour, Meredith was with his friend H. M. Hyndman, and they used to sit outside the Café Florian engrossed in conversation until the early morning. Hyndman was acting as War Correspondent for *The Pall Mall Gazette*, and also of their party, later, at the Hotel Vittoria, Venice, were George Henty of *The Standard*, and George Augustus Sala of *The Daily Telegraph*. It was here that Meredith and Sala had a tremendous quarrel. Sala did not appreciate Meredith's manner and clever, artificial talk, which was probably above his head. From being on the defensive he assumed the offensive, and finally insulted Meredith in a very gross manner. The latter, very wisely, rose and left the table ; in an actual physical struggle he could have demolished the weakly Sala in an instant, so his forbearance was great. At Vienna, by chance, Meredith first met Leslie Stephen, who in later years was to become his very dear friend.

Christmas, 1866, again found Meredith at The Old House, Mickleham, and the new year witnessed the publication of *Vittoria*, enlarged and improved by much observation and

---

[1] Meredith's *Correspondence from the Seat of War in Italy* is reprinted in the Memorial Edition and Edition-de-Luxe of his works.

knowledge acquired during the author's recent visit to Italy. Unfortunately *Vittoria* was not warmly received by the majority of English critics and readers. *The Spectator*, whilst admitting the merits of the book, took care to say that the author had been " hitherto known as a novelist of some ability and a rather low ethical tone "—this, no doubt, in fond memory of the controversy about *Modern Love*. The fairest notice was in *The Pall Mall Gazette*. Meredith was keenly sensitive to what he considered the dense misapprehension of his contemporaries, and in 1883, many years after the first appearance of *Vittoria*, he spoke in a letter (to a correspondent who desired a copy of this book) of how " the effect of public disfavour has been to make me indifferent to my works after they have gone through their course of castigation, and I have copies of only a few. *Vittoria* happens to be of the number, but my children are now getting old enough to claim what can be preserved of them ; otherwise I would send it. I will, when I am next in town, see whether a copy remains with the publisher."

But be it always remembered that *Vittoria* did receive the immediate appreciation of at least one great contemporary and friend—Swinburne, whose *Song of Italy* (1867) was then finding voice from the same inspirational cause that generated the novel. Swinburne, of course, was passionately enthusiastic for the cause of Italian freedom ; when at Balliol he had a portrait of Mazzini hanging in the place of honour in his room, and before this picture he would declaim verses, with gestures of adoring supplication ; and at this period he wrote an *Ode to Mazzini*, which was found in manuscript after his death. He therefore warmly appreciated Meredith's eulogy of his hero's cause and that wonderful description of Mazzini's personal appearance—particularly the eyes—when, at the outset of the story, the patriot is seen standing on the heights amid " the hanging forests ; the pointed crags ; the gleam of the distant rose-shadowed snows that stretch for ever like an airy host, mystically clad, and baffling the eye as with the motions of a flight toward the underlying purple land."

In reply to his friend's praise, Meredith wrote from Kingston Lodge :

" MY DEAR SWINBURNE,—*Vittoria*, as I am told by Chapman and others, is not liked ; so you may guess what pleasure your

P

letter has given me. For I have the feeling that if I get your praise, I hit the mark. It seems that I am never to touch the public's purse. . . . *Vittoria* passes to the limbo where the rest of my works repose. You alone have hit on the episode of the Guidascarpi. I have not seen or heard another mention of it. I would have carried it into fulness, but the vast machinery pressed on me. My object was not to write the Epic of the Revolt—for that the time is yet too new : but to represent the revolt itself, with the passions animating both sides, the revival of the fervid Italian blood ; and the character of the people : Luigi Suracco, Barto Rizzo, etc. Agostino Balderini is purposely made sententious and humorously conscious of it : Carlo Ammiani is the personification of the youth of Italy of the nobler sort. Laura Piaveni and Violetta d'Isorella are existing contrasts. I am afraid it must be true that the style is stiff ; but a less condensed would not have compassed the great amount of matter. I see the illustrious Hutton of *The Spectator* laughs insanely at my futile effort to produce an impression on his public. I suppose I shall have to give up and take to journalism, as I am now partly doing. Yes ! if you could get a place to say something of *Vittoria* ! Morley stated your suggestions to me, and appeared willing that it should be done in *The Fortnightly*, if your or some such good name fathered the article. But his opinion is that it should be a general review of me : the writer could dwell on the work pleasing him best. There is some doubt about giving a special review of a novel that has appeared in *The Fortnightly* pages. Adieu, my friend. . . .

" Your faithful and affectionate

" GEORGE MEREDITH."

Many years later, in 1902, Meredith wrote to Lady Ulrica Duncombe : " Morley touches an unused chord of vanity in me by saying that Gladstone's doings among Italians caused him to re-read my *Vittoria*, which he calls ' a glorious piece of work,' and as it contains some of my best writing, I can well believe he liked it. . . . How I could pray to show you the scenes of Vittoria's wanderings with Angelo Guidascarpi over the sub-Alpine heights from Brescia to Bormio. I was there when, though liking the Austrians, I burned for Italy. I fancy

I did justice to both sides. The young poet, Laurence Binyon, has written to me for permission to make use of the story of the Guidascarpi for a drama he has been commissioned to compose for Mrs Patrick Campbell."

Meredith was here, for once, a correct critic of his own work. The style of *Vittoria* may be stiff, but it does indeed reanimate the Italian Revolt and present that event not only as an historical picture (somewhat incomplete and episodical certainly), but far more as a pulsating momentary drama of passion and blood. *Vittoria* is not so much a novel of intense characterisation as of incident, thereby differing from the majority of Meredithian studies. Apart from the heroine, Barto Rizzo, and Pericles, the characters are not deeply etched : rather are they suggestive types of their respective nations or provinces. The Italians of Meredith utter ringing phrases : " We Italians of this period are children of thunder, and live the life of a flash. The worms may creep on : the men must die." " My faith is in the young. Through them Italy lives." " In the end, a country true to itself and determined to claim God's gift to brave men will overmatch a mere army, however solid its force." " The Fates are within us. Those which are the forces of the outer world are as shadows to the power we have created within us." These are inspiring words for Italy, as fitting for to-day and the future as when they were penned in the glorious times of Mazzini and Garibaldi.

Vittoria herself—the consummated Emilia who has realised her personality and her ideal—is one of Meredith's most characteristic and living creations, on whom he lavished infinite pains. A very woman, contradictory and, so, essentially feminine, she is compact of patriot, musical artiste, passionate lover, and also coquette—as witness her relations with Wilfrid, her former lover, *en route* to Rivoli, and her meditations on Count Karl and his Austrian and enemy attire : " It is a pretty uniform."

But in recalling *Vittoria* it is always the incidents and not the characters which stand out in high relief from the glorious Italian scenic background. Meredith never painted finer pictures than here. The rather tortuous narrative and harsh dialogues may be forgotten, but never those vivid scenes suddenly thrown upon the imagination with all the quivering movement, living momentariness, and realistic fidelity of the kinematograph. The comparison is not altogether an apt one, but it can stand to convey the impression of restless movement and excitement and drama that pulsate in the scene at La Scala on the eve of the Revolt; in the subsequent flight of Vittoria and her night wanderings with Angelo on the hills of the Austrian border; in the duel in the pass; in Wilfrid's escape from the dungeon-house of Barto Rizzo; in the rioting at Milan; in the vengeance of the Guidascarpi on the betrayer of their sister (worthy of Balzac this); in Carlo's death. These, and many similar pictured episodes, are in the front rank of historical romance and bring Meredith into line with Scott and Dumas, though he gets his effects by a different method. And the same with the wonderful pictures of scenery in this story. Without the long detailed descriptions of the earlier school of romancers, the scene is conveyed by a few bold impressionist strokes. The first paragraph of the book, visualising the landscape from the Motterone, is a blaze of colour. Even the mystery of a dark night is a visible picture :

" Nothing was distinguishable . . . save the high-road winding under rock and forest, and here and there a coursing water in the depths of the ravines, that showed like a vein in black marble. . . . At times they were hooded with the darkness, which came on them as if, as benighted children fancy, their faces were about to meet the shaggy breast of the forest. Rising up to lighter air, they had sight of distant twinklings : it might be city, or autumn weed, or fires of the woodmen, or beacon fires ; they glimmered like eyelets to the mystery of the vast unseen land. Innumerable brooks went talking to the night. . . ."

Vittoria ends finely, and that passage where " she drew her dead husband to her bosom and kissed him on the eyes and the forehead, not as one who had quite gone away from her, but as one who lay upon another shore whither she would come," expresses the same thought to be found in Roden Noel's beautiful little poem, *Dying* :

> They are waiting on the shore
> For the bark to take them home ;

> They will toil and grieve no more ;
> The hour for release hath come.
>
> .   .   .   .   .
>
> Now the shadowy bark is come,
> And the weary may go home.

Vittoria, as we have seen, was the link which drew Meredith and Swinburne together again for a time, with the result that Swinburne came to stay for a few days at Kingston Lodge. In the letters, previously quoted from, Meredith had written :

" Why will you content yourself with only writing generously? Why will you not come and see me ? My wife has constantly asked me how it is that you do not come. Must I make confession to her that I have offended you ? It is difficult for me to arrange for spare evenings in town ; I can't leave her here alone. If we meet, I must quit you only too early. I wonder whether Sandys would invite us to dine with him ; when we might have one of our evenings together, and come to an understanding about future evenings at Kingston. . . ."

" I need not say that my wife will be glad to see you. Has she not fought your battles ? . . . I want you to bring Baudelaire when you come ; and anything you may think of besides in the way of verse. I am being carried off from the Singing. I stand on an inexorable current. I shall look forward to meeting you with great pleasure."

This was in March, 1867, and Swinburne's visit to Kingston Lodge is the last incident of any importance connected with Meredith's life there. He was now anxious to leave, owing to his privacy being invaded by the incoming tide of bricks and mortar engineered by that *bête noire* of authors and artists—the speculative builder. He was worried, too, by the notes of a neighbouring church organ, concerning which he once wrote to William Hardman :

" DEAR SIR,—Am I to be damned to all eternity because I curse at a vile organ now afflicting me with the tune of Jack Robinson, presently to be followed by the 100th Psalm, and the simulation of the groans of a sinner.

" Perhaps you will put this before your reverend friend. But you are not to be damned in the present for permitting the infliction, and not at least commanding a fresh importation of organs into Kingston, and the exit of the old.

"This is a matter for you to reflect upon. I am, dear Sir, even as a Chestnut on the Hob, your bursting

"AUTHOR."

Meredith succeeded in disposing of the remainder of his lease of Kingston Lodge to Mr and Mrs Frederick Jones, who were to become his very valued friends. Mrs Jones's first sight of him, when she went to see over the house, was amid the branches of an apple-tree, where he was gathering the fruit, and from whence he made her a profound bow nearly at the expense of Meredithian equilibrium. Meredith now took Flint Cottage, Box Hill, and his furniture was removed to his new house at the close of 1867, but Christmas he spent with his family, as usual, at The Old House, Mickleham, where he remained for most of January until all was ready at Box Hill. During the last months of 1867 he acted as editor of *The Fortnightly Review*, during the absence in America of John Morley, and Meredith's poems *To J. M.* and *Lines to a Friend Visiting America*, which appeared within its pages, relate to this matter :

Now farewell to you ! you are
One of my dearest, whom I trust :
Now follow you the Western Star,
And cast the old world off as dust.

The beggar-king, November, frets :
His tatters rich with Indian dyes
Goes hugging : we our season's debts
Pay calmly of the Spring forewise.

We send our worthiest ; can no less,
If we would now be read aright—
To that great people who may bless
Or curse mankind : they have the might.

Meredith's poem, *Phaëtôn*, had appeared in *The Fortnightly Review* for September of this year ; and during 1867-1869 he also contributed some lengthy criticisms of new books to this Review, among the works he noticed being the *Poems* of Robert Lytton, *The Reminiscences of a Septuagenarian*, by Countess Brownlow, and Frederic Myers's poem, *St Paul*.

Concerning the affairs of the Review, Meredith wrote to Swinburne, in January, 1868 :

" *The Fortnightly* is no longer in the hands of a company but of a publisher who tries to diminish the expenses as much as he can ; the editor being the chief sufferer. I had to pay for the two poems. *The Halt before Rome* has evidently been omitted from the list of what is due to you. When I see Morley I will state your complaints to him [1] ; but from the sum he gets it's scarcely possible to pay more, without doing so out of his own pocket. It will grieve him as it does me to hear that you are dissatisfied. I received for my *Phaëton* (about 150 lines) £5.

" Do—if it's not possible, as I suppose, to buy a copy of Hugo's poem, lend it to me for a day or two. They say that Garibaldi has replied to it in verse. I propose to come and lunch with you some afternoon. Will you have me ? I will stay from two or three to six, and if we are alone, we will give and take, though I shall take ten times the worth of what I give. I have just got your *Blake*. Mr Conway's notice of it is eulogistic, but whether sufficient and warmly critical I can't yet say. My wife and Willie hope to greet you in the warm spring days."

As Meredith's temporary editorship of *The Fortnightly Review* marks his most noticeable position as a journalist, this will now be a convenient time to relate briefly such facts as are known of that phase of his life.

[1] In a letter to Jessopp, Meredith, speaking of John Morley, said : " He is one of the best of fellows, but an editor, and from an editor you must always be willing to take advice and never no."

CHAPTER IX

MEREDITH AS A JOURNALIST AND PUBLISHER'S READER

APART from his early contributions to *Chambers's Journal* and *Household Words*, and later to *Once a Week*, Meredith did not become a professional journalist until he was thirty-two; it was in 1860 that he joined the staff of *The Ipswich Journal*, and his work for the paper continued for more than eight years at a salary, it is reported, of £200 a year. *The Ipswich Journal*, for one hundred and seventy years the leading paper in East Anglia, was founded in 1720. It was acquired by the Jackson family in 1739, and, passing through several generations, it was eventually owned and edited by Stephen Jackson, who died in 1855. His widow (formerly Miss Catharine Cobbold) married, in 1858, Thomas Eyre Foakes, a barrister of the Inner Temple. Foakes thus became possessed of the then valuable property of *The Ipswich Journal*, which he was supposed to conduct, but in reality he delegated his duties to others. He was a friend of R. S. Charnock, and it was probably through the latter that he became acquainted with Meredith. Later they were neighbours in Surrey; Foakes was on and off with his mother at Walton at the time Meredith lived at Lower Halliford; and when the Foakeses took a house on Weybridge Heath, Meredith often came over to see them from Esher. Arthur Meredith was a playmate of Mrs Foakes's son (by her first husband), now the Rev. F. J. Foakes Jackson, of Jesus College, Cambridge, the distinguished historian.

It thus came about that Meredith obtained regular employment on *The Ipswich Journal*: he was never editor of the paper, as has been stated at times: he could hardly have edited from a cottage in Surrey a journal published in Suffolk. The actual editor was Henry Knights. Meredith contributed every week leading articles and a column summarising the week's news in London and abroad. " I have all the writing on a paper now on my shoulders," he told Mrs Ross in 1860. Every Thursday, too, he went up to Foakes's office, transacted business matters with the London agent of the paper, and completed his " copy " there. Some of his letters to friends are amusingly addressed and dated from " Foakes' Den," on " Foakes' Day " ; and occasionally, when he was going away on holiday, his articles were written for him by one of his intimate companions. Thus he requested Hardman in August, 1862, from Ryde :

" Now, Tuck. Will you do this for me ? Will you write for this week's *Ipswich Journal* a summary of the week's news ; and an article—on America, if you like. Follow the Press. Will you call and see Foakes. And if you don't see him, will you, nevertheless, send your work on Thursday, or take it, to Mr Gough, at 1, New Square, Lincoln's Inn, where you sometimes call and see your Robin on Thursdays ; and if you, perchance, don't see Gough, will you post the aforesaid to H. Knights, Esq., *Ipswich Journal* office, Ipswich. I shall write and post one article, but I sha'n't be up to the latest news.

> " For I'll be in a cabin
> Just 3 feet long, 6 square.
> Just ponder on your Robin,
> The figure of him there.
> I don't care a damn, etc.

" You will immensely oblige me by doing this, and I shall then be able to run over to the Channel Islands."

On another occasion he says :

" But for Black Foakes' Day, common to no Calendar save mine, alas ! I would

> " Willy nilly
> Be off with you a jolly Dance
> To Falmouth, Torquay, and Penzance
> Or Scilly."

And when he went abroad a year later, he said : " I think Morley will do my *Ipswich Journal*." Although he wrote in 1865, " I think I shall give up *The Ipswich Journal* which doesn't (really) pay me," he was still working for it three years later, when he told Hardman :

"I have been, so please your Worship, hard at work, old boy, or I should have written to your honourable Bench. Confound this reminiscence of your greatness under which I lived three whole years ! . . . I was going to write, but I had to manage *The Fortnightly* for Morley during his absence in America, and that with incessant composition and pot-boilers kept my hands tied. But I am training my toes (first and second of right foot) to indite epistles and *Ipswich Journal*."

It is not possible, of course, to trace and identify for certain many of Meredith's contributions to the Suffolk paper. Mr Frederick Dolman went to some pains to examine the files, and printed some extracts which undoubtedly bear the impress of Meredith's hand.[1] This was, presumably, the gentleman alluded to by Meredith in a remark he made to Mr Clodd : "I drifted into journalism, my first venture being in the shape of a leader on Lord John Manners, which I sent to *The Standard*. Very little came of that, but I got work on one of your Suffolk papers, *The Ipswich Journal*, which kept me going. Some ghoul has lately threatened to make search for these articles ; may the Commination Service be thundered in his ears ! "

The most interesting feature of Meredith's articles for *The Ipswich Journal*, a strong Conservative paper, was the facile manner in which he, a lifelong Radical of advanced views, advocated Tory principles. It would be amusing if one could establish for certain that he wrote the article attacking Gladstone for ceding the Ionian Islands to Greece, which article caused a great fluttering and outcry in the Radical dovecotes of Ipswich in 1862. It seems certain, however, that Meredith, Champion of Liberty, perverted his principles most egregiously for journalistic requirements or salary by supporting the cause of the South and the Slave Owners, during the American Civil War, in the articles he wrote for *The Ipswich Journal*. Thus :

"Alas ! with a President who cannot write grammar, and generals who lie to the public and snarl among themselves, and

[1] *George Meredith as a Journalist.* *The New Review,* March, 1893.

who all turn tail to the foe, what can the North do but be abject and ask for a master."

And alluding to John Bright's support of the North, he proceeded :

" Mr Bright, *par exemple*, spoke at the Birmingham Chamber of Commerce on Tuesday. His speech contained the necessary ' vindication ' of the North. Their blockade is perfect, wonderful, their greatness should inspire fear, and so forth. We dub him Yankee and bid him good-bye."

A curious article by Meredith was that in which he drew a not very obvious analogy between George III. and Alexandra, then the youthful Princess of Wales :

" George III. would have been the most unpopular Sovereign that ever sat on the throne if he had not dined at one o'clock, had a siesta afterwards, and gone to bed at ten. He was constantly doing things which the nation did not like, and the greater part of his reign was dark with all sorts of disasters. But people forgave him because he conformed to the rules of ordinary life and showed himself, at least at dinner time, to be as other men are. Not the least effective source of the astounding popularity of the Princess of Wales is something of the same kind. She is very comely and graceful, and has the intrinsic attractiveness of youth, and these make her loved. But above and beyond these things are all the stories which reach the popular ear of her thorough geniality, her enjoyment of spectacle and gaiety, and the interest taken by her in everything which interests other people. . . .

" Our ladies wish, they tell us, and we can more decidedly say that every man living who is not a milliner in spirit devoutly desires, that the Princess Alexandra will relieve them from servitude to the Crinoline Empress. The introduction of the crinoline has been in its effects morally worse than a *coup d'état*. It has sacrificed more lives ; it has utterly destroyed more tempers ; it has put an immense division between the sexes. It has obscured us, smothered us, stabbed us."

Finally, the following extract, relating to the rumour that

Lord Palmerston was to figure as co-respondent in a divorce suit, is distinctly Meredithian in phrase :

" But rumour is a wicked old woman. Cannot something be done to stop her tongue ? Surely one who is an octogenarian might be spared ? We are a moral people, and it does not become us to have our Premier, agile though he be, bandied about derisively like a feathered shuttlecock on the reckless battledore of scandal. . . . We are indeed warned that nothing less than an injured husband has threatened and does really intend to lay an axe to the root of our Premier's extraordinary success, in a certain awful court. We trust that rumour again lies, but that she is allowed to speak at all, and that men believe her and largely propagate her breathings, is a terrible comment on the sublime art of toasting the ladies as prosecuted by aged juveniles in office. It is a retribution worthy of Greek tragedy. We are determined to believe nothing before it is proved. It is better to belong to the laughed-at minority who decline to admit that the virtue has gone out of our Premier than to confirm a shameful scandal, the flourishing existence of which is sufficient for our moral."

It is curious that the other paper, *The Morning Post*, for which Meredith wrote a good deal, should also have been of Conservative views. He seems to have commenced his work for this journal in 1862, for he told Mrs Ross in February : " By the way, I write for *The Morning Post* now at odd hours, which pays your poet." As we have seen, Meredith went to the seat of war in Italy, in 1866, as the special correspondent of this paper, and his articles were not particularly noteworthy. He had no military knowledge and no sympathy with a soldier's outlook and temperament. Therefore he could not get to the heart of things, and his war articles were merely narratives of what he saw with his eyes or heard by report. After he left the Italian army he seems to have realised that he was wasting his time as " a correspondent abroad." He wrote from Milan in September, 1866 :

" In all probability I shall be back in Venice for the fêtes, if the delay is not great. *The Morning Post* should have an account of them. Perhaps Borthwick will insist on my doing the work, and I shall not be sorry; for what a correspondent wants is something to describe, and not to continue writing about nothing. . . . I hope very much that *The Times* will take me on. In a settled position (I wish it were in Italy), and with command of news, or the sources of it, I believe I should show the requisite judgment."

Apparently *The Times* project came to nothing, but two years later he was working regularly for another important newspaper. He wrote to Jessopp, on 22nd October, 1868 : " At present I am tied to the pecuniary pen and am not a bright galley-slave. . . . I write almost every week in *The Pall Mall Gazette.* Do you see it ? And did you perchance see the poem of *Phaéton* done in Galliambics in *The Fortnightly Review* of last September a year back ? To my mind they are near on the mark, but as the public is not near it I might as well have missed."

As I have said, Meredith took up journalism merely as a means of making money, and to that extent it served his purpose for the years 1860-1868. But his heart was never in the work, and his results were commonplace and mechanical. His attitude to journalism, and its payment *pro tanto* a column, is thus aptly expressed :

" Above all things I detest the writing for money. . . . Journalism for money is Egyptian bondage. No slavery is comparable to the chains of hired journalism. My pen is my fountain—the key of me ; and I give myself, I do not sell. I write when I have matter in me and in the direction it presses for, otherwise not one word ! " [1]

Meredith secured the position of publisher's reader of manuscripts as a means of making money also in the first place, and indeed it was the staple source of his income for thirty-five years. But he liked this employment much better than journalism ; he was very painstaking and thorough with the work, as will be seen, though his judgments in literary and business matters were sometimes wrong, which was only to be expected when so original a stylist and so highly strung a temperament essayed the rôle of critic and censor.

It was in 1860 that Meredith succeeded John Forster as

---

[1] *The Tragic Comedians,* chap. vii.

literary adviser to the firm of Chapman and Hall, who had published his *Shaving of Shagpat* and *Richard Feverel*. In the early years of his engagement he entered his opinion of the manuscripts he had read—and they comprised nearly all those sent to the publishers—in an official book, which is, of course, carefully preserved. Mr B. W. Matz quoted many extracts from this volume in the interesting article, *George Meredith as Publisher's Reader*, which appeared in *The Fortnightly Review* in 1910. It is possible, therefore, to recover some of the judgments Meredith passed upon the early work and unformed style of writers who have since become famous, and piquant comments upon both those who attained success and those who did not. The first recorded manuscript he read, in August, 1860, was *The Two Damsels : a Spanish Tale*, by C. M. O'Hara, which he dismissed as " Childish : return without comment." Next, Blanchard Jerrold's *The Fleet that brought the Pudding Home* was described as "poor, genial stuff"; and Whyte Melville's *Market Harborough* as " of the order of *Soapy Sponge's Sporting Tour*."

In the following year he performed his famous *faux pas* of the reiterated rejection of *East Lynne*. The story had first appeared as a serial in *The New Monthly Magazine*, 1860-1861, then owned and edited by Harrison Ainsworth, who, as a personal friend of Mrs Henry Wood, did his best to further publication of the work in book form, for he fully perceived the future prospects of popular success in *East Lynne* and its author. He called twice upon Chapman and Hall to urge the advisability of their accepting the manuscript, but " Opinion emphatically against it " was the report of their Reader, George Meredith. Ainsworth pressed the Chapmans to look over the story personally. They did so, and then took the unusual course of returning the book to the Reader for renewed consideration. But Meredith, whose supercilious didactics must ever be emulously envied by the scholastic profession, coolly ignored his employers' wishes, and, being perfectly independent and unmoved by introductions and recommendations of any work, again rejected *East Lynne*, thereby entailing the loss of a vast sum of money to Chapman and Hall. After refusal by Smith and Elder the work was acquired by Richard Bentley, and proved to be one of his most profitable speculations. Since that time considerably over a million copies have been sold. As Ainsworth said to Mrs Henry Wood on one occasion : " Chapman and Hall have never ceased to repent . . . they publish a work that has no chance of success . . . and when such a book as *East Lynne* is brought under their notice they pass it over. I was never more amazed than when Frederic Chapman told me they had returned it to you." Curiously enough, *East Lynne* was started on its triumphant career of success by the review in *The Times* (25th January, 1862) written by Samuel Lucas, the editor of *Once a Week*. Meredith was very indignant at his friend's apostasy from his views, and wrote to the recalcitrant reviewer thus :

" I have read *East Lynne*, and also your notice of it. I have read the latter with almost less pleasure than the novel. It is (the novel) in the worst style of the present taste. What a miserable, colourless villain, Levison : the husband a respectable stick : the heroine a blotched fool : all the incidents forced —that is, not growing out of the characters : and the turning-point laughable in its improbability. Why do you foster this foul taste ? There's action in the tale and that's all."

This was certainly severe criticism, particularly as some of its strictures might well have been applied to the novel, *Rhoda Fleming*, that the writer was then evolving. But Meredith never would admit any merit in Mrs Henry Wood's books. He apparently disliked a certain type of rather sensational novels by women, for this same year, 1862, both *Villiers*, by Ouida, and *Isola*, by Mrs Lynn Linton, were disdainfully marked " Decline " without any reason being given. His disapproval of Mrs Lynn Linton's views continued to the end, and as late as 1894 he wrote of one of her manuscripts : " Very sour in tendency, hard in style. All forced, and exemplify the author's abhorrence of the emancipation of young females from their ancient rules. She has been doing this sort of thing in all directions." [1]

On the other hand, he was always ready to appreciate the unpretentious and conscientious work of young women of literary ability. He would give them much good advice, and though he might not accept the manuscript under consideration, by pointing out its faults he encouraged them to try again and achieve

[1] Presumably he was annoyed in particular by Mrs Lynn Linton's *The Girl of the Period*.

better things. A case in point is that of Miss Jennett
Humphreys. Meredith wrote to her from 193, Piccadilly, the
office of Chapman and Hall, on 22nd November, 1864 :

" The chief fault in your stories is the redundancy of words
which overlays them ; and the chief hope visible in them is the
copious youthful feeling running throughout. Your characters
do not speak the language of nature, and this is specially to be
charged against them when they are under strong excitement
and should most do so. Nor are the characters very originally
conceived, though there is good matter in the old Welshman,
C. Rees. Your defect at present lies in your raw feeling. Time
will cure this, if you will get the habit of looking resolutely at
the thing you would portray, instead of exclaiming about it and
repeating yourself without assisting the reader on in any degree.
We certainly think that you are a hopeful writer, and possibly
we have been enough outspoken to encourage you to believe us
sincere."

In another letter he continued :

" You speak of the exclamatory style as being, you think,
essentially and naturally feminine. If you will look at the
works of the writer of *Adam Bede*, you will see that she, the
greatest of female writers, manifests nothing of the sort. It
is simply a quality of youth, and you by undertaking to study
will soon tame your style. Interjections are commonly a sign
of raw thought, and of vagrant emotion—a literary hysteria
to which women may be more subject than men ; but they can
talk in another tongue, let us hope. We are anxious that you
should not be chagrined by any remarks that we have made.
There is real promise in your work : but remember that the
best fiction is fruit of a well-trained mind. If hard study
should kill your creative effort, it will be no loss to the world
or you. And if, on the contrary, the genius you possess should
survive the process of mental labour, it will be enriched and
worthy of a good rank. But do not be discouraged by what we
say ; and do not listen to the encomiums of friends.[1] Read

[1] In later years Meredith said to Mr Clodd : " Whenever I can I give
honest praise, I will not stint it, although I remind those who hunger
after it that, if they will be drenched with honey, they must expect the
wasps."

the English of the Essayists ; read de Stendhal (Henri Beyle) in French ; Heinrich Zschokke in German (minor tales). Learn to destroy your literary offspring remorselessly until you produce one that satisfies your artistic feeling."

At this date Meredith had adopted the plan of sometimes giving a personal interview to the authors whose work he was considering, and verbally express his opinions and criticisms. He told Hardman, in July, 1864 : " I said to Chapman's I have done much, will do more : will be in Piccadilly three afternoons in the week ; will write all your letters anent MSS. ; will occasion-ally, when imperative, see the authors (my name not being given) and so forth ; thus, as Tuck sees, becoming a chief person, and at no great cost, and with suitable addition to pay. It should be £300. It shall not be less than £250."

It thus came about that Meredith offered to give Miss Humphreys a personal interview after she had sent in another manuscript, which got mislaid.

" 193, PICCADILLY, LONDON, W.
" June 15th, 1866.

" The Reader of Miss Jennett Humphreys's tale of Anwyl Anwyl presents his compliments to her, feeling profoundly guilty—for the blame of this long delay rests entirely upon him. He put the MS. aside, after he had read it ; his intention was to write a long chapter on what to write, blot, and avoid. He can say in personal extenuation that Miss Humphreys could not possibly have made any ' commercial ' use of the tale ; and that if she had published it, it would have done harm to her reputation.

" The Reader is in town on Thursday next, and if it shall please Miss Humphreys to listen to a few of his critical objections to her style, perhaps he may be enabled to do her more good in that direction than if he attempted to write them down. There-fore should she be willing to call at 193, Piccadilly, on Thursday at four P.M., he will endeavour penitently to repair his shameful behaviour. The truth is, he did nothing at all, because of his having intended to do so much.

" If Miss Humphreys should prefer to avoid vocal criticism it shall be written down, but it will possibly not be so effective,

Q

and it may seem more severe. In making this proposal, the
Reader has taken an unusual course by which he trusts to be
able to show his desire to expiate his previous carelessness. It
needs hardly to be said that obscurity is his most comfortable
cloak, whenever he undertakes the thankless duty of looking at
a MS."

Miss Humphreys, accepting the invitation for a verbal
chastening, replied : " She needs no persuading to convince her
of the value, as well as the exceptional favour, of freely-spoken
criticism. Her appreciation of it may be measured by the fact
of her agreeing to throw aside her own cloak and receive a face-
to-face castigation . . .; and she only hopes she shall have sense
and ability enough to derive the benefit from the interview the
Reader kindly intends." Miss Humphreys duly kept the appointment, and her account of the interview incidentally gives
an interesting pen-portrait of Meredith at the age of thirty-
eight, just before he went out to Italy as War Correspondent :

" He was studiously polite to me ; and I have a memory of a
man dressed with great care—leading even to lavender-coloured
kid gloves—his hair of chestnut colour and lying in curls, or
waves, round a handsome face.[1] What he said was patiently
said, my faults being pointed out, and his judgment over what
I had done being several times repeated—' It will not go to
the public.' I asked if I might know to whom I was indebted,
and he said : ' Excuse me '—which, of course, I was bound to
do. We had our talk in a small glass-walled office, enclosed off
from the ground floor at 193, Piccadilly. I brought away my
bundle of MSS. myself, in spite of Mr Meredith's polite desire
that I would let him have it posted."

Not until over forty years later did Miss Humphreys learn
the real identity of the Publisher's Reader. It is curious proof
of how little known George Meredith was in his meridian to find
another author of note apparently quite unaware of his exist-

[1] Curiously enough, the Rev. F. J. Foakes Jackson, who was only
six years old at the time he saw Meredith, when the latter came to
visit his stepfather, T. E. Foakes, of *The Ipswich Journal*, says he mainly
recalls " the yellow dogskin gloves and the reddish whiskers of the
novelist ; the odd thing is that I have any recollections at all, as I
certainly was never given to understand that he was a famous man."

GEORGE MEREDITH
ABOUT THE AGE OF THIRTY-FOUR

ence and confounding his name with the literary pseudonym of
the first Earl of Lytton. Writing to Miss Humphreys in 1871
(at the time *Harry Richmond* was appearing in *The Cornhill
Magazine*), Harrison Ainsworth said : " I fancy the gentleman
whom you saw at Chapman and Hall's must have been Mr Owen
Meredith. I do not know him, but I have heard that he was
their Reader." [1] Harrison Ainsworth's ignorance of the identity
of Chapman and Hall's Reader was the more remarkable as this
firm published nine of Ainsworth's original novels in the years
1861-1870, and the Chapmans were his personal friends. But,
no doubt, Ainsworth's work was accepted without being submitted to the Reader. This is confirmed by the fact that Meredith informed me that he had only read Ainsworth's *Tower of
London* and *Old St Paul's,* and was not acquainted with their
author. It was strange they never met, because from 1871
until his death in 1882 Ainsworth lived principally at Reigate,
and he shared Meredith's love of Surrey scenery, long walks,
good cookery, and old wine. It was another odd coincidence
that Mrs Henry Wood, Mrs Lynn Linton, and Ouida all commenced their literary careers in magazines edited by Ainsworth,
and owed much to his help and advice ; and that the works of
these three ladies should have been unfailingly disliked and
rejected by Meredith when they were before his judgment-seat
of Publisher's Adviser. Evidently the literary opinions of
Meredith and Ainsworth were not in unison. The latter had
been a publisher and magazine owner for many years, and he
could exactly gauge what was likely to be popular and a financial
success. Meredith was, in reality, not suited for his employment. Although his literary judgments may have been correct
in a critical, academic sense, that was not what the publishers
exactly wanted. He was not able to see what would sell well
and be talked about, unless we assume in high alternative that
he deliberately placed what he regarded as the pure interests
of literature before the commercial ones of his employers. And
yet no great writer ever learnt by bitterer personal experience
than he what the public liked or disliked.

Meredith refused another subsequently famous book, *Erewhon,*
by Samuel Butler, with the comment : " Will not do." The

[1] Arthur Symons, writing in *Time,* 1885, thought a novel called *Mary
Bertrand,* by " Francis Meredith," was the work of George Meredith.

author did not bear any malice, and has related how he " took the book to Messrs Chapman and Hall on May 1st, 1871, and on their rejection of it, under the advice of one who has attained the highest rank among living writers, I let it sleep till I took it to Mr Trübner early in 1872. As regards its rejection by Messrs Chapman and Hall, I believe their reader advised them quite wisely. . . . I hope, if I had been their reader and the book had been submitted to myself, I should have advised them to the same effect."

On the other hand, Meredith perceived the promise in the earliest work of William Black, then about twenty years of age, and wrote : " In its way very good. . . . The author's mind evinces strong sense and poetic perceptions ; he has a remarkably clear style, and a power of giving soft pathetic touches, which I commend. He does not know much of life, nor has he the proper artistic feeling for the development of his characters in an interesting way. Write very encouragingly. Don't lose sight of him."

In this same year, 1861, he delivered another perceptive judgment on *Poems* by Edwin Arnold : " I should say this man will do something. . . . He should wait till he has composed a poem likely to catch the public ear. There is no distinct original mark in these poems : not enough to rely on."

The most interesting event of Meredith's Readership was in connection with the commencement of the literary career of Thomas Hardy, who was subsequently, in the eyes of the world, to be his greatest rival ; though, of course, any comparison or rivalry between the two great writers was as absurd a suggestion as that which the previous generation had attempted to establish in the matter of the alleged competition between Dickens and Thackeray. Both pairs of men were distinctively original, and could stand alone as contemporaries of equal merit without any invidious comparisons. In December, 1868, Mr Hardy, then twenty-eight years of age, sent to Chapman and Hall a manuscript entitled *The Poor Man and the Lady*. Meredith, although he did not pass the story for acceptance, saw promise in it, and Hardy was invited, in the manner of Miss Humphreys, to come and see the Reader, which he did, and duly received much good advice : but the advice and sage precepts were not put into practice by Meredith himself in his own books. Mr Hardy has told me that he had his interview with Meredith in a back room at 193, Piccadilly, a house, now pulled down, which stood on the site of the Institute of Painters ; and that Meredith said a novel—or first novel—should have a " plot." Understanding from Meredith's further remarks that he meant what is, or was, called a " sensational " plot, Hardy proceeded to write *Desperate Remedies*—" a story quite foreign to my own instincts, and which therefore, oddly enough, owed its existence to Meredith." However, the work was not published by Chapman and Hall, but by Tinsley, in 1871 ; and, unfortunately, *The Poor Man and the Lady* was never published at all. This first story of Hardy's is said to have been in marked satiric vein. Twenty-six years later, when both Hardy and Meredith were present at a meeting of the Omar Khayyám Club at the Burford Bridge Hotel, in July, 1895, they made interesting reference to their early association. Hardy described his rejected first story as " Very wild," whereupon Meredith called out : " Promising." Hardy went on to say that if it had not been for the encouragement he then received from Meredith, he should never have devoted himself to literature, and that from the time of their first meeting he and Meredith had been friends.

Although not intimate friends, they had a warm regard for each other. Meredith wrote to Frederick Greenwood, in 1892 : " Hardy is one of the few men whose work I can read. I had always great hope of him." And after reading *Tess of the D'Urbervilles* he continued : " The work is open to criticism, but excellent and very interesting. All of the Dairy Farm held me fast. But from the moment of the meeting again of Tess and Alec, I grew cold, and should say that there is a depression of power, up to the end, save for the short scene on the plain of Stonehenge. If the author's minute method had been sustained, we should have had a finer book. It is marred by the sudden hurry to round the story. And Tess, out of the arms of Alec into (I suppose) those of the lily necked Clare, and on to the Black Flag waving over her poor body, is a smudge in vapour— she at one time so real to me." Hardy visited Box Hill in June, 1905, when Meredith told Mr Gosse : " I am always glad to see him, and have regrets at his going ; for the double reason that I like him, and am afflicted by his twilight view of life." Two months before he died, Meredith wrote to Hardy on the publication of *The Dynasts* ; and when his friend lay dead Hardy penned that fine appreciation in verse, *George Meredith*, wherein he recalled their first meeting at 193, Piccadilly and their last at Box Hill :

Forty years back, when much had place
That since has perished out of mind,
I heard that voice and saw that face.

He spoke as one afoot will wind
A morning horn ere men awake ;
His note was trenchant, turning kind.

He was of those whose wit can shake
And riddle to the very core
The counterfeits that Time will break.

Of late, when we two met once more,
The luminous countenance and rare
Shone just as forty years before.

So that, when now all tongues declare
His shape unseen by his green hill,
I scarce believe he sits not there.

No matter.   Further and further still
Through the world's vaporous vitiate air
His words wing on—as live words will.

Another writer who had a personal interview with Meredith at the publishers' office was George Gissing, and he related how Meredith pointed out the faults and merits, and made suggestions for improvement, of his manuscript, which was published under the title of *The Unclassed* in 1884.   This was Gissing's second book, and in his next work, *Isabel Clandon*, 1886, he received even greater help from Meredith, who examined the manuscript two or three times and caused it to be considerably reduced in length.

Olive Schreiner also had interviews with Meredith about *The Story of an African Farm*.   On 2nd May, 1882, the manuscript had been marked : " Return to author for revision," and this being done, it was accepted on 10th August.

Contrariwise, he was not much struck by John Oliver Hobbes's first book, *Some Emotions and a Moral* (1891), which he judged : " Written with some power to exhibit the emotions of the sex

—mainly in the form of whims." And concerning *The Heavenly Twins*, by Sarah Grand, he wrote :

" The author is a clever woman, and has ideas ; for which reason she is hampered at present in the effort to be a novelist. Her characters have ideas, but they are not made to express them, and are incapable of helping the story to move. Such story as there is pertains to their individual fortunes. There is no main current ; Evadne would kill a better work with her heaviness. It matters little what she does—she has her ideas ; the objection is the tedium in the presentation of her. The writer should be advised to put this MS. aside until she has got the art of driving a story. She has ability enough, and a glimpse of humour here and there promises well for the future—if only she will practise, without thought of publishing, until she can narrate, and sketch credible human creatures without harping on such traits as she gives them."

In 1889 he did not strongly advise the acceptance of the Letters of Jane Welsh and Thomas Carlyle. He said : " The authenticity will hardly be contested. But a proof of genuineness that rests so much on a capitulation of domestic trivialities is not a recommendation. . . . I much fear that a chorus of reviewers would cause the public to shun this collection.[1] The little in them concerning Carlyle would plead but poorly on their behalf. . . . I wish I could give a better report. My expectations were lively, and I am disappointed. But if you can just see your way to remuneration, I shall be glad."

Another notable rejection by Meredith was George Bernard Shaw's early work. The first, *Immaturity*, he curtly dismissed with " No." Mr Shaw has given me an interesting report of the matter, and his own views on Meredith, in these words :

" *Immaturity* was my first novel, written in 1879. It was refused by every publisher in London, as were its four successors ; and, unlike them, it remains in MS. (if the mice have not eaten it) to this day. George Meredith shared the guilt of its refusal with John Morley, who read for Macmillan. I fear he repeated the crime with the other four—certainly with *Cashel Byron's Profession*. All my novels were refused everywhere. I have

[1] An example of how badly Meredith judged the public taste.

described the business in my preface to *The Irrational Knot* (the second of the five). For nine years I was rated as unprintable ; and it was only in the case of this hopelessly old-fashioned and ' literary ' *Immaturity* that there was any hesitation. The better I wrote the less chance I had.

" Once, when I had achieved the feat of speaking in the open air at Trafford Bridge (Manchester) for 4 hours at one stretch, a plot was laid by Henry Salt, Clement Shorter, and others, to take me down to Box Hill on the understanding that I should start talking the moment I entered the house and not let George Meredith get a word in edgeways. But it never came off ; and I did not make the pilgrimage and the acquaintance until shortly before his death. I had thought of approaching him in 1898-9, when I lived on Hindhead, through Grant Allen ; but I found that G. A. had given up going to Box Hill. . . . I valued Meredith as a poet and as a cosmopolitan *bel esprit* of a certain mid-Victorian type (represented by Dilke, Laurence Oliphant, Hyndman, etc.); but politically he was a Rip Van Winkle in the Socialist movement ; and the literary life in the Surrey hills was contrary to all my rules of conduct : even as gifted a man as Meredith could not live it as long as he did without becoming a walking anachronism. *Diana of the Crossways* is fifty years behind *Our Mutual Friend* : its social values were all out of date. That is why so many people who, like myself, have a very high opinion of his natural power, can read nothing of his except the poems and *Shagpat*.

" G. Bernard Shaw."

It is a pity that the project of a war of words, if ever seriously contemplated, between Meredith and Shaw was not brought to action. The Lord of Box Hill would certainly have been taken aback by a visitor who dominated the talk and who did not wait upon *his* words.

W. T. Stead also submitted his early literary attempts to Meredith, without much success. He related :

" I had the good fortune to know George Meredith for the last twenty-five years of his life. He was a true friend, not less faithful in criticism than he was cordial in his approbation. Of the former, I remember well the neat way in which he put me

out of conceit with my first attempt to write a story. . . . I
sent him my little effort with fear and trembling. My trepida-
tion was not without warrant. ' I have read *From the Old World
to the New*,' he wrote. ' Some of the characters are interesting
and well drawn. One of them especially reminds me of Cecil
Rhodes. But if any of your friends tell you that he likes the
story as a story, *don't believe him* ! ' How delightfully Meredithian ! Mr Meredith told me once that he had a novel on
the stocks in which Lord Morley, Mr Fred Greenwood, and I
were treated as types of our profession. It was to be called
The Journalist. But it was probably never finished." [1]

Concerning the question of the desirability or the reverse of
introducing living people and actual names into works of fiction,
there is an amusing note in Chapman and Hall's book, 1861, relating to a manuscript entitled *George Meredith : a Tale of the
Merchant Service*, whereof the Reader commanded : " Pray,
speak to this man concerning the impropriety of taking living
names as titles for works of fiction." This was certainly an in-
genious complaint from an author who had pilloried his own
relations and used their Christian names in *Evan Harrington*
the year previously, and who, as we have seen, habitually drew
his characters from his personal friends, with but very trans-
parent disguise. Meredith was the most inconsistent of men,
and his adverse literary judgments on others were generally
applicable to his own faults of style and construction.

I am reminded of a curious coincidence in names by the
following note of William Hardman's in 1862 :—

" Meredith insisted upon giving me a copy of *Over the Straits*,
by Mrs Meredith—no relation of his whatever—but he gets all
books published by Chapman and Hall for nothing, being in some
way connected with that firm. This Mrs Louisa Meredith resides in Tasmania, and wrote to our friend asking if he was not
her husband's long lost brother ; she was with difficulty persuaded that this was not the case. Her letters were impassioned
and full of entreaty ; she and her husband were dying to take
him into their arms. At last our friend favoured them with a
sketch of his life and origin by way of explanation. This

---

[1] It has been stated that the manuscript of this work was burnt at
the author's request, and in his presence, by Dr H. G. Plimmer.

settled the doubts, and extinguished the hopes, of the Tasmanian Merediths, and the correspondence terminated with a hope that if they were not relations they might at least be friends. I should not say ' terminated,' for he still hears occasionally from Mrs Meredith."

This colonial Mrs Louisa Anne Meredith thus bore the same names as George Meredith's aunt, Louisa, who became Mrs Read and the original of the Countess de Saldar, and his grandmother, Anne Mitchell (Mrs Mel.). But more curious still is the fact that this Mrs Meredith, of Tasmania, dedicated another of her books, *Loved and Lost*, to her son, Owen Meredith. It is surely a strange coincidence that her son should have borne the name adopted by the second Lord Lytton—the person who was so often confused with George Meredith and even claimed by ridiculous rumour to be his half-brother.

The most eventful incident of Meredith's work as Publisher's Reader is also connected with family history. After the death of his wife, Catherine Meredith, my grandfather, Sir S. B. Ellis, married again, and by his second wife, Louisa Drayson (sister of General A. W. Drayson, R.A., also an author of note and a pioneer in spiritualism), had a son, the late Sir Alfred Burdon Ellis, K.C.B., Colonel of the West India Regiment, who died of fever during the Sofa Expedition in West Africa, in 1894. My uncle, in addition to his great military ability, had very considerable literary gifts, and wrote equally well both as historian and novelist. About thirty-six years ago he sent some of his first works to Chapman and Hall, and the favourable reports of Meredith procured their publication. The Reader was apparently quite unaware that Colonel—or rather Major—Ellis was a connection of his own, and a son of his " Major Strike," for since the days of *Evan Harrington* there had been no communication with the Ellis family ; but he had the greatest admiration for Alfred Ellis's books. Meredith was always interested in works dealing with travel and foreign countries. Consequently he perceived the value of my uncle's detailed studies of the native races of West Africa, and the immense vocabularies Ellis compiled of the Ewe, Tshi, and Yoruba tongues. *The Land of Fetish*, 1883, was the first work he accepted. *The History of the First West India Regiment* he

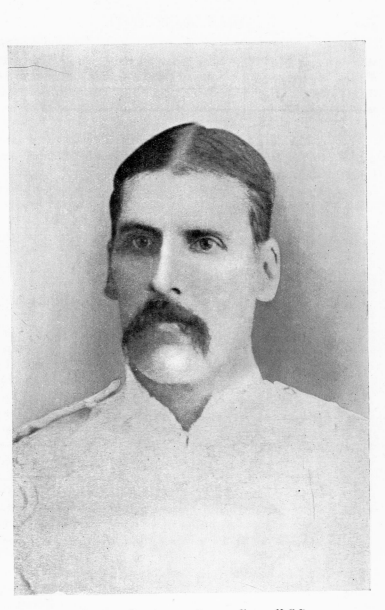

COLONEL SIR ALFRED BURDON ELLIS, K.C.B.

sent back to the author with suggestions, which were adopted before the book was published in 1885. *The History of the Gold Coast* Meredith said was written with A. B. Ellis's " plain but excellent pen. I should be of an opinion that it would be a standard history of the Gold Coast and our possessions about there. It is the one book on the subject." [1]

Later, my uncle wrote a series of short stories based on his experiences in Africa. *South African Sketches*, 1887, proved very successful, but *West African Stories*, 1890, brought trouble to author and Reader and publishers. In his original report of *West African Stories* Meredith seems to have perceived that his unknown " step-cousin " had followed his example and drawn some sketches too markedly from living characters, for he wrote : " Good, charged with local colour : not attractive to readers of romance, but curious, and the author's name as an authority with regard to those parts should help the book. If accepted, it must be with the stipulation that *Mrs Fitzgibbon* be omitted. It is a *sine qua non*." I have the holograph manuscripts of my uncle's works, and *Mrs Fitzgibbon* is the tragic story of an adventuress in Sierra Leone, which ends with the murder of one of her lovers by a jealous rival for the lady's favours. The tale was deleted from the collection, and it was unfortunate that Meredith did not also ask for the elimination of another character sketch, entitled *James Peacock*, the story of a West African trader who by sharp practices acquired a large fortune : for, on the publication of *West African Stories*, a retired West African trader named James Pinnock conceived this sketch to represent his own history (the alliteration in the names gave reason for this supposition), and he brought an action for libel against the publishers, Chapman and Hall.

The case was heard on 8th December, 1891, before Mr Justice Denman. Sir Charles Russell (afterwards Lord Chief Justice) was leading counsel for the plaintiff, and Mr Asquith, the late

---

[1] As lately as 1914, Sir Hugh Clifford, Governor of the Gold Coast Colony, approached me on the question of the republication of my uncle's books, *The Tshi-speaking People* and *The Ewe-speaking People*, at the cost of the Government of the Gold Coast. Sir Hugh Clifford said : " I should be glad to see these works made a text-book for all my administrative officers in the Colony and its Dependencies." So Meredith's judgment of the political value of these books is still justified.

Premier, for the defendants.   It transpired that Major Ellis had seen Pinnock in Brighton, and that their respective wives had some slight acquaintance ; but when Ellis and Pinnock were travelling out on the same steamer to Africa, in 1888, it seems the Major did not appear to care for the plaintiff's company.

On behalf of the author it was urged that no personal description was intended, and that James Peacock's face was described as being of the pugilistic type, which could not be said of the plaintiff's.   On the other hand, it was stated that a Mr Ditchfield had related the facts of Pinnock's life to Ellis, who observed it was a marvel and that a good deal could be done with it to turn it into a good story.

The examination of Lieutenant-Colonel Ellis, taken on commission in Barbados, was then read.   He said *James Peacock* was pure fiction, the ground plan of the story being made up of two stories current in West Africa.   The first he heard at Quittah, in 1878 ; and the second at Bonny, in 1879.   In order to work in both stories he had to bring his " hero " from Sierra Leone to Bonny—a place he knew and could give local colouring to.   The name of James Peacock he had taken from an old Army List ; all the other incidents in the story were imaginary. He acquired his knowledge of trading life in West Africa when he was District Commissioner and Collector of Customs at Quittah and Accra.   His book was written in 1887, and, in September, Meredith, the Reader, suggested alterations.   The revised proofs were sent back in January, 1888, but the work was not published until 1890.

George Meredith, when examined, said he had been Reader to the defendants for thirty years.   Major Ellis's manuscript was submitted to him, and he reported on it on 27th September, 1887.   He had never heard of plaintiff in his life.   He had caused a story entitled *Mrs Fitzgibbon* to be cut out of Major Ellis's manuscript.   As an expert he considered the story to be a work of pure fiction.

Cross-examined by Sir Charles Russell, it transpired he objected to *Mrs Fitzgibbon* as it was not in good taste.   She was a female adventuress.   The description of Peacock's mother he considered the attempt of a serious man to be humorous.   He objected personally to it, but it went down with the public, so he had to pass it.   (*Laughter.*)   It was a sort of elephantine

MEREDITH IN THE BOX
By E. J. Wheeler, Punch, December 19th, 1891

MEREDITH DESTROYING LITERARY FORM
By E. T. Reed, Punch, July 28th, 1894

TWO CARICATURE SKETCHES FROM "PUNCH"

Reproduced by special permission of The Proprietors of Punch

humour. He did not like it, but one would have to object to so much. He was not aware at the time that the two incidents of the clerk and the engineer story were founded on fact. He thought the whole story was fiction. When pressed by Sir Charles Russell to say whether he had ever heard of Pinnock, Meredith replied : " Not since the days of my youth, when I learnt his catechism."

I asked Mr Asquith if he had any recollections of the case, and he replied : " I remember well my dear old friend George Meredith's appearance and demeanour in the witness-box. He had, I think, to stand the most severe ordeal that any witness could be exposed to : cross-examination by Sir Charles Russell, the greatest of advocates ; and he came out well." [1]

However, Mr James Pinnock won his action, and was awarded £200 damages. *The Times* devoted a leading article next day to the case, sententiously observing : " We are grateful to Mr Pinnock for putting limits to the right claimed by certain novelists to mash into literary pulp their friends, acquaintances, and the world in general "—which was a knowing or unconscious slash at Meredith himself. He, indeed, figured as the chief actor in the case. His evidence was parodied by, I understand, Rudolph Lehmann in *Punch* (19th December, 1891) in a skit called *By George !*—a most excellent simulation of Meredith's style. It was accompanied by a clever cartoon by E. J. Wheeler of " George-in-the-Box," showing Meredith popping up as a Jack-in-the-Box before the catechising counsel with Pinnock's manual in hand. In the same issue of *Punch* was a skit entitled *Illegal Fictions*, also dealing with this matter.

Apparently no one engaged in the case was aware that George Meredith and Alfred Burdon Ellis were connected by family ties, involving the history of *Evan Harrington* and " Major Strike," and that it was a curious and unperceived link with the great novelist's early days.

---

[1] " My examination in Court went fairly. I had some fun out of Sir C. Russell. The papers have not printed all," Meredith wrote the next day to Greenwood.

CHAPTER X

MANY pens have described Meredith's house at Box Hill, and it may seem superfluous to attempt to picture once again the situation of Flint Cottage, which became his home at the close of 1867, and remained his loved and fitting retreat until the end, in 1909. It was a fortunate chance that found this ideal setting for the poet-novelist of Nature during his last forty years. The lovely surroundings of his home were reflected and interpreted again and again in the literary work of this long period ; they inspired much that will never die : though he who dwelt there is now dust, the memory of him will attach to the spot evermore.

Flint Cottage, which is far more ancient than it looks, stands on one of the lower slopes of Box Hill against an immediate background of the woods of Juniper Hill and Mickleham. A white gate opens from the rough chalk road of the hill-side on to a garden plot of grass and flower-beds surrounded by tall yew hedges. A few steps under a trellis porch give access to a tiny hall with parlour and dining-room to right and left respectively. When Meredith first came to the house his bed-room was on the east side, overlooking the long sloping garden and a little wooded ravine, and from the window he could see the sun rise over Box Hill. "We do on the left side lean on the wilds," as he told Hardman. After 1876, when his chalet was erected on the highest slope of the garden, with a most picturesque woodland path behind it, he generally slept in the little room opening out of that wherein he lived and wrote in this ideal garden retreat. Around him sang the wild music of the winds he loved, and above floated the wondrous clouds that his favourite South-West brought.

In front of house and garden and chalet the long green slope of Box Hill sweeps up to the left in graceful lines to the tree-

FLINT COTTAGE, BOX HILL, MEREDITH'S HOME AFTER 1867. SIDE VIEW SHOWING MEREDITH'S BEDROOM TO RIGHT. HERE HE WROTE "HARRY RICHMOND" AND "BEAUCHAMP'S CAREER"

Photograph by Mr. Woot

crowned summit. The view from the hill is very lovely, whether to the south-east over a vast tract of champaign country to the downs—" greyhounds in flight," as Meredith imaged them—and almost the sea of Sussex ; or to west and north where rise, challenging the clouds, the hills and hanging woods of Ranmore and Denbies, Norbury Park, with its im- memorial Druid's Grove of yews, and Mickleham Downs. The scene is always beautiful. In winter when the woods are purple under an opal sky, or clothed in gleaming mantles of snow and frost :

> Large and smoky red the sun's cold disk drops,
>   Clipped by naked hills, on violet shaded snow ;
> Eastward large and still lights up a bower of moonrise,
>   Whence at her leisure steps the moon aglow.

In spring, when all the trees are a shimmering green, and the lilacs and laburnums bloom in the nearer gardens :

> Day of the cloud in fleets ! O Day
> Of wedded white and blue, that sail
> Immingled, with a footing ray
> In shadow-sandals down our vale !—
> And swift to ravish golden meads,
> Swift up the run of turf it speeds . . .
> To where the hill-top flings on sky.

Glorious is the landscape in the full pride of summertide ; but loveliest of all, perhaps, as I saw it last, when the woods put on their autumn robes of russet, red, and innumerable shades of dark green, and the clouds are broken at close of day by bars of blood-red fire as the sun sets behind the hills :

> Autumn's sunset skies,
> When at a waving of the fallen light
> Sprang realms of rosy fruitage o'er her eyes.
> A lustrous heavenly orchard hung the West,
> . . . then, here and there,
> A golden harp lost strings ; a crimson shell
> Burnt grey ; and sheaves of lustre fell to air. . . .
> A green-edged lake of saffron touched the blue,
> With isles of fireless purple lying through :
> And Fancy on that lake to seek lost treasures sailed.

" Come down," wrote Meredith to Comyns Carr one October day, " Come down and see our Indian summer here. A dozen

differently coloured torches you will find held up in our woods."
The torches still burn there at the fall of the year, though he
who hymned the beauty of the scene has passed.

Such was Meredith's loved home. His first letter written
from Box Hill, on 31st January, 1868, voices the inspiration
the spot was to bestow on him for the remainder of his
life : " I am every morning on the top of Box Hill—as its
flower, its bird, its prophet. I drop down the moon on
one side, I draw up the sun on t'other. I breathe fine
air. I shout ha ha to the gates of the world. . . . G. M. of
Box Hill."

Here he, at last, found a home in the real sense of the word ;
here he knew domestic happiness. His daughter, Marie
Eveleen, was born at Flint Cottage in June, 1871, and she and
her brother passed their childhood here. And here Meredith
reached the maturity of his literary powers and produced his
most profound and thoughtful work. As Mr J. A. Hammerton
well expressed it : " The tide is making for his greatest period
of joyous and successful literary labour. Visits abroad, long
tramps among the downs of his own homeland, increase of
friends, the fireside haven of afterwork, love and the glow of
good health ; all these now mark his days, and this period
of tranquil delight is to continue for a good many years, and
out of it shall come the ripest fruits of his genius."

He was very busy in December, 1868, when he wrote to his
" Dear Baron Tuck " :

" I find this, O My Lord ! that I must work like Cerberus and
the man who invented umbrellas—who was it, Tuck ? It was
not Danaë, you know (forgive me for mentioning her if you think
her improper : she was a king's daughter). I say I must work
with three heads to keep off the drenching shower of Xmas ripe
fruits. Art acquaint with 'em ? Sweet William ! Now . . .
in very truth, Tuck, I do hate these bills. They are, I protest,
the obscene artillery of the stinking pit. I am no sooner
touched by one than I have sensations of the damned. It is a
proof whence they come. . . . I have no more to say. I love
thee. Give an oboli or so of that to thy wife, an thou dar'st,
and believe me Yours the Vagabond and Harper
                                        " GEORGE MEREDITH.

" Nursery Chronicle : or call it *The Standard* with the venom exhausted.

" Willie Maxse Willikins is well. He sings many songs. He works the wheelbarrow merrily. Ben yesterday cut his hind paw on a bit of some cockney's glass bottle on Box Hill. Our cat is growing the handsomest in the world."

Thus work and domesticity went happily hand in hand, but he did not forget the old days at Copsham. In his next letter to Hardman he said :

" Your letter, my dear Tuck, reached me in London and smelt of the old time like moss of the woods, with here and there a lurking violet ; likewise I caught in it glimpses of wood nymphs, and of a Faun that did wantonly trip. . . . Needs not to say how refreshed I was. A breath from those coverts is eternally reviving. We live, we battle, but there grow our medical herbs. Art yet a Knight ? [1] For me is no distinction. As for the world, it has wagged till it waggles. Opposite the Memorial to the Great and Good, I have meditated on Princes, Peoples, and Widows. We were lodged at Prince's Gate. I salute you according to your three characters—the Justice with round capon lined, the host of an exceeding warm embrace, and (between them, seen by few) the florescent Son of Pan. Adieu. Your loving

" GEORGE MEREDITH."

To 1870 belongs the exquisite *Dirge in Woods* :

> A wind sways the pines,
>   And below
> Not a breath of wild air ;
> Still as the mosses that glow
> On the flooring and over the lines
> Of the roots here and there
> The pine-tree drops its dead ;
> They are quiet, as under the sea.
> Overhead, overhead
> Rushes life in a race
> As the clouds the clouds chase ;
>   And we go,
> And we drop like the fruits of the tree,
>   Even we
>   Even so.

---

[1] This was prophetic : but Hardman was not knighted until 1885.

R

The similar, but more pregnant, poem, *In the Woods*, was written three years later.

When spring at Box Hill came round, Meredith remembered his visits to the nightingale-haunted Vale of Mickleham in former years with Bonaparte Wyse, and wrote off to that valued friend to come down and renew old memories.

"*April* 20*th*, 1870.

"MY DEAREST OF DEAR FELLOWS,—The Mickleham Nightingales, believing in your vows of affection, invite you to a concert here as early as you can come. If you bring your wife, whom mine will joyfully welcome, and I greet irradiated, we will quarter you for the nights at an adorable inn, framed to figure in the annals of co-respondency. Come you alone, perhaps you will condescend to the old hammock-cot I used to sleep in at Copsham. Let me know the day you are to arrive in town. I can't tell you how glad I shall be to grasp your hand. You and I awaken from a winter like that in the planet Jupiter, so let the thaw smite the rocks to torrents.

"I've no photograph of myself and shall not have one. Take instead my thanks for yours and *Li Parpaioun Blu*, which I have been spelling over with astonishment at your facility, and delight in its effects. More of it by and by. I am trying to get a copy of my review of *Mirèio* for you. I wrote in *The Pall Mall Gazette* of the great meeting of the Félibres, little imagining that you were one of them and much their host!

"Adieu for the moment, and to our meeting! With compliments and affectionate regards to your wife,

"I am your loving,

"GEORGE MEREDITH."

"13*th May*, 1870.

"MY DEAREST BTE.,—A word to say how much I regret that we shall not have you here on your return. The Reverend received his copy of the *Parp. Blu* and sends you enclosed acknowledgment. I shall give the other copy to Swinburne, I think. Am reading *Bread of Sin* [1]; moderately interesting,

---

[1] An English translation by Bonaparte Wyse of Théodore Aubanel's *Lou Pan de Pécat*, drama in Provençal.

but not so exciting as an ordinary adultery case in the news-papers, and without the dignity of the tragic drama. Phaedre was excusable, but Fanette's longings are beneath expression in verse. You see, she has no character, no quality of mind. It is an attempt to make a dramatic poem out of the irritation of this female's gender. A strong young man and a middle-aged wanton are not enough to compose a poem. Fanette is the Provençal Madame Bovary, conceived provincially. . . . No, we do not allow your wife to make such a stretch of gener-osity as to part with the *Moans*.[1] We read it and shall return it. As to her fear that we see nothing but the ludicrous in them, let her be aisy. Only laughter is precious and is for company : the rest sinks deep. None can fail to feel the awful tragedy of the situation, and the triumph of fetching poetry of any kind out of it. Adieu—I am very busy. Shall be glad to hear from you, and with very kind regards to your wife and three kisses to the little Lucien,

" I am your affectionate

" GEORGE MEREDITH."

In October, 1868, he had stayed at Holly Hill to help his friend Maxse, who was the Radical candidate in the Southampton election—" a dismal business, but I take to it as to whatever comes," he wrote to Jessopp ; and in the summer of 1869 Meredith went abroad with Lionel Robinson to see his son Arthur. He writes : " Of Arthur I have good news to tell you. I had him with me (old Poco a third) on the Rieder Alp : then away to Stuttgart, where I left him housed with a Professor to attend the Gymnasium. He writes quaintly of the Suabian folk, is marching well forward in Latin and Greek. I believe really working. He is bold on the ice and endures fatigue well ; projects his head and chin. The lad is evidently a shrewd observer."

In 1870 Mrs Meredith's father, Justin Vulliamy, died. This summer Meredith paid a visit to his friend Maxse and had some yachting. Next, he and his wife stayed with the Cotterills at Tongswood, and then took rooms at 21, Cavendish Place, East-bourne. From here he wrote amusingly to Hardman :

---

[1] *Moans of a Moribund*, sonnets by Bonaparte Wyse, privately printed.

" Eastbourne is on the whole pleasant. The bathing is delightful . . . you see half a dozen fat men at a time scampering out of the machines. . . . Then they dive, they rise, there is a glistening on the right cheek and the left—too distant to offend the most gingerly. I opine so, for I have beheld antique virgins spy-glass in hand towards the roguish spot. This salt water fetches me round, Tuck. It is the next best to mountain air."

William Hardman was always extending his civic activities, and becoming a Justice of the Peace, a member of City Companies, and what not. When he accepted the office of Mayor of Kingston he inspired Meredith thus :

" Box Hill. *Dec.* 11*th*. 1870.

" MY DEAREST TUCK,—I would not write until I had thoroughly mastered the state of amazement I was thrown into by your last communication—used as I am to see you swell like a balloon and away to the empyrean ! The vision of you in the robes obfuscates me still. Gods ! what a sight. But we shall have it in a picture. Of all the list of dignities I have conceived for you as sure to fall to your lot, that of Mayor of the town of your adoption was alone beyond my prophetic ken. And I dare say you walk as composedly as a common man ! For the moment I am not quite equal to meeting you on the terms of ancient friendship I know you will, sated with earthly grandeurs, insist upon. I must first go through a preparatory course of some sort, and I mean to write to a Committee of the New Educational Board for the receipt. I love to enter my friend's house, but should the appalling reflection come on me, without my being prepared for it, that I am in a Mayor's nest, I am certain I shall give way.

" You are rapidly destroying the sense of wonder in me, Tuck. Where will you stop ? Are there bounds to you ? I might vision you ultimately taking flight as one of the cherubim host, discarding the robes of blue and yellow, but that imagination never could deprive you of what you are so largely endowed with. . . ."

In other letters he continued :

"Shall you have your Gold Barge on the Mole to float down to Kingston in? If so, I should like to accompany you. I have often desired to eat a swan on board, and see my countrymen kneeling on the tow-path as the procession goes by." [1]

"*February* 15*th* [1871].

"I read of you at the recent Kingston festival.

> "Cool you proceed at speed
> From station unto station,
> While I but in giving heed
> Shed drops of perspiration!

"But I say, tell me you're not going to wear the robes: I can't stand it: the fate of Semele warns me.

"Godson has had bad influenza, which he bequeathed to his father, flooring me completely. I am still a little nosey. . . . Adieu. My love to D. Troïa and the fair fruit of the siege, now stately tall as pines on Ida."

"*October* 17*th* [1872].

"MY DEAR LORD TUCK,—Coward capsized me before I left London for France with intelligence of another of your transformations.[2] I went back on my heels. What do you say to the Presidency of Honduras next? . . .

"Willie Godson grows tall and good. Our Babbles is in her present stage the awfullest roarer! We had a nice time in France, *but* that we were upset (Theodore, Ned, Billy, Rose Vulliamy, and your friend). Ned V. nearly killed, and I with a crack on my funny-bone, which sang and wouldn't heal for a fortnight exactly. Marie and Will were in a coach behind. We hurled out of a wagonette.

"Illustrious and Astonishing One! I am, Tuck! the admirer of the former, fast friend of the latter."

During his first two years, or more, at Box Hill, Meredith was leisurely finishing *The Adventures of Harry Richmond*, which commenced to appear serially in *The Cornhill Magazine*,

---

[1] See also *Letters of George Meredith*, p. 221.

[2] Presumably Hardman's position as editor of *The Morning Post*, which rôle he assumed in 1872. He then gave up Norbiton Hall and went to live in Montague Street, Bloomsbury.

September, 1870, illustrated by George du Maurier with unsatisfactory designs.[1] The story ran for the long period of fifteen months here, and was published in three volumes by Smith and Elder in the winter of 1871. But the work had been commenced as far back as 1861, and in May, 1864, the author told Jessopp, at the time he was writing *Vittoria* : " I have also in hand an autobiography, *The Adventures of Richmond Roy and his Friend Contrivance Jack : Being the History of Two Rising Men* : and to be a spanking bid for popularity on the part of the writer." Apparently his first intention was to write a book on the lines of Borrow, dealing entirely with the road and the heath, for he continued a few weeks later : " A series of wayside pieces for *The Cornhill*, Sandys illustrating, is on the tapis. These will ultimately form a volume special and I hope popular."

It is to be regretted that the project for Sandys's illustrations never materialised. He was a Norwich man, and could have given the Borrovian touch to scenes of nomadic life. And he evidently had some influence on Meredith's story, for it was a gipsy model of Sandys's named Kaomi who was the original of Kiomi in *Harry Richmond*. How fine was her presentation there is testified by Watts-Dunton, himself a profound student of Romany life :

" The pictures of gipsy life . . . in all other novels are the merest daubs compared with the Kiomi of George Meredith's story *Harry Richmond*. Not even Borrow and Groome, with all their intimate knowledge of gipsy life, ever painted a more vigorous picture of the Romany chi than this. The original was well known in the art circles of London at one time, and was probably known to Meredith, but this does not in any way derogate from the splendour of the imaginative achievement of painting in a few touches a Romany girl who must, one would think, live for ever." [2]

Meredith's great romance of the open road and the wild heath

---

[1] One of them, *Janet Ilchester with Harry and his Father*, illustrates a scene in the text that is omitted in later editions.

[2] *Harry Richmond* was regarded by Watts-Dunton as Meredith's best work, and he re-read it not long before his death. Kaomi was the model for Sandys's picture of Judith (1864), and another of his portraits of the girl was in the collection of the late Lord Battersea.

lands of Hampshire had for setting that portion of the county adjoining Sussex, south of Petersfield. Riversley Grange was seven miles from " Ewling," which may be identified with Harting—the country, in fact, of *Evan Harrington* and Beckley Court. When little Harry Richmond was carried away from Riversley Grange by his imperial father : " The soft mild night had a moon behind it somewhere ; and here and there a light blue space of sky showed small rayless stars ; the breeze smelt fresh of roots and heath. . . . So strange an aspect had all these quiet hill-lines and larch and fir-tree tops in the half-dark still-ness . . . beyond the park, among the hollows that run dipping for miles beside the great high-road toward London."

The Portsmouth Road. And in *Harry Richmond,* as in *Evan Harrington,* there are suggestions of Meredith's early life and family characteristics. *Harry Richmond* is, in my opinion, the " Autobiography " mentioned by the author in his letters, and which some of his commentators have stated was never written. But Meredith never asserted that the " Autobiography " was to be a plain actual account of his own life—a Book of Memoirs in the Rousseau sense. On the contrary, in 1864 he called it the " Autobiographic Tale "—that is to say, it is written in the first person like Dickens's *David Copperfield,* Charlotte Brontë's *Jane Eyre,* and William De Morgan's *Joseph Vance* (bearing the sub-title " An ill-written Autobiography "). All these books reflect memories and experiences of their authors, and present transcriptions of actual characters known to them in the past : but they are not strictly autobiographies, for they all contain much that is purely imaginative. It is thus with *Harry Richmond* too. The word " Autobiography " applies to him and not to Meredith ; but granting that, and the fact that some prominent characters, such as the Princess Ottilia and the life-like Squire Beltham, may be fictitious creations, it is also true that much of the book is founded on actuality. The Richmonds, father and son, are a sort of melange of four generations of Merediths. Undoubtedly the great Richmond Roy was in-spired by Melchizedek Meredith in the first place. Was not the latter reputed to have passed as a Marquis at Bath, where Roy also strutted one of the many glorious hours of his life ? But Meredith's stupendous creation of his Micawberian Prince of Adventurers and Impecunious Impostors far transcended the personality of his own grandfather, dashing, thriftless, handsome, and pretentious as the latter was. Meredith's characters were realities to him, and he would, it is said, hold communion and talk aloud with them in the retirement of his study where they were born. Thus he told Marcel Schwob: "When Harry Richmond's father first met me, when I heard him tell me in his pompous style about the son of a duke of blood royal and an actress of seventeen years of age, I perfectly roared with laughter!" The claims of Richmond Roy to royal birth were perhaps suggested to his creator by the absurd stories which, as we have seen, attributed to the novelist himself a similar lineage: or it may be the latter legends were caused by *Harry Richmond*, when somebody, reading the story, detected a reflection of some actual facts of Meredith history and imagined more. Richmond Roy also has some characteristics of Augustus Meredith, and Harry himself resembles both George Meredith and his son Arthur.

I have already pointed out that Meredith endowed Harry Richmond with his own gift as a boy of reading the thoughts and characters of his companions, and that Rippenger's school was a picture of the one George went to, in Hampshire, as a boarder after he left St Paul's, Southsea, in 1841. Harry Richmond's travels with his father on the Continent suggest those of Meredith and his small son Arthur, whose juvenile friendship with Miss Janet Duff Gordon resembled Harry Richmond's with Clara Goodwin. In this book, the living lady named Janet seems to have again been used as a model, this time for physical characteristics and not character; Meredith's description of Janet Ilchester certainly coincides with the Watts portrait of Miss Janet Duff Gordon: "The face was mobile, various . . . the profile was less assuring than the front, because of the dark eyebrows' extension and the occasional frown, but that was not shared by the mouth, which was a charming bow, running to a length at the corners like her eyebrows, quick with smiles." And both the Janets were skilled horsewomen.

The problem of *Harry Richmond* is the same as that of *Evan Harrington*—the love of a young man for a girl above him in social rank, and his (and his author's) conflict with snobbery and pride. Thus Harry says:

" Ottilia's station repelled and attracted me mysteriously. I could not separate her from it, nor keep my love of her from the contentions into which it threw me. In vain I raved, ' What is rank ? ' There was a magnet in it that could at least set me quivering and twisting, behaving like a man spellbound. . . . Perhaps it has already struck you that one who takes the trouble to sit and write his history for as large a world as he can obtain, and shape his style to harmonise with every development of his nature, can no longer have much of the hard grain of pride in him."

The early part of *Harry Richmond* is certainly the best : it is too spun out after the hero comes to man's estate. The boys of the book are delightful. As Janet Ilchester remarks : " English boys are unrivalled. Honesty, bravery, modesty, and nice looks ! They are so nice in their style and their way of talking." But it is a pity that, having created his nice boys, Meredith sometimes makes them talk in his style and not that of boyhood. Boys who talk " of our horses' hic-hæc-hocks getting strained on this hard nominative-plural-masculine of the article road " from conversation should be " expunged "— to use another unlikely expression emanating from a boy in this book. Meredith's good things come far better from the mouth of Richmond Roy : " ' Idiots, insects, women, and the salt sea ocean ! ' said he, to indicate a list of the untameables." And " Things printed can never be stopped, Richie. Our Jorian compares them to babies baptized. They have a soul from that moment, and go on for Ever."

The character of Janet Ilchester can be regarded as either a very subtle study or a failure. At the outset she is a scheming, unpleasant little girl, with a greed for other people's property : in the end a noble, generous woman, and it is not clearly marked in the story when and how her character changed. Up to the period when she successfully conspired to separate Ottilia and Harry in the Isle of Wight she ever appears unlovable and selfish, for her own obvious and paramount purpose was to secure the hero herself. A pale " hero " certainly, one who never accomplished anything except by aid of his father and friends ; a squanderer of money provided by others ; and inconceivably weak at the crisis of his fate. Why he should be debarred by high scruples of honour from marrying the Princess when she and her father were " in the net " of Richmond Roy is not apparent, in view of the fact that Harry had not hesitated to compromise Ottilia's reputation by a midnight assignation in Germany. It cannot be contended that in the meantime his character had advanced, for, despicable to the last, he accepts the bounty of Riversley (of which he had been disinherited) and only discovers he " loves " Janet Ilchester when that astute young lady is the heiress of the millions he had reckoned upon in the past as his future inheritance. In the imbroglio of the renunciation of the Princess, sympathy goes most to Richmond Roy at the collapse of all his schemes ; and his retributive fall, at the vengeful hands of the blackguardly Squire, is too heavy and complete for one who had ever before sailed his glittering bark of personality gaily over the seas of adversity. Meredith does not account for this sudden collapse of character either, and thus the final impression of the tale is disappointing and vague. This nebulosity of intention, which envelops much of the book throughout, explains the contradictory criticism it has received. Thus Arthur Symons found it a romance " rousing, enthralling, exciting, full of poetry, and a serious and masterly study in character. On a first reading we are fairly swept away and carried along by the racing tide of the narrative. . . . Brilliant and fantastically lighted pictures flit past, like the slides of a magic lantern." But W. L. Courtney pronounced : " Perhaps in no novel do we find the absence of joy more conspicuous than in *Harry Richmond.* Here is a young man who goes through a series of surprising adventures quite removed from the sphere of probability. . . . The only literary excuse for such extravagance would be the rollicking character of the hero, such a one, for instance, as was endeared to our childhood by Captain Marryat or Kingston. But Harry Richmond does not rollick ; he is never young, but talks about himself with the *maladie de la pensée* of a modern age."

I think Mr Courtney is right, though some, no doubt, find the story rollicking, and have even regarded it as of the school of Lever, the Prince of Rollickers. Thus, Meredith wrote to Hardman when the tale was first appearing in *The Cornhill* : " So you do both care for *H. Richmond.* I hoped it. I wish some one like Shirley Brooks would let it be known it's mine.

Lethbridge tells me he has seen it attributed to Lever! A word from you, Tuck, in the august ear of Punch, anon, anon, Sir. Mind and tell me how you like it as you go on. I shall have another to follow when *Richmond* ceases, and so by drumming may make the public hear me at last. Really, Tuck, I feel pleasure in my work when I hear you like it. I have an audience of about a dozen, but if they're satisfied I am too, and no man speaks so heartily as you do."

There are some interesting references to *Harry Richmond* in two letters to Jessopp from Meredith (not included in the published Correspondence) :

" I am busily finishing a novel for *The Cornhill Magazine*, one of three or four that are carved out and waiting. . . . The English public will not let me probe deeply into humanity. You must not paint either man or woman ; a surface view of the species flat as a wafer is acceptable. I have not plucked at any of the highest or deepest chords. Hence possibly those who have heard some of the chapters say it must be the best novel I have written."

" DEAR AND MOST REVEREND DOCTOR OF D., and of L. too, I trust, and may'st thou be ever a charm against him who so begins and ends the letters of his name, without whom thy craft is nothing ! . . . Don't speak of *Richmond* till you have read the whole. When you have done that, say what you like. I shall be glad of criticism. Consider first my scheme as a workman. It is to show you the action of minds as well as of fortunes —of here and there men and women vitally animated by their brains at different periods of their lives—and of men and women with something of a look-out upon the world and its destinies : the mortal ones ; the divine I leave to Doctors of D. . . . As for recognition of the stuff in my writing, and the system it goes on, I care little for it now, and when I thrust myself into the pillory by publishing, the smack in the face and the pat on the shoulder are things in the day's order."

In another letter to Hardman he continues to deal with the subject :

" It struck me that a perusal of the book without enforced pauses might lead you to see that the conception was full and good, and was honestly worked out. I resisted every temptation to produce great and startling effects (after the scene of the Statue, which was permissible in art, as coming from a boy and coloured by a boy's wonder). Note, as you read, the gradual changes of the growing Harry, in his manner of regarding his father and the world. I have carried it so far as to make him perhaps dull towards adolescence and young manhood, except to one studying the narrative—as in the scenes with Dr Julius. Such effects are deadly when appearing in a serial issue. I was here and there hand-tied, too, by gentlemanly feeling in relation to the reigning Royal House, sweet Tory Tuck ! or I should (and did on paper) have launched out. The Speech at the City Banquet [1] would have satisfied a Communist Red originally. And I had planned startling doings for the season of the Grand Parade. But I constrained myself. I suppose I am unlucky, for I hear that the novel does not move. It is confounded by Mudie with the quantity coming out."

Maxse told Meredith that he knew a lady—a great novel reader—who found *Harry Richmond* quite unintelligible in parts. But the German scenes of the book ought to have appealed to the public of that time (1870-1871), for they were topical in view of the contemporary Franco-Prussian War. Meredith, however, is always topical, whatever the lapse of years since he wrote, and his revelations of German character in *Harry Richmond* could be cited as apt to-day as they were forty-seven years ago. Thus the views of Prince Hermann :

" He talked of the littleness of Europe and the greatness of Germany ; logical postulates fell in collapse before him. America to America, North and South ; India to Europe. India was for the land with the largest sea-board. Mistress of the Baltic, of the North Sea and the East, as eventually she must be, Germany would claim to take India as a matter of course, and find an outlet for the energies of the most prolific and the toughest of the races of mankind,—the purest, in fact, the only true race, properly so called, out of India, to which it

[1] When Richmond Roy replied to the Royal toast.

would return as its source, and there create an empire magnificent in force and solidity, the actual wedding of East and West ; an empire firm on the ground and in the blood of the people, instead of an empire of aliens, that would bear comparison to a finely-fretted cotton-hung palanquin balanced on an elephant's back, all depending on the docility of the elephant (his description of Great Britain's Indian Empire)."

And then Professor von Karsteg as interpreted by the Princess :

" ' You forgive him his irony. It is not meant to be personal to you. England is the object and partly, I may tell you, it springs from jealousy. You have such wealth ! You embrace half the world. You are such a little island. All this is wonderful. The bitterness is, you are such a mindless people—I do but quote to explain my Professor's ideas. " Mindless," he says, " and arrogant, and neither in the material nor in the spiritual kingdom of noble or gracious stature, and ceasing to have a brave aspect." He calls you squat Goths. . . . And to his conception, you, who were pioneers when the earth had to be shaped for implements and dug for gold, you will turn upon us and stop our march ; you are to be overthrown and left behind, there to gain humility from the only teacher you can understand—from poverty.' "

But Ottilia rightly says at another time : " Nations at war are wild beasts. The passions of these hordes of men are not an example for a living soul. Our souls grow up to the light : we must keep eye on the light, and look no lower. Nations appear to me to have no worse than a soiled mirror of themselves in mobs. They are still uncivilised : they still bear a resemblance to the old monsters of the mud. Do you not see their claws and fangs ? "

The war of 1870 deeply affected Meredith, who was torn asunder by conflicting sympathies for both belligerents. France he ever loved, but he blamed the Emperor ; and he liked much that was German. At first he cherished the hope of seeing something of the conflict in his old rôle of war correspondent, but this did not come about. Writing to John Morley in the summer of 1870, he said :

" On the whole, I side with France, or so incline. The instinct of the people in seizing an opportunity to dispute the aggrandisement of Prussia is right : it is not a Vanity war nor a King's, but a People's war—war of Germans and Frenchmen ; a trial of actual strength for supremacy : and it was nonsense to think of postponing it, ruinous to delay. . . . It's possible that I may start to French quarters for Borthwick. . . . The war of '70 is a direct issue of '66. Just as we abused the Prussians then we howl at the French now, but the tremendous armaments on both sides were meant for this duel, and it mattered very little what was the pretext for the outbreak. . . . Here we have it ; and if we are energetic and wise it may be the last of the great fights of Europe. The two foremost States in war and intellect may well be committed to cut the bloody tangle. I feel deeply for the Germans ; I quite understand the ardour of the French. I think their cause, from their point of view, thoroughly good, and not likely to succeed. Armies can't do it : they can't check the tide of a great nation. I would not mind our language if it came from an unselfish people : but a people notoriously craving peace for comfort's sake, and commerce's—they do but scold, they provoke contempt. I regret bitterly that I am not out on a post of observation. I may still go for a month."

By the autumn, Meredith attached more blame to France, and writing to his son Arthur, whose sympathies were entirely for the French, he said :

" This war is chargeable upon France, and the Emperor is the Knave of the pack. Two generations of Frenchmen have been reared on the traditions of Napoleonism, and these meant the infliction of wrongs and outrages on other nations for the glory and increase of their own. They elected a Napoleon for chief because of his name, and in spite of his known character. It is said the French peasantry did not want war ; that their ignorance offended in electing this man ; but who can deny that it was the Napoleonic prestige which gave him his first step to the throne by overwhelming votes ? This man was the expression of their ignorance or folly, or vanity ; he appealed to the Napoleonism in them, and had a prompt response. A more ignoble spectacle than the recriminations of Emperor and people upon one another as to the origin of the war, after defeat, history does not show. The Germans, on the contrary, reap the reward of a persistently honourable career in civic virtue. . . . As to German boasting, why the English also are great boasters. See the best in those about you. I say this, and I admire and respect the Germans, and God knows my heart bleeds for the French. But my aim, and I trust it will be yours, is never to take counsel of my sensations but of my intelligence. I let the former have free play, but deny them the right to bring me to a decision. . . . Try not to be let into some degree of injustice to your host,[1] the German people, out of pity for France. . . . And when on a tour have a care of your tongue and your company. The Professor says you do not consort with Germans at all. I am grieved at this. I am sure you do not altogether underrate the fine qualities of German youth ; but perhaps your immediate sympathies, and a somewhat exaggerated sensitiveness, stand in your way. It will be a pity if this is so. . . . If you do not cultivate the people you are living amongst in your youth, you will fail in having pleasant places to look back on—landmarks of your young days.[2] And besides, the Germans are your hosts, and you owe them at least a guest's thankfulness. I esteem them deeply for their fine moral qualities. Just now they are abusing us roundly, but that will pass away. I know they have the capacity for friendship, and that as a rule English friendships are not so lasting. Look around you, and try to be accessible to your German associates. Consider whether you are not yielding to luxurious predispositions in your marked preference for English ones. . . . Captain Maxse is out and out French ; Mr Morison intensely German ; Mr Morley and I do our utmost to preserve an even balance."

To Hardman he wrote :

" The Vulliamys at Nonancourt, I fear, have the Uhlans quartered on them by this time. Relatives of their wives at Jouy (near Versailles) have housefulls of occifers. But I bear in mind, as a corrective to wrath at the conquerors, that the

---

[1] Arthur was at Stuttgart.
[2] Meredith spoke from experience of failing to adopt this advice himself in youth.

brutallest invader in the world has always been the Frenchman.
The Germans are going beyond the mark in their despoliations,
for which they also must suffer. . . . I know you don't like the
Germans. They are not amusing, but they have their good
side."

" I suppose the French are for peace now. They rage and
foam at it like the Devil. I am in sorrow about them, but I
fear they have too many of the devil's passions to float, though
they have many a noble turning, and are always a picture good
for study."

Consequently Meredith was able to write at this same time,
in seeming contradiction of sympathies and views, his Ode,
France, December, 1870, which appeared the following month in
The Fortnightly Review :

> They lie like circle-strewn soaked Autumn-leaves
> Which stain the forest scarlet, her fair sons !
> And of their death her life is : of their blood
> From many streams now urging to a flood,
> No more divided, France shall rise afresh.
> Of them she learns the lesson of the flesh :—
> The lesson writ in red since first Time ran,
> A hunter hunting down the beast in man :
>
> .   .   .   .
>
> Immortal Mother of a mortal host !
> Thou suffering of the wounds that will not slay,
> Wounds that bring death but take not life away !
> Stand fast and hearken while thy victors boast :
> Hearken and loathe that music evermore.
>   . . . Soaring France !
> Now is Humanity on trial in thee :
> Now mayest thou gather humankind in fee.

But again, two months later, in February, 1871, he wrote to
Maxse of France in phrases which are applied to Germany in
1918 :

" Can you pretend to believe that France was not in need of
the bitterest of lessons ? Her philosophers said one thing
but military glory stuck to the passions of her people. And
many of her philosophers allowed themselves to be hoodwinked
by the idea that France should be dominant ' for the good of
mankind,' instead of seeking to make her dominant by virtue

and a bright example. She trusted to the sword without even testing her steel. She is down. I grieve for her; I detest the severities practised upon her. But I cannot forget that she appealed to the droit du plus fort. Nor can I forget that she has always been the perturbation of Europe. The Germans may be. That is to be seen. They are at least what they pretend to be. A considerable number of cheap prophets have followed their triumphant march howling. I prefer to wait without prophesying. Let France train a virtuous democracy, and she will spring a mine in Germany amply to be revenged on the Hohenzollerns. Her cries of vengeance now are after the pattern—too shockingly similar!—of Ancient Pistol. She ' eats and ene she swears.'

" What I wish is that you and I should look to the good future of men with some faith in it, and capacity to regard current phases of history without letting our sensations blind and bewilder us. I am neither German nor French, nor, unless the nation is attacked, English. I am European and Cosmopolitan —for humanity! The nation which shows most worth is the nation I love and reverence.

" Confess that the French have conducted themselves like mere children throughout. The probation may accelerate their growth and bring their practice up to their best professions. The Germans have behaved as the very sternest of men, caring more for their Fatherland than for the well-being of men in the mass. I am susceptible of admiration of their sterling qualities, holding nevertheless that they will repent of the present selfish restriction of their views. . . . I think with pain that the Germans enter Paris this very day! But the City is not a ' holy City ' for me. The astonishing delusion which makes Frenchmen think it is so is one proof of rudderless brains. Morley is not ' German.' He agrees with me that it would have been a silly madness to create a terrible and a justly wrathful enemy for ourselves (looking to the origin of this war), on the chance of securing a frenzied, fantastical ally."

Thus, in 1871, Meredith did not advocate a British alliance with France, or intervention in that country's quarrels with Germany. But at the close of his life he foresaw that England would be involved in a war that would devastate all Europe.

S

Speaking in 1909 to the Rev. D. Owen, a Welsh bard, he said :

" I am by temperament an optimist. I believe in the future of the race, in the progress of mankind, and in the inviolability of the soul. But I am a pessimist in one direction, because I see looming in the distance, not the very far distance, a great tragedy, the Armageddon of Europe. You belong to the generation of thunder and lightning. Think of it : Europe a medley of blood and thunder. You will live to see it ; I shall not. I am too old, not in spirit but in years. I shall not see Armageddon. But, with all the talk of peace, the signs of the times are for war. We in Britain need a great stirring up, a great crisis, to rehabilitate the qualities of our race. We have become limp, lax, and fearful. We are afraid of death. Militarism in Germany would produce a sort of barbaric courage, dead to all the higher instincts of man. War waged by a nation obsessed by militarism would be horrible and ruthless."

To M. Photiadès, a year earlier (1908), Meredith expressed these opinions :

" The Englishman, his intelligence dulled by his wealth, will not awaken unless a German invasion occurs, or a slaughter upon his northern shores. We have no army. The army in India is marvellously equipped and disciplined, but what purpose does it serve as regards England ? Besides, India is our weak point. We neglect our own European England. One day, when it has crumbled still further, we shall say adieu to our colonies, to the vast continents of the antipodes, to the archipelago spread abroad upon the equatorial seas. We shall not then have enough of our matchless navy to defend ourselves. And if Germany were to beat us, as she has beaten France, should we revive ? I doubt it. France possesses wealth of many kinds ; the wealth of England is strictly commercial. Should anyone extort from us a crushing war indemnity, we are ruined unless we can re-establish our industries and the power to protect our commerce and our food supplies."

To Frederick Greenwood, too, he said this same year (1908) :

" Those who know the German mind are of opinion that there is an intention to try conclusions with England when Germany has ships to protect a landing (thought to be quite possible), and while the huge army is kept from the corruption of a long peace. Not for nothing did the German stipulate at The Hague for the right of mining the sea ways. With the use of mines an inferior Navy can match the giant for temporary purposes."

And in his letter to *The Daily Telegraph* of 17th February, 1903, he wrote :

" Pan-Germanism challenges many foes, and a Power ambitious to be preponderant in a great Navy as well as a great Army will find its adversary within, besides those that press around it. A slumbering England will offer it the chance it craves before the inevitable financial strain brings it to the ground. A watchful England may look on calmly for that certain issue."

Although Meredith was thus truly prophetic concerning the coming war, the effects of militarism on German character (once renowned for intellectual achievement), and, let us hope, the final course of events in the great struggle, he did not correctly judge the characteristics of his own countrymen and how they would behave when the trial came. The English did not require a German invasion of their shores to " awaken " them, and they have not proved " afraid of death," either as soldiers in the field or civilians under murderous outrages at home. But Meredith was always too prone to write disparagingly of the English, especially in his letters. This trait seems to have originated from what he considered their lack of appreciation of his work ; and so, to the end, he would use such phrases as : " The English cure one early of a desire for applause. . . . I have worked without thought of that and the profit coming of it." " On the theme of laughter, you should have dealt with the great stomach laugh of the English—on which they found their possession of the sense of humour." " I am, I mean to think, disdainful of an English public, and I am beset by the devils of satire when I look on it." " The English have hardened me outside, and there has been a consequent process within." " The notion of stirring Englishmen with verse is comic. Foemen in the guts might do it. Or Brighton bombarded, or

supplies of fresh meat failing.   We have an inefficient navy.
. . . And Invasion is an acknowledged possibility."   " Do
impress upon your pudding-headed English that if they want
security for peace, they must get into the habit of settling
questions instead of shuffling them on to the next Party in office
or generation."   " If I could quit England, hold off from paper,
and simply look on for the remainder of my term—mountains
near—I would ask for no better.   To be mixed up with them is
hard, these English are so astonishing to my ideas of dignity
and valour."

These references and others (particularly in *One of our
Conquerors* and *Celt and Saxon*) to England and the English
might be the growls of a dyspeptic foreigner.[1]   It may be
contended, of course, that Meredith wrote thus critically of the
English in his assumed rôle of a pugnacious Welsh-Irishman
constitutionally antagonistic to England.   But despite his frequent assertion that he was Celtic, his Welsh and Irish descent,
as previously demonstrated, was remote, his progenitors for
several generations, on both the paternal and maternal side,
having been Hampshire people.   It must be conceded with
regret that Meredith's strictures upon his fellow-countrymen
were based upon a compound of personal pique and that
very English characteristic—self-depreciation, which latter
trait still finds expression in certain foolish newspapers, who
continue to assert that England, the amazement merchant
for " The Intelligent Foreigner," has not yet contributed her
share of sacrifice in the great war or borne a burden com-
measurable with that of " Our gallant Allies."

Thirteen years ago Meredith sympathised with Russia's
aspirations for liberty, and desired the fall of the Tsardom.
But that also he did not live to see.   To an interviewer he said,
in January, 1905 :

" Russia cannot, it is certain, long escape the spirit of Liberalism that has swept over Europe.   The sympathy of the British
people with the brave fellows who are fighting an uneven, an
almost hopeless battle, as it seems, is very great.   And it should

[1] It is true that in *Lord Ormont and his Aminta* Meredith gave
expression to admiration for many characteristics of English schoolboys
and their creed, and the dogged pluck of Englishmen as soldiers.

be practical. . . . Everybody should spare what he can, and the money should be telegraphed immediately to one of the leaders who are not in prison. We must help them, and this is our only way. They cannot expect much help from Germany. Germany ever since 1870 has been an armed camp, waiting behind a fortress to be attacked. But no doubt the German people will sympathise with these poor fellows. France is in a difficult position. She was forced into an alliance with Russia by the Triple Alliance, before she came to a good understanding with us. Her people were attracted by the undeveloped riches of Russia to invest their money in that country. And France has her bondholders to consider. But she has a great spirit of humanity. I do not like the word humanity, but it will be understood—and the French people also will have much sympathy with the aims of the Russian revolutionaries."

At this same time he wrote his poem, *The Crisis* :

> Spirit of Russia, now has come
> The day when thou canst not be dumb.
> Around thee foams the torrent tide,
> Above thee its fell fountain Pride.
> The senseless rock awaits thy word
> To crumble ; shall it be unheard ? . . .
> Those rulers in all forms of lust
> Who trod thy children down to dust
> On the red Sunday, know right well
> What word for them thy voice would spell,
> What quick perdition for them weave . . .
> A soul ; that art thou. It remains
> For thee to stay thy children's veins,
> The countertides of hate arrest,
> Give to thy sons a breathing breast,
> And Him resembling, in His sight,
> So to thy land, let there be Light.

The latter aspirations of the poet have not been realised, for though Russia has broken her ancient chains she has not found salvation or liberty. It is curious that Meredith, a lifelong Radical and champion of liberty, and one who fully perceived the dangers of militarism, should have been in favour of the greatest evil of militarism—conscription. When the question of the Russian advance in Asia was prominent in 1878, Meredith wrote to Hardman, editor of *The Morning Post*:

" *The Morning Post* has fought well beside *The Pall Mall*, but the sentimental or party-ridden English have spoiled the hour. It is now too late to oust the Russians. No country like ours can afford to fight at so terrible a disadvantage as they offer us. . . . Meanwhile press for an army. . . . Ultimately it will come to a Conscription, and the sooner the better. The volunteering system gives us a scum of men no match for countries that bring their best into the field, and in overpowering hosts."

In 1874 he had urged the same view on Frederick Greenwood for propagation in *The Pall Mall Gazette*:

" I am troubled about various outlooks for the country, and do hope you will be at work on the subject of a conscription—your own subject years back. . . . Our stiff-necked people must pass under this yoke."

And in 1890 he wrote, in *One of our Conquerors*:

" The journals are trading engines. Panics are grist to them ; so are wars ; but they do their duty in warning the taxpayer and rousing Parliament. . . . We go on believing that our God Neptune will do everything for us, and won't see that Steam has paralysed his trident . . . if we won't learn that we have become Continentals, we shall be marched over. . . . Well, then conscript them, and they'll all be of a better pattern. The only thing to do, and the cheapest."

At the end of his life his views seem to have been modified to an approval of a system of military training. He wrote to his friend Hyndman, in January, 1909 :

" I was pleased to see you and Blatchford in union for a national army. A poem of mine, *The Call*, in *The Oxford and Cambridge Review* raised the same cry. One may fear that a landing of foreign artillery on our shores alone will touch the mercantile class. Doubtless, also, there is an apprehension as to the prudence of schooling the toilers in the use of arms. We are not yet a people."

In the poem he mentions, *The Call*, he pleads :

> Our people one !   Nor they with strength
> Dependent on a single arm :
> Alert, and braced the whole land's length,
> Rejoicing in their manhood's charm
> For friend or foe ; to succour, not to harm.

> . . . .

> It cannot be declared we are
> A nation till from end to end
> The land can show such front to war
> As bids a crouching foe expend
> His ire in air, and preferably be friend.

In conclusion, it must be conceded that, on the whole, Meredith's outlook upon public affairs was remarkably sane and far-seeing, and that his words, when dealing with such subjects, are as appropriate to-day as when they were written in past years. Despite his pose of criticising the English, he admitted they were " a kind-hearted people " ; he sincerely loved his native country and would, however much he loved Germany, or France, or Italy, have supported her in any supreme crisis of her fate.   As he wrote in the poem just quoted from :

> The grandeur of her deeds recall ;
> Look on her face so kindly fair :
> This Britain ! and were she to fall,
> Mankind would breathe a harsher air,
> The nations miss a light of leading rare.

CHAPTER XI

"BEAUCHAMP'S CAREER." THE SHORT NOVELS. SOME LATER LITERARY FRIENDSHIPS

DURING the decade of the "seventies," Meredith formed some additional and notable friendships, in particular with Leslie Stephen (whom he had first met in 1866), Comyns Carr, R. L. Stevenson, and Frederick Greenwood, the projector and first editor of *The Pall Mall Gazette*. To the last-named he writes, on 1st January, 1873 :

"Open your heart a minute to receive a greeting of the New Year from me. May you fight as victoriously—bravely you always will—this year as last ! May suppressed gout go limping on the other side of the river ! May you be touched with the wand of wisdom to throw off your one blindness and see the virtues of my pen as with a flash of revelation."

At this date he was contributing to another paper. He told Hardman :

"If you chance to see the commencement of a set of Dialogues in *The Graphic* you will know that your Robin, ex of Copsham Forest, has been taken on board that prosperous ship as one of the Stewards. And should you like any part of it, *quote it*, for that will fortify me. I never ask favour for novel or poem, but my pot-boiler I long to see praised, seeing that it is written for nothing else than the yellow flood that bursts through the Gates of Praise. I have sent copy for this next week. Encourage me, if you can, to think it will do, and also advise me. In no way better than by coming and administering the same with the live voice. Alack ! our cook is a lame 'un, but will we not put up prayers for her works on Sunday ? "

The Dialogues by Meredith appeared in *The Graphic*, December, 1872, and January, 1873, in five parts, and were entitled *Up to Midnight*. Seven characters discuss the topics of the day, the recent Franco-Prussian War, and the political situation abroad and at home. Recent floods and their influence on crops introduce a typical little bit of scenic painting :

" Jove was coming from the eastward, and the strip of a moon was in a cloud itself. . . . Dian veiled and tossing away fragments of dusky-coloured vapour to the gale ; there was a space of untroubled blue, darkening about the setting star, and the vast calm sheet of the invading water, with its line of river-side sallows and field-dividing elms and hedgerows, reflected all."

This leads on to a discussion of the picturesque and poetry, when Mr M'Nimbus says he prefers good boots to bad poems. Whereupon, in a passage flavoured with the genuine Meredithian tang, Mr Helion observes :

" ' These versicles of the half-literate come frequently of a restless craving for the jam-tarts of society. A kind clergyman fancies he has caught a Chatterton, and a reviewer anxious to expend an ebbing literary enthusiasm in the purchase of a situation as benefactor in a biography, lifts the victim on a puff. Ladies pet the victim. He gets his bit of jam-tart and some blanc-mange ; but it is discovered that he is not a Chatterton, and he is let down again. Clergyman, reviewer, and victim are chiefly to blame in about equal proportions ; the world and the picturesque are not ; and there will always be the picturesque to console the poor fellow, if his passion for it was originally genuine.'

" ' Eh, if he can see the picturesque through the bedraggled drab of a thriftless non-cooking British wife ! ' " breaks in Mr M'Nimbus.

" The English have an extraordinary sense of when it is respectable to put on the *undertakerly* air " is another typical remark ; and of course Meredith's favourite wind is mentioned :

" When the South West blows it is summer in England, and I confess I prefer it."

Since 1871 he had been engaged on the composition of *Beauchamp's Career*. In the spring of 1874, when the work was ready, it was not found acceptable as a successor to *Harry*

Richmond in *The Cornhill Magazine*. " I want work," the author wrote to Greenwood. " My poor *Beauchamp* is not thought good for the market by George Smith." [1] This was a disappointing omen for the story, and, perhaps, contributed more than anything else to consolidate Meredith's disgust at the lack of appreciation he thought he received (it must be remembered that he was ever appreciated by a select few of his contemporaries) and his resultant criticism of the English which we considered in the last chapter. For he was now on the flood tide of his literary powers, and *Beauchamp's Career* merited an enthusiastic reception and immediate success. Here he gave of his very best—himself, and his creations were living realities to him. He had approached and carried out his task with the most intense seriousness—too serious, I suppose, for a "popular" novel. In a letter to Dr Jessopp, dated 8th April, 1873, he said :

" I am at present too busy on *Beauchamp's Career* to spend a day in town. . . . It will run on with me through June. And it is already full to bursting—it and I. ' The world is too much with me ' when I write. I cannot go on with a story and not feel that to treat of flesh and blood is to touch the sacredest ; and so it usually ends in my putting the destinies of the world about it—like an atmosphere, out of which it cannot subsist. So my work fails. I see it. But the pressure is on me with every new work. I fear that *Beauchamp* is worse than the foregoing in this respect. The centre idea catches hold of the ring of the universe, the dialogues are the delivery of creatures of this world, and the writing goodish. But altogether it will only appeal (so I fear) to them that have a taste for me ; it won't catch the gudgeon world."

He judged only too correctly that it would not be generally popular. When the story was eventually accepted for *The Fortnightly Review*, on the condition of drastic condensation, he wrote to the editor :

" MY DEAR MORLEY,—I thank you very much for stepping over the obstruction for our mutual convenience in the matter

---

[1] *The Cornhill Magazine* had, however, published Meredith's rather obscure poem, *The Song of Theodolinda*, in September, 1872.

of *Beauchamp*. Greenwood and Maxse told me that the work pleased you. I need scarcely assure you that I look upon your appreciation of my labour as a good reward of it. I write for you and men like you. Consequently when the greater pay-master failed me,[1] I hoped the work might be accepted where it would be more suitably accommodated, feeling quite certain that you would allow nothing to stand in the way of your estimation of it on its merits. Your reluctance to undertake the burden of so lengthy a production, I cannot but think reasonable, and I gladly meet your kind proposal that I should cut it short as much as I can, without endangering the arteries. . . . It strikes me that the parts to lop will be the letters, a portion of the Visit to Normandy, the heavier of the electioneering passages, introductory paragraphs to chapters, and dialogues passim that may be considered not vital to the central idea. That which may be stated to be the personal abnegation coming, in spite of errors here and there (and as it were in spite of the man himself), of a noble devotion to politics from the roots up, I think I can retain uninjured—possibly improved by the exclusion of a host of my own reflections.

" The ' mutilation ' does me no hurt ; but hitherto I have merely looked at it to see that it could be done ;—but with shudders to think how much more there was to do ! The central portion, I fear, must be cut to pieces, condensed, re-written."

But, of course, he did feel acutely the " mutilation " of his work, for to hack at a created thing is the most painful task that could be assigned to its author. He wrote rather sadly and despondently to Moncure D. Conway, who was negotiating for the American publication of *Beauchamp's Career*, in June, 1874 :

" I am engaged in cutting down my novel for *The Fortnightly Review*. The task is hard, for I have at least to excise a third of my work, which appears to be a full three-vols. measure . . .
" I feel bound to warn you of the nature of my work. It is

---

[1] For his previous work, *Harry Richmond*, Meredith had received from *The Cornhill Magazine* £500, and a further £100 after the sale of 500 copies.

not likely to please the greater number of readers. . . . It is philosophical-political, with no powerful stream of adventure : an attempt to show the forces round a young man of the present day, in England, who would move them, and finds them un-utterably solid, though it is seen in the end that he does not altogether fail, has not lived quite in vain. Of course, this is done in the concrete. A certain drama of self-conquest is gone through, for the hero is not perfect. He is born of the upper class, and is scarcely believed in by any class, except when he vexes his own, and it is then to be hated. At the same time the mild spirit of a prosperous middle class, that is not extremely alarmed, is shown to be above persecuting ; so that the un-fortunate young man is in danger of being thought dull save by those who can enter his idea of the advancement of Humanity and his passion for it. In this he is a type. And I think his History a picture of the time—taking its mental action, and material ease and indifference, to be a necessary element of the picture.''

It is well known that the character of Beauchamp was drawn from the author's friend, Captain Frederick Maxse, R.N., to whom it was written : '' I have just finished the History of the inextinguishable Sir Harry Firebrand of the Beacon, Knight Errant of the 19th Century, in which mirror you may look and see—My dear Fred and his loving friend, George Meredith.'' Maxse's emotional, mercurial temperament passed through many changing phases. It is an interesting study to compare and collate *Beauchamp's Career* with the extensive series of letters addressed by Meredith to the prototype of his novel, for these letters analyse and advise on all those warring qualities exhibited by Beauchamp, some of them penned long before the book was written. *Beauchamp's Career* is a study of the combat in a man of his hereditary aristocratic instincts and passions with a sincere, if rather hysterical, realisation of the wrongs and needs of the democracy, with various personal feuds and fads as corollaries. So in the letters are politics (public and private) and fads—such as Maxse's abstention at one time from meat and strong drink—pregnantly or humorously dealt with, followed by many comments on the exemplar's character. To take a few extracts :

FREDERICK MAXSE, R.N. THE ORIGINAL OF NEVIL IN
"BEAUCHAMP'S CAREER"
From a contemporary photograph

" I note with dismay your tendency to extremes. You are right just now. Nevertheless you must needs lay down positive principles as if your existing state were the key of things. You will become a fanatical Retired Admiral advocating Maine Liquor Laws for every natural appetite on earth, and dogmatically refusing to hear an opinion." " I think you altogether too impetuous : 500 years too fast for the human race." " There was a report in London yesterday that you had given up Meat. I hope this is not true, though I know I used to tell you that we consume too much meat, and you (I remember) appeared to reflect on my words. The determination, which you hinted, that you would by and by abstain from clothing yourself, will not I trust be carried into effect. . . . I shall correct you very gently. Don't forget that mental arrogance is as a fiery wine to the spirit—a little of it gives a proper pride : but you carry too much." " What I dread most is that you are boiling, or simmering, yourself down to a sort of human type and engine. When you think you think suddenly, vehemently—with the force and swiftness of a meteor, and perhaps with the result, but in any case your apparent incapacity to listen to the wisdom thrust in your way is fraught with incalculable evils, and more and more I feel Fred going and an eccentric Force usurping his place." " I'm persuaded, too, that you're in error in supposing you belong to this Century, and it's only by courtesy the fellows of it don't tell you so ; it's the next you belong to, and you will find it out ; and you were not made for a Club, but for mankind." " Though the demure look you assume is very becoming and eclipses all the curates ever dreamed of by a pulpit-stricken virgin . . . still I demur . . . when I bear in mind your late extraordinary oration against One who turned the Water into Wine—in which you so violently denounced Him for having done so."

Although Meredith thus spoke his criticisms plainly, only once was he on the point of rupture with his friend, and then he said : " I am glad of the old time, am always proud of you, always heart in heart with you on all the great issues of our life, and in all that concerns your health and fortunes." The passing cloud soon blew over. Meredith fully realised his friend's fine points and shared many of his political views : " I could have no wish but to stick by you, and the more so as your views are mine." He actively assisted in canvassing for Maxse, who was the Radical Candidate in the Election of 1868 for Southampton (the Bevisham of the novel), and after the defeat told his son, Arthur Meredith : " We were badly beaten at Southampton. . . . I fancy Captain Maxse had to pay about £2000 for the attempt. He acted simply in a spirit of duty, that he might enter Parliament to plead the cause of the poor."

As the years went on, the Radical sailor became a Unionist and moderated many of his early views. His friendship with Meredith endured to the end, and when he died, in 1900, the author of *Beauchamp's Career* paid him that fine tribute : " The loss to me is past all count. . . . A light gone out. But still it cannot be quite death for a man so good and true as he. The unsuffering part of him lives with those who knew him. Nobility was his characteristic, and always where that is required in life I shall have him present. . . . Be sure that nothing good is ever lost."

Of course, Maxse must not be identified too literally with Beauchamp beyond his vivid crusading nature and his early political and social views ; though Meredith had a disconcerting way of blending actual traits and facts and names with the entirely imaginary doings of his characters.[1] As we have seen, this was brought to a fine art in *Evan Harrington*; and, as in the other novels, it is demonstrated to a slightly lesser degree in *Beauchamp's Career.* Putting aside the obvious facts of the Southampton Election and that Captain Maxse married a lady named Cecilia, daughter of Colonel Steel (Cecilia Halkett, in

[1] Comyns Carr has a suggestive comment to offer on this matter. He said, in *Some Eminent Victorians* : " Meredith could talk and walk after a fashion that I have known in no one else. Sometimes he would occupy the whole of our ramble in a purely inventive biography of some one of our common friends, passing in rather burlesque rhapsody from incident to incident of a purely hypothetical career, but always preserving, even in the most extravagant of his fancies, a proper relevancy to the character he was seeking to exhibit. On one occasion I remember he traced with inimitable humour, and with inexhaustible invention, a supposed disaster in love encountered by an amiable gentleman we both knew well ; and as he rambled on with an eloquence that never halted, he became so in love with his theme that I think he himself was hardly conscious where the record of sober fact had ended and where the innocent mendacity of the novelist had begun."

the story, being also the daughter of a Colonel), let us particularly examine the case of Beauchamp's uncle, Everard Romfrey, that delightful old Whig, who was drawn, both as to physical and mental characteristics, from Captain Maxse's maternal uncle, Grantley Berkeley (a younger son of the 5th Earl of Berkeley). It will be remembered that Everard Romfrey thrashes Dr Shrapnel with " a gold-headed horsewhip." Just so—for similarly a lady's name was involved—did Grantley Berkeley act in the famous case of his assault on James Fraser for the libellous review which appeared in *Fraser's Magazine* of his, Berkeley's, novel, *Berkeley Castle*, dealing with his family history in a peculiar manner. Grantley Berkeley felled the offending publisher to the ground and beat him savagely with a heavy gold-headed hunting-whip. Less fortunate than Shrapnel, James Fraser eventually died from an illness brought on by the injuries he had received. Grantley Berkeley's brother, Craven, was present when the assault took place : Meredith mentions the name Craven twice in his account of the Romfrey family, and he accurately describes Berkeley Castle, in Gloucestershire.

Henry Murray detected in Dr Shrapnel a physical resemblance to Meredith himself, with the same obstinate tuft of grey hair bristling up over his forehead—" the tall old man whose extreme leanness made him appear of more than his actual height . . . the face of more than feminine delicacy with an almost angelic softness of expression." Meredith certainly told Maxse that he as well as his friend could be seen in this " mirror " of a book.[1]

However this may be, there is no doubt that in Blackburn Tuckham we have an authentic and amusing picture of William Hardman. The very name at the outset establishes that. Hardman came from the Bury and Blackburn district of Lancashire, and was not " Tuck " the name bestowed by Meredith upon his friend at the very beginning of their delightful companionship ? And then, sketched with a few deft touches, is presented the figure and ruddy complexion, the north-country energy and assurance of the man ; his personal traits, his love of life and good living, and that hearty laughter which has echoed through all the letters that Meredith addressed to

[1] See *ante,* page 284.

Hardman : " This, my Friar, whom I love, must be the Rosey Boy, well plumped on British fare."

" It was amusing to find an exuberant Tory in one who was the reverse of the cavalier type. . . . Mr Tuckham had a round head, square flat forehead, and ruddy face ; he stood as if his feet claimed the earth under them for his own, with a certain shortness of leg that detracted from the majesty of his resemblance to our Eighth Harry, but increased his air of solidity ; and he was authoritative in speaking. ' Let me set you right, Sir,' . . . and that was his modesty. ' You are altogether wrong ' . . . which was his courtesy. . . . He told stories incidental to his travels now and then, commended the fishing here, the shooting there, and in some few places the cookery, with much bright emphasis when it could be praised. . . . His laughter was catching, and somehow more persuasive of the soundness of the man's heart and head than his remarks."

Beauchamp's Career was, perhaps, Meredith's favourite among his own works. He told Mr Clodd : " Sometimes *Harry Richmond* is my favourite, but I am inclined to give the palm to *Beauchamp's Career*. There is a breezy, human interest about it, and the plot has a consistency and logical evolution which *Feverel* lacks. Then, a thing that weighs with me, the French critics liked it ; they said that Renée is true to life."

Renée was very real to him. He said to Marcel Schwob : " Was she not a sweet girl ? I think I am a little in love with her yet." That was twenty years after her creation.

There was no very remarkable outburst of contemporary appreciation to greet this work, written at the height of the author's power, when it was published in three volumes by Chapman and Hall at the close of 1875. It has been stated by one prominent critic that Meredith's reputation was not materially advanced by this story, " overlaid by political disquisition," with " its somewhat monotonous hero." I understand it was at this date that Mark Pattison warned his readers against opening a volume which bore on its cover the name of George Meredith. However, H. D. Traill praised Meredith in *The Nineteenth Century* of October, 1875 ; in later years *Beauchamp's Career* has been ably noticed by Arthur Symons and other literary men ; and both Justin McCarthy and T. P.

O'Connor have declared it to be their favourite Meredith novel. James Thomson's appreciation I will deal with presently.

Presumably the popular objection to *Beauchamp's Career* is that it is neither a tale of mystery nor a love story with a happy ending. Meredith no doubt foresaw that profound criticism, for in a passage in the book where he says he envies " those happy tales of mystery," he goes on to state his own case :

" My way is like a Rhone island in the summer drought, stony, unattractive and difficult between the two forceful streams of the unreal and the over-real, which delight mankind—honour the conjurors ! My people conquer nothing, win none ; they are actual, yet uncommon. It is the clockwork of the brain that they are directed to set in motion, and—poor troop of actors to vacant benches !—the conscience residing in thoughtfulness which they would appeal to ; and if you are there impervious to them, we are lost : back I go to my wilderness, where, as you perceive, I have contracted the habit of listening to my own voice more than is good."

Although Meredith is reported to have said to York Powell : " Thank God I have never written a word to please the public," it needs no argument to prove that even in *Beauchamp's Career* there are many good sayings to please the densest public : " Property and titles are worth having, whether you are ' worthy of them,' or a disgrace to your class." " Two men in this house would give their wives for pipes, if it came to the choice. We might all go for a cellar of old wine. After forty, men have married their habits, and wives are only an item in the list and not the most important." " He escapes his nation's scourge, in the shape of a statue turned out by an English chisel." " If Providence is to do anything for us it must have a sea-worthy fleet for the operation."

Again this book also, forty-five years old though it be, is strangely topical and appropriate for to-day. The very first chapter, with its excellent allegory of the Spinster Panic aroused from her bed by letters to the papers, and lulled again by " inspired " leading articles, has been applicable to certain stages of the Great War by merely substituting Germans for French as the foes possibly invading these shores :

T

" Their spectral advance on quaking London through Kentish hop-gardens, Sussex corn-fields, or by the pleasant hills of Surrey, after a gymnastic leap over the riband of salt water, haunted many pillows. . . . We saw them in imagination lining the opposite shore ; eagle and standard-bearers, brandishing their fowls and their banners in a manner to frighten the decorum of the universe. . . . But where were our armed men ? Where our great artillery ? Where our proved captains, to resist a sudden sharp trial of the national mettle ? Where was the first line of England's defence, her navy ? These were questions, and Ministers were called upon to answer them. The Press answered them boldly, with the appalling statement that we had no navy and no army. . . . We were in fact as naked to the Imperial foe as the merely painted Britons. . . . There ensued a curious exhibition that would be termed, in simple language, writing to the newspapers : in reality, it was the deliberate saddling of our ancient nightmare of Invasion, putting the postillion on her, and trotting her along the highroad with a winding horn to rouse old Panic. . . . She turned in her bed at first like the sluggard of the venerable hymnist : but once fairly awakened, she directed a stare towards the terrific foreign contortionists, and became in an instant all stormy nightcap and fingers starving for the bell-rope. Forthwith she burst into a series of shrieks, howls, and high-piercing notes. . . . The Press, which had kindled, proceeded to extinguish her with the formidable engines called leading articles. . . . It turned out that we had ships ready for launching, and certain regiments coming home from India ; hedges we had, and a spirited body of yeomanry ; and we had pluck and patriotism, the father and mother of volunteers innumerable. Ministers were authoritatively summoned to set to work immediately. They replied that they had been at work all the time, and were at work now. They could assure the country, that though they flourished no trumpets, they positively guaranteed the safety of our virgins and our coffers. . . . Government launched a big ship with hurrahs, and ordered the recruiting-sergeant to be seen conspicuously."

The main thesis of the book, too, the author's mordant study of the ineffectual character—fine in its individual elements, but marred and stultified by waywardness, lack of balance, and the impossible ambitions of the visionary, as exemplified in the personality of Nevil Beauchamp—is a signpost of warning at this time of national stress, when clarity of reason and stability of character are essential (and alas ! how lacking) in men of politics and government and public affairs in general.

There are lovely scenic descriptions in this book—the night on the Adriatic, and sunrise upon the Alps, near Venice ; and those vivid, unforgettable scenes where Beauchamp joins Renée in Normandy, and they ride through valley and wood till they come upon the little river at Tourdestelle with its trembling poplars and rustic bridge and mill bright in the silver moonlight. That is the picture I always see when *Beauchamp's Career* is mentioned ; and no doubt Meredith described an actual landscape which he had seen during his visit to his Vulliamy relatives in Normandy during 1872.

Some points open to criticism the story must plead—such as the failure of Beauchamp to mete out adequate punishment to his enemy, Cecil Baskelett ; the seemingly impossible behaviour (though founded on fact) of Everard Romfrey, Colonel Halkett, and other " gentlemen," in permitting the private letter addressed to Beauchamp by Shrapnel to be read and ridiculed in public ; and the author's annoying method of relating important incidents, like the flogging of Shrapnel and the death of Beauchamp, by the conversations of other characters instead of in detailed and direct narrative. But these minor objections are blotted by the fineness of the literary work. Here, in this book, Meredith writes primarily *for* men and *of* women in an exquisite way. Singularly subtle is the creation of Renée's personality—half beneficent, half malign star when in conjunction with the exemplar's career. The problem of Beauchamp's relations with the four women who not so much influenced as intertwined his life is of absorbing interest ; the tragedy of his loss of Cecilia Halkett—one of the most lovable characters in Meredith's great gallery of female portraiture—brings a sense of personal regret rarely experienced in the reading of fiction. " It had stolen into him that he and she were not walking on the same bank of the river, though they were side by side ; a chill water ran between them. . . . Incredible as it was, the icy sense of his having lost her benumbed him."

Futile was Beauchamp in his wooing—" too late "—of Cecilia, and futile in his death. Pathos and tragedy here in full measure. What a flashlight of genius illumines that last scene by Hamble river : the drowned Beauchamp and the muddy, snivelling urchin he died to save : " This is what we have in exchange for Beauchamp." Poignant, splendid futility *in excelsis.*

But beyond all this, and the sense of Tragic Fate, and the graphic power of the literary artist who draws these pictures, there rises paramount a perception of Meredith's clear, sane outlook upon life, of the essential robustness of his views upon national affairs and man's duty to man. Surely *Beauchamp's Career* is the most successful accomplishment of the goal the author desired to reach ; here he voiced his message with penetrating notes, not lost upon the wind of pretentious verbiage as was sometimes the fate of his winged words.

Before leaving *Beauchamp's Career* it is of interest to recall that the book brought Meredith into personal association with James Thomson (" B. V."), the remarkable poet of the sombre *City of Dreadful Night* and the sparkling *Sunday up the River,* whose wasted gift of life and talents so sadly resembled the case of E. A. Poe. Curiously enough, the same absurd legend which bestowed Bulwer Lytton as a parent upon Meredith was attached also to the paternity of Thomson, but probably all three men were unaware of the lying rumour which propounded this literary relationship.

James Thomson was the son of a sailor and born at Port Glasgow in 1834. His profession as an army schoolmaster brought him, when stationed at the dreary barrack-village of Ballincollig, near Cork, the friendship of Charles Bradlaugh, who in those early days was a trooper in a dragoon regiment. Bradlaugh afterwards obtained various kinds of employment for his friend, and as editor of *The National Reformer* gave first publication to Thomson's poems during the years 1862-1874. It was in 1874 that *The City of Dreadful Night* appeared, and brought some meed of recognition to the poet. Thomson was one of the early admirers of Meredith's work, and *Beauchamp's Career* inspired him to contribute his able and characteristic

Note on George Meredith, in 1876, to *The Secularist*. This was followed by an equally appreciative article in *Cope's Tobacco Plant*, in May, 1879. At the same time Meredith was reading with equal appreciation the poems of Thomson, whom he only knew as " B. V." Eventually the identity of the poet with the critic was revealed by G. W. Foote to Meredith, who wrote, in May, 1879 :

" I have read Mr Thomson's article on my book with the singular pleasure we feel when it is evident that we have been loved of old date, and by the very worthiest, and that nothing but love can have that way of speaking. The mental stature of the critic is the point ; after which the sincerity. He who does me the honour to praise me in this instance, is to be valued in both respects."

And to Thomson himself he wrote :

" I am glad to be in personal communication with you. The pleasant things you have written of me could not be other than agreeable to a writer. I saw that you had the rare deep love of literature ; rare at all times and in our present congestion of matter almost extinguished ; which led you to recognise any effort to produce the worthiest. For when a friend unmasked your initials, I was flattered. For I had read *The City of Dreadful Night*, and to be praised by the author of that poem would strike all men, able to form a judgment upon eminent work, as a distinction."

There was much of Thomson's work in sympathy with Meredith's outlook upon life and his poetical expression of thought. Consequently the latter was able to give very high praise to his new friend's volume of verse in 1880 :

" In writing to you about this admirable and priceless book of verse I have wished to be competent to express my feeling for your merit, and as much as possible the praise of such rarely equalled good work. My friends could tell you that I am a critic hard to please. They say that irony lurks in my eulogy. I am not in truth frequently satisfied by verse. Well, I have gone through your volume, and I have not found the line I would propose to recast. I have found many pages that no other English poet could have written. Nowhere is the verse feeble, nowhere is the expression insufficient; the majesty of the line has always its full colouring, and marches under a banner. . . . I have not time at present to speak of the City of Melancholia. There is a massive impressiveness in it that goes beyond Dürer, and takes it into upper regions where poetry is the sublimation of the mind of man, the voice of our highest. . . . I am in love with the dear London lass who helped you to the ' Idyll of Cockaigne.' You give a zest and new attraction to Hampstead Heath." [1]

The two poets only met twice in life. In September, 1881, Thomson visited Flint Cottage and relates :

" Tuesday I spent with George Meredith at Box Hill ; a quiet, pleasant day, cloudy but rainless, with some sunshine and blue sky in the afternoon. We had a fine stroll over Mickleham Downs, really park-like, with noble yew-trees and many a mountain-ash (' rowan ' we Scots call it) glowing with thick clusters of red berries. M. read me an unpublished poem of considerable length. He says that having suspended work on a novel, poems began to spring up in his mind, and I am glad that he thinks of bringing out a new collection."

Meredith endeavoured to help Thomson and further his literary prospects by introducing him to John Morley, the editor of important papers. But it was too late ; his efforts were in vain, like those of Thomson's other friends. The melancholy poet's intemperance was a form of madness engendered by morbid depression and despair of the most appalling kind. It was periodical in attack, and made him too weak and unfit to carry out any literary employment given to him. The last tragic months found him wholly in the power of his foe, and he died in University College Hospital on 3rd June, 1882, at the age of forty-seven. In subsequent letters to Thomson's biographer, Mr H. S. Salt, Meredith further expressed his appreciation of the unhappy poet :

[1] *Sunday up the River* was " An Idyll of Cockaigne " : *Sunday at Hampstead* " An Idle Idyll."

" Few men have been endowed with so brave a heart. He did me the honour to visit me twice, when I was unaware of the extent of the tragic affliction overclouding him. . . . I have now the conviction that the taking away of poverty from his burdens would in all likelihood have saved him, to enrich our literature ; for his verse was a pure well. He has, almost past example in my experience, the thrill of the worship of valiancy as well as of sensuous beauty. . . . But he inherited the tendency to the thing which slew him. . . . He was a man of big heart, of such entire sincereness that he wrote directly from the impressions carved in him by his desolate experience of life. . . . No Inferno could be darker. But the poetical effect of a greater part of the Poems is that of a litany of the vaults below. . . . Bright achievement was plucked out of the most tragic life in our literature. . . . Now and then I have had in me jet of an endeavour to hit the delicate balance which would give the just portrait of a brave good man and true poet, hapless in his birth, fighting his best, and not failing, though baffled."

Meredith's association with James Thomson, and his unfailing sympathy with him, is one of the most charming episodes in the records of literary friendships.

Following the publication of *Beauchamp's Career*, Meredith did not produce very much during the next few years. He was writing some short stories and poems, and studying the idea of Comedy, which was to bear fruit in the Essay on the subject and in *The Egoist*. Life at Box Hill was very pleasant in these days. In August and September, 1874, he writes :

" Latterly I have been rising here at half-past five, and have enjoyed the tonic morning air immensely, yet more the fresh loveliness of the downs and fields, the velvet shadows, sharp and thin, and the exquisite sky. . . . I am finishing a Poem, *The Nuptials of Attila*—about forty pages : Jacob [1] at my foot, an accustomed pigeon on the window-sill, bees below humming. . . . For a week we have had fine S. W. skies : yesterday was quite wonderful with scaling clouds. I went up the hill with Will and his mother and sister (Jacob of course) and we flew a kite and dreamed. It was on the whole as good as Switzerland while it lasted."

[1] A dachshund presented by Maxse.

In June, 1875, he invites Morley : " Come on Wednesday in
time for a French breakfast in the garden about ¼ past 11.
You have no idea how nice it is.   We tried it on Sunday with
three good men and an ancient Hock, and I assure you that
staid and formal day danced to its end like an ecclesiastic that
has received the promise of a bishopric."

Meredith had always loved choice food and good wine, as we
have seen, but unfortunately he suffered from a weak stomach,
which constrained him to try for a time the vegetarian regimen
he had so stoutly warned Maxse against but a few years earlier.
Mr Hyndman, in paying a tribute to the merits of Meredith's
second wife, makes amusing allusion to the vegetarian trial
which the victim pursued with characteristic ardour.

" I have heard some of Meredith's friends speak rather
slightingly of this lady, as if she were intellectually quite unworthy of her husband.   Genius has no mate.   But Mrs Meredith
was a charming, clever, tactful and handsome Frenchwoman,
a good musician, a pleasant conversationalist, a most consider-
ate, attentive and patient wife, and an excellent mother.
Nobody who knew her could fail to admire, esteem, and like
her.   Her care of her husband was always thoughtful but never
obtrusive, and Meredith, with all his high qualities, was not by
any means an easy man to live with.   Writing men mostly are
not.   At one time he would persist in turning vegetarian.   It
was well-nigh the death of him.   But he had persuaded himself
that that was the right sort of food to give the highest development to body and mind, and persist in it he would.   What was
to be done ?   Meredith was a man who took a tremendous lot
out of himself, not only intellectually but physically.   He was
always throwing about clubs or going through gymnastic
exercises, or taking long walks at a great pace, not allowing an
ounce of fat to accumulate on his body or his face.   It was the
same with his writing.   He never pretended to take matters
easily.   So poor Mrs Meredith had a hard time during this
bread and roots period.   She saw her husband gradually going
down hill, and becoming every day more gaunt and hungry-eyed
and skeletonic ; yet if she or anyone else ventured to suggest
that this meagre diet was unsuited to a man of his habit of life
and work, and that—this very gently—his increasing acerbity

was caused by sheer lack of sustenance and his energy consequently sawing into his exposed nerves—well, it was a case of
' stand from under ' very quickly."

Mrs Meredith endeavoured to remedy the situation by
introducing shredded meat, with the connivance of the
local baker, into the bread intended for her husband's
consumption.

Although Meredith always appreciated good wine, his enthusiasm for rare vintages, which often sparkle in his works, seems
to have been modified with advancing age, probably because
he found that stimulants did not agree with him. He told
Mr W. G. Collings, in 1887 :

" I do not abjure wine, when it is old and of good vintage.
I take it rarely. I think that the notion of drinking any kind
of alcohol as a stimulant for intellectual work can have entered
the minds of those only who snatch at the former that they may
conceive a fictitious execution of the latter. Stimulants may
refresh, and may even temporarily comfort, the body after
labour of brain ; they do not help it—not even in the lighter
kinds of labour. They unseat the judgment, pervert vision.
Productions cast off by the aid of the use of them, are but
flashy trashy stuff—or exhibitions of the prodigious in wildness or grotesque conceit, of the kind which Hoffman's tales
give, for example ; he was one of the few at all eminent
who wrote after drinking. Schiller in a minor degree—not to
the advantage of his composition. None of the great French
or English."

But as late as 1891 he expatiated on the joys of Old Veuve
and Burgundy in *One of our Conquerors* ; and in a letter of
June, 1908, he wrote : " I drink wine and I smoke."

During 1876 he wrote several poems for *The Fortnightly
Review*—" Pecks of poetry have been coming from me " —
including his fine *Ballad of Past Meridian* :

> Last night returning from my twilight walk
> I met the grey mist Death, whose eyeless brow
> Was bent on me, and from his hand of chalk
> He reached me flowers as from a withered bough :
> O Death, what bitter nosegays givest thou !

> Death said, I gather, and pursued his way,
> Another stood by me, a shape in stone,
> Sword-hacked and iron-stained, with breasts of clay,
> And metal veins that sometimes fiery shone :
> O Life, how naked and how hard when known !
>
> Life said, As thou hast carved me, such am I.
> Then memory, like the nightjar on the pine,
> And sightless hope, a woodlark in night sky,
> Joined notes of Death and Life till night's decline :
> Of Death, of Life, those inwound notes are mine.

In December, 1876, he seems to have received a visit from Bonaparte Wyse and R. H. Horne—his " deep-hearted friend " in early manhood, for writing to the former he says :

" I find it is quite impossible for me to spare a morning to come to you, but you can I am sure manage to come to me. The truth is, I am very busy with divers bits of work. . . . I shall be able to attend on you for I rarely write after one P.M.

" Pray, if you think fit, ask Horne, with my compliments to him. Only, he should be made to know, as you do, that the sort of entertainment I am able to give here is very poor, anything but attractive. I have no bed to offer, and not much of a cook to fortify a friend in winter for the long return journey."

Meredith had now completed his essay *On the Idea of Comedy and the Uses of the Comic Spirit*, and he was induced to deliver it in the form of a lecture at the London Institution, Finsbury Circus, on 1st February, 1877, which was, I think, his first and last appearance as chief actor at a public function of this description. " I hate it," he said of lecturing ; " and it does not pay me, it makes me nervous and I have to give up my inner mind's work to it. But I have the question going on whether I ought to decline anything, I unlucky, portionless, ill-paid."

The lecture seems to have been quite a success. " All went well," he wrote Morley. " Audience very attentive and indulgent. Time 1 h. 25 m. and no one left the hall, so that I may imagine there was interest in the lecture. Pace moderate : but Morison thinks I was intelligible chiefly by the distinctness of articulation." The Essay was soon after published, in *The New Quarterly Magazine*, April, 1877—" cursed with misprints that made me dance gadfly-bitten . . . some, I am afraid, attributable to me. I am the worst of correctors of my own writing."

It is needless to recapitulate the argument of the Essay and Meredith's plea that an atmosphere of mental equality between the sexes is required before pure Comedy can truly flourish. One characteristically comic extract may be quoted, that relating to the national reaction from the dissolute Restoration comedies :

" Our tenacity of national impressions has caused the word theatre since then to prod the Puritan nervous system like a satanic instrument ; just as one has known Anti-Papists, for whom Smithfield was redolent of a sinister smoke, as though they had a later recollection of the place than the lowing herds. Hereditary Puritanism, regarding the stage, is met, to this day, in many families quite undistinguished by arrogant piety."

Meredith had contributed also to *The New Quarterly Magazine*, for January, 1877, his first short novel, *The House on the Beach*. This story, as I have previously related, was commenced as far back as 1861, under the title of *Van Diemen Smith*, and contained Meredith's impressions of Seaford. When he resumed the narrative fifteen years later he seems to have amplified the character of Martin Tinman with some particulars of a civic quidnunc at Kingston, whose doings were related to him by Hardman. He writes to the latter, on 28th September, 1876 :

" DEAR LORD MAYOR TUCK,—. . . At your leisure, write out for me briefly the case of the man Busbey or Busby, and his conflict with your Board of town-councillors, Aldermen and what not : being careful to give the exact titles to them, and his position. It strikes me that I may make something of it ; and no man can put such things more succinctly than you. If I am right, you will have some entertainment, and I as ever shall be bound in gratitude to you. Let me have the official title of your convenings for general, for special, and for extraordinary occasions. Also how you are attended, whether by policemen or other constables, and in what halls you meet. In fact I am desirous to have the local colouring—but not of Kingston proper, you understand."

Meredith's second short novel, *The Case of General Ople and Lady Camper*, which followed in *The New Quarterly Magazine*, for July, 1877, was also based on an affair which had occurred in Kingston, when General Hopkins, a distinguished soldier, living at 1 Park Gate Villas, Queen's Road, Norbiton, was compelled to take action against his neighbour at No 2, Lady Eleanor Cathcart, an eccentric person, who persisted in annoying him by sending caricatures of himself engaged in gardening and otherwise. Needless to say, the end of the case was not the matrimonial one of the story. Hardman was a friend of General Hopkins, and Meredith wrote to him : " Run your eyes over *The Case of General Ople and Lady Camper*. I think you will recognise the General and remember the case." He transferred the scene of the tale to Norbiton Hall and Kingston Lodge, the houses previously occupied by Hardman and himself. In General Ople's " gentlemanly residence " there is a very accurate picture of Kingston Lodge, with its entrance lodge like " two sentry-boxes," its garden and privacy. And the opening description of how the General came to the place " across a famous common " (Wimbledon) and by " a lofty highway along the borders of a park " (the Kingston Hill side of Richmond Park) is topographically correct.

Meredith's third, and best, short novel, *The Tale of Chloe*, appeared in *The New Quarterly Magazine*, July, 1879.[1] This little tale of Tunbridge Wells in the eighteenth century is one of the most perfect things he ever wrote. It is a masterpiece of construction and accomplishment, and makes one regret that he did not essay miniatures of this description again. Both the period of the story and the tragic end were unusual for Meredith, but he traverses both triumphantly. The characterisation is admirable. Beau Beamish is a kind of adaptation of the autocratic Nash translated from Bath, but Chloe is a brilliant creation. For her, Meredith must have " dug down to the very roots of human nature," as Sir J. M. Barrie said.[2]

Sir J. M. Barrie has ever been one of the staunchest Meredithians. His admiration dated from his early manhood, and

[1] The original manuscript was sold for £171 at Sotheby's in 1910. It was entitled *The Lamentable Tale of Chloe*.

[2] *The Lost Works of George Meredith*, by J. M. Barrie, in *The Scots Observer*, 24th November, 1888. His plea for the republication of Meredith's short novels has, of course, been carried out in several editions since then.

the story of how he went down to Box Hill to try to get a glimpse of Meredith, and how he fled when the author appeared on the garden path, is true. I asked Sir J. M. Barrie if the legend followed facts, and he replied : " The first time I went down I sat on the bank gazing at what I was told was *the* window, and then he came to the door, and I drank my fill. Then he slowly came down the path and then I fled. If that's the story, it is ' gospel.' " That was about 1885, and he later became one of Meredith's most valued friends. Another interesting friendship between Meredith and a young Scotsman destined for literary fame was that with Robert Louis Stevenson.

It was in 1878 that Stevenson and his mother came to pass the summer at the Burford Bridge Hotel. Through the introduction of Mrs J. E. H. Gordon he met Meredith, and would listen with rapt attention to the novelist's talk. Mrs Gordon relates (in *The Bookman*, January, 1895) :

" I well remember the eager listening face of the student Stevenson, and remember his frank avowal that from henceforth he should enrol himself ' a true-blue Meredith man.' He was an inspiring listener, and had the art of drawing out the best of Mr Meredith's brilliant powers of conversation. . . . My sister, I remember, was much interested in Stevenson, and even in those early days expected great things from him in the future. And I well remember her satisfaction one afternoon when . . . Mr Meredith trumpeted down our feeble utterances by informing us that some day he felt sure we should all be proud to have known him, and prophesied success and fame for him in the future."

To Mr W. M. Fullerton, Meredith said : " I knew Stevenson long before he was known to you all. I saw what was in him and knew that he would do good work."

It was Stevenson who was destined also to do " good work " of another kind in conjunction with W. E. Henley, Grant Allen, James Thomson, and others, and that was in compelling public recognition of Meredith's superlative literary work by means of forceful and enthusiastic criticism, raising his standard and proclaiming his title to fame. It is a mistake, however, to think that these new champions introduced or " made " Meredith, or even " boomed " him—to quote the unpleasant phrase of one of them : they simply made him known to the wide outside public which takes its instruction from the Press and reads what its neighbour recommends.　As we have seen, Meredith had always had the approval of a select band of cultured readers, even if the professional critics were adverse.　And young Oxford had discovered him without any extraneous introductions. "My dear boy, we read Meredith in the early seventies at Oxford," York Powell said to Professor Oliver Elton ; and a decade later, Mr F. T. Bettany relates : "We were all madly in love with George Meredith in my undergraduate days at Christ Church. . . . For us youngsters George Meredith was what Dickens had been to our seniors, and our joy in him was, I fear, just a little enhanced by his being—then, at least— caviare to the general." [1]

Oscar Wilde was at Oxford in the seventies, and it would be interesting to know if he was of the company who read and appreciated Meredith.　Most probably he was, for it was only some ten years later (1889) that he wrote his famous criticism in *The Decay of Lying* :

"Ah ! Meredith ! Who can define him ? His style is chaos illumined by flashes of lightning.　As a writer he has mastered everything except language : as a novelist he can do everything, except tell a story : as an artist he is everything except articulate.　Somebody in Shakespeare—Touchstone, I think—talks about a man who is always breaking his shins over his own wit, and it seems to me that this might serve as the basis for a criticism of Meredith's method.　But whatever he is, he is not a realist.　Or rather I would say that he is a child of realism who is not on speaking terms with his father.　By deliberate choice he has made himself a romanticist.　He has refused to bow the knee to Baal, and, after all, even if the man's fine spirit did not revolt against the noisy assertions of realism, his style would be quite sufficient of itself to keep life at a respectful distance.　By its means he has planted round his garden a hedge full of thorns, and red with wonderful roses."

And two years later, 1891, Wilde wrote in *The Soul of Man under Socialism* :

[1] Mr F. Schiller tells me that Meredith was widely read by the undergraduates of Cambridge also at this date.

" One incomparable novelist we have now in England, Mr George Meredith. There are better artists in France, but France has no one whose view of life is so large, so varied, so imaginatively true. There are tellers of stories in Russia who have a more vivid sense of what pain in fiction may be. But to him belongs philosophy in fiction. His people not merely live, but they live in thought. One can see them from myriad points of view. They are suggestive. There is soul in them and around them. They are interpretative and symbolic. And he who made them, those wonderful quickly-moving figures, made them for his own pleasure, and has never asked the public what they wanted, has never cared to know what they wanted, has never allowed the public to dictate to him or influence him in any way, but has gone on intensifying his own personality, and producing his own individual work. At first none came to him. That did not matter. Then the few came to him. That did not change him. The many have come now. He is still the same. He is an incomparable novelist."

This passage, I think, is one of the most acute observations ever penned on Meredith's art and his attitude to himself and the public. Unfortunately, Meredith was not able to offer any appreciation in return to the poet who had termed him " a prose Browning," and whose poetry was so often akin to his own in its passionate expression of beauty in Nature. On one occasion, in September, 1892, Meredith met Wilde. " I was with the Walter Palmers at Reading last week for a couple of days, met among others Oscar Wylde (*sic*), who is good company," he wrote to a friend. But he was not favourably impressed by the paradoxical man himself, so Watts-Dunton told me, and apparently in view of the fact that he misspelled Wilde's name, he was not familiar with the work of the author of *Dorian Gray*.[1] Otherwise his critical judgment should have given a guerdon of praise to *The Garden of Eros* and *The Burden of Itys*, poems which were inspired by the same spirit that had found expression in song in the older poet's *Poems and Lyrics of the Joy of Earth*.

[1] Mr Frank Harris, in his *Contemporary Portraits* (1915), states that Meredith regarded Wilde as a *poseur* and by no means in the front rank of literature, and that he peremptorily refused to sign a memorial for the remission of some portion of Wilde's sentence in 1895.

CHAPTER XII

" THE EGOIST." " THE TRAGIC COMEDIANS "

IT was in the early spring of 1877 that the chalet in the garden of Flint Cottage was ready for occupation, and Meredith wrote to Morley: "I want you to see my cottage-annexe-chalet on the terrace. I think you will agree with me that it is the prettiest to be found, the view is without a match in Surrey. The interior full of light, which can be moderated; and, while surrounded by firs, I look over the slope of our green hill to the ridges of Leith, round to Ranmore, and the half of Norbury. . . . I am very hard at work, writing a 5 Act Comedy in verse, besides tales, poems, touches of a novel, and helping my wife with a translation.[1] But in this room of mine I should have no excuse for idleness. In truth, work flows with me. You should know, I work and sleep up in my cottage, at present, and anything grander than the days and nights at my porch you will not find away from the Alps: for the dark line of my hill runs up to the stars, the valley below is a soundless gulf. There I pace like a shipman before turning in. In the day, with the S. West blowing, I have a brilliant universe rolling up to me.

> " My study, flanked with ivied fir
> And budded beech with dry leaves curled."

The first-fruits of this ideal work-place were *The Tale of Chloe*, and then *The Egoist*—the most brilliant of all his novels, wherein a spirit like that of champagne—or shall we say the tonic air of Ranmore and Box Hill?—bubbles and froths and scintillates in a prodigal outpouring of wit and epigram, comedy and mordacity. His surroundings were the scenic setting of *The Egoist*. "Patterne Hall" is not far from Denbies and Ranmore and Dorking ("Rendon"), and in this book Meredith gives his grandest picture of his beloved South-West in stormy mood and his own joy in his own Surrey hills:

[1] Probably *The Life of Cavour*.

304

THE CHALET IN THE GARDEN OF FLINT COTTAGE. HERE
"THE EGOIST," "DIANA OF THE CROSSWAYS," AND THE LATER
BOOKS WERE WRITTEN
Photograph by Mr. Wood

" Rain was universal ; a thick robe of it swept from hill to hill ; thunder rumbled remote, and between the ruffled roars the downpour pressed on the land with a great noise of eager gobbling, much like that of the swine's trough fresh filled, as though a vast assembly of the hungered had seated themselves clamorously and fallen on to meats and drinks in a silence, save of the chaps. A rapid walker poetically and humorously minded gathers multitudes of images on his way. And rain, the heaviest you can meet, is a lively companion when the resolute pacer scorns discomfort of wet clothes and squealing boots. South-western rain-clouds, too, are never long sullen : they enfold and will have the earth in a good strong glut of the kissing overflow ; then, as a hawk with feathers on his beak of the bird in his claw lifts head, they rise and take veiled feature in long climbing watery lines : at any moment they may break the veil and show soft upper cloud, show sun on it, show sky, green near the verge they spring from, of the green of grass in early dew ; or, along a travelling sweep that rolls asunder overhead, heaven's laughter of purest blue among titanic white shoulders : it may mean fair smiling for awhile, or be the lightest interlude ; but the watery lines, and the drifting, the chasing, the upsoaring, all in a shadowy fingering of form, and the animation of the leaves of the trees pointing them on, the bend-ing of the tree-tops, the snapping of branches, and the hurrah-ings of the stubborn hedge at wrestle with the flaws, yielding but a leaf at most, and that on a fling, make a glory of contest and wildness without aid of colour to inflame the man who is at home in them from old association on road, heath, and moun-tain. Let him be drenched, his heart will sing. And thou, trim cockney, that jeerest, consider thyself, to whom it may occur to be out in such a scene, and with what steps of a nervous dancing master it would be thine to play the hunted rat of the elements, for the preservation of the one imagined dry spot about thee, somewhere on thy luckless person ! The taking of rain and sun alike befits men of our climate, and he who would have the secret of a strengthening intoxication must court the clouds of the South-West with a lover's blood."

Commenced in 1877, and said to be " on the way to a con-clusion " in June, 1878, *The Egoist* was in reality not completed

U

until February, 1879 : " I finished a 3 vol. work rapidly, and as it comes mainly from the head and has nothing to kindle imagination, I thirsted to be rid of it soon after conception, and it became a struggle in which health suffered, and my unfailing specific of hard exercise was long in resting me." During the last three months of composition he wrote late into the night.

Apparently Meredith was a little doubtful of the effect the blinding brilliance of his cleverest work would have upon his friends, for he told Stevenson :

" I don't think you will like it : I doubt if those who care for my work will take to it at all. And for this reason, after doing my best with it, I am in no hurry to see it appear. It is a Comedy, with only half of me in it, unlikely therefore to take either the public or my friends. This is true truth, but I warned you that I am cursed with a croak."

The work was published in three volumes, by Kegan Paul and Co., in October, 1879,[1] and without the author's leave it made a serial appearance under the title of *Sir Willoughby Patterne, the Egoist*, in *The Glasgow Weekly Herald*. Writing from Goldrill House, Patterdale, Westmorland, where, in July, he was staying with John Morley, Meredith told Stevenson : " The diplomatic Kegan has dealt me a stroke. Without a word to me, he sold the right of issue of *The Egoist* to *The Glasgow Herald*, and allowed them to be guilty of a perversion of my title. I wrote to him in my incredulous astonishment. He replied to me, excusing himself with cool incompetency. He will have to learn (he is but young at it) that these things may be done once —not more."

With the publication of *The Egoist* Meredith took possession of his kingdom. He could no longer complain of ignorant and unappreciative reviewers. There was a chorus of praise in the Press. Within a few days *The Spectator*, *The Examiner*, *The Pall Mall Gazette*, and *The Athenæum* all paid their tribute of warm appreciation.[2] The reviews in the two last-named papers

---

[1] A second edition, in one volume, followed in 1880.

[2] As James Thomson put it in his Diary : " At length ! Encouraging ! A man of wonderful genius and a splendid writer may hope to obtain something like recognition after working hard for thirty years, dating from his majority ! "

INTERIOR OF THE CHALET, SHOWING ALSO THE COMMUNICATING ROOM WHERE MEREDITH SLEPT

Photograph by Mr. Wood

were written by W. E. Henley, who also contributed the notice in *The Academy*—all three appearing in November, 1879. He and Stevenson were, of course, radiantly delighted that their perspicacity concerning Meredith's genius was at length justified and admitted. The two kept up their airy Badminton of praise of their idol, and particularly of *The Egoist*, until the end of life. It was in April, 1882, that Stevenson wrote that well-known letter :

" MY DEAR HENLEY,—. . . Talking of Meredith, I have just re-read for the third or fourth time *The Egoist*. When I shall have read it the sixth or seventh, I begin to see I shall know about it. You will be astonished when you come to re-read it ; I had no idea of the matter—human red matter—he has contrived to plug and pack into that strange and admirable book. Willoughby is, of course, a pure discovery ; a complete set of nerves, not heretofore examined, and yet running all over the human body—a suit of nerves. Clara is the best girl I ever saw anywhere. Vernon is almost as good. The manner and faults of the book greatly justify themselves on further study. Only Mr Middleton does not hang together ; and Ladies Busshe and Culmer *sont des monstruosités*. . . . I see more and more that Meredith is built for immortality. . . .

" I am, Yours loquaciously,

" R. L. S."

Certainly *The Egoist* must be immortal, for despite its cold glittering artificiality and intellectual and philosophical preciosity, the sheer cleverness of the book, its wealth of epigram, the riot of outrageous simile, the concatenation of antithesis and antiperistasis, make it unique, a towering alpine peak in literature, crested with eternal gleaming snows.

This is the most quotable of Meredith's books. Open it anywhere at random and an acute phrase will spring to light. " Life is duty ; duty to parents, duty to country. But friendship is the holiday of those who can be friends. Wives are plentiful, friends are rare." " Personal ambition. I have it no more. And what is it when we have it ? Decidedly a confession of inferiority ! That is, the desire to be distinguished is an acknowledgement of insufficiency." " Cleverness in women is not uncommon. Intellect is the pearl. A woman of intellect is as good as a Greek statue ; she is divinely wrought, and she is divinely rare." " Women have us back to the conditions of primitive man, or they shoot us higher than the topmost star." " The fact that she was a healthy young woman, returned to the surface of his thoughts like the murdered body pitched into the river, which will not drown and calls upon the elements of dissolution to float it." " Literary men, it is notorious, even with the entry to society, have no taste in women. The house- wife is their object." Then Dr Corney's comment on his patient's last superstitions : " Pill and priest launch him happy between them." And how aptly the Court of Charles II. is summed up in these few words : " Oh ! it was a naughty Court. Yet have we dreamed of it as the period when an English cavalier was grace incarnate ; far from the boor now hustling us in another sphere ; beautifully mannered, every gesture dulcet. And if the ladies were . . . we will hope they have been traduced. But if they were, if they were too tender, ah ! gentlemen were gentlemen then—worth perishing for ! "

To revert to the history of the book. There was some question of dramatising the story for the stage as late as 1898. Meredith told friends : " A man named Sutro [1] came here from Forbes Robertson some days back with the proposal to drama- tise *The Egoist*, as Forbes has taken to the notion of personating *Sir Willoughby*. It may be done. Sutro brings me the sketch of the Comedy shortly." And " I have to prepare *The Egoist* for the boards and can go nowhere." But the project was abandoned later.

It is curious that the work has not appealed to actor-managers more, for it would make a superlative comedy of manners, and the part of Sir Willoughby could be made very picturesque in appearance, due attention being given to his " leg."

To pass to the prototypes of the novel. It is unnecessary to seek for an actual original of Sir Willoughby Patterne (although Meredith said he had a certain man in mind), for he is a universal type, a lay-figure from which everyone can study certain traits and qualities common to all humanity. He is as accurately constructed from the original (up to a certain stage) as Tartuffe,

[1] Alfred Sutro, subsequently to be well-known as the author of *The Walls of Jericho* (1904) and other successful plays.

and is, as Henley said, " a companion figure to Arnolphe and Alceste and Célimène . . . a compendium of the Personal in man." There is the story, told by R. L. Stevenson, of how a young friend of Meredith's came to him in a rage and cried : " This is too bad of you, Willoughby is me ! " " No, my dear fellow," replied the author of *The Egoist*, " he is all of us." To which Stevenson added the comment : " I am like the young friend of the anecdote—I think Willoughby an unmanly but a very serviceable exposure of myself."

We are all egoists, and consequently we can all see some aspects of ourselves in Willoughby Patterne ; and all those who have loved—or desired—as he, where love—or desire— was not responsive, but only toleration or repulsion, can realise the pangs he suffered in his relations with Clara Middleton, whom at the same time he adored and yet longed to punish and wound in his baffled agony of mind.

This universality of Willoughby Patterne makes him a verit- able mirror wherein poor humanity can see itself in the manner desiderated by Burns ; but he is a figure of pathos rather than one of comedy. He is almost tragedy sometimes, as in the scene where he is foiled in obtaining possession of the letter Clara has left with her maid on the morning of her intended flight :

" Struck by the ridicule of his posture of expectation and of his whole behaviour, he went to his bedroom suite, shut himself in and paced the chambers, amazed at the creature he had become. Agitated like the commonest of wretches, destitute of self-control, not able to preserve a decent mask, he, accustomed to inflict these emotions and tremors upon others, was at once the puppet and dupe of an intriguing girl. His very stature seemed lessened. The glass did not say so, but the shrunken heart within him did, and wailfully too."

I see nothing comic in Willoughby, this unhappy man with- out a true friend, except his stilted phraseology, which is where he fails to resemble universality, and in the ridiculous final imbroglio, which is simply farcical and unworthy of Meredith. As we have seen, he finished the story hurriedly and with health affected. Unhappily, many of Meredith's novels go to pieces and improbabilities at the close, for he did not possess the craft of the real cohesive tale-teller, and in this case the art which

had embellished the earlier part is smashed into as many fragments as Colonel De Craye's unlucky porcelain vase. The
behaviour of Lady Busshe, Lady Culmer, and even Mrs Mountstuart Jenkinson is a preposterous perversion of the type they
are supposed to represent ; Clara Middleton's acquiescence—in
view of her previously obstinate character—to Willoughby's
arrangement to marry her off alternatively to Whitford is a
hard strain on the probabilities ; and Willoughby's final loss
of all sense of dignity and decency in his desperate attempt to
secure the faded and ailing Lætitia is in complete contradiction
to the presentment, up till then, of his proud and sensitive
nature. It may be charged to be a cynical reflection on the
female sex, but in actual life a baronet, good-looking and
generous, with fifty thousand a year, would not have to look
far for a wife, and would not be reduced to implore, on his
knees, a poor and plain and aging spinster in ill-health, and a
disappointed " poetess " to boot, to take pity on his unmarried
situation and thereby save his face in the eyes of the world. As
a work of art *The Egoist* should have ended with Willoughby's
loss of Clara Middleton, and he left alone with the dead sea fruit
of his reflections. Meredith, speaking perhaps from experiences of his own first marriage, thought to condemn him to an
even bitterer retribution : " But he had the lady with brains !
He had : and he was to learn the nature of that possession in
the woman who is our wife."

What all the commentators of *The Egoist* seem to have missed
is the fact that almost the whole gallery of characterisation in
the book is a study of egoism : young Crossjay Patterne, Dr
Corney, and the Ladies Eleanor and Isabel are the only exceptions. In this mordant unveiling of people seeking their own
benefit and the gratification of personal desires, here is Dr
Middleton looking out for his own ease and quiet and superlative port, and a great establishment for his daughter ; the
same ambitions, in other aspects, affect the valetudinarian Mr
Dale ; Lætitia Dale merely marries her shattered idol to obtain
wealth and power ; Willoughby's disloyal friend, the despicable
De Craye, plots to rob him of his affianced wife ; Vernon Whitford is selfishly immersed in his own studious ambitions, and
does not show much solicitude for the cause of his cousin and
benefactor, whom he criticises slightingly ; Flitch longs only for

the port and flesh-pots of the Hall kitchen ; the aim of the great
" ladies " is to gratify their love of meddling in other people's
affairs and their love of gossip ; and Clara Middleton is as
complete an egoist as Willoughby himself. True, she has the
grace to admit it at the end (*after* she has got her own way in
every desire) : " I was the Egoist. I am sure, if I had been
buried, I should not have stood up seeing myself more vilely
stained, soiled, disfigured. I need purification by fire."
" Call me anything but good."

I do not subscribe to the general enthusiasm and admiration
for Clara Middleton which places her as " Meredith's most
perfect heroine." If she be so, it is a strange reflection on his
other admirable and true female creations, such as Rosamund
Culling, Nesta Radnor, Cecilia Halkett, Ottilia, Sandra Belloni,
Chloe, and Diana. As Dr Middleton says to his daughter :
" Epitome that you are of all the contradictions and muta-
bilities ascribed to women from the beginning," so she is. A
selfish, wayward girl, moody and unreasonable, never knowing
her own mind ; an undutiful and disobedient daughter ; de-
ceitful and prevaricating ; ungrateful—even to Vernon Whitford when she dubs him " a Triton ashore " ; she is always
seeking her own mental and physical comfort, untruthful whenever occasion requires—" fibs, evasions, the serene battalions
of white lies parallel on the march with dainty vague falsehoods. . . . Clara's fibs and evasions disturbed her not in the
least." And yet this is the perfect character described by the
late Miss Hannah Lynch, in her study of Meredith, thus :

" In all fiction there is not another girl so enchanting and
healthily intelligent as Clara Middleton—none described like
her. In addition to the attractions of birth, breeding, and
beauty . . . are those of . . . singular *good taste and tact*, and
honesty of soul . . . *without any shabby tricks of mind or
habit.*"[1]

---

[1] It is perhaps superfluous to regard Miss Lynch seriously as a critic,
as it was this lady who committed herself, in reply to Mr Le Gallienne's
suggestion that Mrs Berry, of *Richard Feverel*, would have been a feather
in the cap of Dickens, to the egregious statement : " Doubtless, but
that is not a compliment to Mr Meredith, for what would do honour to
Dickens cannot be said to be worthy of him."

The italics are mine. The fact is, the cold brilliance, the scintillating arts and crafts of *The Egoist*, have blinded the partial critics to the irony that underlies the whole conception of the work. They perceive the beauty and youth, so artistically suggested, of Clara Middleton, the wit of De Craye, but they do not see that these and other prominent characters are as egotistical as Willoughby, and more contemptible than he, inasmuch as they lack his generosity and strength of will. Otherwise how could even Henley write : " Its characters, from Sir Willoughby downwards, are brilliantly right and sound ; it has throughout the perfect good-breeding of high comedy." Perfect good breeding : Horace De Craye and Lady Busshe !

Dr Middleton often suggests an echo of Meredith's father-in-law, Thomas Love Peacock, with his scholarship, his fine taste in food and wine, and his love of ease and quiet :

" The Rev. Doctor was a fine old picture ; a specimen of art peculiarly English ; combining in himself piety and epicurism, learning and gentlemanliness."

Thus, when compelled to give a verdict on Mrs Mountstuart Jenkinson's wine, torn between disapproval and politeness : " Ladies, he said, were famous poisoners in the Middle Ages. His opinion was that we had a class of manufacturing wine-merchants on the watch for widows in this country. . . . ' Our hostess is not responsible. But widows should marry.' "

It is through the Doctor that Meredith pays his most anacreontic tribute to the King of Wines :

" Of all our venerable British of the two Isles professing a suckling attachment to an ancient port-wine, lawyer, doctor, squire, rosy admiral, city merchant, the classic scholar is he whose blood is most nuptial to the webbed bottle. The reason must be that he is full of the old poets. He has their spirit to sing with, and the best that Time has done on earth to feed it. . . . Port hymns to his conservatism. It is magical : at one sip he is off swimming in the purple flood of the ever-youthful antique. . . . He is worthy of the wine, as are poets of Beauty."

In Lieutenant Patterne, the officer of Marines, Meredith vented another attempt at ridicule upon his uncle by marriage, S. B. Ellis ; but that officer was now long dead, and the passing years had softened the bitterness he felt towards his relative. In *The Egoist* he freely acknowledges my grandfather's bravery, particularly in China, and there are several sentences like "Captain Patterne is as brave a man as ever lived. He's a hero!" But the Royal Marines are always brave and ready to save a desperate situation, *per mare per terram*, as their motto proclaims; consequently, Meredith's humours at the expense of that gallant Corps are a trifle obscure and can only be attributed to unfamiliarity with naval and military history.

Crossjay Patterne the younger, one of the most natural boys in all fiction—for he talks and acts like a boy, which is rarely the case in novels—was, as I previously mentioned, a very accurate picture of Meredith's first cousin, George Hasted Ellis, a troublesome, high-spirited lad:

"Vernon . . . stalked off to Devonport, and brought back a rosy-cheeked, round-bodied rogue of a boy, who fell upon meats and puddings, and defeated them, with a captivating simplicity in his confession that he had never had enough to eat in his life. . . . The pranks of the little fellow, and his revel in a country life, and muddy wildness in it . . . would have enlivened any household. He was not only indolent, he was opposed to the acquisition of knowledge through the medium of books. But his passion for our naval service was a means of securing his attention to lessons after he had begun to understand that the desert had to be traversed to attain midshipman's rank. He boasted ardently of his fighting father."

The young original, George Ellis, spent his boyhood at Stonehouse, which is part of Devonport, and no doubt he and his brothers and sisters *were* "all hungry" there at times, for at that date the family of Sir S. B. Ellis were dependent on his pay as a captain. Owing to the inartistic haste with which *The Egoist* was concluded, Crossjay suddenly vanished from its pages; his future naval career was not adumbrated. But George Ellis duly entered the Royal Navy, and, after roving adventures in all parts of the world, eventually fought as a volunteer in the Southern Army during the American Civil War, when he was killed at the Battle of Bull's Run, in 1861.

The most interesting portrait in *The Egoist* is, of course,

Vernon Whitford, drawn from Leslie Stephen—"'A Phœbus Apollo turned fasting friar' painted the sunken brilliancy of the lean and long walker and scholar at a stroke." And Meredith told a correspondent : "Vernon Whitford is a sketch of L. Stephen, but merely a sketch, not doing him full justice, though the strokes within and without are correct."

Leslie Stephen, born in 1832, came to London from Cambridge in 1864, to follow a literary career. He was editor of *The Cornhill Magazine*, 1871-1882, and wrote the first volume, on Johnson, for the English Men of Letters series in 1878. He was also the first editor of *The Dictionary of National Biography*, 1882-1891. He married Thackeray's youngest daughter, Harriet, in 1867, and, after her death, in 1875, Miss Duckworth became his second wife. Leslie Stephen was always a redoubtable pedestrian. He walked from Cambridge to London, fifty miles, in twelve hours, and was a famous Alpine climber. His walking prowess is recorded in *The Egoist*, and it was in the autumn of the year the book was published (1879) that Stephen founded The Sunday Tramps. This was a pedestrian coterie which met every other Sunday from October to June, the walks taken being generally in Surrey, Kent, and Hertfordshire. The original members included Lord Justice Romer, Sir Frederick Pollock, Sir Herbert Stephen, John Collier, R. B. (subsequently Lord) Haldane, Cotter Morison, D. MacColl of *The Athenæum*, and, of course, Leslie Stephen, who acted as leader. His was an " unlimited paternal despotism " ; and when collecting his tramping flock at the railway station he had " the solicitous look of a schoolmaster." Meredith was a kind of ex-officio member. His health was beginning to fail now, and he was not often able to accomplish the full distances essayed by the Tramps, but whenever they came to his part of Surrey he would meet them at an appointed spot on the hills and escort them back to his house. " Tramping with them one has the world under review, as well as pretty scenery." After dinner at Flint Cottage the guests started for London by train at ten P.M. These pleasant excursions are often mentioned by Meredith. Thus he tells Stevenson, in June, 1880 :

" The Sunday Tramps visiting us were L. S. for leader or Pied Piper, Morison, Fredk. Pollock, Croom Robertson, Edgeworth,

LESLIE STEPHEN. THE ORIGINAL OF VERNON WHITFORD IN
"THE EGOIST"

From a contemporary photograph

and another. Will and I shouldered a sack of cold sausages, 'Polinaris and Hock, and met them at old Dorking station. Thence away to Leith Hill, where, in splendid sunlight, we consumed the soul of the sack, talked spiritedly (you may have been mentioned among the brilliant subjects), rolled and smoked. Then down the piny clefts of the hill by Friday Street into the sloping meadows each side the Tillingbourne leaping through Evelyn's Wotton, along under Ranmore to our cottage and dinner. To this day the walk has a bubbling memory : L. S. in a recent number of *The Pall Mall* has described it in the philosophic manner." [1]

In September, 1882, he wrote to Stephen : " It is desired and hoped by the Box Hill family that the Captain of Tramps will bring his troop to us at the end of October, or in the first week in November, to see the red and yellow of the leaf in the valley. Please bear our wishes in mind."

The occasion of the Tramps' Centenary Walk was celebrated by a dinner at Flint Cottage. Professor James Sully, in his account of these meetings, says of Meredith :

" From his occasional participation in a part of the walk and still more, perhaps, from the readiness to fall in with our mood of playful lawlessness, we grew accustomed to regard him as one of ourselves. It seems to some of us now that we were never more penetrated with the essence of trampdom than when in one of those delightful summer evenings we sat and smoked after dinner in the Swiss Chalet above the Box Hill Cottage, and listened to our host as with exuberant force and brilliant

---

[1] *Peripatetics*, I.   *Pall Mall Gazette*, 12th June, 1880. Leslie Stephen did not forget to refer to the cold sausages brought by Meredith : " The most brilliant passage in our annals was the discovery by our poet— for it need hardly be said that without poetry and philosophy one could never attain the essence of commonplace existence—of the singular harmony between lovely scenery and cold sausages." He goes on to speak of the view from Leith Hill : " In front of us rises the old mansion of the Evelyns, in such perfect harmony with its surroundings, that for the moment I feel myself a cavalier in spirit, and a loyal subject of Charles II. I look round instinctively for an oak-apple to stick in my hat." Albury suggested some inevitable humour at the expense of Martin F. Tupper, whose complacent " philosophy " has made him the butt of many gibes.

wit he richly clothed our poor attempts to ridicule the ways of the over serious." [1]

But the ever fleeting years and the toll of advancing age all too soon brought these pleasant walks and talks to an end both for Meredith and the founder of the Tramps. Leslie Stephen resigned, owing to reasons of health, from the leadership in 1891, but he sometimes joined the band up till 1895. After that he walked no more with them. Nothing can exceed the pathos of those last letters exchanged between Stephen and Meredith—those two mighty walkers of hill and dale in " good days gone "—when the former lay dying, and his friend, in hardly better case, weak and prostrate after long illness, wrote : " We who have loved the motion of legs and the sweep of the winds, we come to this. But for myself, I will own that it is the Natural order. There is no irony in Nature. God bless and sustain you, my friend."

Shortly before his death, in February, 1904, Stephen wrote to Meredith :

" MY VERY DEAR FRIEND,—I must make the effort to write to you once more with my own hand. I cannot trust to anybody else to say how much I value your friendship, and I must send you a message, perhaps it may be my last, of my satisfaction and pride in thinking of your affection for me. Your last bunch of violets is deliciously scenting my prison house.

" Always your

" L. STEPHEN."

And when all was over, Meredith wrote to his friend's daughter : " One of the most beloved of my friends has gone from sight, and though I feel that he remains with me and has his lasting place in our literature, this day's news darkens my mind. Last Autumn I was near to going. The loss of my friend spurs the wish that I had preceded him."

---

[1] *The Cornhill Magazine*, January, 1908. Meredith appreciated this article which recalled happy days of a quarter of a century before, and wrote to Professor Sully : " Your sketch of the Tramps will be a memorial and that of Leslie is a portrait that brings him living before me. Good days gone ! My mind is bent on the future (little for myself, as you may imagine), but in this case I look back with regret, with more than the breath of a sigh."

Thus passed the original of Vernon Whitford. The decline of Meredith's own health dated from the arduous work, day and night, which he forced upon himself in order to finish *The Egoist* rapidly. He told his son Arthur, in 1881 : " My health is now far from good. I finished the last volumes of a novel two years back by writing at night for three months. An attack of whooping cough followed on the lowered nerves. I have never been well since then. My digestion is entirely deranged, and still I have to write—and for a public that does not care for my work. . . . Hitherto my lungs have worked soundly. Nothing but the stomach has ever been weak. Unhappily this is a form of weakness that incessant literary composition does not agree with."

A visit to France in the late summer of 1879 did not re-establish his health. He left his family in Normandy, and crossed Touraine and the Cevennes country to Nîmes, and so to Marseilles and Bordighera, before proceeding to Dauphiné. He came back to England, and his mental and bodily state were not improved by the atmospheric conditions which greeted him. He told Jessopp : " Old galley-slave England has punished us all for our infidelity to fog and bad summers ; as we landed at Dover from temperate cordial France (stepping from a cabin redolent of beer and stale crumbs and brandy-breathing steward) a chill fog seized on us and sowed coughs in each bosom."

It was one of the sad perversities of Meredith's life that the same cause, *The Egoist*, which brought to him success and appreciation should have sown the seeds of illness that was fated in his latter years to develop into chronic invalidism, and thereby rob him of what he loved best in life, the power of walking far in the English country-side and of mountain-rambling in the Alps.

He told Bonaparte Wyse, on 5th January, 1881 :

" I am slightly coming round to be able to write, but for several months I have been incapable ; and I loathe the pen so much that I shun the plain duty of immediately replying to letters. The malady, as of old, is bradypepsy influenced by the nervous excitement of composition continued too long.

" You are in arms and fighting for your own,[1] but you have always a general head besides the personal, and you will let me say that my sympathies are with the Government. I regret that the Opposition should have defeated its mediation between the land owner and the Land League. The former has ever been in Ireland and elsewhere (when not controlled by a Richelieu) tyrannical and witless. In this instance, you have a case to plead. I am glad that the children are all well. You are at any rate blest with a comrade of proved good courage to stand by you. Give her my warm regards."

By the end of 1881 he was constrained to admit of his illness : " The malady seems to be nervous, affecting the spine, and I begin to feel my legs labouring after an hour of motion."

Despite his affected health, Meredith set to work upon *The Tragic Comedians* in the year following that of *The Egoist*, and arduous work too. He wrote to Bonaparte Wyse, in May, 1880 :

" You propose a delightful holiday, but it happens that I, slave of the pen, have just accepted work which binds me to the desk for the next six months. And temporarily worse, for I should like to see you, we are without a cook. Our last one, a good one, whiskified and flared up, and there is no dining here. By combination of all the forces of the Cottage we obtain a kind of cat's meal, but the amenities of cookery are absent . . . I am really a slave and not in love with my chains."

However, he completed his term of " slavery " within the specified six months, for *The Tragic Comedians*—a short book for Meredith, it is true—was published in December, 1880, after the story had commenced an abbreviated serial appearance in *The Fortnightly Review* in October.[2] As usual, he felt dubious as to its reception. He told Hardman, in February, 1881 : " I have a book for you—not to be reviewed : only to be read at your entire leisure. I fear you will not care for it. But it is history, and a curious chapter of human nature." He might have said one of the most curious chapters of human nature.

[1] In the Irish Land troubles of that date : Gladstone passed the Irish Land Act in 1881.
[2] The original manuscript of fifteen chapters (the book contains nineteen) realised £220 at Sotheby's in 1910.

It is scarcely necessary to say that *The Tragic Comedians* is based on the amazing history of Ferdinand Lassalle and Hélène von Dönniges—one of the great love stories of the world. And yet there was more of tragedy than love in the drama, for both the protagonists failed to rise to the crisis of their fate and, lacking entire devotion to the other's need, wasted the golden moments in futile procrastination and quixotic scruples of duty and honour. The motto for such as they, *amor vincit omnia*, was blotted out in blood. Their story is more startling and pathetic and dramatic than that of any invented novel or stage play. As Meredith wrote :

" Their acts are incredible : they drank sunlight and drove their bark in a manner to eclipse historical couples upon our planet. Yet they do belong to history, they breathed the stouter air than fictions, the last chapter of them is written in red blood."

Ferdinand Lassalle was " a wonderful and ideal man : so great, so generous, heroical, giant-like, that what he wills must be." But, like Samson of old, he was brought to death by a woman. He, a Jew and a great potential force in the political future of Germany, met, and fell in love with at first sight, this young girl, Hélène von Dönniges, who was already engaged to a youthful Roumanian Prince, Yanko von Racowitza. She was swept away by this new force which enveloped her, and there was made manifest " the dream of poets rarely witnessed anywhere, and almost too wonderful for credence in a haunt of our later civilisation. Yet there it was : the sudden revelation of the intense divinity to a couple fused in oneness by his apparition . . . love at first sight was visible." But the race and religion, the political views, and the past reputation of Lassalle were all abhorrent and anathema to the parents of the girl, and they violently refused to listen to even the idea of his becoming their son-in-law. At first, Hélène would have sacrificed everything for her lover. She fled from her home, came to Lassalle at his hotel, and if he had then grasped his fate firmly, all would have been well. But his wayward temperament suddenly shot forth egotistical and quixotic decisions. He, the super-man, would conquer the objections of the Dönniges family, and he, the past profligate, would wed a wife in the normal way out of her parents' house. So, he was capable of the absurd folly of sending the girl back to her home, and then employing as one of his intermediaries an old woman, the Countess Hatzfeldt, with whom he had had an affair in the past. This person now played a malign rôle in the drama somewhat akin to that of the Countess Platen in the great love tragedy of Königsmarck and Sophie Dorothea, wife of George I., which also ended in blood for the man and long remorseful years and bitter tears for the woman.

When Lassalle sent Hélène back to her parents he lost her for ever ; he never saw her again. The Dönniges family refused to treat with him, and the father, a typical German officer, broke his daughter's spirit by confinement and methods of terrorism—even to physical violence. He actually compelled her, against her own will, to send letters of renunciation to her lover. It is then Meredith puts into the mouth of Lassalle that bitter indictment :

" O that woman ! She has murdered love. She has blotted love completely out. She is the arch-thief and assassin of mankind—the female Apollyon. He lost sight of her in the prodigious iniquity covering her sex with a cowl of night, and it was what women are, what women will do, the one and all alike simpering simulacra that men find them to be, soulless, clogs on us, bloodsuckers ! "

But he, Lassalle—" He was like some great cathedral organ foully handled in the night by demons "—now realised his folly too late, and yet proceeded to an act of extreme folly. He had always been opposed to the practice of duelling : his lion-like nature placed him above the charge of physical cowardice. But in his baffled agony of mind he sent a challenge to Hélène's father, who refused it on the plea of age. But the challenge was taken up by Racowitza, her earlier lover. The two men met, and, by the most tragic irony of fate, Lassalle was mortally wounded by his boyish rival. He lingered in horrible agony for three days, and then the end :

" He met his fate like the valiant soul he was. Haply if he had lingered without the sweats of bodily tortures to stay reflectiveness, he might have cast a thought on the irony of the fates felling a man like him by a youngster's hand and for a shallow girl. . . . Silent was that house of many chambers. That mass of humanity profusely mixed of good and evil, of generous ire and mutinous, of the passion for the future of mankind and vanity of person, magnanimity and sensualism, high judgment, reckless indiscipline, chivalry, savagery, solidity, fragmentariness, was dust."

Lassalle died on 31st August, 1864, and his slayer broke the news, with sobs, to Hélène : " He is dead." She had confidently expected that Racowitza would be the one to fall, and had resolved then to fly to Lassalle once more. But Fate denying this, she rose to the supreme height of Tragic-Comedy and a few months later married the man whose hands were stained with the blood of her lover. The outrageous union was of short duration, for Fate shot another bolt, Prince Yanko von Racowitza dying within five months. One need not apportion any blame to him in this amazing drama : he was merely a puppet ground beneath the juggernaut of the Eternal Feminine.

Thus far the story as known to Meredith and utilised by him. He did not live to learn the last act of his Tragic Comedy, which befitted what had been enacted throughout. The widowed Princess von Racowitza, hated by the populace as the cause of the death of the idolised Lassalle, and disinherited by her parents, became a female Ishmael and a nomad. She went on the stage, without much success, consoled herself with many lovers, and married a second husband, Siegwart Friedmann, an actor. Divorce ended her connection with him five years later, and eventually she married a third husband in America, Baron Schewitsch, whose estates in Russia had been confiscated owing to his complicity with Nihilism. He and Hélène returned to Munich, and earned a precarious living by journalism.[1] The Baron died in October, 1911, and the dramatic Hélène, fearing to face the prospect of old age, loneliness, and poverty, ended her mortal career a few days later by means of poison. To the last, it is said, she retained the inscrutable, Mona Lisa type of face, and those

[1] The Princess von Racowitza wrote her own astonishing *Autobiography*. An English translation was published by Constable in 1910.

x

wonderful masses of Titian-red hair which had brought so many men to ruin.

She was a profoundly interesting exemplar of (not to) her sex, and Meredith, with better health and inclination, might have achieved a greater study than he did in *The Tragic Comedians*. He did not allow himself sufficient time and scope to develop the characters of the protagonists, and the work suffers from the unusual fault in Meredith of being too short. Nevertheless, it needs must hold attention through the course of perusal, and there are many caustic sayings. How good is the definition of Light Literature :

" The garden and the orchard, the fountain, the rainbow, the far view ; the view within us as well as without. Our blood runs through it, our history in the quick. The Philistine detests it, because he has no view, out or in. . . . We are the choice public, which will have good writing for light reading. Poet, novelist, essayist, dramatist, shall be ranked honourable in my Republic. . . . I have learnt as much from light literature as from heavy—as much, that is, from the pictures of our human blood in motion as from the clever assortment of our forefatherly heaps of bones. Shun those who cry out against fiction and have no taste for elegant writing. For to have no sympathy with the playful mind is not to have a mind : it is a test."

And how good, too, Alvan's comment on widows' weeds prophetically suggested to him by the dark lichen-killed fir-tree :

" By the way, my fair darling, let me never think of you wearing this kind of garb for me, should I be ordered off the first to join the dusky army below. Women who put on their dead husbands in public are not well-mannered women, though they may be excellent professional widows, excellent ! "

Excellent is the vignette of Bismarck introduced in this work ; and very apt the credo of the demagogue and unscrupulous politician, which might be professed to-day by some who have, unhappily, risen to supreme power in the destinies of England :

" I have the secret of how to head the people—to put a head to their movement and make it irresistible, as I believe it will be beneficent. . . . I am no empty theoriser, no phantasmal speculator. . . . I stand for index to the people of the path they should take to triumph—must take, as triumph they must sooner or later : not by the route of what is called Progress—pooh ! That is a middle-class invention to effect a compromise. With the people the matter rests—with their intelligence ! Meanwhile my star is bright."

The Tragic Comedians is thus topical : but, as I have often said before, Meredith is always strangely topical. This book reminds me of an amusing discussion I had, both verbally and by correspondence, with Sir Francis Burnand, who, although a friend of fifty years' standing, could never read Meredith's work. He took exception to my statement in an article that Dickens and Meredith were " two of the most distinguished men in English literature." He said :

" No, emphatically, no, when Meredith is styled ' *one of the most* . . . ' He will eventually be nowhere near the high niche *where he placed himself*. Will he be above *Peacock* ? He had not Peacock's originality of humour. But I forget we are bounded and limited by Dickens who, *when in his own line of romance*, stands alone. *Out of that line* even Dickens is not on a par with Jerrold, nor in *pure romance* can he equal Ainsworth (who was of his time)—I do not mention Thackeray—they stood quite apart. Thackeray gave us ' living pictures '— *real* men and *real* women. . . . Meredith's conceit killed him, or rather his work. . . . I wish you would pursue the subject, but whether worth while is questionable. *Your* method and style of treatment make me utter the wish. I have all Meredith's works but I can*not* read them with the exceptions mentioned. . . . Last night I made another *bonne volonté* trial attempt at reading *The Tragic Comedians*. *Impossible*—for *me* at least. I shall try another of G. M.'s : but I believe that, except with *Evan Harrington*, a poem or two, *Modern Love*, *The Ordeal of Richard Feverel*, I shall find them *now*, as I found them *at first*, writ in a ' language not understanded of the people '

and certainly not of *this* singular person signing himself,
Yours,   F. C. BURNAND."

Thus the extensive gamut of Meredithian criticism: from
Burnand, who found him unreadable and conceited, to Stevenson, who aligned him with Shakspere and immortality.

CHAPTER XIII

*T*HE *Tragic Comedians* finished, Meredith for some time devoted himself to his favourite muse, Poetry, though he well knew the scant rewards it would bring. "The dreadful curse of Verse is on me, and has been for two months," he wrote in March, 1881. " Poetry comes easier than prose and bedevils me." The result of this particular bedevilment was made manifest in the spring of 1883, when Macmillan published *Poems and Lyrics of the Joy of Earth*. The volume was inscribed to James Cotter Morison, and contained twelve poems and twenty-five sonnets. It included the famous *Woods of Westermain*, inspired by the poet's walks in Deerleap Woods, near Abinger, and also to a large extent by Norbury Park, renowned for its ancient trees and sylvan glory. Here, too, appeared Meredith's finest poem, *The Lark Ascending*, written in 1881, wherein he trod the heights with Shelley and as his compeer, both exquisitely singing the immanence of Nature in all things beautiful, the lark being but the symbol :

> For singing till his heaven fills,
> 'Tis love of earth that he instils,
> And ever winging up and up,
> Our valley is his golden cup,
> And he the wine which overflows
> To lift us with him as he goes :
> The woods and brooks, the sheep and kine,
> He is, the hills, the human line,
> The meadows green, the fallows brown,
> The dreams of labour in the town ;
> He sings the sap, the quickened veins ;
> The wedding song of sun and rains.
> He is the dance of children, thanks
> Of sowers, shout of primrose-banks,
> And eye of violets while they breathe ;
> All these the circling song will wreathe.

> And you shall hear the herb and tree,
> The better heart of men shall see,
> 　Shall feel celestially, as long
> 　As you crave nothing but the song.

The setting for " the silver chain of sound . . . an ecstasy to music turned " was, of course, the Box Hill Valley, just as *The Orchard and the Heath* suggests Ranmore Common :

> My footpath left the pleasant farms and lanes,
> Soft cottage-smoke, straight cocks a-crow, gay flowers ;
> 　Beyond the wheel-ruts of the wains
> 　Across a heath I walked for hours,
> And met its rival tenants, rays and rains.
>
> ·　　·　　·　　·　　·　　·　　·
>
> I turned and looked on heaven awhile, where now
> The moor-faced sunset broaden'd with red light ;
> 　Threw high aloft a golden bough,
> 　And seemed the desert of the night
> Far down with mellow orchards to endow.

In the same volume was the revised and extended version of *Love in the Valley* (reprinted from *Macmillan's Magazine*, October, 1878) ; and here, too, appeared *Phœbus with Admetus* with its stately cadences and momentary pictures, such as the vivid :

> Bulls, that walk the pastures in kingly-flashing coats !
> Laurel, ivy, vine, wreathed for feasts not few !

Mrs Grant Allen told me that one of her most memorable experiences at Flint Cottage was when Meredith declaimed this poem in sonorous tones to a few friends assembled in his chalet.

Shortly before the volume appeared, the poet, bitterly anticipating lack of appreciation once more, told Maxse :

" I confess with shame that I am at work correcting, preparatory to bringing out a volume of poems. . . . Truly the passion to produce verse in our region is accursed. I ask myself why I should labour, and, for the third time, pay to publish the result, with a certainty of being yelled at, and haply spat upon, for my pains. And still I do it. At heart, it is plain, I must have a remainder of esteem for our public. . . . I scorn myself for my folly. Where he can get no audience a spouting Homer would merit the Cap and Bells."

Still, after publication, he was constrained to admit that "my little book is moving"; and it did more to bring him recognition as a poet than any of his previous or subsequent volumes of verse. *Poems and Lyrics of the Joy of Earth* contains Meredith's best-known and oft-quoted poetry.

To revert a trifle chronologically, in 1882-1883, Meredith was a good deal in London, and went about and to the theatre more than was his usual custom. He saw Mrs Langtry in *Ours*, and pronounced her "The ideal shepherdess of the chromolithographs. Very handsome—not a shade of mystery or variableness: the heroine for bold dragoons. She has to make love, and does it with all her arms and breasts." Of Irving as Romeo he said: "The Love Play ceases to present a sorrowful story, and becomes a pageant with a quaint figure ranting about." He liked Albani in *The Flying Dutchman*. At Browning's request he dined with the poet in July, 1883. A year earlier he had the pleasure of Robert Louis Stevenson's company at Box Hill again, when the two had several long after-dinner talks. Later this summer (1882) he went abroad. He told Bonaparte Wyse:

"I crossed the Simplon to meet Arthur at Stresa. We were a week together over Lugano—drenched. Thence to Milan. He is now at Naples, winters in Sicily. My health forbids much writing, and as I have no ambition I chiefly read."

But he was now planning *Diana of the Crossways*. As early as December, 1881, he said: "I am in harness to my novel." He wrote to Leslie Stephen in September, 1882, at the time when there was a hope the new story might appear in *The Cornhill Magazine* (which project, however, was not realised):

"When I have done the work I will hand it to you and await your opportunity, supposing you judge it to be fitting. I begin rather to feel that I shall write when I try—that is, in a manner to please myself, which has not been in my power for several months of late, though curiously I found no difficulty in verse. I am a bit stronger, less nerve-shaken after holding the pen in earnest for a couple of hours. If things go well I shall have the story ready by the Spring, but I dare not forecast very hopefully."

The work was destined to take him over a year longer than he anticipated. In October, 1883, he reported to Cotter Morison :

" I am queerish at times, ill-balanced over the common pit, but working at a splendid pace. Ever since I took to your prescription in diet—from the first day miraculously—I sprang to the pen, and am producing rapidly. But I can't walk much. A mile beyond the right distance cripples me. And as soon as I feel better I fall in the old ways and am lamed again."

In February, 1884, " *Diana* rather in the Doldrums " : but the following month he had recovered his creative energy and, despite his health, was able to tell R. L. Stevenson :

" I have developed a spinal malady and can walk not much more than a mile. On the other hand, I can work passably, and am just finishing at a great pace a two-volume novel, to be called *Diana of the Crossways*—partly modelled upon Mrs Norton. But this is between ourselves. I have had to endow her with brains, and make them evidence to the discerning. I think she lives. She appears by instalments in *The Fortnightly Review*, commencing May or June.[1] I hope to have done with her—have her out of me—in April."

And to Mrs Leslie Stephen he wrote, the same day :

" I am now writing daily very hard, and though the work flows to its end in full view, my health at present is of a kind hardly to bear the strain. . . . I hope to finish with the delivery of the terrible woman afflicting me (a positive heroine with brains, with real blood, and demanding utterance of the former, tending direction of the latter) by the end of April."

But in May he had to tell the same friend :

" *Diana of the Crossways* keeps me still on her sad last way to wedlock. I could have killed her merrily, with my compliments to the public ; and that was my intention. But the marrying of her sets me traversing feminine labyrinths, and you know that the why of it never can be accounted for."

[1] Only about two-thirds of the story, twenty-six chapters, appeared in *The Fortnightly Review*, June to December, 1884.

In June his work was interrupted by the serious illness of his wife, who had to undergo a severe operation in London. Mrs Meredith's health improved temporarily after a stay at East-bourne, and, in August, Meredith having resumed his work, told Mrs Leslie Stephen :

" My *Diana* still holds me ; only by the last chapter ; but the coupling of such a woman and her man is a delicate business. She has no puppet pliancy. The truth being that she is a mother of Experience, and gives that dreadful baby suck to brains. I have therefore a feeble hold of her ; none of the novelist's winding-up arts avail ; it is she who leads me. But my delay of the conclusion is owing to my inability to write of late."

Diana of the Crossways is, perhaps, the most psychological of Meredith's books. This was a very subtle study of the complex character of his heroine,[1] and even the title of the story was allegorically apt. The character of Diana was mostly Meredith's creation, for her prototype, Mrs Norton, was erratic rather than complex, and it was her eventful life and not her mind that Meredith borrowed. " She wouldn't be a bad heroine of romance," said Percy Dacier, derisively of the Romantic, after he had broken with Diana ; and certainly Caroline Norton, if not a heroine in life, had a romantic career, tarnished though it was by dust from the sordid arenas of Grub Street, Politics, and the Law Courts.

Caroline Sheridan was an interesting example of the warring influences of heredity. Granddaughter of Richard Brinsley Sheridan, she inherited his literary talents and *espièglerie* and Irish carelessness ; she had the good looks of her father, Tom

---

[1] See the interesting exposition of Diana the author gave to Lady Ulrica Duncombe, in *Letters of George Meredith*, pp. 530-532, 542-543. " She is one of the women dear to me," he said. On another occasion, when asked to estimate the value of his books, he wrote : " *The Egoist* comes nearer than the other books to the proper degree of roundness and finish. In *Diana of the Crossways* my critics own that a breathing woman is produced, and I felt that she was in me as I wrote. *Rhoda Fleming* is liked by some, not much by me. *Richard Feverel* was earnestly conceived, and is in some points worthy of thought. *Beauchamp's Career* does not probe so deeply, but is better work on the surface."

Sheridan ; she possessed the musical and artistic gifts of her Linley grandmother. It was her fate to have her name coupled with several notable men : her first husband, George Norton (a younger brother of the 3rd Lord Grantley), was the least remarkable of them. As early as 1828, when she was twenty years of age and a bride of but one year, there was some gossip in London about the frequent and lengthy visits the Honourable Mrs Norton paid to 27 Old Bond Street, to see her young and handsome literary adviser, William Harrison Ainsworth, who superintended the production of her first book of poems, *The Sorrows of Rosalie*. In 1836 came the famous case concerning her relations with the Premier, Lord Melbourne. The accused parties established their innocence ; and it is possible that political conspiracy had some share in involving Melbourne in this scandal, which might well invalidate his influence in the counsels of the female sovereign whose succession was imminent. Mrs Norton's resultant invidious and uncertain position, and her conflicts with her husband in the Law Courts and in print, tended much to ameliorate the laws and ancient conventions governing the social condition of women. In 1845 occurred the most painful incident of Mrs Norton's life, when she was charged by rumour with having sold to *The Times* a political secret concerning the immediate impending repeal of the Corn Laws—information supposed to have been confided to her by Sidney Herbert, who had just joined the Cabinet. The accusation was undoubtedly false, for it seems clear by later evidence that it was Lord Aberdeen who prematurely imparted the momentous intelligence to Delane, the editor of *The Times*, in the course of what is vulgarly called " a deal." Obtaining her long-desired marital freedom in 1875, when she became a widow, Mrs Norton, true to her illogical temperament, assumed the yoke again two years after, when she married Sir William Stirling-Maxwell, who, however, had been her faithful friend for many years. She died three months later, in June, 1877

Such, in briefest outline, were the salient incidents of the stormy course of this lifelong victim of gossip, " The Byron of her Sex," as Mrs Norton's contemporaries regarded her ; and it will be seen that Meredith followed rather closely the facts of her life in his story of *Diana of the Crossways*, with, of course, a good deal of author's licence and transposition of dates and incidents. He commenced his work four years after her death.

As I mentioned in passing, when dealing with Copsham days in 1859-1860, Meredith had previously known Mrs Norton, then a woman of about fifty, as he met her at the house of his friends, the Duff Gordons, at Esher. Mrs Ross told me that Mrs Norton did not much care for the rising author of *Evan Harrington*, and this, perhaps, throws some light on what follows, for *Diana of the Crossways* recalls an echo of Meredith's life in earlier years. Copsham no doubt suggested the name of " Copsley," the estate of the Dunstanes so frequently mentioned and described in the story, though the actual house and its high situation seems like a picture of Denbies, near Dorking. Lady Dunstane was another presentment of Lady Duff Gordon, who was an enthusiastic defender of the character of her friend, Mrs Norton (always called " Aunt Carrie " by her daughter, Janet Duff Gordon) ; but the foolish Sir Lukin in no way resembled Sir Alexander Duff Gordon, who was a man of fine character. Most of the other personages of the novel could be fitted with prototypes ; some are obvious, and it will suffice here to draw attention to the interesting fact that Arthur Rhodes was more or less an auto-portrait of Meredith himself in young manhood, the period of his life of which so little, unfortunately, is known. To establish the corollary, I must recall a little of what I have previously related in an earlier chapter.

When about eighteen, Meredith was articled to Mr Charnock, a solicitor ; but the handsome boy disdained the law and gave his time and attention to the study of literature ; to long rambles in Surrey devoted to Nature worship ; and to the cultivation of the society of literary people he met in the circle of Thomas Love Peacock. Soon after, he published his first volume of poems. Just so in *Diana of the Crossways* Arthur Rhodes was " a young poet, rather good-looking, and well built." Diana said of him : " I received a volume of verse. . . . He seems a nice lad . . . mad for literature, and he must have talent. . . . I may have a chance of helping him. He was an articled clerk of Mr Braddock's." (A name which is almost an anagram of Charnock.) When Arthur Rhodes walked out from London to Copsley, he descanted with rapture on " the objects he had noticed along the road-side and through the woods, more sustaining, closer with Nature than her compulsory feeding on the cream of things." When, later, Diana advised Arthur Rhodes to consider the prudence of his resuming the yoke of the Law, he laughed, and said he had some expectations of money to come. George Meredith about 1849 inherited a small legacy from a relative in Portsmouth. Arthur Rhodes, in his friendship with Diana, " treasured her sayings. . . . She gave him more than she knew of a present that kept its beating heart into the future ; a height of sky, a belief in nobility, permanent through manhood down to age."

Whether it is permissible to deduce from this that Mrs Norton had some influence upon Meredith's career is a matter for individual opinion. If it was so, then it is regrettable that he should have revived in *Diana of the Crossways* the scandalous accusation that charged his friend with betraying a political secret. To Mrs Norton's other and more staunch friends this matter in his book gave great offence. It very nearly caused a rift with the Duff Gordon family ; but it was only subsequent to 1896 that the prefatory note was added to later editions of the novel stating that the charge in question was a calumny, and that Meredith's version of the story was to be read as fiction. This was done at the urgent insistence of Lord Dufferin and Ava, who informed Mrs Ross in that year :

" Meredith has promised to introduce an adequate refutation of the story he has so powerfully helped to promulgate into the next edition of *Diana of the Crossways*, so that I have had the pleasure of vindicating ' Aunt Carrie's ' memory of this atrocious accusation."

Much has been written and said about the impenetrability of the first chapter of this book. But as a matter of fact there is nothing very difficult in it. Inartistic it certainly is, and probably no other fine novel has such an unusual and untempting introduction, except *The Egoist* in a lesser degree. In brief, it is merely a review of the contemporary comments upon Mrs Norton to be found in the Greville and other memoirs, and a plea for philosophy in fiction. Incidentally it contains an apt and caustic *mot* on Charles Greville and his famous diary : " He had by nature a tarnishing eye that cast discolouration."

In addition to the forbidding introduction, there are many improbabilities in the story. The conversations are often on too pretentious a height both in the dining-room and in the servants' hall (Danvers, the lady's-maid, uses the word "invidious"!); and the author's views on the emancipation and rights of women are introduced at a tangent, without much regard to the unities. But these are unimportant criticisms, and are forgotten in the appreciation that must ever be the meed of the major portion of this brilliant work. There are many memorable phrases in it in addition to the famous "A high wind will make a dead leaf fly like a bird." How fine is "Friendship, I fancy, means one heart between two." And "That is life—when we dare death to live." Meredith nobly voiced his own aspirations in the sentence : "The art of the pen (we write on darkness) is to arouse the inward vision, instead of labouring with a drop-scene brush, as if it were to the eye ; because our flying minds cannot contain a protracted description. That is why the poets, who spring imagination with a word or a phrase, paint lasting pictures."

But in his novels also, Meredith could paint lasting pictures with a few vivid strokes. They stand out pre-eminently in this book and in memory after the reading—Redworth's November night ride to The Crossways (the actual house being The Crossways Farm, near Abinger Hammer), "a dark mass of building, with the moon behind it, shining in spires through a mound of firs. . . . The Downs were like floating islands, like fairy-laden vapours " ; Diana lighting the fire at The Crossways ; Diana's night watch by the body of her dead friend ; Diana on the wind-swept ebb-sands beyond Caen ; the great scene of Diana's confession and parting with Dacier. And all through the story, like a musical motif, recurs Meredith's love for Surrey scenery and those wonderful flaming sunsets, changing "from a saffron to intensest crimson," which gild the lily of that county's loveliness of hill and heath and woodland. With a few strokes he paints the well-known characteristics of the familiar scenery :

"A gateway led to the turf of the Down, springy turf bordered on a long line, clear as a racecourse, by golden gorse covers, and leftward over the gorse the dark ridge of the fir and heath country ran companionably to the South-west, the valley between, with undulations of wood and meadow sunned or shaded, clumps, mounds, promontories, away to broad spaces of tillage banked by wooded hills, and dimmer beyond and farther, the faintest shadowiness of heights, as a veil to the illimitable. Yews, junipers, radiant beeches, and gleams of the service-tree or the white-beam spotted the semicircle of swelling green Down black and silver. The sun in the valley sharpened his beams on squares of buttercups, and made a pond a diamond."

Ever his beloved South-West wind blows upon the exquisite scenes he pictures. Sometimes, as when Diana and Redworth walked to Selshall, the South-Wester dons the robes of rude force—" great surges of wind piping and driving "; but more often he is in gentle mood, as when Diana drove out with Lady Dunstane " on one of those high mornings of the bared bosom of June, when distances are given to our eyes and a soft air fondles leaf and grass blade. . . . Here and there hung a milk-white cloud with folded sail. The South-West left it in its bay of blue and breathed below. . . ."

The South-West winds and Surrey sunsets, great and worshipped symbols of Nature to Meredith, stir and irradiate the pages of *Diana of the Crossways*, the novel pre-eminently of Meredith's own county and cloudland :

> Sunrays, leaning on our southern hills and lighting
> Wild cloud-mountains that drag the hills along,
> Off ends the day of your shifting brilliant laughter
> Chill as a dull face frowning on a song.
> Ay, but shows the South-West a ripple-feathered bosom
> Blown to silver while the clouds are shaken and ascend
> Scaling the mid-heavens as they stream, there comes a sunset
> Rich, deep like love in beauty without end.

Dedicated to Sir Frederick Pollock, one of The Sunday Tramps, and published in three volumes by Chapman and Hall early in 1885,[1] *Diana of the Crossways* received full recognition

[1] The use of the copyright was for five years. See *First Editions of George Meredith*, by Luther Livingston, and *The Sphere*, 4th May, 1912, where Mr Shorter mentions the strained relations between Meredith and his publishers in 1893, which led soon after to a severance of their long association.

GEORGE MEREDITH
From the photograph by Thomson

in the reviews without delay. That in *The Academy* for 28th February, written by James Ashcroft Noble, propounded Meredith as a brilliant social essayist paradoxically using the form of a novelist; W. E. Henley, in *The Athenæum* of 14th March, compared Meredith's art with Shakspere's, and ranked Diana with Rosalind; and Cosmo Monkhouse, in *The Saturday Review* of 21st March, declared that in Diana the author had created a living woman dowered with exceptional gifts of blood and brains. Nevertheless, in spite of these and other generous criticisms, Meredith preserved his usual attitude to the world and professed to believe that his latest work had met the fate of its predecessors and received appreciation only here and there from some friendly pen. Thus he wrote to Frederick Greenwood in June, 1885:

" I do not reply to reviews of my work, favourable or the reverse. But the friendliness of your little note in *The St James's* of yesterday is out of the regions of criticism, and I may notice it to thank you. Innovators in any department have a tough struggle to get to the field through the hedge for a hearing. Mine has lasted about thirty-five years, and still I have only to appear for the bawlers to be in uproar. As I know the world I do not complain. I am sensible not the less of generous voices."

And to another friend he said:

" I have had several letters concerning reviewers and the review you mention. But I take habitually a bracing bath in my own criticism of my work, so that these East winds cause no catarrhs to me, though apparently my friends are doomed to be afflicted by them."

But he was in no mood to pay attention to reviews, favourable or the reverse, for his book had appeared just as his wife was struck down again by illness, this time to be fatal. After an operation in February, 1885, Mrs Meredith was removed to Avalon House, Upperton, Eastbourne, in April, and her husband was with her there on and off until she was brought back to Box Hill in June. All hope was now abandoned: " Here I am in the very pits of tragic life. My wife is desperately ill. There is no hope "; and " I live for the day, trying to work, though the machine has latterly got crazy," Meredith wrote.

For three months longer the sad and painful trial continued, until the end came, on 17th September. Meredith wrote several beautiful letters to his friends when all was over. Here is one to the Hardmans :

" She died on Thursday at 10 minutes to 6 P.M., peacefully, with one sigh, in her sister's arms, after a long struggle of 16 months, two operations, and a period of afflicting speech-lessness. Since the end of May we had no word from her mouth—nor at the last. I found her hand warm in mine, 40 minutes after the end. Never an old pressure in return. Death was a release to her. As for me, I shall not be long away from her remains. I have her spirit with me. I know your warmth of heart as if you were speaking here beside me now. God bless you and spare you suffering."

This was an irreparable loss. " She was the best of wives, truest among human creatures." Meredith, after his son went to Normandy and his daughter to Mr John Morley's house at Wimbledon, was alone in the home of sad memories. " This place of withered recollections is like an old life to be lived again without sunshine. I cross and recross it. Sharp spikes where flowers were. . . . When the mind shall be steadier, I shall have her calmly present—past all tears."

This was the mood in which he wrote his beautiful poem, *A Faith on Trial*. At first, in sorrowful reminiscence, he recalls the past :

> On the morning of May
> Ere the children had entered my gate
> With their wreaths and mechanical lay,
> A metal ding-dong of the date !
> I mounted our hill, bearing heart
> That had little of life save its weight :
> The crowned Shadow poising dart
> Hung over her : she, my own,
> My good companion, mate,
> Pulse of me : she who had shown
> Fortitude quiet as Earth's
> At the shedding of leaves. And around
> The sky was in garlands of cloud,
> Winning scents from unnumbered new births,
> Pointed buds where the woods were browned
> By a mouldered beechen shroud.

He pictures his wife's early home in Normandy, and the happy days at Box Hill :

> When we two stood overnight
> One, in the dark van-glow
> On our hill-top, seeing beneath
> Our household's twinkle of light
> Through spruce-boughs, gem of a wreath.

So far Nature has been unable to blot the bitterness of his personal grief, but now the sudden vision of beauty of the wild-cherry tree in flower strikes a message of hope through the darkness :

> Now gazed I where, sole upon gloom,
> As flower-bush in sun-specked crag,
> Up the spine of the double combe
> With yew-boughs heavily cloaked,
> A young apparition shone :
> Known, yet wonderful, white
> Surpassingly ; doubtfully known,
> For it struck as the birth of Light :
> Even Day from the dark unyoked.
> It waved like a pilgrim flag
> O'er processional penitents flown
> When of old they broke rounding yon spine :
> O the pure wild-cherry in bloom ! [1]

Now all is clear, despair is vanquished, and Faith in the ultimate good of all things restored :

> A shaft of the blossoming tree
> Was shot from the yew-wood's core.
> I stood to the touch of a key
> Turned in a fast-shut door.

The rest of the poem is devoted to the profession of the Faith of the God of Nature, whose truths are unlocked by the " handmaiden " Earth. *Change in Recurrence* also voices Meredith's loss of his wife and his now empty home :

> I stood at the gate of the cot
>
> .   .   .   .   .   .
>
> I gazed : 'twas the scene of the frame
> With the face, the dear life for me, fled.
> No window a lute to my name,
> No watcher there plying the thread.

---

[1] See also chap. xi. of *The Egoist*.

Y

Many other poems of this date also reflect the poet's great sorrow, and his ultimate consolation, as in *Hymn to Colour* :

> But Life ere long
> Came on me in the public ways and bent
> Eyes deeper than of old : Death met I too,
> And saw the dawn glow through.

And the epitaph *M. M.* (Marie Meredith) gives it final expression :

> Who call her Mother and who calls her Wife
> Look on her grave and see not Death but Life.

The poems we have been noticing, together with twenty-four additional pieces, including *The South-Wester* and *The Thrush in February*, appeared in the volume entitled *A Reading of Earth*, published by Macmillan in 1888. The same firm had issued the previous year Meredith's volume of verse, *Ballads and Poems of Tragic Life*, containing nineteen items.[1] These books are characteristically alluded to by their author in a letter, to Mr George Stevenson, of February, 1887 :

" The volume . . . should be ready for issue by the end of March—if the Germans do not force on a war. I call it *Ballads and Poems of Tragic Life* ; and there will be another to follow, of more spiritual flavour. Perhaps, if I am not driven to the novel, I shall be at a Poem treating of all the Explosives in the modern mind and manufactories : *The Anarchiad*. The hero, Karl Onyx, has as many adventures as Odysseus. I am at times moved strongly by the theme. Neither would fill the purse, and so I look at them as a lean lover looks at damsels that sit gazing over his uncrowned pate upon the wreathed and portly. The novel is my brawny scullery Jill."

Yet all through his life Meredith would have preferred to be a poet, and it was his poetry that he regarded as his best work. He told Mr Clodd :

" Chiefly by that in my poetry which emphasises the unity of life, the soul that breathes through the universe, do I wish

---

[1] He wrote in June, 1887 : " My last poor volume continues to receive drubbings from reviewers, while I have private letters from distinguished persons, meant for balm."

to be remembered : for the spiritual is the eternal. Only a few read my verse, and yet it is that for which I care most. . . . I began with poetry and I shall finish with it."

But he had to pay for his preference. As he put it : " A fit of my cross old Fairy, who condemned me from the cradle to poverty, through my love of verse." That is an exaggerated statement, like another he made on the same subject : " As to publishing books of verse, I have paid heavily for that audacity twice in Pounds sterling. I had for audience the bull, the donkey, and the barking cur." This refers to his first two volumes of verse, which, as we have seen, had many admirers, and he was never in " poverty " after 1860. Still, the fact remains that until 1896 his books of poetry were published at his own expense ; and he would not have the later ones sent out for review.

Meredith's least attractive poetry was written about 1892, the period of *The Empty Purse*, which the author himself, in later years, admitted to be prosy. He told Mrs Sturge Henderson, in a letter of 1906 : " I regret that I have written didactic verse, such as *The Empty Purse*, which is not poetry. The muse shuns that pædagogue. But I had to convey certain ideas that could not find place in the novels." Even in 1892, however, there were poems that contained much of the old beauties of thought and imagery, such as *The Lesson of Grief, Night of Frost in May*, and *Breath of the Briar*.[1]

> O briar-scents, on yon wet wing
> Of warm South-West wind brushing by,
> You mind me of the sweetest thing
> That ever mingled frank and shy :
> When she and I, by love enticed,
> Beneath the orchard apples met.

The curious production, *Jump-to-Glory Jane*, belongs to 1889, and by some is regarded as a burlesque on the methods of the Salvation Army, whose activities and persecutions were prominent at that date. It will be remembered that Meredith introduced a Salvationist, Matilda Pridden, in *One of our*

---

[1] This book of verse seems to have sold well ; the author told Mrs Walter Palmer, " the hundreds of bound copies being all sold out. It is good news."

Conquerors, written in 1890. The published version of *Jump-to-Glory Jane* differs very much from the original manuscript. The poem appeared first in *The Universal Review*, and to the editor, Harry Quilter, Meredith vouchsafed some " exposition " of *Jump-to-Glory Jane* which may be taken seriously or, more advisedly, as a typical example of intense and strained Meredithian humour at its slyest. He said :

" It is a grave narration of events in English country life. Jane, though a jumping, is a thoughtful woman. She has discovered that the circulation of the blood is best brought about by a continual exercise, and conduces to happy sensations, which are to her as the being of angels in her frame. She has wistful eyes in a touching but bony face. . . . Yes . . . a Satire, but one of the pictures of our England as well. Remember Mrs Girling and her following, and the sensations of Jane, with her blood at the spin with activity, warranted her feeling of exaltation. An English middle class Blavitzkey maniac would also be instructive, though less pathetic, than poor Jane."

Originally it was proposed that Linley Sambourne should illustrate *Jump-to-Glory Jane*, but he did not see his way to do so ; then Bernard Partridge was engaged for the work, but, according to report, " his heart failed him " and he resigned the commission ; eventually Laurence Housman executed some very fine and sympathetic designs, which were reproduced in the 1892 edition of this remarkable poem, dedicated to Meredith's friend, John Morley, by Mr Quilter, who also furnished a foreword on Meredith's " unpopularity."

Meredith's *Odes in Contribution to the Song of French History* belong to the year 1896. He wrote in December to Mrs Seymour Trower : " I am at work, a series of Three Odes. The First, *The French Revolution*, is done. I am midway in the *Napoleon*. The Third is *Alsace-Lorraine*. You will catch the idea in the sequence. It is History—my view ; and I make History sing ! Clio in Calliope." [1] The Odes were not published until 1898, when they appeared in *Cosmopolis* and in book form.

[1] " They will need to be read twice—and that is much against them in this country," he said of these Odes later on.

His last volume of verse, *A Reading of Life*, was published in 1901. This contained twenty-five poems, and among much that was harsh there sounded an echo of the poet's early and musical note from the past in the beautiful little *Song in the Songless* :

> They have no song, the sedges dry,
>   And still they sing.
> It is within my breast they sing,
>   As I pass by.
> Within my breast they touch a string,
>   They wake a sigh.
> There is but sound of sedges dry ;
>   In me they sing.

To revert briefly to the decade of the " eighties," in August, 1886, Meredith had the pleasure of a visit, at Flint Cottage, from R. L. Stevenson. Although some of his older friends were passing, Meredith had new friends he much valued, one of the most intimate to the end being Mr Edward Clodd, whom he first met in 1884. He much appreciated the society of the Misses Lawrence and Mrs Walter Palmer. Grant Allen and his wife, who were then living at Dorking, were always welcome at Flint Cottage. They introduced, on one occasion, William Watson, who, despite his article, *Fiction—Plethoric and Anæmic*, was graciously welcomed by Meredith. Various politicians also came to Box Hill : Haldane, Dillon, and, later, Mr Asquith. In April, 1887, Meredith dined with the Eighty Club, when he was introduced to Gladstone, "who favoured me with the pleased grimace of the amiable public man in the greeting of an unknown, and heard a speech from him enough to make a cock robin droop his head despondently. We want a young leader. This valiant, prodigiously-gifted, in many respects admirable, old man is, I fear me, very much an actor. His oratory has the veteran rhetorician's artifices—to me painfully perceptible when I see him waiting for his effects, timing those to follow." In June, 1888, Meredith mentions an engagement to dine with Haldane and Asquith at the Blue Posts, sitting between A. J. Balfour and Morley. This was the dinner given in honour of Parnell.[1] In the following year Meredith

---

[1] A little sketch of Meredith at this dinner, by Sir F. C. Gould, was reproduced twenty-one years later in *The Westminster Gazette*, 4th January, 1909.

attended several of the sittings of the Parnell Commission, when the banqueted idol of a few months earlier had fallen.

In the summer of 1887, he and his family stayed for a month at 4 Draycot Terrace, St Ives, Cornwall, where, in addition to fine scenery and good bathing, there was the pleasure of the society of the Leslie Stephens. The following summer he and his daughter went to Wales, where his son, W. M. Meredith, was then working as an electrical engineer, in partnership with Mr J. C. Howell, of Llanelly.

" We were at Tenby for 17 days, and had Cole [1] down, who caught a big conger ; we drove to ancient castles and sea-fowl rocks, bathed, surfeited on cream, became green as Neptune, and were alternate days drenched. Thence to Llanelly. Next day to Llandilo, on the Towy. . . . Thence to Llandrindod. Thence to Brecon. . . . I went through a term of extreme probation. We were at hotels in all the places, and it was English hotel cookery. Rain usually at night, walks not possible except in penitence. No places of amusement. I had in desperation to go to bed at half-past nine. . . . Not a chair gave repose for reading or writing. However, I saw pretty sea-side, noble rocks, briny birds, fair vales, Baronial this and that ; mountains and Welsh eyes : also I learnt some Welsh."

At Ferndale, Meredith and the rest of his party went down a coal shaft, accompanied by the owner, Mr Frederick Davis, and Mr Frank Edwards, M.P. The novelist had some conversation with the miners below the surface.

1889 found him at work on *One of our Conquerors* : " My work (I cannot go at it for a certainty continuously, as in other times) holds me to it with rigour ; and I have much to say ; and my time on the surface of our sphere is short." And " Health only middling, and hard at work. Why do I work ? I am not obliged, and might survey mankind from the top of Fiesole. But the habit is on me. I have besides things to say which friends would forget." Such was his report, and the following year was much the same with him. He told Hardman, in the last letter he was to address to that companion of the old time :

[1] The gardener at Flint Cottage.

" *April 14th*, 1890.

" My dear Friend,—I fondly hoped to greet you all on Helen's Saturday, but my work has me in its grip and is dragging the poor author in travail, so that he has no will or way of his own. This would matter little if I were not somewhat worn. I am, I believe, Mus giving birth to Mous. At least, no occupation is absorbing enough. . . .

" The word of your illness has dealt me a shock. Lady Lawrence had spoken of it—as a thing past. I supposed you to be fully restored. Beg of your wife to send me news of you. I shall certainly call the first day of freedom that I have. We go for two months to Loch Earn in July. I am promised a steam-yacht to take me up to Oban. So it is not Bayreuth this year. Besides the novel, I have been translating choice fragments of the *Iliad* into Hexameters. You see I want a holiday. God bless you and our dear D : Troïa.

" Know me ever your constant loving friend,
" George Meredith."

Sir William Hardman died five months later, on 12th September, 1890, and the previous year Meredith had lost his other old friend and neighbour at Norbiton a quarter of a century before—Frederick Jones. He felt the snapping of these firmly forged and trusty links with the past. He wrote to Mrs Jones :

" All yesterday I was thinking of you and your husband and the old times—the stay with you, the welcoming here, the songs. . . . You are right as to my affection for him. He was one of the few true men I have known. And, my friend, these men live on in us. . . . They have the eternal in them. I do not look on death as a victory over us. Death and life are neighbours, each the cause of the other : and the Task for us, under stress of deprivation, is to take our loved ones into the mind, and commune with them, spirit to spirit—so will they be wedded to us faster, closer about us, than when we had the voices and eyes. . . . In the soul of true love there is no parting. Our dearest go from touch and sight—not, nor ever, from the lastingly vital of us. I say this, with full consciousness of the loss I too have sustained."

Meredith could write very exquisitely in times of sorrow with real heart-felt words of sympathy, though he had the sensitive artist's horror of death and the grim ceremonies that follow it. Consequently he did not feel able to be present at the funeral of his son, Arthur Meredith, whose death on 3rd September, 1890, preceded Sir William Hardman's by nine days.[1] It was a sad coincidence that the two personalities most intimately associated with the old days at Copsham should have passed almost together, and it must have struck poignantly the chords of memory. Perhaps his *Ode to Youth in Memory* was an expression of what Meredith felt in this retrospective time :

> Days when the ball of our vision
> Had eagles that flew unabashed to sun ;
> When the grasp on the bow was decision,
> And arrow and hand and eye were one ;
> When the Pleasures, like waves to a swimmer,
> Came heaving for rapture ahead !—
> Invoke them, they dwindle, they glimmer
> As lights over mounds of the dead.
>
> .   .   .   .
>
> Darkness is wedded and the waste regrets
> Beating as dead leaves on a fitful gust,
> By souls no longer dowered to climb
> Beneath their pack of dust,
> Whom envy of a lustrous prime,
> Eclipsed while yet invoked, besets,
> And dooms to sink and water sable flowers,
> That never gladdened eye or loaded bee.
> Strain we the arms for Memory's hours,
> We are the seized Persephone.

---

[1] Browning's funeral at Westminster Abbey, on 31st December, 1889, was one of the few services of this description that Meredith ever attended. He was also present at Tennyson's funeral in the same building in October, 1892, of which he wrote : " It was unimpressive, except among the thoughts. The Poet's own words in the anthem were good to hear, the music hardly so.''

CHAPTER XIV

"ONE OF OUR CONQUERORS." "LORD ORMONT AND HIS
AMINTA." "THE AMAZING MARRIAGE"

THE decade 1885-1895 is supposed, popularly, to be the
most " difficult " of Meredith's literary output : it was
the period when he accomplished his literary vengeance
on his critics, of whose hostile activities, as we have seen, he
took a perversely exaggerated view. As late as 1887 he told an
American admirer of his work : " In England I am encouraged
but by a few enthusiasts. I read in a critical review of some
verses of mine the other day that I was ' a harlequin and a
performer of antics.' I am accustomed to that kind of writing,
as our hustings orator is to the dead cat and the brickbat flung
in his face—at which he smiles politely ; and I too ; but after
many years of it my mind looks elsewhere."

But now that he was financially independent, and had a considerable following both in America and England, as even he
was constrained to admit,[1] he resolved to flail those reviewing
animals, or insects rather, who had bit and tormented him in
the wilderness. As a literary force and influence, the critics
would be obliged to wrestle with his verbal mystifications and
perverse juggling with the English language, and to swallow
the indigestible preliminaries of *Diana of the Crossways*
and *One of our Conquerors* by way of *hors d'œuvre* before
the meat he deigned to offer them was served. Such was
the author's intention in his last, and so-called " difficult,"
novels.

[1] He wrote in 1888 : " Yesterday I had a startler in the shape of a
Draft on Baring's from the publishers of my works in Boston, U.S.A.,
by way of Royalty. I had heard of large sales over there. The touch
of American money has impressed me with concrete ideas of fame. I
have not been writing much. I must soon be doing or the trick will
quit me." And later : " The run of the novels started from American
appreciation. . . . The English, unlike the Americans, have not
accepted me in the form of a poet."

There is an interesting reference to one of these books in a
late letter (1906) of Meredith's to a critic of his work :

" You mention *One of our Conquerors* with revulsion.   It is
a trying piece of work.   I had to look at it recently, and remembered my annoyance in correcting proofs.   But, strange
to say, it held me.   A doctor of the Insane wrote to my
Publishers from Australia that the opening chapter showed
all the intimations of incipient lesion of brain, and he wondered
whether I had studied the disease.   Had I done so, I should
not have written of it.   The novel has value, for containing
the characters of Nesta Radnor, little Skepsey, and Dartrey
Fenellan, and an Irish Gentleman, of a type different from
Colonel De Craye of *The Egoist*.   Also, I found in it much that
is now made manifest of the malady afflicting England."

When M. Photiadès visited Meredith in 1908, and spoke
appreciatively of *One of our Conquerors*, he was complimented
by the author for having ventured upon his most difficult book.
Meredith went on to say :

" I have observed, since my earlier works, that nothing
bewilders the critics so much as that which, avoiding banality,
demands a surfeit of attention.   When I was about sixty, and
I had inherited a small sum of money which made me independent, it pleased me to put before these critics a strong dose
of the most indigestible material.   I presented to them, slyly,
Diana of the Crossways and the novels which followed.   But
nothing enraged them so much as *One of our Conquerors*.   These
poor fellows knew not by what saint to swear.   How could
they give an account of the cursed volume ?   It was necessary
to commence by understanding it, and they groped blindly in
their own great darkness."

The critics must answer for themselves.   One certainly, Mr
J. M. Robertson, confessed : " With the exception of Zola's
La Terre—hard reading for a different reason—*One of our
Conquerors* was the hardest novel to read that I ever met with." [1]
Without in any way seeking to pose as a person who van-
quishes difficulties admitted by more experienced critics, I may

[1] *Concerning Preciosity.   The Yellow Book*, April, 1897.

say that, personally, I find no difficulty in reading *One of our Conquerors* : on the contrary, owing to the extreme interest of the problem presented and the flow of incidents, regarded as a novel I find it easier to read than some of Meredith's earlier work, such as *Sandra Belloni,* where nothing in particular happens beyond the mental convolutions and consequent actions and reactions of the characters, whereas there is full store of dramatic happenings in *One of our Conquerors,* particularly at the close, and the final interview with Mrs Burman is astonishingly vivid. Possibly the effect is gained by contrasting the intense emotions of the actors in the scene with the familiar setting, which Victor Radnor finds the same after the absence of long years : the white and gold furniture ; the scent of Maréchale ; the French clock, with the swinging gilt Cupid, which was always wrong as to time—as momentous and sinister a horologe as the French clock, with its alarmed ticking and cheerful brass group of the sacrifice of Iphigenia, appeared to Amelia, of *Vanity Fair,* when she found herself in the drawing-room of Osborne's house in Russell Square, another funereal mansion like Mrs Burman's in Regent's Park.

There is, indeed, a sort of Thackeray-London atmosphere throughout *One of our Conquerors,* permeated as it is by the odours of Armandine's superlative cookery and the sound of popping corks of Old Veuve. How picturesque is the opening scene, the view from London Bridge—" London's unrivalled mezzotint " ; and then the smoky splendours of sunset over Trafalgar Square in *The Walk Westward* :

" There is immensity, swinging motion, collision, dusky richness of colouring, to the sight ; and to the mind idea. London presents it. If we can allow ourselves a moment for not inquireing scrupulously (you will do it by inhaling the aroma of the ripe kitchen hour), here is a noble harmony of heaven and the earth of the works of man, speaking a grander tongue than barren sea or wood or wilderness. . . . Clouds of high colour above London City are as the light of the Goddess to lift the angry heroic head over human. They gloriously transfigure. A Murillo beggar is not more precious than sight of London in any of the streets admitting coloured cloud-scenes. . . . And if haply down an alley some olive mechanic of street-organs has quickened little children's legs to rhythmic footing, they strike on thoughts braver than pastoral."

And in twenty-three words he paints the picture of Hyde Park at night : " The grandeur of that black pit of the benighted London, with its ocean-voice of the heart at beat along the lighted outer ring." [1]

In contradistinction to *The Egoist*, the characters of *One of our Conquerors* are almost without exception lovable and delightful. Surely Nesta Radnor is the most charming of all Meredith's heroines. Though gifted with intellect and musical talent, she is ever an unaffected and affectionate girl—the symbol by whose acts and words Meredith expressed his noble compassion for women who have erred and suffered. Very real and human, too, are Victor Radnor and Nataly, the two Fenellans ; most amusing Skepsey, Beaves Urmsing, the Duvidney ladies and their disconcertingly perfumed lap-dog, Tasso. The unctuous parsons of the book, the rival confessors of Tunbridge Wells, that Paradise of the Elect, and the Rev. Septimus Barmby, and the Rev. Groseman Buttermore, give another Thackeray touch, for they belong to the school of the Rev. Charles Honeyman. The character of Dartrey Fenellan may have been suggested by Colonel Frederick Burnaby, author of *The Ride to Khiva*, who was killed at Abu Klea in 1885. In Colney Durance, I imagine, Meredith provided a ventriloquist's doll who could enunciate his own satiric observations at the expense of England and the English ; Durance's serial, *The Rival Tongues*, appeared in a magazine unappreciated and misunderstood, much in the manner accorded, in his own estimation, to Meredith's work in *The Fortnightly Review*. Certainly Durance speaks with the tongue of the Celtic Meredith as revealed in the letters of the latter when alluding to the English. Thus Colney :

" They beg for the privilege of pulling the forelock to the bearers of the titles of the men who took their lands from them

[1] Had Meredith lived to read *The Story of Francis Horatio and His Three Companions*, by Hillel Samson (1912. Dent), he would have delighted in the exquisite descriptions this book contains of atmospheric effects in London, particularly of autumn skies and mists over the river and trees.

and turn them to the uses of cattle. The Saxon English had,
no doubt, a heavier thrashing than any people allowed to
subsist ever received : you see it to this day ; the crick of the
neck at the name of a lord is now concealed and denied, but
they have it and betray the effects ; and it's patent in their
Journals, all over their literature. Where it's not seen, another
blood's at work. The Kelt won't accept that form of slavery.
Let him be servile, supple, cunning, treacherous, and to all
appearance time-serving, he will always remember his day of
manly independence and who robbed him ; he is the poetic
animal of the races of modern men. . . . He does not offer
the other cheek or turn his back to be kicked after a knock to
the ground. Instead of asking him to forgive, which he cannot
do, you must teach him to admire."

Which may be taken as a parable for the government of
Ireland.

Colney Durance utters many pungent sayings in the manner
of Meredith's table-talk, as when he advises love as a cure for
stoutness. " Obeseness is the most sensitive of our ailments :
probably as being aware that its legitimate appeal to pathos is
ever smothered in its pudding-bed of the grotesque." And
when he is annoyed by Brighton : " These lengths of blank-
faced terraces fronting sea ! . . . So these moneyed English
shoulder to the front place ; and that is the appearance they
offer to their commercial God ! . . . The face of a stopped
watch !—the only meaning it has is past date ! "

Other typical Meredithian remarks are uttered by Victor
Radnor : " After all, a caged wild beast hasn't so bad a life.
. . . To be well fed while they live, and welcome death as a
release from the maladies they develop in idleness, is the condition of wealthy people—creatures of prey." And : " These
are the deluge days when even aristocracy will cry blessings
on the man who procures a commercial appointment for one
of its younger sons offended and rebutted by the barrier of
Examinations for the Civil Service."

In this book, too, Meredith tilted at his favourite windmill of
the inefficient British Army ; voiced his views on conscription
and the scandal of young officers who, as soon as they were
trained, resigned their commissions :

"He expects the title soon, will leave the army—the poor plucked British Army, as you call it !—and lead the life of a country squire, hunting ! Well, it's not only the army, it's all over Great Britain, with this infernal wealth of ours !—and for pleasure or Paradise for a sugar plum ! Upon my word, it appears to me, Esau's the Englishman, Jacob the German, of these times. . . . If we're not plucked, as your regiments are of the officers who have learnt their work, we're emasculated :— the nation's half made up of the idle and the servants of the idle. . . . Ay, and your country squires and your manufacturers contrive to give the army a body of consumptive louts fit for nothing else than to take the shilling. It wouldn't so much matter if they were trained to arms and self-respect."

All this, in view of recent history, now seems strangely out of date, and here, for once, Meredith was not a true prophet. But, as I have said before, depreciation always finds its mouthers in England, even from Downing Street with sneers at " kilometric advances " against " impenetrable barriers," and from Episcopal Palaces with rescripts announcing that never again will *We* tolerate the spectacle of healthy young men serving as footmen or drapers' assistants. Perhaps : perhaps not. Anyway, the despised lackey and counter-jumper, who has managed to fight all right for the protection of the spouters, will decide for himself whether he resumes, or not, his former employment. He will require no direction or interference from those whose knowledge of battle and sudden death is confined to rides in motor cars behind the lines for purposes of exhortation, and to seeing from the windows of a special train " shrapnel bursting " over London—a spectacle not vouchsafed, it would seem, to other dwellers in the city.

Although a bishop might find confirmation of his views upon the young men of England in *One of our Conquerors*, he would also find speedy cause for corybantic commination at the sympathetic laxity expressed in the same book for breaches of the marriage law and the Seventh Commandment. The whole problem of the novel is concerned with those matters, and it was in *One of our Conquerors* that Meredith first adumbrated his quasi-humorous and much reprobated plea for " leasehold marriages " determinable by the contractors after a term of years if so desired :

" Awful thing, marriage, to some women ! We chain them to that domestic round ; most of them haven't the means of independence or a chance of winning it ; and all that's open to them, if they've made a bad cast for a mate—and good Lord ! how are they to know before it's too late !—they haven't a choice except to play tricks or jump to the deuce or sit and ' drape in blight ' as Colney has it ; though his notion of the optional marriages, broken or renewed every seven years . . . ! "

Elsewhere he expressed his theory more seriously, but probably he was still half in jest, so ineradicable always was the Comic Spirit within him :

" No man and no woman should be inexorably tied together for more than a ten years' trial. I fix ten years as a fair period of probation ; a shorter period would be too little, longer would be too much. In ten years they will find each other out. Under the most favourable circumstances there will be some bickerings and disagreements. There will be surprises and disappointments. The man will find out that the girl is not quite the angel he thought, and the girl will find out that the man is not the god that she believed. But these surprises and disappointments will not justify separation ; the couple have to pass through their period of disillusionment. The dreams of courtship have to be dispelled. The couple have to be hardened to the married life."

One of our Conquerors has its faults, of course, like all other books. The extracts from Colney Durance's imaginary work, *The Rival Tongues*, are intolerably dull—to me, the dullest thing Meredith ever wrote ; and it is curious that his sense of humour did not save him from making the villain of his story, Worrell, a Major. Wicked Baronets and Majors ! Who shall ever compile the full list of you in fiction and drama and the indictment of your villainies for the entrapment of Female Virtue ? And who were the progenitors of your long lines ?

One of our Conquerors commenced a triple serial appearance in October, 1890, in *The Fortnightly Review*, *The Australasian*, and *The New York Sun.* It was published in three volumes by Chapman and Hall in 1891.[1] One of the few references to the story in Meredith's correspondence is contained in a letter to an admirer of the author living in Glasgow—Mr George Stevenson, who was dubbed " Glasgowgo " : " The Novel has been knocked about by Reviewers as I expected, and clearly there is no further chance of peace between us. What they call digressions is a presentation of the atmosphere of the present time, of which the story issues."

So, having declared war with the critics, the veteran set about preparing his next bomb for their confusing in the shape of *Lord Ormont and his Aminta.* But for those who have read Meredith in his literary progression, this book and *The Amazing Marriage* can have no difficulties.[2] Compared with the didactics of *Beauchamp's Career* and the subtleties of *The Egoist*, they are simple—tales merely of vagaries in the Holy Estate of Matrimony. Why Swinburne, for instance, could not read them is inexplicable. Perhaps the real objection to these books is not directed to any obscurity of plot or tortuosity of narrative, but rather to the perverse use of words and simile. This point of view has been very trenchantly expressed by Mr J. M. Robertson in his article, *Concerning Preciosity*, before mentioned :

" It is indeed impossible for a reader who respects Mr Meredith's genius to read him—or at least his later works—without irritation at his extraordinary ill-usage of language. Old admirers, going back to his earlier works, never free from the sin of preciosity, recognise that there has been an almost continuous deterioration—the fatal law of all purposive preciosity. In the earlier novels there were at times signal beauties of phrase, sentences in which the strain towards utterance was transmuted into fire and radiance, sentences of the fine poet who underlay

---

[1] The original draft of the manuscript was entitled *A Conqueror in our Time* ; 440 pages of this were sold for £260 at Sotheby's in 1910.

[2] Meredith himself seems to have regarded *Lord Ormont and his Aminta* as " easier " reading than *One of our Conquerors*, for alluding to the latter in a letter to C. K. Shorter, dated 25th May, 1891, he said : " If the run against this novel should put my present men out of pocket, I shall feel bound to give them a chance of indemnification with the offer of a more generally readable. But they may have become incredulous on that point."

and even now underlies that ever-thickening crust of preciosity and verbal affectation. Even in *One of our Conquerors* there seemed, to the tolerant sense, to be still some gleams of the old flame flashing at long intervals through the scoriæ of unsmelted speech. But in *Lord Ormont and his Aminta* neither patience nor despair can discover in whole chapters aught but the lava and cinders of language. . . . After a few chapters I no longer sought to read Mr Meredith. I made a hand-to-mouth précis of nearly every page, and soon got over the ground, only pausing at times tò reassure myself that all was ill. Hardly once, so far as I have read, do we find an important sentence really well written ; never a paragraph ; for the perpetual grimace of expression, twisting the face of speech into every shape but those of beauty and repose, is in no sense admirable."

Mr Robertson showed no mercy to the famous " Marine Duet " chapter of *Lord Ormont and his Aminta,* which he said was merely " the imagination of a man who either never knew what swimming is or has forgotten what he knew.[1] The occurrence, as related in the novel, is an impossible dream. In this, indeed, there is pathos, and perhaps the ideal reader would only see pathos or literary picturesque in the kindred aberration of the novelist's prose."

For thirty-five years Meredith's female creations had been " swimming " metaphorically in his works, and now, according to this critic, when, at last, a lady takes to the water in reality and kicks out and splashes and swims for miles, talking the while, the whole thing is an impossibility ! Meredith's fondness for the simile of a woman swimming is surely the most irritating of his recurrent affected phrases ; it can probably be found in every one of his stories, and even in *Love in the Valley* " she swims to me on tears," which suggests anything but a romantic experience and inclines to raise the spectacle of a damp nightmare. When Mrs Doria or Diana " swim " to the door or the tea-tray, the mental picture conjured up is not graceful or dignified : one seems to see the ladies face downwards, kicking out their heels and sprawling on the floor. Only on one occasion do I find the expression tolerable, and that is when the

[1] The swimming scene was placed at Felixstowe, where Meredith used to stay, over forty years previously, with his first wife.

Countess de Saldar " swam in the pleasure of a nobleman's compliment." Here we *can* picture the harassed dame, splashing about and diving and bobbing up again, and showing off, so to speak, during one of the few pleasant moments of that unlucky dinner at Beckley Court.

In *Lord Ormont and his Aminta* Meredith again attacked his favourite problem of a woman placed in an invidious and dubious position by some flaw in her matrimonial chains, though the thesis in this book that the heroine's marriage might be irregular owing to the ceremony having been performed in a British Embassy abroad is not very convincing. Provided the necessary formalities had been carried out and an authorised clergyman or official had performed the service, a marriage in an embassy abroad, a place regarded as " British soil," should be as legal as any other, whether contracted in church or registry or drawing-room. Meredith seems to have based his presentment of the relations between Lord and Lady Ormont on the celebrated case of Charles Mordaunt, 3rd Earl of Peterborough (1658-1735), Admiral and General, who, after a stirring and stormy Service career, was supposed to have married Anastasia Robinson, the singer, in 1722. The lady quitted the stage and lived in a villa at Parson's Green provided by the Earl. Being very ill in 1735, and perhaps pricked by the recollection of the three capital crimes he owned to committing in his youth, Lord Peterborough at length acknowledged his wife and " remarried " her before his death in October, 1735.

But the characteristics of Lord Ormont were undoubtedly drawn from the Earl of Cardigan (1797-1868), the gallant leader of the Light Brigade of Cavalry at Balaklava, and the most popular hero of his time in England. He was very wealthy, and a noted duellist, his most notorious affair being that with Harvey Tuckett, whom he wounded, on Wimbledon Common, in 1840, as by that date duelling was going out of favour. In his later years Lord Cardigan was inclined to pose as an ignored hero. All this, it will be seen, coincides with the career of Lord Ormont, " our general of cavalry, whose charge at the head of fifteen hundred horse in the last great battle shattered the enemy's right wing, and gave us the victory." Lord Ormont was married in the British Embassy at Madrid. Lord Cardigan's remarkable second marriage took place in 1858 at Gibraltar, and he and his beautiful bride (formerly Miss Adeline de Horsey) proceeded to Madrid.　Like Aminta, Miss de Horsey had excited much comment when she rode in Hyde Park by the side of the Cavalry hero.[1]　But the analogy collapses at the ridiculous ending of the book, where Lord Ormont, who throughout has been represented as a fire-eater and deadly duellist, not only fails to call out or horsewhip Weyburn, the " betrayer " of his wife, but actually and meekly arranges to send his young grand-nephew to the school conducted by this erring gentleman and lady, both so calmly oblivious of law and honour, living together in the Unholy Estate of Adultery.　It seems impossible to believe that Meredith intended this farcical finale to be taken seriously, and yet there is no evidence that he ever alluded to it as a trap for the tripping of his loathed critics, which would seem the most reasonable explanation.

The character of Lady Charlotte Eglett, who presents admirably a certain type of arrogant but kind-hearted *grande dame* peculiar to the nineteenth century, is one of the most clearly depicted and humorous portraits in the Meredith gallery.　She is said to have been suggested by Lady Caroline Maxse, who died in 1886.[2]　As the mother of his intimate friend, Admiral Maxse, Meredith had often met her, and some confirmation of the supposition alluded to is provided by the fact that the name of Lady Caroline's grandson, Leo (Maxse), is bestowed upon Lady Charlotte's grandson in the book.

Although Lady Charlotte Eglett is an entirely successful creation, the same cannot be said of Aminta.　One never quite sees the springs which govern her erratic actions or what causes her sudden mutations of conduct.　Except on the principle that " the glory fades in possession," it is not clear why her hero-worship for Lord Ormont faded; and it is not clear why her original contempt for the scholastic profession, as exemplified in the person of the unheroical Matey Weyburn, should be transmuted into an ardent desire to share his duties in that

---

[1] Compare chap. xi. of *Lord Ormont and his Aminta*, and p. 99 of *My Recollections*, by the Countess of Cardigan.

[2] Meredith noted her strong character in his epitaph, *Lady C. M.*

> To them that knew her, there is vital flame
> In these the simple letters of her name.
> To them that knew her not, be it but said,
> So strong a spirit is not of the dead.

sphere of work, and the world well lost, except on the plea of the instability and irrationality of the sex when caught in the toils of Cupid. It is curious that Meredith should have given his schoolmaster the name of Weyburn, which so nearly resembles in sound that of Wrayburn, the character in Dickens's *Our Mutual Friend* who is so insulting and contemptuous to the schoolmaster, Bradley Headstone, and his calling, in that book. Matey Weyburn cuts but a poor figure as a hero when he escorts Aminta up from Steignton and hides from Morsfield in " The Jolly Cricketers " Inn—though the progressive incidents of the journey are very vivid and in Meredith's best narrative style, recalling the scenes of south-western high-roads and wayside taverns in *Evan Harrington* and *Harry Richmond*—" the food and service of the little inn belonged in their unpretentious honesty to the kind we call old English : the dear old simple country English of the brotherly interchange in sight of heaven —good stuff for good money, a matter with a blessing on it."

Again in this book Meredith re-harped on his old theme of the invasion of this country and the supineness of the English to the possibility, but for once he paid the reprehensible islanders a few compliments by the mouth of Lord Ormont :

" They fall well. Yes, the English fall like men. . . . Bodies knocked over, hearts upright. That's example ; we breed Ironsides out of a sight like that. . . . An army's shipped to land without commissariat, ambulances, medical stores, and march against the odds, as usual. . . . Our men can spurt, for a flick o' the whip. They're expected to be constantly ready for doing prodigies—to repair the country's omissions. . . . Our men are good beasts ; they give the best in 'em, and drop. More's the scandal to a country that has grand material and overtasks it. A blazing disaster ends the chapter."

There, in brief, is the parable of the Dardanelles and Mesopotamia disasters in the Great War. The words were written a quarter of a century ago, but the late and present Governments can take this unction to their souls, that Meredith unerringly foresaw how the Ministerial caste would inevitably fall to the occasion whenever The Great Emergency arose for England.

There are many mordant flashes in the old style of *Richard Feverel* in *Lord Ormont and his Aminta* :

" She was a married woman, and she probably regarded the wedding by law as the end a woman has to aim at, and is annihilated by hitting ; one flash of success, and then extinction, like a boy's cracker on the pavement." " The sedentary professions corrupt men : bad for the blood. Those monastery monks found that out. They had to birch the devil out of them three times a day and half the night, howling like full-moon dogs all through their lives, till the flesh was off them." " Published Memoirs indicate the end of a man's activity, and that he acknowledges the end." " How preach at a creature on the bend of passion's rapids ! One might as well read a chapter from the Bible to delirious patients."

Lord Ormont and his Aminta was completed in 1893. In June, Meredith told Mrs Walter Palmer : " I am writing every day from 10.30 to 6 P.M., and am tired at the end. I hope— rather think—you will like the novel for its own sake—not in your gentleness for mine." It commenced to appear serially in *The Pall Mall Magazine*, December, 1893, and was published by Chapman and Hall, in three volumes, in 1894. The book was " Gratefully inscribed to George Buckston Browne, Surgeon " (a Dr Buxton figures in the story), who had very successfully performed an operation for stone upon Meredith in 1892. Mr Buckston Browne has given an account of his first meeting with the author :

" I had for some years wished to see or to know Mr George Meredith, and had often tried to imagine the personality of the author of *The Egoist* and *The Ordeal of Richard Feverel,* when one morning a letter came asking me to give him a professional appointment at my house. On June 20th, 1892, Mr Meredith plumped himself down in what has been called the victim's chair in my consulting-room. He was then sixty-four years old and ataxic, and literally threw himself into chairs or on to couches with alarming precipitancy. His first words were : ' Mr Browne, I am a writer,' and I was able to say at once : ' Mr Meredith, you need no introduction here,' and opening a bookcase immediately in front of him, I showed him a complete edition of his works. We became great friends. He gave me his entire confidence, and although exceedingly sensitive in every possible way, he proved an excellent patient."

On 22nd June, Meredith wrote to Frank Harris :

" It may be you who sends me marked on a page the *Revue d. d. Mondes*. I take in the Review and saw with pleasure the translation of your *Modern Idyll*—I suppose by Madame Bentzon. It is not ill done. Let her now tackle *Elder Conklin*, which is as powerful and not quite so acid. Pray, more of them. They give me a sense of fulness that I don't get from other work of our time. And how I need a dose of recreation you will understand when I tell you that I come to town to-morrow to lie for a week under the hands of Buckston Browne, and can't write ; can but read, with this devilish critical spirit of mine which you are of the few that can appease."

As Meredith said of Buckston Browne, " No victim of sharp instruments could be in skilfuller or kinder hands . . . he is the ablest as well as one of the best of men " ; and when, owing to his ataxic condition, another operation had to be endured four years later, he told Frank Harris : " Science has abolished pain, and with pain even the need of steeling oneself : the doctors have made the ford easy, we can't even feel the chill of the water."

Buckston Browne, and his wife and daughter, became the ever-welcome friends of Meredith at Box Hill ; and the dedication of *Lord Ormont and his Aminta* to this distinguished surgeon ranks in literary and medical annals with Thackeray's tribute to Dr John Elliotson, to whom *Pendennis* was dedicated in recognition of " constant watchfulness and skill " during a severe illness of the author in 1849.

In February, 1892, the degree of LL.D. was conferred by St Andrews University on Meredith. His presence was waived owing to ill-health. Writing to George Stevenson, he said : " I prefer to pay the usual fees and beg you to let me know where I am to address myself when my new title is patent. . . . St Andrews confounds my wits and makes me question what I have done to deserve her notice."

On 4th October of this year his son, William Maxse Meredith, was married to Margaret (Daisy), daughter of Ralph Elliot, and granddaughter of Sir George Elliot, 1st Bart., M.P. for North Durham and Monmouth, and step-daughter of Colonel T. H. Lewin, of Parkhurst, Leith Hill.[1] The author's first grandchild, George Meredith the younger, was born in November, 1894.[2]

In April and May, 1893, Meredith sat to G. F. Watts, R.A., for the portrait presented by the artist to the nation. At first he refused the request : " Watts has written a most generous offer to paint my head for the list among his gifts to the nation. It is distressing, for I could not consent to absorb any of his precious time, or to sit for such a purpose. I am ashamed to say I have no ambition to provoke an English posterity's question, Who is he ? And my grizzled mug may be left to vanish." But he relented, and mentions a few months later : " Just home from Loseley,[3] near G. F. Watts, to whom I have been sitting for a portrait—which, I am told, is good. But why a grizzled head is wanted for posterity to see, is the riddle to me. I dare not hint it, or I shall hear the retort that I am thinking . . . Once and in truth there was a presentable phiz, when no one cared for it."

In July, 1894, Meredith's only daughter, Marie Eveleen, was married to Henry Parkman Sturgis, of Givons, Leatherhead— not far distant from Box Hill, which was a happy mitigation of the sense of separation for the author now alone at Flint Cottage. He was still in full mental force, and engaged upon his last published novel, *The Amazing Marriage*. This had been commenced, and then laid aside, fifteen years earlier. He told R. L. Stevenson, in 1879 : " I am about one quarter through *The Amazing Marriage*, which, I promise you, you shall like better." In 1893 he resumed the story at the suggestion of his friend, Frederick Jameson (to whom it was fittingly dedicated). In June, 1894, he told Mrs Walter Palmer he was " Dreadful busy. A Novelist's prolonged delivery is a terrible matter." In August he stated : " My work will want a chapter or two for finish at the end of the month. Never enter on the composition of a novel with a light heart. I have had to drive two dozen

[1] Her younger sister, Miss Mabel Elliot, was married the following year to Sir Alexander Mackenzie, K.C.S.I., late Lieutenant-Governor of Bengal.

[2] George William Lewin Meredith, now an officer in the 18th Hussars, has served with distinction in the war and won the Military Cross.

[3] A house near Guildford rented by the Palmer family.

characters as two, making all run together to one end." In
January, 1895, he gave up his intention of being present at the
first night of Irving's production of *King Arthur* owing to the
pressure of his work. He wrote to Mrs Palmer :

" I can hardly feel the pen in my hand, the chalet is a re-
frigerator. It will be better for you to exclude me from the
Lyceum festival. I find that the strain of my prolonged work
has made me a crazy machine, and I doubt of being able to sit
through the performances."

And to Frederick Greenwood he wrote, in April :

" Come for a night or two. The daffodils are over our
banks, the cowslips beginning to crowd, and a South-Wester in
prospect for weeks ; which means a variation of high skies
and low, glooms and glories. What better, to speed sweet converse ? And novelists are worth talking with, you should
learn. . . . You will greatly revive a creature resting from the
enfantement of two novels without a pause."

The Amazing Marriage had a condensed serial appearance in
Scribner's Magazine throughout 1895, and the complete work [1]
was published the same year, in two volumes, by Constable and
Co. The author's son, W. M. Meredith, had become a partner
in that firm, who henceforth issued the reprints of Meredith's
books, and published posthumously the work he left unfinished
at his death.

Unfortunately R. L. Stevenson did not live to read *The*

[1] An early version of the manuscript of *The Amazing Marriage* was
sold for £96 in 1910. The manuscript of the published version (lacking
the first eight chapters), together with those of *Lord Ormont and his
Aminta* and *Diana of the Crossways*, were given in his lifetime by Meredith to Frank Cole, for thirty years his gardener and faithful attendant,
and one of the familiar institutions of Flint Cottage to the author's
visitors. The gift was intended to provide future benefit for Cole, who
accordingly, in 1909, disposed of the three manuscripts to Mr J. Pier-
pont Morgan for the sum of £800. With regard to the missing chapters
of *The Amazing Marriage*, it is possible they were a sacrifice to Nicotine,
for Meredith frequently used pages of his manuscripts as spills to light
his cigars, which accounts for the generally incomplete state of his
holograph work. Meredith presented copies of many of his books to Cole.
One bears the inscription : " Frank Cole, from his friend, George Meredith.
A good servant cancels the name of master. Dec. 19th, 1897."

Amazing Marriage, in which he was much interested from the fact that the character of Gower Woodseer, in its earlier stages, was drawn from him :

" Outwardly simple, naturally frank, though a tangle of the complexities inwardly, he was a touchstone for true aristocracy."

And as he is made to describe himself :

" ' I care for open air, colour, flowers, weeds, birds, insects, mountains. There's a world behind the mask. I call this life ; and the town's a boiling pot, intolerably stuffy. My one ambition is to be out of it. . . . I slept beside a spring last night, and I never shall like a bedroom so well. I think I have discovered the great secret : I may be wrong, of course.' And if so, he had his philosophy, the admission was meant to say."

In an interesting letter to Meredith, written from Vailima, Samoa, on 17th April, 1894, Stevenson said :

" I hear we may soon expect *The Amazing Marriage*. You know how long, and with how much curiosity, I have looked forward to the book. Now, in so far as you have adhered to your intention, Gower Woodseer will be a family portrait, age twenty-five, of the highly respectable and slightly influential and fairly aged ' Tusitala.' You have not known that gentleman ; console yourself he is not worth knowing. At the same time, my dear Meredith, he is very sincerely yours—for what he is worth, for the memories of old times, and in the expectation of many pleasures still to come. I suppose we shall never see each other again ; flitting youths of the Lysaght [1] species may occasionally cover these unconscionable leagues and bear greetings to and fro. But we ourselves must be content to converse with an occasional sheet of notepaper, and I shall never see whether you have grown older, and you shall never deplore that Gower Woodseer should have declined into the pantaloon ' Tusitala.' It is perhaps better so. Let us continue to see each other as we were, and accept, my dear Meredith, my love and respect. ROBERT LOUIS STEVENSON."

[1] Sidney R. Lysaght, author of *The Marplot*, who had recently presented a letter of introduction from Meredith. Stevenson much liked him.

This letter was sadly prophetic, for Stevenson died eight months later, and a few days before *The Amazing Marriage* commenced in *Scribner's Magazine*. In his later development of the character of Gower Woodseer, as I have intimated, Meredith was not drawing upon his recollections of Stevenson.[1]

In this last novel, Meredith reverts to the easier style of his earlier work, and it contains much of the spirit of *Evan Harrington* and *Harry Richmond*. Like those books, it is a novel of Meredith's own counties, Surrey and Hampshire, of English life. There are passages in it which recover the point of view that environed him in his boyhood at Portsmouth and near Petersfield when the nineteenth century was still young in its second quarter :

" We lived a happy domestic life in those old coaching days, when county affairs and county people were the topics of firesides, and the country enclosed us to make us feel snug in our own importance. My opinion is, that men and women grow to their dimensions only where such is the case. We had our alarms from the outside now and again, but we soon relapsed to dwell upon our private business and our pleasant little hopes and excitements ; the courtships and the crosses and the scandals, the tea-parties and the dances, and how the morning looked after the stormy night had passed, and the coach coming down the hill with a box of news and perhaps a curious passenger to drop at the inn. I do believe we had a liking for the very highwaymen, if they had any reputation for civility. What I call human events, things concerning you and me, instead of the deafening catastrophes now afflicting and taking all conversation out of us, had their natural interest then. We studied the face of each morning as it came, and speculated upon the secret of the thing it might have in store for us."

Hindhead, Richmond, and many a spot in the south-west land beloved of Meredith come into this book :

"They were on the level of the vale, going along a road between farms and mansions, meadows and garden-plots and park-palings. A strong warm wind drove the pack of clouds

---

[1] Further reference to the subject will be found in *The Sketch*, 27th November, 1895.

over the tree-tops and charged at the branches. English scenery, animating air ; a rouse to the blood and the mind."

Lofty Croridge seems to be intended for Crowborough.

Apart from his trips abroad and visits to Seaford, to near Southampton, to Wales, and to East Anglia, it is a curious fact that Meredith's long life of eighty-one years was spent in that portion of England which may be roughly defined on the map by drawing a more or less straight line from Portsmouth to London, with some slight divergences right and left. From Portsmouth he went to school near Petersfield, and then (Neuwied intervening) to London. Thence to Weybridge, Lower Halliford, Esher and Copsham, Kingston, and finally Box Hill. This topographical definition of where he lived also comprises the topography of the novels and much of his poetry. Hampshire and Surrey are synonymous with Meredith primarily ; and in a lesser degree the places he visited at home and abroad are all, as I have endeavoured to show throughout in this book, transcribed in his literary work, for Meredith ever drew faithfully from Nature both in the human and scenic sense.

Thus in *The Amazing Marriage* there are reflections of his visit to Wales a few years earlier, and tributes to the race he liked, in his later years, to identify himself with—" owning to a considerable infusion of Welsh blood in the composition of him " :

" Now, to the Cymry and to the pure Kelt, the fact is at their elbows continually. The past of their lives has lost neither face nor voice behind the shroud ; nor are the passions of the flesh, nor is the animate soul, wanting to it. Other races forfeit infancy, forfeit youth and manhood with their progression to the wisdom age may bestow. These have each stage always alive, quick at a word, a scent, a sound, to conjure up scenes, in spirit and in flame. Historically, they still march with Cadwallader, with Llewellyn, with Glendower ; sing with Aneurin, Taliesen, old Llywarch ; individually they are in the heart of the injury done them thirty years back,[1] or thrilling to the glorious deed which strikes an empty buckler for most of the sons of Time. An old sea rises in them, rolling no phantom

---

[1] Perhaps this throws some light on the animus against his relatives which Meredith expressed in *Evan Harrington*.

billows to break to spray against existing rocks of the shore. That is why, and even if they have a dose of the Teuton in them, they have often to feel themselves exiles when still in amicable community among the preponderating Saxon English."

There is mention more than once of how the Welsh love their native mountains, seen or in exile. This book, indeed, is a pæan of mountains, for in addition to those of Wales, the heights of Germany and Styria are extolled. How beautiful is the picture of dawn in Carinthia's name-land :

" The plumes of cloud now slowly entered into the lofty arch of dawn and melted from brown to purple-black. The upper sky swam with violet ; and in a moment each stray cloud-feather was edged with rose and then suffused. It seemed that the heights fronted East to eye the interflooding of colours, and it was imaginable that all turned to the giant whose forehead first kindled to the sun : a greeting of god and king. . . . The armies of the young sunrise in mountain-lands neighbouring the plains, vast shadows, were marching over woods and meads, black against the edge of golden ; and great heights were cut with them, and bounding waters took the leap in a silvery radiance to gloom ; the bright and dark-banded valleys were like night and morning taking hands down the sweep of their rivers. Immense was the range of vision scudding the peaks and over the illimitable Eastward plains flat to the very East and sources of the sun."

The Amazing Marriage and its two immediate predecessors form and complete the trilogy whereby Meredith voiced his sympathy for the wrongs of women, particularly for those who find themselves yoked to unsuitable partners and those who are —or rather were—debarred from realising their personalities and gifts in the world of endeavour and achievement. As he said to Lord Morley : " I have been oppressed by the injustice done to Women, the constraint put upon their natural aptitude, and their faculties, generally much to the degradation of the race."

In *The Amazing Marriage*, of course, the moral is conveyed with a Barrie-like touch of phantasy, for the two protagonists are bathed in a light that never was on sea or land. It is an impossible and delightful story, but if it is supposed to hold a mirror to Human Nature, it is as one of those warped freak glasses beloved of trippers in exhibitional " Halls of Mystery." The whole episode of The Amazing Baby belongs to the realm of French farce, and even granting the possibility of the cryptic matrimonial ladder left at the window of the inn, it is not clear how Lord Fleetwood came to use it, inasmuch as there is never a hint of his having returned from Canleys the first night or any other night.   On the contrary, he is made to muse : " Of course, he could not return to her.   How would she receive him ? There was no salt in the thought of it ; she was too submissive." To spring suddenly a joke of this kind—an infant born to a couple who separated on the day of their marriage—in the midst of what professes to be a normal novel may be an amusing literary harlequinade, but it has no pretence to claim consideration as literature or art.   And one regrets this Jack-in-the-Box intrusion the more, because the problem of Fleetwood's reconciliation with his wife would have been of intense interest if treated seriously.   Even as it is, when the improbabilities and absurdities of the story are put aside, there are moments when it is possible to be moved acutely by this tragedy of love—love that came too late on the man's side, love that had been killed in the woman.   What a fine story it might have been : the pity of it.   Fleetwood's character had great possibilities of development ; a flood of suggestive tragedy is revealed in the words :

" He took love unmanfully ; the passion struck at his weakness ; in wrath at the humiliation, if only to revenge himself for that, he could be fiendish ; he knew it, and loathed the desired fair creature who caused and exposed to him these cracks in his nature, whence there came a brimstone stench of the infernal pits.   And he was made for better."

That last simile is an example of the mysterious power of Meredith to hammer home an impression or suggestion.   " A brimstone stench of the infernal pits " : a wild and outrageous metaphor, but how appropriate and vivid for the meaning intended.   Perhaps the final fate of Fleetwood as a monk was the right one for a man of his extreme temperament, and Meredith, with his insight into character, knew the consolations that the Roman Catholic faith can offer to an emotional and sensitive person who has suffered much in contact with the world, and who in return for the abnegation of free will finds peace in mystic symbolism :

" It is natural to worship, and only the Catholics can prostrate themselves with dignity. That is matter for thought. . . . For estimable language, and the preservation of self-respect in prostration, we want ritual, ceremonial elevation of the visible object for the soul's adoring through the eye. So may we escape our foul or empty selves."

Although *The Amazing Marriage* was Meredith's last complete novel, he left, at his death, an unfinished work, which was published posthumously in 1910 under the title of *Celt and Saxon*. The character of Richard Rockney was drawn from Frederick Greenwood :

" Richard Rockney takes front rank. A journalist altogether given up to his craft, considering the audience he had gained, he was a man of forethought besides being a trenchant writer, and he was profoundly, not less than eminently, the lover of Great Britain."

Celt and Saxon was another sympathetic study of the Welsh temperament in the person of Adiante, and of the Irish as represented by the three O'Donnells—the two races of which Meredith liked to consider himself a compound. There is, at times, a lightness of touch in this story, particularly in the delineation of Patrick O'Donnell and of Captain and Mrs Con, that reminds one of the later and subdued Lever, of the period of *The Barringtons* and *The Martins of Cro Martin* ; and it is a pity that the original basis of the tale, the fate of Adiante and Philip, was never worked out. Instead, the author fell into the pit of his own digging and wandered in a morass of the most precious Meredithese, which reached high-mud mark in the tilting at the symbol of England, the long chapter *Of the Great Mr Bull*, whereof this is a specimen :

" Banish Bull. . . . Decline to let that old yeoman turned Alderman stand any longer for the national man. Banish him from your revels and your debatings, prohibit him your

Christmas, lend no ear either to his panics or his testiness, especially to his rages ; do not report him at all, and he will soon subside into his domestic, varied by his pot-house, privacy."

Another fragment of novel which it is much to be regretted Meredith never continued was *The Gentleman of Fifty and the Damsel of Nineteen*.[1] The six short chapters are very amusing, and the Vicar and Vicaress might have developed into most humorous creations : " She cast on him a look of a kind that makes matrimony terrific in the dreams of bachelors."

The scene of the story, Ickleworth, was no doubt intended for Mickleham, and perhaps the opening incident of the capsizing of the Vicar and his wife into the muddy river was suggested by a similar accident mentioned by Meredith in a letter to Mrs Walter Palmer :

" The Comtesse de Montesquieu and another dame, with husbands and lap-dogs, were shot into the water last week, and had to kick legs hanging on to oars for minutes."

The story of Louise de Riverolles promised to bear some resemblance to that of Renée in *Beauchamp's Career*, and the setting of it was in like manner placed in Normandy and Dauphiné.

Many pens have described the personal characteristics of Meredith in this decade of 1885-1895. Perhaps the most succinct and yet graphic portrait is that drawn by Mr Frank Harris :

" A most noble and inspiring personality, perhaps the widest and deepest mind born in England since Shakespeare. . . . I was astonished by the Greek beauty of his face set off by wavy silver hair and the extraordinary variety of ever-changing expression, astonished, too, by the high loud voice which he used in ordinary conversation, and by the quick glancing eyes which never seemed to rest for a moment on any object, but flitted about curiously like a child's."

Meredith never spoke in the low, remote tone usual to deaf people. And as early as 1894 he suffered acutely from this

[1] It will be found in vol. xxxiv., *Miscellaneous Prose,* Constable's Collected Edition of Meredith.

affliction, for Lord Morley notes that year : " Found Meredith very deaf : he was less turbulent and strained than he used to be."

Although his temper became milder in the latter years, Meredith preserved to the end his loud, drawling voice, mouthing his words in the manner now associated with Lord Dundreary, but which had been the prevailing habit of speech among gentlemen, particularly officers, in the days of his youth.   And now the days of old age are come.

NOTE TO *THE AMAZING MARRIAGE*

The character of Captain Kirby, the Old Buccaneer, in *The Amazing Marriage*, was drawn from that of Captain Edward John Trelawny (1792-1881), the friend of Shelley and Byron. Several incidents in the life of Kirby were based on the experiences of Trelawny. See his *Adventures of a Younger Son*. One of the best portraits of Trelawny is that by Millais in *The North-West Passage*.

CHAPTER XV

THE LAST YEARS. DEATH

FOURTEEN years of Meredith's life remain, but I do not propose to describe them in full detail, as apart from the publication of his last volume of poetry, *A Reading of Life*, in 1901, and writing a few other poems, his literary work was done. He realised this himself, for he wrote in January, 1901, to Professor W. A. Knight, who had requested a contribution to *Pro Patria et Regina* : " I have just sent a volume to the press, and also verse to special Charities. I have nothing that I can offer you. Believe me that I hold it a matter for regret. My store and my present powers of production are exhausted. Whatever the opinion with which you favour my work, you may be assured that the public will not miss it in your collection."

To note briefly the interesting incidents of the author's last years. In May, 1895, Alphonse Daudet and Henry James paid a visit to Flint Cottage. In July he was induced by Mr Clodd to attend a meeting of the Omar Khayyám Club held at the Burford Bridge Hotel. Meredith's health did not permit him to be present at the dinner, but he came at the close, and was conducted by Mr C. K. Shorter to the seat of honour on the right-hand side of the chairman. It was in reply to Mr Clodd's words of welcome that Meredith made his maiden speech at this late hour of life, and in tribute to the sly and artful beguilement which had doubly drawn him from kennel or covert retirement and to " give tongue " this friend was ever after dubbed " Sir Reynard." [1] A very interesting speech was made by Mr Thomas Hardy, who recalled the history of his first meeting with Meredith, as Publisher's Reader. George Gissing also

[1] Ten years later (1905) Meredith wrote to Mr Clodd : " You will represent me at the dinner on Saturday and air your eloquence, as when you pitchforked me over the table of the Omar Khayyámites."

spoke in similarly reminiscent vein of his meeting with Meredith in the office of Chapman and Hall.[1]

At this date (1895-1896) Meredith was still able to visit London occasionally, to attend a concert with his friends, the Misses Lawrence, or to go to Dr Plimmer at Sydenham : " He has got the score of *Otello*, to play it me ; says it is Wagner and water ; would seem to say it is the Verdi-gris of Wagner." He also enjoyed the water-parties of Mrs Seymour Trower, who was styled " Lady BytheWey " and her husband " Gondolier " in memory of pleasant times on the Wey.

In the summers of 1896 and 1897 Meredith stayed with Lord and Lady Battersea at Overstrand, near Cromer. In 1898 his seventieth birthday was marked by the presentation of an address signed by thirty notable people, mostly writers, including J. M. Barrie, Austin Dobson, Thomas Hardy, Henry James, W. E. H. Lecky, and A. C. Swinburne. It was worded :

" Some comrades in letters who have long valued your work send you a cordial greeting upon your 70th birthday.

" You have attained the first rank in literature after many years of inadequate recognition. From first to last you have been true to yourself and have always aimed at the highest mark. We are rejoiced to know that merits once perceived by only a few are now appreciated by a wide and steadily growing circle. We wish you many years of life, during which you may continue to do good work, cheered by the consciousness of good work already achieved, and encouraged by the certainty of a hearty welcome from many sympathetic readers."

Meredith in reply said :

" The recognition that I have always worked honestly to my best, coming from the men and women of highest distinction, touches me deeply. Pray let it be known to them how much they encourage and support me."

At the same time he said caustically and privately to Mr Clodd : " I know what they mean, kindly enough. Poor old devil, he *will* go on writing ; let us cheer him up. The old fire isn't quite out ; a stir of the poker may bring out a shoot of gas."

[1] See *ante*, p. 244.

Feby 20th

Miss Nellie!

We violets are
modest flowers. but not the
Queenly Rose is surer of
welcome where she appears.
So, pray withold acknowledgements
of our transmission to you,
I we shall be flattered
the more by knowing you
pleased of course.

Facsimile of Meredith's holograph, 1899. Lines sent to Miss Buckston Browne
(Mrs Lett) with some flowers.

This tribute, and the fact that he was chosen to succeed Tennyson as President of the Society of Authors in 1892, should have convinced Meredith that he had no longer cause for complaint that he was unappreciated and unacknowledged in England. But he liked to preserve the little mental myth, and continued to describe himself as " an unpopular novelist and unaccepted poet."

He did not approve of the South African War, and perceived faults on both sides. He wrote to Hyndman in October, 1899 :

" This hateful war tears me in two. I have to wish for the success of our men in the cause that I condemn. The Demon is in that mount of Gold. I had always the dread that the first steps of Imperialism would be bloody. Greenwood has written excellently. But the tide of Brummagem policy was too strong ; Cairo to the Cape of Mighty Hunger."

Further, in 1902, he addressed letters to *The Daily News* and *The Daily Mail* on the subject of Kritzinger's case, in which he pleaded for more humane treatment of the Boers.

In September, 1903, Meredith was very ill, and near to dying. Later, he stayed for several months with his daughter at Givons, and did not return to Flint Cottage until March. During this illness, a newspaper having stated that so critical was his condition that he only had " periods of partial consciousness," the veteran was roused to voice one of his mordant claims to unimportance in England. He wired :

" Dorking report of me incorrect ; though why my name should be blown about, whether I am well or ill, I do not know. The difficulty with me is to obtain unconsciousness ; but sleep, on the whole, comes fairly. I am going on well enough. This for friends who will have been distressed by the report."

This year (1904) Meredith's seventy-sixth birthday was marked by the fine sonnet addressed to him by Watts-Dunton :

This time, dear friend—this time my birthday greeting
Comes heavy of funeral tears—I think of you,
And say, 'Tis evening with him—that is true—
But evening bright as noon, if faster fleeting ;

Still he is spared—while Spring and Winter, meeting,
   Clasp hands around the roots 'neath frozen dew—
To see the " Joy of Earth " break forth anew,
And hear it on the hillside warbling, bleating.
Love's remnant melts and melts ; but if our days
   Are swifter than a weaver's shuttle, still,
Still Winter has a sun—a sun whose rays
   Can set the young lamb dancing on the hill,
And set the daisy, in the woodland ways,
   Dreaming of her who brings the daffodil.

In 1905, the Order of Merit was bestowed upon Meredith by King Edward VII. He could, of course, have had an hereditary title if he had so desired, but as he said : " I wished for no distinction. A title would have sunk me." A special concession excused him from attending at Buckingham Palace, although the King offered to receive him and bestow the decoration privately. Sir Arthur Ellis came down to Flint Cottage as the King's representative, and invested Meredith with the Order of Merit there in December, 1905.

In July and August of this year Meredith had rented Alma Cottage, Aldeburgh, for the sake of sea air and the society of his friend, Edward Clodd. He found the little town and flat Suffolk scenery as dull as Seaford had been fifty years agone, and wrote amusingly to his daughter :

" There is no scenery, dead flat land, a long line of shingly beach with bathing sheds marked for the sale of Holloway's Pills and Ointment—which Bessy Nicholls [1] declines daily for the in and outside of her, although they are offered freely at my expense. . . . All that can be given by Aldeburgh in exchange for amenities is a grand sea often peopled with shipping, and strengthening air. The Dearie will, if she deigns to visit the place, yawn a jaw-cracker at the end of the first day ; manacles and hobbles and anæsthetics will be required to retain her at the end of the second. And my poor little ones will soon be aweary of the monotony. Sir Reynard is good for a sail on the Salt Alde. There is nothing else. This has to be stated to you. For the rest, your coming would be a refreshment to me."

Nevertheless, he returned to Aldeburgh the following summer, for the air was good and probably he had grown to like the drear

---

[1] His faithful nurse and attendant during his last years.

yet fascinating marshlands of Suffolk which offer such vast expanse of sky, beautiful atmospheric effects, and splendid sunsets. But at Aldeburgh itself he still continued to gird. He wrote to his daughter :

" This (butter) of Aldeburgh bawled Margarine as it entered my mouth. The vegetables grow apparently in the shops that sell them ; the fruits on the shingle. Rank and Fashion have not yet arrived ; hotel windows gape, and every second house raises the lamentable cry of Apartments. Strange fowls or clever semblances send me eggs for breakfast. They commit suicide on the way, and appear before me inside out, in the manner of ancients. They are interesting for having a IXth Century flavour. The absence of Sandie [1] is felt severely. . . .

" An Omnibus arrives on the Parade, with luggage piled high. Excitement. An Omnibus departs, with luggage piled high. Depression. The good people will not see their heavy charges combined with the poor attractions are forbidding. They plead that they have a season of only two months. But such a place should never have counted on a season at all. . . . Owing to my condition, I am not allowed to stay more than 5 minutes watching the old ferryman—my one intellectual amusement here."

Mr Clodd notes on the latter point :

" When Meredith was last at Aldeburgh it was his delight to be wheeled to the ancient quay along which Crabbe had rolled the barrels of salt which were under his father's charge as collector of duties. . . . With a bunch of bladder-weed, plucked from the sodden timbers, and held to his nose as if fragrant as the choicest attar, he would watch John, the old ferryman, plying oars which he averred were dipped twice in the same water. ' I am certain,' he said, ' that there are Nereids under the keel to help the boat across.' "

A pathetic contrast, this restricted, inactive life with the old days of great walks over the hills, and the soaring " beetle." But he still found pleasure in studying human nature, particularly as represented by elemental toilers, and John of

[1] His dog.

GEORGE MEREDITH AT ALDEIURCH
Photograph by Mr. C. K. Shorter, reproduced by his permission and by courtesy of " The Bookman "

Aldeburgh Ferry was to Meredith as the tinkers of Copsham Common he had delighted to converse with nearly half-a-century before, and the " Friendly Tramps " of *A Stave of Roving Tim*.

Meredith was now a confirmed invalid, and since an accident in the autumn of 1905, when he slipped and broke his right leg, he could only move abroad in his bath-chair. The little procession of the author drawn by his donkey " Picnic," led by Cole, and Miss Nicholls bringing up the rear, became a familiar sight at Box Hill. The favourite route was ever up the zigzag path to the summit of " our green hill," whence he could see the view which had delighted and inspired him for two-thirds of a long life. Owing to his difficulty of movement, it was found necessary to convert the dining-room at Flint Cottage into a bedroom for him after the accident in 1905. This put an end to entertaining his friends to luncheon or dinner, which hospitalities he had always warmly extended : but he was glad to see those who came. He often had visitors ; earlier this year (1905) they included Haldane and Lloyd George. Rarely now was he able to enter the chalet where so much great work had been achieved, and during the last year of his life he did not do so at all. But he faced all his deprivations and losses, the sadness of old age, and approaching Death itself with calm resignation and unflinching bravery. " The worst of a long life is the seeing our friends drop by the way, and leave in our minds the flickering rushlight of them in memory." As he wrote to Mr Meynell : " For me, I drag on, counting more years and not knowing why. I have to lean on an arm when I would walk, and I am humiliated by requiring at times a repetition of sentences. This is my state of old age. But my religion of life is always to be cheerful." And to others he said : " Nature is my God, and I trust in her. Without doubt, lovers of Nature, as long as they have contact with men, cannot escape suffering ; but their burdens will be lightened since they themselves turn towards Nature. . . . I am never alone. My daughter and my son often pay me a surprise visit, and friends come almost every day. Even if no one comes I never feel lonely. I have my books and my own thoughts. And besides, I am never lonely with Nature and the birds and beasts and insects, and the woods and the trees, in which I find a constant companionship. . . . Death ? I have lived long enough, I do not fear it ; it is but the other side of the door ; to die, is to pass from one room to another. . . . We have come to the time of life when the landscape surrounding, ' *haec data poena diu viventibus*,' the tombstones of our beloved and the narrowing of our powers, throws a not unpleasant beam on the black gateway, as we take it to be in the earlier days. . . . I find nothing to regret in the going at my age."

And yet, inevitably, there must have been some regret, as for him darker grew the valley, at parting with the fair glory and joys of earth and sky which he had loved and hymned all his life. Mountain and valley, sunset and starlit eve, the moon on a forest pool, woods aflame with autumn glory, the eternal miracle of the loveliness of spring, the song of birds, distant lightning quivering behind a cloud-rack on a hot summer's night, the threnody of the winds of winter sighing around the house firelit and warm, friends, a faithful dog, a kitten at play, wine and books and flowers—no imaginative artist and lover of beauty can resign all these without a sigh of regret.

> Love eyed his rosy memories : he sang :
> O bloom of dawn, breathed up from the gold sheaf
> Held springing beneath Orient ! that dost hang
> The space of dewdrops running over leaf. . . .
>
> Of thee to say behold, has said adieu :
> But love remembers how the sky was green,
> And how the grasses glimmered lightest blue ;
> How saint-like grey took fervour : how the screen
> Of cloud grew violet. . . .

One consolation was granted to Meredith in old age. His mind did not fail him and his heart remained young. As he said : " I do not feel to be growing old either in heart or mind. I still look on life with a young man's eye. I have always hoped I should not grow old as some do—with a palsied intellect, living backwards, regarding other people as anachronisms, because they themselves have lived on into other times, and left their sympathies behind them with their years."

This wish was realised to the end. His sympathies were ever with new movements for freedom and progress both in nations and individuals. The Franchise for Women was a cause that had his warm approval, though he, of course, like all other sane people, reprobated the absurd activities of the enthusiasts termed " Suffragettes," who injured and retarded their movement some years ago. Meredith addressed a long letter on the subject to the editor of *The Times*, dated 1st November, 1906 ; and a year before his death he further expressed his views to a well-known authoress thus :

" As to the request, I am not in harmony with the present militant movement for the reason that I am, as I have for long been, in favour of the suffrage for women. I like them for the high spirit they show, but think them erratic in policy. They are quite unaware of the sturdy hostility they are exciting. Well, you will have to pardon me, if you can, years hence, perhaps. You are in the heat of the fray, counting him who is not with you as against you. Nothing will stop the advance of your feet, but the cause will be retrograding. Or else men can be worried or wheedled or frightened into granting what they dislike, which would seem to be the calculation."

Quite in his last years, he, who had " loved the motion of legs and the sweep of the winds " in the days of active health, now found some compensation in the rapid motion and opposing wind of motoring. " To vary my growls when I am out on the road with ' Picnic,' I hire a motor and have a spin of 100 miles, a way of ensuring appetite and prolonged sleep." In the autumn of 1908, he motored in Sussex a good deal ; and in his very last letter, written a month before his death, he spoke of motoring over to Putney to see Watts-Dunton : but that was not to be.

Meredith's eightieth birthday, on 12th February, 1908, was celebrated by his friends and admirers with every demonstration of affection and respect. In the morning, after his usual pilgrimage up Box Hill, drawn in his chair by " Picnic," and accompanied on this occasion by Lady Edward Cecil (the daughter of his old friend, Maxse), Meredith received Mr and Mrs C. K. Shorter and Mr Edward Clodd, who came to present the congratulatory address signed by some two hundred and fifty representative names. It was worded :

" Many of your fellow-countrymen will join in felicitating you upon the health and happiness that are yours upon this your eightieth birthday. We desire on our own behalf to thank you for the splendid work in prose and poetry that we owe to your pen—to say how much we rejoice in the growing recognition of this work—and to thank you for the example you have set to the world of lofty ideals embodied not only in books but in life. Most heartily do we wish you a continuance of health and happiness."

The signatories included Thomas Hardy, A. C. Swinburne, Rudyard Kipling, John Morley, A. J. Balfour, Sir Edward Grey, Professor J. B. Bury, Holman Hunt, H. Beerbohm Tree, and Miss Ellen Terry.

In the afternoon, Mr Anthony Hope, Mr Herbert Trench, and Mr I. Zangwill arrived to present an address from the Society of Authors to the President. Meredith also received the representatives of various newspapers, and seems to have talked in an animated manner :

" He was sitting in an armchair between the fire and a window that looks on to his beloved Downs, surrounded by his books. On every table were dozens of telegrams of felicitation. In each corner of the room and out in the little hall were bouquets of flowers. A wonderful old leonine man, with a face like Hermes grown old, the long white hair lying loosely about his ears, with a rug round his knees and his hand to his ear. . . . In repose the face took on an almost feminine grace of expression. When he spoke the deep, rich, resonant voice, and the animation of the countenance, seemed to give added stature to the aged frame. . . . In everything that concerned himself and the homage being paid to him on his birthday, Mr Meredith was characteristically modest. ' I have been climbing the stairs for eighty years,' he exclaimed, ' and I have done with the pulpit.' " [1]

But nevertheless he proceeded to express his views on the Suffrage for Women and universal military service. More interesting was his characteristic badinage about an imaginary novel to be called *The Benefactor of the Race.*

[1] *The Daily Telegraph,* 13th February, 1908, which gives an excellent account of the day's proceedings.

His eightieth birthday placed Meredith, for the first time in his career, in the centre of the public stage with a profusion of unwelcome limelight illuminating the privacy of his life and home. The newspapers seemed to be possessed by a belated epidemic of hero-worship for " The Sage of Box Hill." Leading articles and memoirs and " appreciations " of his work, written up by people quite unacquainted hitherto with their subject, appeared in bewildering confusion. " Interviews " with the great man were urgently desired, and so, as Mr J. A. Hammerton excellently put it :

" A motley crowd of reporters haunted the precincts of Box Hill, as keen as if a murder had been committed at Flint Cottage. . . . Photographers had been busy ' snapping ' him when he came forth in his donkey-chaise ; pages of illustrations—most of them deplorable—were given in the papers. . . . Never, in sooth, was so much written and printed in the space of one week about any man who had not achieved the distinction of committing a singularly revolting crime. So magnificent a tribute to mere literary genius and intellectual greatness made one feel that the British press had taken leave of its senses."

Meredith, no doubt, regarded his week of fame in its right proportions ; and despite the fact that he had lived to see himself described in flaring headlines as " The King of Novelists " and " The Last of the Great Victorians " and " Our Greatest Author," and so forth, he still continued to speak of himself as an unappreciated and unpopular writer. When M. Photiadès visited him at Box Hill in September, 1908, seven months after the clash of the birthday cymbals, Meredith said :

" The press has often treated me as a clown or a harlequin— yes, really ! And with such little respect that my fellow-citizens can scarcely put up with me. . . . Certainly at this late hour they accord me a little glory ; my name is celebrated, but no one reads my books. As for Englishmen, I put them to flight because I bore them. With regard to foreigners, I am but an illustrious unknown. . . . No one has bought my books—my novels or my poems."

And eight months before his death he wrote : " I have no claim to popularity in England." [1] These were certainly controvertible statements ; but, as I have said, he chose to preserve this little illusion to the last.

He, of course, felt the fatigue and boredom of the vast correspondence the birthday celebration had entailed :

" This eightieth of mine comes but once, thank the Lord ! Since that day I have been writing letters by the score ; and as our Poet says, still they come ; many demanding answers :— letters naming plays from novels, begging letters, letters of great gush, idiotic letters ; one from a piteously-voiced bankrupt clergyman ! No one knowing me can imagine that I like to be trotted out before the public. And I have had to bear it and smile."

In his replies to tried and trusty friends his mind travelled back to old days in their company. To Sir Francis Burnand he wrote of those good times gone :

" It is hard that one should strike the solemn peal of 80, and not be able to caper with the legs though the mind and heart are elastically harlequin. However, good things come at this big age, and among them your reminder that the old days are not forgotten by you. As to the calculation of the years, I think it is pretty correct. And would either of us have thought, when walking the Esher roads, that we should look back with mortal eyes over such a stretch of time [2]—and you a burnished Knight, and I receiving Deputations. And there is Hyndman wielding the Socialistic baton to ravishing discords."

And to Hyndman, too, he wrote :

" I am, it would appear, a discovered man. I think of the old days, my visit to Cambridge, your performance on the flute ; remembering well the little bit of Beethoven, and your fine stand in the cricket field—some 50 !—and the Hauptman duets with my wife at the piano—all as yesterday. For all

[1] See also letter of 19th February, 1909, to Herr Frey, in the published *Letters*.

[2] Nearly fifty years.

GEORGE MEREDITH AND HIS DOG, SANDIE: THE DAILY DRIVE ON BOX HILL

Photograph by Bolak, and by courtesy of "The Bookman"

through the years backward I conjure at with the senses and feelings by the day. And now you are among the foremost in the fray, while I do but sit and look on. I am accused sharply by myself, and yet am helpless. You can imagine, therefore, what my thoughts are when congratulations come showering under the note of ' happy returns.' Cheerfulness has not forsaken me, but Nature has cast me aside, and I do not like this mere drawing of breath without payment for it."

By April he was able to report :

" The shower of letters since my oppressive 80th is abating ; still daily I have one or two for answer. It is hard at my age to be pitchforked up in the public eye. Some would like it. I am not a Martin Tupper who said, when he had been flung on the accustomed heap after much pitchforking, that he would rather be an object of abuse than not be mentioned at all. And I have had to write a poem—for the Union Jack Club's Album, while undergoing the torments of a heavy cold, all because of ' my great name ' which the Album must have. . . . Also a sitting to Mr Strang on behalf of the King for members of the Order of Merit to be hung in the Library at Windsor—my worn old features ! "

The aftermath of the birthday celebrations took the form of the Press seeking Meredith's views on every conceivable public question, which were duly published : it did not matter whether the subject was one on which he was qualified to speak or the reverse.

His last and eighty-first birthday, in 1909, was spent quietly. In the morning he took his usual drive up Box Hill, drawn by " Picnic," and attended by Miss Nicholls, and Cole, with his favourite dog " Sandie " barking a joyous accompaniment. In the afternoon the numerous congratulatory letters and telegrams received were read to him. In the evening his daughter and son and daughter-in-law, together with Mr and Mrs J. M. Barrie, and Dr and Mrs Plimmer, dined with him. Mr Haldane had visited Flint Cottage the previous Sunday, and Lord Morley also came at this time. To him, almost the last survivor of his early intimate friends, Meredith said laughingly :

" Going quickly down, no belief in future existence." But perhaps that negation of the future was his final mordant paradox, for about this date, when another friend asked him what was his favourite extract from his own works, he quoted :

> Full lasting is the song, though he
> The singer passes : lasting too,
> For souls not lent in usury,
> The rapture of the forward view.

The singer was passing, but to the end his vigour of mind and love of Nature remained in full force—" till the last long sigh." If he looked backward he had a long vista of years to retrace, marked by many regrets but many joys. He had spanned the whole of the Victorian Era. Born nine years before it commenced, he lived for eight years beyond its close.

Quietly the last months passed, and he saw and heard for the last time the magic of Spring. In February he heard the thrush :

> He sings me, out of Winter's throat
> The young time with the life ahead ;
> And my young time his leaping note
> Recalls to spirit-mirth from dead.

He saw " the butterflies roaming abroad on the sunny March day, the pine-cones opened " ; April with its " budding leafage and fresh green pastures " ; and then, as he had written in the far-away days of youth :

> Fixing my dying eyes for aye
> On the dawning brows of maiden May.

On Friday, 14th May, 1909, he went in his usual health for his customary drive. He contracted a chill, which was aggravated by going out again the next day—the last time he was to traverse Box Hill. He was taken seriously ill on the Sunday and, despite every attention, the action of the heart failed, though he was conscious almost to the end. His son and daughter, and his faithful attendant, Miss Nicholls, were with him. And he remembered his dog " Sandie " almost to the last.

With face to the dawn, George Meredith died on 18th May

1909, at that early hour of the morning he had so exquisitely pictured :

> . . . When the white star hovers
> Low over dim fields fresh with bloomy dew,
> Near the face of dawn, that draws athwart the darkness,
> Threading it with colour, like yewberries the yew.
> Thicker crowd the shades as the grave East deepens
> Glowing, and with crimson a long cloud swells . . .

He died in " green-winged spring," when the lovely surroundings of his home were clothed in their most beautiful vestments. There was an exceptional ecstasy of blossom that year in the Surrey gardens and lanes, lilac and laburnum and horse-chestnut and hawthorn blending with the glorious sunshine in harmonious blaze of colour to light the last journey of him whose credo was Nature, and who had been Nature's supreme Singer for sixty years.

It is needless to discuss here the illogical decision which denied to George Meredith's cremated ashes a resting-place in Westminster Abbey while at the same time it provided a memorial service there for this Naturist whose views were unorthodox to clerics of the Higher Criticism. Far better was it to bury him, as he wished, beside his second wife in Dorking Cemetery. " Sweeter the green grass turf than Abbey pavements," he said.

He rests in his own loved valley, guarded by Ranmore, Leith Hill, Norbury, and Box Hill. Rightly, Surrey holds Meredith in death as in life.

INDEX

edith.

	DATE DUE		

22 May '7